SUBMISSION: The Danger of Political Islam to Canada – With a Warning to America

Thomas Quiggin, Tahir Gora, Saied Shoaaib, Jonathon Cotler and Rick Gill

Copyright © 2017 by Canadian Centre for the Study of Extremism (CCSE)

All rights reserved. The use of any part of this publication reproduced, transmitted in any form or by any means, electronic, mechanical, photocopying, recording, or otherwise, or stored in a retrieval system, without the prior written permission of the publisher – or, in case of photocopying or other reprographic copying, a license from the Canadian Copyright Licensing Agency – is an infringement of the copyright law.

Library and Archives Canada Cataloguing in Publication
is available upon request

ISBN - 978-0-9952235-3-0

Cover photo – Ikhwan web

Layout and format by Rick Gill

ABOUT THE AUTHORS

Thomas Quiggin, MA, CD

Thomas is a court-qualified expert on terrorism (criminal court and federal court) and has had his expertise on the "the reliability of intelligence as evidence" recognized by the Federal Court of Canada. He has also testified as a court expert to the Immigration and Refugee Board of Canada. He was a Senior Fellow at S. Rajaratnam School of International Studies at the Nanyang Technological University, Singapore. Thomas has 25 plus years of practical intelligence experience in a variety of positions. These include the Royal Canadian Mounted Police (NSIS/INSET); the Bank of Canada; the Canadian Armed Forces; the United Nations Protection Force in Yugoslavia; Citizenship and Immigration Canada (War Crimes); the International Criminal Tribunal for the former Yugoslavia (ICTY) in The Hague, and the Privy Council Office of Canada. He was also a qualified arms control inspector for the Conventional Forces in Europe Treaty and the Vienna Document. He has also testified to a Senate Committee on intelligence matters (The Kelly Commission, 1998); the Air India Inquiry (2007) as well as providing testimony to the Special Senate Committee on Anti-terrorism (2010) and to the House of Commons on 25 March and 28 May 2015.

Thomas holds a Master's Degree in International Relations and is a certified knowledge management practitioner. He has also provided three training sessions to the Canadian Department of Justice as part of the special advocates program with the focus being on intelligence and evidence. Thomas also has been a guest lecturer at the Canadian Police College with the lectures on terrorism and intelligence. He has spoken at various conferences in Europe, Southeast Asia, and Australia on related matters. Thomas has authored many publications on security and terrorism matters in Germany, the Netherlands, the UK, USA, Canada, and Singapore. He has previously published a book on national security titled **Seeing the Invisible: National Security Intelligence in an Uncertain Age**, (2007, World Scientific).

Tahir Gora

Tahir is a Director General and founder of Canadian Thinkers' Forum (CTF), a Think Tank focusing on complexities of diversity in Canada. He is recipient of the Queen's Diamond Jubilee Medal for his services.

He contributes regularly to various well-known Canadian newspapers and web-based forums including The Huffington Post. He is a strong proponent of freedom of speech and has developed various initiatives to bring about the much-needed changes in the representational and communal aspects of Canadian Muslim Community.

Tahir is a prominent writer, novelist, poet, journalist, editor, translator, publisher and TV Host (for South Asian TV Channels) with over 30 years of experience in the industry. He is recognized as a bold social activist who has initiated many interfaith and pluralistic streams to bring Muslim community of Canada together to support progressive ideas and actions. He is an author of two novels, three collections of short stories and three collections of poems in the Urdu and Punjabi languages. One novel and a collection of poems have been translated and published in Russian and Uzbek languages.

Tahir is also a founder of the online multicultural TAG TV. Some of his shows in Urdu-Hindi languages have received millions of views in South East Asia.

Saied Shoaaib

Saied is a writer and researcher who has specialized in Islamic movements. Originally from Egypt, he has previously served as the editor/manager of the Alyoum 7 news website (www.youm7.com). Saied has also been the manager of "United Journalists" which is a human rights organization that works in the training and protection of the rights of journalists. He also been the editor-in-chief of the Sada Albalad news website, the Editor/Advisor of the Vetogate news website and the Editor/Advisor of the Albasaba News website. Saied has also taught electronic journalism at the Canadian University of Egypt.

His work in Egypt has earned him fatwa death threat in Egypt and online death threats in Canada.

Saied has written several books, which include:

- **"Lovers of Death": Islamist extremism in our Canadian mosques, schools, and libraries** (2016) co-authored with Thomas Quiggin about the sources of Islamic terrorism in Canada, and
- **How to be a successful journalist and how to profit from the electronic media**, (2014) Dar Awrak;
- **The Demise of the State of the Muslim Brotherhood**, (2013) Dar Awrak;
- **Toz in Egypt: The Sins of the Muslim Brotherhood in Egypt**, (2010) Sesafa.
- **Where does Egypt Go?** (2001)
- **State rigging - confessions of the first police officer of election fraud** (2000) in conjunction with Mahmood Kotry, published by the Centre for the Future;

Saied also wrote a play titled **Do not be Satisfied**, 1990.

Jonathon Cotler

Raised mainly in Canada, Jonathon has travelled extensively in the Middle East. His B.A. was from McGill University in Montreal and his law degree is from the New York Law School.

Rick Gill, CD

Rick is a 38-year veteran of the Canadian Armed Forces, 32 years of which were served in military intelligence as an intelligence analyst, intelligence plans staff officer, instructor, training developer, and analytic methodologist. He has over ten years' experience as an intelligence analytic instructor and training developer. Rick has served in numerous strategic, operational, and tactical environments, both domestically and abroad, including deployments to Bosnia-Hercegovina, Kosovo and Afghanistan. Since retiring from the Canadian Armed Forces in 2012, Rick has worked in both the public and private sectors, focusing on the development and delivery of tools, training, and education for intelligence analysts.

DEDICATION

This book is dedicated to the victims of the Islamist ideology – both Muslims and non-Muslims.

Islamist extremism and its accompanying conflict will be to the 21st Century what fascism and communism were to the 20th Century. It will be the defining civilizational struggle in the Middle East, Europe, North America, North Africa, South East Asia, South Asia, Central America and much of South America.

Islamists believe they have both the right and an obligation to force their political/religious beliefs on all other persons and systems. The evidence at this point suggests the Islamists will continue to be successful in growing at a frightening pace. Conflict and confrontation are the natural outcome of the growth of Islamist beliefs, as can be seen in areas as diverse as Canada, France, Belgium, the United Kingdom, Egypt, India, the USA, the Philippines and Australia.

Western governments are often intellectually weak, cowardly, and suffer badly from delusions of their own competency. Fascinated by visions produced by global elitism and progressive philosophies (cultural Marxism), they fail to defend even the most basic of Western values. They do this in the name of political correctness and progressive "social justice."

The results are clear now as the bodies pile up in the UK, France, Germany, Canada and elsewhere while the social fabric of societies is torn asunder. Barbaric practices such as Female Genital Mutilation, the killing of apostates and gays, and wife beating continue to grow. They are becoming normalized by the government, the media, and judiciary. More victims are being created in their wake.

It is these victims, many of whom suffer in an enforced invisible silence, that this book hopes to comfort and assist.

FOREWORD BY RAHEEL RAZA

In this well researched and well referenced book, Thomas Quiggin, and four other authors who are experts in their own fields, have laid out facts that are no longer open for discussion due to political correctness. However, these facts are extremely important not only to Canadians, but to the international community as we deal with a global Islamist insurgency which few people are brave enough to address head on.

As aptly noted in the opening dedication "Islamist extremism will be to the 21st Century what fascism and communism were to the 20th Century. It will be the defining civilizational struggle in the Middle East, Europe, North America, North Africa, South East Asia, South Asia, Central America and much of South America."

This book is dedicated to the victims of terrorism. As President George Bush said in a recent speech, "the further we get away from 9/11, the further people are getting away from the lessons learned from 9/11". This book is a wake-up call and reminder that 9/11 changed the world in unimaginable ways and unless we face the truth, we will never be able to fight the war of ideas that the world is faced with.

The authors address many questions that are on the minds of North Americans (both Muslim and non-Muslim) but which they are hesitant to ask. The various chapters cover such important issues as:

- Is the false narrative of Islamophobia silencing people? The book discusses M103 and asks the simple question – how do you know if you are being critical of evil or Islamophobic? Is speaking out about violence against women, racist?
- The book exposes those organizations that are creating a victim ideology amongst Muslim youth and pretending to be "the voice of all Muslims"
- In a chapter on reform Muslims, the authors address challenges faced by Muslims who speak out against the radical Islamist ideology
- In a fearlessly frank chapter, the authors address media bias and how many real issues dealing with rising Islamist agendas are not reported

With signs of candid humour and unabashed honesty, the authors in this ground-breaking work have done all Westerners a favour by opening avenues for major discussion and debate that should have taken place right after 9/11 but which could not happen due to vested subversive agendas of the regressive left and the extreme right.

With great risks to their lives, these authors have dared to say what many Canadians need to hear – like yesterday.

Raheel Raza

President, Council for Muslims Facing Tomorrow – Toronto October 2017

QUOTES

"It is the nature of Islam to dominate, not to be dominated, to impose its law on all nations and to extend its power to the entire planet."

- Hassan al-Banna, founder of the Muslim Brotherhood.

"Islam wishes to destroy all states and governments anywhere on the face of the earth which are opposed to the ideology and programme of Islam regardless of the country or the Nation which rules it."

- Abul A'la Maududi, founder of Jamaat-e-Islami.

"Conquest through dawah, that is what we hope for. We will conquer Europe, we will conquer America! Not through sword but through dawah."

- Yusuf Qaradawi, International Union of Muslim Scholars (IUMS).

"Therefore, prepare for jihad and be the lovers of death. Life itself shall come searching after you. You should yearn for an honourable death and you will gain perfect happiness. May Allah grant myself and yours the honour of martyrdom in His way!"

- Hassan al-Banna, founder of the Muslim Brotherhood as quoted by the Islamic Circle of North America (ICNA) Youth Wing of Canada.

"Here, we follow the teachings of the Muslim Brotherhood."

- Dr. El-Tantawi Attia, Executive Director, Dundas Street Mosque, Muslim Association of Canada, Toronto, Ontario, Canada.

"Islam is <u>not incompatible</u> with free and open Western secular democracies."

- Prime Minister Justin Trudeau, Ottawa, Ontario, Canada, January 2016.

"Islam is <u>totally incompatible</u> with Western democracy."

- The Islamic Circle of North America (ICNA) Brampton, Ontario, Canada, February 2016

"Much of the philosophy and vision of the Muslim Association of Canada derives from the heritage of the Muslim Brotherhood. Our commitment to the model of individual self-development expressed in communal organization is based largely on the vision of the Muslim Brotherhood and Hassan Al-Banna... We believe that the efforts of Al-Banna and subsequent generations of the Muslim Brotherhood remain the truest reflection of Islamic practice in the modern era."

- The Muslim Association of Canada (MAC) web site.

"We do not work for anything else and anybody else but the establishment of Allah's government."

- Maulana Asad Jafri, Toronto, Ontario, Canada.

CONTENTS

About the Authors 3

Dedication 5

Foreword by Raheel Raza 6

Quotes 7

Contents 8

Chapter 1: The Global Struggle for the Soul of Islam 10

Chapter 2: Death Threats, Fear, and Self-Censorship 16

Chapter 3: Canadian Values and the Social Fabric of Society 18

Chapter 4: Modernist Muslims and Why They are Losing 25

Chapter 5: Political Correctness and the Damage to the Social Fabric of Other Countries 28

Chapter 6: Extremism, Violent Extremism, and Terrorism 35

Chapter 7: Can We Eliminate the Dangers of Political Islam? 40

Chapter 8: The False Narrative of Islamophobia, Racism, and Victimization 68

Chapter 9: A Helpful Guide on Being Islamophobic in Canada 77

Chapter 10: Being Beaten is a Sign of Love and Concern - Women and Islamist ideology 85

Chapter 11: M-103 – How islamist style blasphemy laws may be coming to canada 92

Chapter 12: The Trudeau Party, Entryism and Extremist Islam 100

Chapter 13: A Partial Overview of Front Organizations in Canada 128

Chapter 14: The Muslim Student Association 160

Chapter 15: Charitable Status Revoked for Connections to Extremism 177

Chapter 16: The Killing of Apostates and Non-Believers 188

Chapter 17: Reporting of Islamists and Extremism by the Canadian Press 189

Chapter 18: Intelligence, Law Enforcement, and the Mullah Syndrome 208

Chapter 19: The Montreal Kidnapping 215

Chapter 20: The Quebec City Mosque Shooting and the Cycle of Violence in Canada 222

Chapter 21: It's not a defect! It's a feature! Anti-Semitic and Anti-Christian Messages in Canadian Mosques 228

Chapter 22: Will Hassan al-Banna and the Muslim Brotherhood Destroy Islam? 232

Chapter 23: Submission or Free Will? 234

Chapter 24: A Warning to America 244

Chapter 25: What is to be Done? 248

Annex A: Lexicon 254

Annex B: Source Reliability and Information Credibility Rating System 259
Annex C: Structured Analytic Techniques (SATs) 263
INDEX 274

CHAPTER 1: THE GLOBAL STRUGGLE FOR THE SOUL OF ISLAM

Thomas Quiggin

Key Points

- An intense and inherently brutal global struggle is ongoing for the soul of Islam.

- Islam may emerge as a unified modern faith or it may fragment into an ever-increasing number of factions. Most probably, Islam may continue to digress to a Salafist past which enforces a supremacist theocratic political system. Those who advocate and fight for this are referred to as Islamists.

- Two of the most important blocs of Islamists are led by the Muslim Brotherhood (Sunni) and its spinoffs while the other bloc is led by the Iranian Khomeneists (Shia). They are growing rapidly.

The Islamists

An Islamist is one who would impose any given interpretation of Islamic religious law (called Sharia) over society. For current Islamist groups such as the Muslim Brotherhood, Hizb ut-Tahrir, ISIS, al Qaeda, Boko Haram, and others, this means a politicized form of Islam. In short, it is a theocracy that has a distinctive relationship with confrontation and, on occasions, violence. The intent of the Islamists, as noted by major ideological writers such as Hassan al Banna, is to force all others, Muslims and non-Muslims, to submit to their will.

Islam can be translated as either submission or peace. In the Islamist context, the term very much means submission. Either Canada and the West begin to resist the Islamists, or we continue to make acts of submission. Hence the title of the book.

Islamist adherents can be described as:

- Jihadists: They believe in the selective use of violence to achieve aims, including offensive jihad;

- Takfirists: They believe it is acceptable to call a dissenting Muslim a non-believer or an apostate. By doing so, they are calling for the death of that individual;

- Supremacists: To them, no other form of Islam or any other belief system is allowable; and

- Misogynists: Despite claims to the contrary, violence against women is used to enforce Islamist conformity within their community.

- Salafists: They increasingly advocate a return to the traditions of the "salaf" or "devout ancestors" who existed at the time of the Prophet Mohamed;

By contrast, reformist Muslims believe Islam must integrate science and democracy into Islamic life and drive the faith into the future. They believe that without the opening of Islam, the Islamic world and the Middle East will continue to slide into the past. A reasonable assessment would suggest the reformists are losing the struggle as they are under attack from the Islamists and most Western government are sidelining them in favour of Islamist front groups.

Hassan al-Banna, the founder of the Muslim Brotherhood said that "It is the nature of Islam to dominate, not to be dominated, to impose its law on all nations and to extend its power to the entire planet." Syed Abul A'la Maududi was the founder of Jamaat-e-Islami, the south Asian based sister organization of the Muslim Brotherhood. His belief was that "Islam wishes to destroy all states and governments anywhere on the face of the earth which are opposed to the ideology and programme of Islam regardless of the country or the nation which rules it."[1]

Those who follow a political form of Islam – the Islamists – believe in the views of al-Banna and Maududi. They insist that it is their natural right to dominate all others. As they gain strength in any given society, they will continue to come into conflict with those who believe in basic human rights, democratic systems and those who believe woman can play an equal or leading role in society.

Islamists wish to promote their version of Islam through dawah and ideology.[2] To the Islamists, dawah is an aggressive process of proselytizing, along with the intent of forcing existing Muslims to remain in their fold, and silencing others (i.e. forcing others into submission). Yusuf Qaradawi, the leading theocratic voice of the Muslim Brotherhood, stated:

> "I expect that Islam will conquer Europe without resorting to the sword or fighting. It will do so by means of **dawah** and ideology. Europe is miserable with materialism, with the philosophy of promiscuity, and with the immoral considerations that rule the world - considerations of self-interest and self-indulgence. It is high time Europe woke up and found a way out from this. Europe will find no life saver or life boat other than Islam. Islam will save Europe from the raging materialism from which it suffers."[3] (Emphasis added)

Dawa is also described as a process of the "re-Islamization of Muslim minorities in the West.[4]" The Islamists see Muslim minorities as being oppressed because they have been integrated into Western ways of thinking.

Confrontation and communal conflict are the natural consequences of a society that has a growing population of Islamists. When one group of people believes that their religiously inspired political system

---

[1] *Jihad in Islam* by Maulana Abul A'la Maududi. The full book can be seen online at: http://www.muhammadanism.org/Terrorism/jihah_in_islam/jihad_in_islam.pdf. See pages 6 and 22. Viewed 7 April 2017. **Rated A1.**

[2] See, among many others, *From Dawa to Jihad: The various threats from radical Islam to the democratic legal order*. This paper by the Dutch AIVD can be seen online at https://fas.org/irp/world/netherlands/dawa.pdf. Viewed 19 October 2017. **Rated B3**. See also Ayaan Hirsi Ali, *The Challenge of Dawa: Political Islam as Ideology and Movement and How to Counter It,* 21 March 2017. An executive summary can be seen at https://www.hoover.org/research/challenge-dawa-political-islam-ideology-and-movement-and-how-counter-it and the full document can be seen at https://www.hoover.org/sites/default/files/research/docs/ali_challengeofdawa_final_web.pdf. Viewed 19 October 2017. Not rated.

[3] Yusuf Qaradawi Profile. The profile can be seen online at http://www.investigativeproject.org/profile/167/yusuf-al-qaradawi. Viewed 9 April 2017. **Rated B2.**

[4] *From Dawa to Jihad: The various threats from radical Islam to the democratic legal order,* December 2004, The AIVD, The Hague, Netherlands. This intelligence agency document can be seen online at file:///C:/Users/User/Downloads/fromdawatojihad.pdf. Viewed 23 October 2017. **Not rated.**

has the right to dominate all others, they will create the political and social space necessary for confrontation and violence to emerge. This is one desired outcome of their methodology, as they then can claim that they are the victims of oppression, even as they oppress others.

A society with a growing population of Islamists has limited choices. It can resist the Islamists by using Western value systems, or commit an act of submission and accept the loss of freedom that comes with being dominated. Submission, or appeasement, has not worked out well historically for those who practice such schemes. Britain's Prime Minister Chamberlain tried appeasement with Nazi Germany in the 1930's with disastrous results. France and Belgium have tried submission to the Islamists, which may help explain why France currently has 10,000 troops on the streets on any given day (Operation Sentinelle[5]) trying to prevent further Islamist attacks.

M-103 – The Islamophobia Motion

The Parliamentary Motion 103 on Islamophobia, put forth by Member of Parliament Iqra Khalid, is very much following in the Islamist tradition described above, including their advocacy of Sharia. Muslims are not the victims of regular violence or oppression in Canada. The reality is that Blacks, Gays, and Jews are on the receiving end of most of the hate crimes in Canada.[6] The artificial furor of Islamophobia, including repeated false claims about non-existent attacks[7], is nothing more than a smokescreen on the battlefield, used to confuse and distract attention away from the real intentions of the Islamists.

Islamophobia is not defined in the M-103 Motion and with good reason. The Islamists, however, absolutely need to advance the concept of Islamophobia and the M-103 Parliamentary Motion. Their belief systems and practices are so alien to Western civilization that they could never defend them in public debates. Is a beating a form of education for women? Should we kill all the non-believers? Is death required for someone who leaves a religion? Is the way a woman is dressed a justification for rape? Should we kill all the Jews and the polytheists?

Islamist ideology also lies at the roots of the recent radicalization, terrorism, and the recruiting of youth to die here in Canada and overseas. Canada has produced a series of suicide bombers, jihadi fighters and propagandists who have died in ISIS, Algeria, Somalia, and other areas of Islamist conflict. Among those were suicide bomber Salman Ashrafi from the University of Calgary and ISIS propagandist John Maguire from the University of Ottawa. Also from the University of Ottawa was Ahmed Said Khadr, the infamous al Qaeda funder, embassy bomber and "martyr" as described by al Qaeda itself. These individuals are the products of a series of deep networks which have the structure and resources to create the social and political spaces where Islamist ideologies can flourish.

This book will expose these Islamist networks, including the most effective ones: the Muslim Brotherhood front groups. Beginning in Canada in 1958, the Muslim Brotherhood (the Ikhwan) have created a series

---

[5] An explanation of Operation Sentinelle can be seen on the French government's defence website at http://www.defense.gouv.fr/operations/operations/france/operation-sentinelle. Viewed 19 October 2017. Not rated.

[6] *Police-reported hate crime in Canada*, 2015, Statistics Canada, 13 June 2017. This government report is available online at http://www.statcan.gc.ca/pub/85-002-x/2017001/article/14832-eng.htm . Viewed 26 July 2017. **Rated B2.**

[7] See chapters eight and nine in this book for more information about false claims of Islamophobia.

of fronts[8] designed to advance their globalist cause of "settlement" and "civilization jihad" (See Annex D). This includes a policy of Entryism into the political and social structures of Canada. It will also briefly examine others such as Hizb ut-Tahrir and the Iranian sponsored Khomeneists.

The information provided to the reader will raise questions as to the most basic direction of Canada. This refers to Canadian values as expressed through the Constitution of Canada and the Charter of Rights: pluralism, freedom of speech, freedom of thought and the rights of women.

The Ideology

Ideas change the world. The Muslim Brotherhood was founded in 1928 by Hassan al-Banna. Its ultimate impact is still unknown, but its Islamist ideology has sparked both an intellectual and physical struggle which is potentially as important the Reformation. The most basic Western concepts such as the Westphalian state, freedom of speech, pluralism and individual freedoms are at the centre of the conflict. They are being lost now and this trend may be terminal. Alternatively, Hassan al-Banna's founding of the Muslim Brotherhood may either destroy Islam or a new modernist and humanist Islam may arise from the death, fire, and ashes.

Perhaps the greatest difference between the Islamist view and that of Western intellectual traditions is how the individual is placed at the centre of the ideology. In Western belief systems, individual rights and freedoms are considered paramount and sovereignty lies within the individual, not the sovereign. In the Islamists view, this is inverted, and the collective is all consuming. The individual is left with no concept of agency.

While the future is grim, the outcome is not predetermined. Violent conflict at the personal, organizational, sub-state and state level will continue to occur. Large portions of the Middle East and North Africa as well as South Asia are falling into conflict while hopes for a "future spring" appear to have died. Europe is suffering from an ever-increasing wave of Islamist inspired attacks and there does not appear to be the will to challenge this ideology, at least not in the corridors of government power. Canada and the USA are following Europe down a rather dark path.

Already, our courts in Canada are ruling in favour of individuals who work for and represent Muslim Brotherhood front groups such as the ICNA (Islamic Circle of North America). Tens of millions of "charity" dollars have been misappropriated to fund terrorist groups. It was Canadian taxpayer's money that funded al Qaeda when it was desperately seeking funding after its return to Afghanistan, much of it through the hands of Ahmed Said Khadr. IRFAN raised tens of millions of dollars in cash and services for Hamas before being shut down,[9] although the extensive RCMP criminal investigation into this fraud was quietly dropped by the current government.[10]

---

[8] Muslim Brotherhood groups can be defined as Pure Brothers, Brotherhood Spawns or organizations influenced by the Muslim Brotherhood. For more on this see Dr. Lorenzo Vidino, *The Muslim Brotherhood in Austria*, Program on Extremism at George Washington University and the University of Vienna, August 2017. The article can be seen online at https://extremism.gwu.edu/sites/extremism.gwu.edu/files/MB%20in%20Austria-%20Print.pdf . Viewed 3 October 2017. **Rated B2**.

[9] For more on the role of IRFAN, see Chapter 15 of this book.

[10] The RCMP operation was known as Project Sapphire. Its status is unclear, but the page on the RCMP website has disappeared.

Many in Canada have tried to deny an Islamist ideology issue exists, or they have sought to conceal the problems through fuzzy language. By refusing to name Islamism or to use clear language to describe it, they pretend the problem does not exist.

Another "intelligence failure in the making" is developing. The intelligence community, captured by process rather than outcomes and using a collectivist mindset, remains resistant to a changing threat environment. They continue to focus on terrorism rather than extremism. They serve short term perceptions rather than long term realities. Information sharing silos and analytical mindsets, as always, remaining the crippling underpinnings. Much as Pearl Harbour, the collapse of the Soviet Union and 911 were all missed, Entryism and the spread of the Islamist ideology is being missed or willfully ignored.

Implications

It remains unclear if Canada (and the USA) can learn the lessons of the United Kingdom, France, Belgium, the Netherlands, and Germany before the costs become unbearable. Our personal freedom may already be damaged beyond recovery. The next few years will be critical as the future course of the country and its social fabric are charted.

Western governments (Europe and North America) have been captured by their own complexity and pursue endless debates driven by identity politics, political correctness, progressivism (i.e. cultural Marxism) and the meaningless concept of "social justice." Currently, Islamists (not reformist or secular Muslims) outrank all others, including women, on the scale of social justice warriors and "progressive" politicians. Western politicians in general have no discernable values, no definable goals and no sense of the citizens and the civilization they are alleged to serve. Many, if not most of the current leadership class, are little more than experts in getting elected. Few have any real-world experience or meaningful education. Beyond words and virtue signaling, they have little to nothing on offer.

Islamists, on the other hand, have clear messages which they pursue at all costs. Their message of domination is clear. Islamists have distinct goals as defined by their ideology and from this they are building up a series of strategies, tactics, and organizational methods.[11] Their simplicity and clarity allows them to drive ahead and succeed in the face of Western politicians who confuse themselves with their lack of values. It is little wonder than voters in the West appear to be driven by anger towards government in general.

The value systems of the Islamists are barbaric, and their leadership is often unpolished, but they can advance their cause because they understand the inherent weakness of their opposition. Western values are clearly superior, but losing is a real option for societies broken down by their own lack of will, moral authority, and courage. Western politicians have, in general, become confused by delusions of their own adequacy. This is not a new problem. As Thucydides noted some 2400 years ago in his classic work The Peloponnesian War, those who consider themselves as educated or among the "intelligentsia" often lose in such conflicts. He stated: Generally, those of weaker intelligence prevailed, boldly resorting to action, not wanting to fall prey to fine words and ingenious plots. On the other hand, their more intelligent opponents fell prey to the delusion that they had plenty of time, so they perished in disproportionate numbers.

---

[11] For an earlier example of this sort of development see: Thomas Quiggin, *Understanding al-Qaeda's Ideology for Counter-Narrative Work,* Perspectives on Terrorism, Vol 3, No 2 (2009). The article is available online at http://www.terrorismanalysts.com/pt/index.php/pot/article/view/67/html . Viewed 16 August 2017. **Not rated.**

Thucydides is also noteworthy for his statement Wars spring from unseen and generally insignificant causes, the first outbreak being often but an explosion of anger. Given the anger being expressed on the streets of France, Belgium, the UK, Germany, and Canada (etc.), perhaps now is the time to return Canada to the values of the Constitution and the Charter of Rights. Otherwise, globalist policies and progressivism will lead us to wars between neighbourhoods as well as war between nations.

CHAPTER 2: DEATH THREATS, FEAR, AND SELF-CENSORSHIP

Thomas Quiggin

Key Points

- Freedom of expression and speech are under attack in Canada.
- When researching or publishing on the subject of Islamists, death threats and law suits are a constant.
- The Government of Canada is working to silence those who oppose the Islamists.

Chapter 15 of this book does not exist. The intended title was "The Killing of Apostates and Non-Believers." The intended author, a former Muslim, chose not to write the chapter about life in Canada after you leave Islam – the life of an apostate. The reason was fear. The fear of having family members harassed or killed in Canada. This is the reality of Canada today when it comes to freedom of religion, conscience, thought and expression.

No full chapter exists in this book on the horrors that face Muslim girls and women in Canada. These girls and women face death threats and fear in Canada from the oppressive Islamist ideology. Honour killings, or forced suicides as they are sometimes called, are under reported and under investigated. Police at the front lines are trying to move forward on these issues, but they speak of the problems of resistance. This resistance does not come from their (primarily white) supervisors, but from a lack of will and resources from city councils and police boards. Few are willing to speak on these issues due to the prevailing atmosphere of political correctness. One of the best-informed women in Canada has gone silent and will not publish on these matters anymore.[12] Fear is the weapon that is silencing these voices.

On the issue of the normalization of the subjugation of women, the true silence comes from the PIFs (Pro Islamist Feminists). Statements in Canada are regularly made to justify wife beating, child marriages and sexual slavery. Girls and women are women forced of out the room when they are "unclean" in Canadian public schools. But the (primarily white) PIFs remain silent. Perhaps their progressive values and social justice warrior ethics preclude them from commenting on why it is OK to beat women? Do they believe women like being beaten? (Chapter 10)

The Prime Minister's Office (PMO) has used its influence to attempt to silence a reporter on such issues. Why? Because the reporter had accurately reported on the Prime Minister's speech to a segregated mosque that has direct ties to terrorism. The PMO could not identify a single fault in the story, but chose to make a hostile call to the intimidate the reporter. (Chapter 17)

Virtually no main stream media reporting exists on the background of the mosque that was attacked in Quebec City in early 2017. However, plentiful open source information exists to show that the mosque's leadership had extensive Muslim Brotherhood ties. Was the attack against the mosque carried out because it was or because it was "Muslim Brotherhood?" Why the silence? Is the media afraid to raise the issue out of fear, or out of political correctness? (Chapter 20)

---

[12] Interview with the author.

In addition to missing chapters, this book also suffers from a certain degree of self-censorship. Two of the writers in this book are already the subjects of fatwas and/or death threats. Consequently, the use of imagery has been restricted. Fear is the reason.

But perhaps the greatest cloud hanging over writing such a book is not the Islamists and their instance on enforcing "Islamophobia" and threatening those who oppose their domination. The biggest single fear here may be from the Government of Canada. Free speech is under attack in a variety of arenas in Canada. The various motions on Islamophobia and the Heritage Canada M-103 hearings on these motions are clear indicators. The current government has chosen to champion the agenda of the Islamists over the Canadian values found in the Constitution and the Charter of Rights and Freedoms. Among those values most at risk are freedom of expression, conscience, thought, and opinion.

Prime Minister Trudeau says that Canada is now a new kind of country. We are not defined by our history or our European national origins (read Judeo/Christian/Greco values) but by a new kind of "pan-cultural heritage" (read globalist/progressive/Islamist values). His admiration for the "basic dictatorship" of China and his glowing review of Cuban dictator Fidel Castro are just two more warnings about the future of Canada.

Prime Minister Trudeau has openly cooperated with the Islamists; funded them; defended them; deflected criticism away from them and openly stated that he identifies with their vision and their beliefs. He has never met with a reformist or secular Muslim group such as Muslims Facing Tomorrow, the Muslim Reform Movement, or the Canadian Thinkers' Forum. (Chapter 12)

Implications

The enemy of Canadian society is not just the Islamists, but the triumph of the lack of will on the part of Canadians to reject the progressive/Islamist (Red/Green) alliance. This direction, aided by the Government of Canada and Prime Minister Trudeau, will lead in one direction: Submission.

CHAPTER 3: CANADIAN VALUES AND THE SOCIAL FABRIC OF SOCIETY

Tahir Gora

Key Points

- Faced with an increasing Islamist ideology problem, UK Prime Minister David Cameron ordered an integration study[13] in 2015. The author of the study, Dame Louise Casey, looked at the levels of integration between various communities in the UK.

- Some of Canada's multicultural policy-makers don't want to see Canada as a country with its own values and norms.

- Islamist groups such as the Muslim Brotherhood and Jamaat-e-Islami are paving their way to introduce Sharia law here in Canada.

Dame Louise's UK based study on integration accused public bodies of ignoring or promoting divisive and harmful religious practices because of their fear of being called racist. It also clearly stated that "Misogyny and patriarchy has to come to an end…"[14] She accepted that she is putting Muslim communities under the spotlight in her report. But she argued that bringing a community or an individual that lags behind closer to rest of the society, is a service to that community or individual.

Responding to this report, British Communities Secretary Sajid Javid said "Civil servants and other holders of public office should swear an oath to British values."[15] The study also produced the conclusion that "an oath of integration with British values and society" should be administered for new immigrants and that school children be taught "British values."

Canadian Values

When Conservative MP Kellie Leitch asks for a screening test for "Canadian values," should it sound odd to us?

It should not. What's wrong with promoting Canadian values in terms of integrating new immigrants?

---

[13] Louise Casey, "*The Casey Review: a review into opportunity and integration*." (2016). The article can be seen online at https://www.gov.uk/government/publications/the-casey-review-a-review-into-opportunity-and-integration. Viewed 16 August 2017. **Not rated**.

[14] BBC News, *"Segregation at 'worrying levels' in parts of Britain, Dame Louise Casey warns,"* 5 December 2016, accessed 14 May 2017. http://www.bbc.com/news/uk-38200989 . Viewed 16 August 2017. **Not rated.**

[15] Matt Dathan, *"Everyone employed in public office will have to swear an oath of allegiance to British values under plans to fight extremism,"* The Daily Mail Online, 18 December 2016. The article can be seen online at http://www.dailymail.co.uk/news/article-4045902/Everyone-employed-public-office-swear-oath-allegiance-British-values-plans-fight-extremism.html . Viewed 16 May 2017. **Not rated**.

The question, of course, arises: What are Canadian values? And what do we mean by integration? We could certainly write a book on Canadian values such as politeness, being sorry for everything, and elevating hockey to a religion. But our core values based on the founding principles of the country are:

- Democracy,
- Separation of religion and state,
- Gender equality including LGBT communities,
- Freedom of expression, conscience and thought;
- Individual freedom, and
- Non-acceptance of violence.

If an individual or community coming to Canada doesn't endorse these values, it's absolutely a problem for Canada, or for any democratic society.

Accepting and working with these core values would be called integration, no matter what the original cultural heritage of those concerned. Any person, from whatever faith or culture can be regarded as integrated when they live in accordance with these values.

But unfortunately, we are making this simple task difficult by playing political and religious cards. We should not support those who ask for gender segregation, mixing of religion with state affairs and curbs on the freedom of speech.

Unlike the UK which had the courage to address the issues and "call a spade a spade," Canada is burdened with reports such as that by Gerard Bouchard and Charles Taylor. Their 2008 report titled BUILDING THE FUTURE: A Time for Reconciliation[16] is a feel-good bureaucratic effort.

Then Quebec Premier Jean Charest announced the establishment of the consultation commission on accommodation practices related to cultural differences on 8 February 2007.

In their findings, Bouchard and Taylor emphasized the importance of Canadians understanding immigrants' cultures rather than urging immigrants to learn about their host country. This appears to be consistent with the post-modernist belief that all cultures are somehow "equal" and that something is wrong with "us" if we insist that "they" adapt to the rules of our house. As an aside, this is consistent with Prime Minister Justin Trudeau's belief that we not only have to tolerate the practices of other cultures, but we must accept them.

The general public's lack of knowledge or interest in this report indicated one more reality; that ordinary people don't feel such solutions work on the ground. Our governments should have understood by now

---

[16] Bouchard, Gérard, and Charles Taylor. *"Building the Future." A Time for Reconciliation. Report* (2014). The article can be seen online at http://red.pucp.edu.pe/wp-content/uploads/biblioteca/buildingthefutureGerardBouchardycharlestaylor.pdf . Viewed 16 May 2017. **Not rated.**

that such reports don't make much sense to the public. By importing the cultures and problems of other countries, we shift the area of trouble from the national border down to the neighbourhood.

Many citizens have strong negative feelings about some immigrant communities looking for different laws and norms in this country. They especially react to the demands of some fundamental Islamist groups. The angry outbursts at the Peel Regional Board of Education are examples of this.[17]

It looks like some of our multicultural policy makers don't want to see Canada as a country with its own values and norms, especially those based on the founding cultures. PM Justin Trudeau is one of those as he insists that Canada is a "post national state." Similarly, feel-good academics, policy-makers and their associated commissions want to present Canada as a role model to the world, a country where one can regularly see veil/burka-wearing Muslim female drivers, delivering a message across the world how great a multicultural society this country is.

Such commissions, suffering from delusions of their own competence, remain fascinated by their illusions. They do not understand the fragmentation level within those religion-bound immigrant communities. Rather, these commissions are causing more division. They have no clue that the rights they are advocating in certain communities are already bones of contention within those circles.

They don't know that very few Sikhs are looking to overrule the laws. The bureaucrats, politicians and commissions show their pride in turning Canada into a country of hodgepodge laws where some Sikhs are walking to school with their kirpans (ceremonial knives) and some Sikhs are asking Canadian law to be overturned so they can wear turbans instead of motorcycle helmets or safety hard hats.

They don't understand that most Muslim women don't dream of wearing burkas. Nor do most Muslim women want to be beaten in their homes, nor do they think being beaten is a type of education. They do not see being beaten as a sign of "love and concern." Very few Muslim men are looking to create prayer places in the corridors of their work places.

Why then are governments spending millions of dollars on commissions and consultants to prepare reports of hundreds of pages? Why do the governments consider special accommodation, but only for the highly vocal and visible minorities? Do we hear any unusual and abnormal demands by the Chinese, the biggest immigrant community? Do we hear of requests by Filipinos, Latinos and eastern Europeans? No.

We have large immigrant communities from those parts of the world as well. Why do we give so much importance to the demands of a few members of just some immigrant groups?

The time and effort spent on these reports and hearings could be much better spent on teaching immigrant groups about cultural norms of their Canada, their host country and new home. This of course, assuming our governments believe in Canadian values any more.

Such are the challenges we face in our changing social fabric.

---

[17] See, among many others, Caroline Alphonso, *Ontario school board's Muslim support fuels hate, threats*, the Globe and Mail, 18 April 2017. The article can be seen online at https://beta.theglobeandmail.com/news/toronto/peel-school-boards-muslim-support-fuels-hate/article34746614/?ref=http://www.theglobeandmail.com& . Viewed 16 May 2017. **Not rated**.

Canadians react to another recent issue, Anti-Islamophobia Parliamentary Motion 103.

Islamist groups such as the Muslim Brotherhood and Jamaat-e-Islami are paving their way to introduce Sharia law here in Canada. Federal parliamentary motion number 103 (also known as M-103) on Islamophobia is part of this activity. It seems that Islamist groups in Canada are trying their best to prove that Islamophobia is a big issue here. Some Muslim Canadian MPs are working hard in our federal parliament on behalf of the Islamist cause.

Under the guise of "eliminating systemic racism and religious discrimination," MP Iqra Khalid tabled only the second motion[18] of this type in parliament to curb "Islamophobia" in Canada.

M-103 is unnecessary. If there would have been islamophobia, Canadians would have not elected 11 members of the Muslim faith to the Canadian Parliament (Ten Liberal and one Conservative).

Progressive Muslims find it difficult to raise questions about this loose motion. It's against the wind of populism. Since the Liberal Government passed M-103, opponents to modernist Muslims are calling them traitors and infidels. But modernist Muslims are the voice of the voiceless. It is also they who suffer at the hands of Islamists.

Canadians of diverse religious backgrounds are also concerned about mixing religion with politics. Unfortunately, most politicians are playing with this motion for their short term political gain, but they are unable to understand the magnitude of damage they are causing to our own beloved Canada. They are unable to understand the damage to Muslims in Canada. This motion has put Muslims' safety and security at risk. Now, Muslims in Canada are selected targets of backlash and retaliation.

If MP Khalid was concerned about the "root causes" of Islamophobia, she might find broader support. Islamophobia is generally defined as a "dislike of or prejudice against Islam or Muslims, especially as a political force." So why are the Islamists seen so poorly and what are the root causes of disliking Islam and Muslims in Canada and elsewhere?

Could it be groups such as the Islamic Circle of North America? For instance, what Canadians see in the Islamic Circle of North America education syllabus is regarded as offensive. They believe that:

- Women are inferior to men;
- Western civilization is the enemy of Islam;
- Songs, music, jesters, buffoons are satanic work;
- A Muslim wife must obey her husband when he calls her to bed;
- A majority of the dwellers of hell are women; and
- A pregnant adulteress is to be stoned after giving birth.

---

[18] House of Commons, *Iqra Khalid – Private Members' Motions – Current Session*, Parliament of Canada. http://www.ourcommons.ca/Parliamentarians/en/members/Iqra-Khalid(88849)/Motions?sessionId=152&documentId=8661986 . Viewed 16 May 2017. **Not rated**.

This mindset, and many others like it, are the basic root cause for any potential "Islamophobia."

But our Canadian Muslim organizations and Muslim Members of Parliament (MPs), such as Iqra Khalid, fail to condemn this syllabus. Iqra Khalid and her family, however, do appear to have good relations with this group.

One possible request for MP Iqra Khalid would be to have her ask the Islamic Circle of North America remove this offensive syllabus from their website.

Would Muslim and non-Muslim parliamentarians, who are striving to denounce Islamophobia, strive equally hard to denounce and remove this mindset from the larger part of my Muslim community?

Similarly, when Canadians see Canada's Security Intelligence Report about how over 180 Muslim Canadians have joined ISIS abroad, what message does that send to Canadians about my Muslim community?

What about our Muslim MPs, such as Iqra Khalid, Salma Zahid or Omar Alghabra, who have close ties with all the Islamic establishments in Canada? They speak very loudly about the need to protect the reputation of Muslim community and Islamic centers. But what about the need to curb radical mindsets and distance themselves from the concept of armed jihad?

None of our Muslim MPs condemned any of the Islamic preachers who recently chose to sit down during Canada's national anthem in Mississauga.

None of our Muslim MPs have questioned the role of the Muslim Student Association, affiliated with the Muslim Brotherhood, and who are active in 17 out of 19 high schools in Mississauga. They are seeking the right to preach in the schools.

Every year, various Islamic centers together arrange a hateful Al Quds Rally in Toronto against the Jewish community and Canada's best friend and ally in the Middle East, Israel. What message do Canadians get through this ugly rally? Will Muslim MPs challenge the hateful messages of this rally?

Our Muslim MPs, who are advocating more for their Muslim communities than their own country, should not appear as hypocrites by asking Canadians to change their mindset while not asking their own communities to leave certain hateful practices behind.

How would Canadians react to a conference of over 20,000 Muslims in Toronto in which some speakers talked about killing homosexuals? Similarly, how would they feel about acts ranging from my Muslim community's general conspiracy theories as well as men and women being segregated? What about adherence to Sharia values? Would this make our neighbors and fellow Canadians comfortable with us?

In short, faith is a personal matter to every individual. Communities should not bring these sorts of beliefs into our social fabric.

The Burka Debate

The advocates for the right of Muslim women to wear veils ignore one basic reality: This is not about Islamic faith. If wearing the veil was a faith-oriented right, every Muslim woman should be striving for it.

But most Muslim women, in Islamic countries and in the West, don't practice this tradition, which was traditionally imposed by Muslim men.

It seems ironic to me that some Western feminists and intellectuals speak loudly in favour of Muslim women's right to put the veil over their faces. No sensible person is in favour of forcing women to take off their veil, but many Muslim scholars and women's groups are opening a debate on whether the veil represents Islamic values.

Since veil-wearing women and their proponents have a right to state their opinions, those who oppose this trend have the same right. The clear majority of Muslim opponents think that the traditional veil is clearly a mark of separation, and consider it an element of the fanatical side of Islam.

Should anyone have a problem with the consensus of most Muslims? If most Muslims call the veil tradition an "attempt at separation" (not only in the West but in their own Islamic countries, too), should this statement be called -- as it has been -- absurd?

If Western proponents of the veil see that as absurd, they may also appreciate the actions of suicide martyrs waging jihad, encouraged by the minority of literalist, fanatic Islamists.

Hold on for a minute. I do understand there is a difference in the degree of fanaticism between the veil issue and suicide attacks. But both fall into the core category of fanaticism. The opponents of the veil do not want to snatch them from women's faces. But they will keep exercising their right to denounce it just as they denounce other fanatical elements of the Muslim world.

There is a need to understand the difference between being separate and being moderate. There is also a need to understand that most Muslim women who don't wear these emblems are still followers of Islam. The conclusion of this debate should be that wearing a particular item of dress should be a person's choice. But showing yourself -- your identity -- should be a choice made by society.

If a woman wants to show a hardcore Islamic religious symbol, she can be modest and wear a headscarf. When a woman puts on a niqab (a head-covering with a slit for the eyes), a burka (a full-body garment that hides the eyes as well) or a face veil, then she must grant society the right to decide whether that is appropriate to wear in public.

It seems obvious to me that a secular society can't accept citizens concealing their identity. Just as the Netherlands, France, Austria and Germany are banning the burka and veil in public places, so women's rights groups need to understand the reasons -- which seem simple and logical to me -- behind the decision.

There is no harm if Canada goes the same way (although there is no plan to do so). Such a decision wouldn't be against the multicultural mosaic of Canada. It would help us Canadians show our secular and moderate face.

What is Multiculturalism? And what is the Canadian version of it?

These are among the hottest debates in our society these days. Does multiculturalism mean blending all cultures in one pot, or does it increasingly mean keeping all ethnic communities separated from each other?

According to the Department of Canadian Heritage definition, "Multiculturalism ensures that all citizens can keep their identities, can take pride in their ancestry and have a sense of belonging." But belong to what? To one's own ethnic community or to Canadian society?

This definition states further, "The Canadian experience has shown that multiculturalism encourages racial and ethnic harmony and cross-cultural understanding, and discourages ghettoization, hatred, discrimination and violence." This is less than clear on the ground, when attacks in St Jean sur Richelieu, Ottawa, Edmonton and Toronto seem to indicate.

How does this discourage ghettoization? It is hard to explain this part while saying the multiculturalism also encourages the "sense of belonging" to one's own ethnicity.

Critics often attack this contradiction, saying this is a particularly Canadian form of multiculturalism. Visible minorities, such as Chinese, South Asian, Arab, Black and South American communities are across Canada, congregated mainly in big cities such as Toronto, Montreal, Vancouver, Calgary, Edmonton, Ottawa and Hamilton.

But the Canadians from (or descended from) European Caucasian nations, who have long had a strong feeling of "owning" this country, raise the questions and concerns. "Hey, we have made the rules of laws of this land. Hello newcomers, welcome. But make no mistake: stoning or burning women alive won't be tolerated and faces are not to be covered except at Halloween."

In our multicultural mosaic, none of the ethnic communities except Muslims have fundamental clashes with "Canadian values" such as women's liberties, openness, separation of religion from community or questioning religious scriptures, etc. Drinking alcohol or sexual freedom is equally shared by the majority and most other minority communities. Killing the non-believers is not acceptable.

The Islamists clash with multiculturalism is not due to cultural reasons but on the mixing of Islamic religious orders with cultural values.

In our definition of multiculturalism, though, we didn't endorse religious scriptures. We need to make it clear that our model of multiculturalism should be structured based on multiple cultures not multiple religions. There is a separate debate to be had on how religion reflects culture and to what extent. But religion must be made separate from culture; otherwise it is hard to reach a harmonious and practical model of multiculturalism.

Our multicultural model weakens when we try to introduce religious ethnicity into it. That's the point where we don't understand why things don't go smoothly. Instead of blending different religions, the mixing up of cultures could be the right path to multiculturalism.

Implications

True multiculturalism and integration can only flourish when cultural values - not religious restrictions - come together. Agree to disagree

CHAPTER 4: MODERNIST MUSLIMS AND WHY THEY ARE LOSING

Tahir Gora

Key Points

- Islamists in Canada insist on being Muslims in the first place, while denying all other national, ethnic and heritage lineages.
- Islamists in Canada are getting funding from Saudi Arabia, Iran, Qatar and Kuwait.
- Modern Muslim groups have huge challenges ahead of them to get their voices heard. Without their success, the social fabric of our Canadian society will continue to tear.

Who are Humanists and Modernist Muslims? How do we define them? These were the type of questions I began posing to myself in the early 1990s while living in Pakistan. At that time, I had identified myself as a follower of Punjabi Sufi Islam that was a manifesto of living in harmony with all diverse communities such as Shias, Ahmaddies, Christians and Hindus.

At that same time, the Islamists group Jamaat-e-Islami had their own perception of what it meant to be a "Muslim." They would commonly harass, attack and torture those people who they did not believe were "their kind of Muslims." They were Islamists, which is to say they were insisting on being a Muslim in the first place, while denying all other national, ethnic and heritage lineages. They also attempted to dominate all others into their political and ideological view of Islam. Jamaat-e-Islami were quite hostile towards Ahmaddies, Christians and Hindus in particular. The Islamists were pushing 'us' to leave all other identities behind and forcing individuals to stick to one identity: Islam.

I narrowly escaped their torture a couple of times. I could never relate with their type of Islam. To the contrary, I started counting myself among those who were identifying themselves as a humanist first, then along ethnic identity lines such as Punjabi, Sindhi and Pashtun etc. We were not identifying ourselves Muslims in the first place.

That was the point where I first realized the difference between being an Islamist or a modern humanist Muslim. An Islamist believed in being a Muslim only and forcing all others to accept their politicalized view of Islam. By contrast, a humanist and modern Muslim was the one who could be a nationalist, proud of one's own heritage and having faith in Islam.

Canada

I arrived in Canada in April 1999 with a hope that I will be able to identify myself as a Canadian Pakistani Punjabi of Indian heritage and a follower of Sufi Islam. Much to my surprise, however, Canadian Islamist organizations fiercely confronted me. They started labelling me a kind of an infidel, anti-Islam and anti-Muslim. I was none of these, but nonetheless I was being described as an apostate.

For the past 30 years, I have been at forefront of confronting the Islamists and their ideology. During this time, I have worked with several modernist Muslim groups and individuals in Canada, the USA and Europe. This has also led me to contacts in South Asia and Australia as well.

Such modern Islamic groups have never been large in numbers and resources. There maybe two dozen leadership figures around the globe.

This was noted in a New York Post article[19] by Dr. Daniel Pipes on 23 September 2003, when he wrote that:

> "Other outspoken academics include Saadollah Ghaussy formerly of Sophia University in Tokyo, Husain Haqqani of the Carnegie Endowment for International Peace, Salim Mansur of the University of Western Ontario and Khaleel Mohammad of San Diego State University. Journalists such as Tashbih Sayyid of Pakistan Today and Stephen Schwartz (who has written for The Post and The Weekly Standard, among others) are on the front lines against militant Islam in the United States, as is the writer Khalid Durán. Tahir Aslam Gora has the same role in Canada."

Death Threats and Fatwas

I founded the "New Islam Movement" in 2000. Merely forming this group landed me into a wave of fatwas, death threats, harassment, and bullying.

Interestingly, I am also witness to some of our so-called "Modern Muslim" groups and leaders who became tools in the hands of those who were anti-Muslims. Some of them went far to attack Muslims to gain media hype. Others made it a business model. Some turned themselves into celebrities so that they could travel the globe while lecturing about Islam. Others left Islam and joined different ex-Muslim organizations. Those in the latter category tend to be relatively honest people.

However, some individuals opted to stay within the orbit of Islam and keep fighting with the Islamists from within. These are the individuals whose lives are in danger.

Currently, the modernists are losing their ground to the larger and better funded Islamist groups in Canada, the USA and other Western countries. This is due not just to less numbers and resources, but also their rejection by Western governments, political parties, media and policy makers.

The modernists and humanists represent many "ordinary" Muslims but they don't yet the offices, mosques or Islamic Centers to expand their base. As such, they do not attract attention.

Most of the mosques and Islamic Centers in Canada are run by those groups who are affiliated with the Muslim Brotherhood and Jamaat-e-Islami. Hence, they are not only getting funding from Saudi Arabia, Iran, Qatar and Kuwait etc., but also raise millions of dollars every month by the growing number of Muslim visitors. The Government of Canada funds them directly through cash grants as well as indirectly by giving their front groups charitable status through the Canada Revenue Agency.

Because of this foreign and domestic funding, the Islamists with their exclusionary and supremacist ideology are attracting individual politicians, their parties as well as policy makers and the media.

Implications

---

[19] Daniel Pipes, *"[Moderate] Voices of Islam," New York Post*, September 23, 2003. The article can be seen online at http://www.danielpipes.org/1255/moderate-voices-of-islam. Viewed 24 July 2017. **Rated B2.**

Modern Muslim groups, who are in the middle, have a long road ahead of them. They need to attain the resources and develop the strategies to handle the extremist Islamists such as the Muslim Brotherhood and Jamaat-e-Islami front groups. At the same time, they need to confront the growing wave of opportunist anti-Islamists. The fabric of society depends on their success.

CHAPTER 5: POLITICAL CORRECTNESS AND THE DAMAGE TO THE SOCIAL FABRIC OF OTHER COUNTRIES

Thomas Quiggin

Key Points

- The West suffers from Harry Potter Syndrome when dealing with the Islamist aspects of Islam. If you cannot name your problem, how can you challenge it? This is the Voldemort Effect.
- Political correctness and the fear of "rocking the multicultural community boat" resulted in the rape and trafficking of some 1,400 girls aged 11 to 14 in the United Kingdom.
- Political correctness, when wielded by Islamists and their apologists, is nothing more than a cudgel used to silence critics into submission.

Introduction

It is reasonable to believe that terrorism is not yet an existential threat to Canada. The Islamist ideology, however, can be assessed as a threat to Canada, as it has begun to erode our most basic values.

But the greatest threat to Canada is not terrorists with bombs or guns. It may net even be the ideological groups that radicalized them. We might be able to defeat them.

The greatest single threat to Canada may be political correctness. The values of Canada, expressed by the Constitution, the Charter of Rights and Freedoms and the Criminal Code of Canada are the bulwarks of our lives. The fundamental freedoms, as expressed in the Charter, are freedom of conscience, freedom of religion, freedom of thought, freedom of belief, freedom of expression, freedom of the press and of other media of communication, freedom of peaceful assembly, and the freedom of association.

Each one of these fundamental values has already been harmed by political correctness. For instance, it is a fact that publicly funded forums in Canada, such as universities, are being used to advance wife beating as an acceptable practice, not least because women view it as a sign of love and concern.[20]

To see the damage that has occurred, we can look at the democracies in Europe. Political correctness is tearing the social fabric of society and damaging lives. The response to mass rapes in the UK was originally silence, as those who enforced the will of political correctness believed that abstract values such as community balance outweighed fundamental rights such as the right to stay alive and unmolested. The rapes of Rotherham and the 2015 New Year's Eve attacks in Cologne highlight the issue.

Rotherham UK and Mass Rape: Political Correctness, Community Balance, and Criminal Cover-ups

It is a fact that community leadership figures, such as feminists, mayors, city councilors, police, and Members of Parliament can exist in a culture of denial. At the same time, they will suppress reports on criminal activity to maintain community balance.

---

[20] *A Tale of the Handmaidens – Violence Against Women in Canada.* The article is available in Annex J.

The facts in this situation are that the Jay Report in the United Kingdom (26 August 2014) detailed how a wide variety of officials in the City of Rotherham deliberately covered up the grooming and mass rape of 1400 girls to avoid issues of racism. The report, which was accepted by the Parliament of the United Kingdom,[21] even details how one individual who attempted to address the mass rapes was sidelined, threatened with dismissal, and sent on a two-day ethnicity and diversity course.[22]

In Rotherham, between 1997 and 2013, a conservative estimate suggests that 1,400 primarily white girls between the ages of 11 and 14[23] (but some as young as nine[24]) were groomed[25] in Rotherham and then "raped by multiple perpetrators, abducted, trafficked to other cities in England, beaten and intimidated."[26] The perpetrators of the institutionalized abuse of the girls were, as the official report noted, primarily Pakistani-Kashmiri Muslim men. The fact that 1,400 girls could be forced into sexual slavery in a British town of 257,280 while no one noticed staggers belief.

It is also a fact that a variety of civic officials, town councilors and a Member of Parliament had been aware for years of the abuse, but had remained silent or punished those who spoke out. It was also noted that the three of the previous inquiries from 2002, 2003 and 2009 had found similar issues, but those reports were "effectively suppressed."[27] One researcher who reported the rapes faced hostility from the city council. Her records and information were stolen and destroyed by an unknown person who also likely worked for the council.[28]

The Home Secretary at the time of the report was Theresa May. She blamed the failure of the authorities in Rotherham on "institutionalized political correctness."[29] The Victims' Commissioner, Louise Casey, followed up with a report that stated, "misplaced political correctness" and "a staggering culture of denial" allowed more than 1,400 vulnerable girls to be routinely abused. "Some councilors have not lived up to the high standards expected of those in public life or their positions of responsibility."

---

[21] For the full report see http://www.parliament.uk/business/committees/committees-a-z/commons-select/communities-and-local-government-committee/inquiries/parliament-2010/jay-report-rotherham/ Viewed 19 June 2017. **Rated A1.**

[22] *Rotherham Whistleblower 'Sent On Diversity Training For Saying Most Abusers Were Asian,'* Huffington Post, 2 September 2014. The report can be seen online at http://www.huffingtonpost.co.uk/2014/09/02/rotherham-abuse-researcher-diversity-course_n_5750560.html . Viewed 19 June 2017. **Rated C2.**

[23] For the full report see www.rotherham.gov.uk/.../independent_inquiry_cse_in_rotherham.pdf

[24] http://www.telegraph.co.uk/news/uknews/crime/11391314/Rotherham-child-sex-abuse-scandal-council-not-fit-for-purpose.html . Viewed 19 June 2017. **Rated A1.**

[25] For one personal account of the grooming and abuse process, see *A Rotherham Abuse Survivor Speaks Out*. It can be seen online at: http://s.telegraph.co.uk/graphics/projects/rotherham/index.html . Viewed 19 June 2017. **Rated C2.**

[26] Page 7/159 of the PDF version of the Jay Report. This can be seen online at www.rotherham.gov.uk/.../independent_inquiry_cse_in_rotherham.pdf *Viewed 19 June 2017.* ***Rated A1.***

[27] *Rotherham child abuse scandal: 1,400 children exploited, report finds*, BBC News, 26 August 2014. http://www.bbc.com/news/uk-england-south-yorkshire-28939089 . Viewed 19 June 2017. **Rated B2.**

[28] Alison Holt, *Rotherham abuse: Researcher 'faced council hostility'* BBC Panorama, 1 September 2014. The article can be seen online at http://www.bbc.com/news/uk-england-south-yorkshire-29012571 . Viewed 19 June 2017. **Rated B2.**

[29] *May blames 'institutionalised political correctness' for Rotherham scandal.* The Guardian. 2 September 2014. The article is online at: http://www.theguardian.com/uk-news/2014/sep/02/theresa-may-political-correctness-rotherham-abuse . Viewed 19 June 2017. **Rated C2.**

Ms. Casey further wrote: "The issue of race is contentious, with staff and members lacking the confidence to tackle difficult issues for fear of being identified as racist or upsetting community cohesion.[30] The Jay Report notes that a known deep-rooted problem exists with Pakistani-heritage perpetrators targeting young white girls. Ironically, when a city councilor of Pakistani heritage wanted to tackle the issue head on, he was over ruled by the other largely white, Labour Party councilors.[31]

The issue of widespread sexual abuse of young girls had also been raised by Ann Cryer, the Labour MP for Keighley. Unfortunately, her attempt to address the issue of young girls being groomed for sexual abuse resulted in her being attacked and shunned by her own party. Frustrated by the lack of a response from politicians, social workers, and the police, she finally found one city councilor (of Pakistani heritage) to take the names and addresses of 35 of the offenders to the local elders and Imams. According to The Guardian newspaper report, the councilor tried but with no results:

> "He said to the imams, 'Ann Cryer would like you to go around to these families and explain that this behaviour is totally un-Islamic.' But the upshot was that the elders allegedly said, 'Go back to Ann Cryer and tell her it's nothing to do with us.' "[32]

Perhaps the most stunning admission of all came from the Member of Parliament for the Rotherham area. Denis McShane, the former Labour MP, was questioned by the media the day after the Jay Report was released. He made a stunning statement concerning the role of multiculturalism in the UK. Speaking to the BBC, he stated:

> "I think there was a culture of not wanting to rock the multicultural community boat if I may put it like that."[33]

Mr. McShane also said he was aware of the problem of cousin marriages and the oppression of women within parts of the Muslim community in Britain. He added, however that:

> "Perhaps yes, as a true Guardian reader, and liberal leftie, I suppose I didn't want to raise that too hard."

A reasonable opinion can be formed that a culture of political correctness, denial and cultural relativism led the officials responsible to abdicate their responsibilities. Faced with the rape and abuse of 1,400 white girls on one hand, and the fear of being called racist or Islamophobic on the other, a wide range of officials chose to allow the destruction of young lives to continue, rather than risk their own moral high ground upon which their belief in political correctness had placed them.

---

[30] Evans, Martin, *Rotherham Council Ignored Child Abuse by Asian Gangs Because of 'Misplaced Political Correctness'*, Report Concludes." The Daily Telegraph, 4 February 2015. The article can be seen online at http://www.telegraph.co.uk/news/uknews/crime/11391314/Rotherham-child-sex-abuse-scandal-council-not-fit-for-purpose.html . Viewed 19 June 2017. **Rated B2.**

[31] Pages 99 and 100 of the PDF version of the Jay Report of above. (Pages 93 and 94 of the text version).

[32] Helen Pidd, *Rotherham report 'reduced me to tears', says MP who exposed abuse decade ago*, The Guardian, , Saturday 30 August 2014 23.01 BST. The article can be seen online at: http://www.theguardian.com/uk-news/2014/aug/30/rotherham-girls-could-have-been-spared-ann-cryer . Viewed 19 June 2017. **Rated B2.**

[33] Gordon Rayner, *Denis MacShane: I was too much of a 'liberal leftie' and should have done more to investigate child abuse,* The Telegraph, 5:35PM BST 27 Aug 2014. The article can be seen online at: http://www.telegraph.co.uk/news/uknews/crime/11059643/Denis-MacShane-I-was-too-much-of-a-liberal-leftie-and-should-have-done-more-to-investigate-child-abuse.html . Viewed 19 June 2017. **Rated B2.**

Cologne Germany: Breaking the Wall of Silence

The attacks and sexual assaults against women in Cologne Germany on New Year's Eve (2015/16) were not new.

It is a fact that such attacks, featuring coordinated actions against local women by largely Islamist/Muslim migrants, had occurred for years in Europe. What was new was that the main stream media in Germany was finally forced into reporting on the events. The original response from the Cologne Police was that the evening had been "largely peaceful" and had occurred in a "relaxed atmosphere."[34] It has not yet emerged if the police in Cologne, like many others, had been pressured into adopting politically correct narratives rather than factual reporting.

By 15 February 2016, the "peaceful" event had resulted in 1,075 complaints to the police of which 467 involved sexual assaults. Most of the rest of the complaints involved assaults and robbery. Most damning was that some of the complaints accused the police of denial of assistance to the victims[35] although it may be that the police were simply overwhelmed. At least one female police undercover officer was sexually assaulted during the evening.[36]

A variety of political officials attempted to downplay assaults by saying the Cologne attack was an isolated event that was not organized, nor were their large numbers of migrants involved. Their politically correct narratives were subsequently destroyed in the following weeks.

Cologne was not the only city to suffer such widespread sexual attacks on women by migrants on that evening. Similar attacks were carried out in Hamburg, Frankfurt, Dortmund, Düsseldorf, Stuttgart, and Bielefeld.[37]

The attempt to say that the attacks were not organized was destroyed by the Deputy Chief of Police of the Finnish City of Helsinki. As with Cologne, Helsinki suffered a wave of sexual assaults on New Year's Eve 2015/2016. However, unlike Cologne, it appears the police in Helsinki were partially prepared for the

---

[34] The report that the evening had been largely peaceful (Ausgelassene Stimmung - Feiern weitgehend friedlich) came from the Twitter account of the Cologne (Koln) Police and was released on the morning of 1 January 2016. For more on this, and an image of the original Tweet, see the Der Spiegel article *Übergriffe an Silvester: De Maizière wirft Kölner Polizei Versagen vor* published on 5 January 2016. The article can be seen online at: http://www.spiegel.de/politik/deutschland/koeln-innenminister-thomas-de-maiziere-kritisiert-koelner-polizei-a-1070651.html . Viewed 19 June 2017. **Rated B2**.

[35] For more on the number of assaults and complaints about the police, see the N-TV article *Vorwurf: Unterlassene HilfeleistungAnzeigen gegen Kölner Polizei eingegangen* which was published on 13 January 2016. The article can be seen online at: http://www.n-tv.de/politik/Anzeigen-gegen-Koelner-Polizei-eingegangen-article16761856.html . Viewed 19 June 2017. **Rated B2**.

[36] RP-Online, *Angriffe auf Frauen in Köln: Täter packte Zivilpolizistin in die Hose*, 4 January 2016. The article can be seen online at: http://www.rp-online.de/nrw/staedte/koeln/uebergriffe-auf-frauen-in-koeln-taeter-packte-zivilpolizistin-in-die-hose-aid-1.5667697 Viewed 19 June 2017. **Rated B2**.

[37] For more on sexual assaults and violence on New Year's Even 2015/2016, see the following online articles: http://www.faz.net/aktuell/politik/inland/koeln-meldet-inzwischen-106-anzeigen-nach-uebergriffen-an-silvester-14000124.html , http://www.welt.de/politik/deutschland/article150798244/Hunderte-sollen-Bielefelder-Disco-attackiert-haben.html , http://www.rp-online.de/nrw/panorama/bielefeld-junge-frauen-durch-antanztrick-sexuell-belaestigt-aid-1.5671781 and http://www.stuttgarter-nachrichten.de/inhalt.uebergriff-auf-frauen-in-silvesternacht-weitere-mutmassliche-opfer-in-stuttgart.dfe30c13-9ce5-4bc3-b80f-eac86485ae96.html Viewed 19 June 2017. **Rated C3**.

outbreaks. Helsinki police broke up New Year's Eve attacks before they got started based on intelligence collected from asylum centres. As they believed would happen, approximately 1,000 asylum seekers had gathered in the tunnels surrounding the central railway station by 11pm.[38] Notwithstanding the preparations, Ilkka Koskimaki, the deputy chief of police in Helsinki stated that "We have never before had this kind of sexual harassment happening at New Year's Eve." The Deputy Chief also added that "sexual assaults in parks and on the streets, had been unknown in Finland before record 32,000 asylum seekers arrived in 2015..."[39]

A series of sexual assaults also occurred on New Year's Eve 2015/16 against women in the Swedish cities of Malmö, Helsingborg, Karlstad, and Kalmar.[40] However, the most damning information, appears to have come from Stockholm where widespread sexual assaults against Swedish women at a major summer festival appeared to have gone deliberately unreported for at least two and a half years and perhaps since the year 2000.[41]

After the Cologne attacks became widely discussed in the European press, the Swedish newspaper Dagens Nyheter reported events in Stockholm at previous events, but then became involved in a scandal where they were accused of having hidden information about previous attacks in the summer of 2014 and 2015. The entire event became tangled with the police and the newspaper blaming each other for failing to report the events.[42] The Swedish Prime Minister blamed the police.

While who is to blame remains unresolved, Swedish women were sexually attacked and robbed at a summer festival called "We are Sthlm."[43] Police reports about the festival had reported that the events "proceeded calmly" but a later report by the newspaper Dagens Nyheter review shows that internal emergency reports have been hushed up. The attacks were against girls as young as 11 and 12 and were

---

[38] For more on the intelligence gathering prior to the attacks and the events of New Year's Eve 2015/16 in Helsinki, see the article by Richard Orange, *Unprecedented sex harassment in Helsinki at New Year, Finnish police report*, The Telegraph, 8 January 2016. The article can be seen online at: http://www.telegraph.co.uk/news/worldnews/europe/finland/12088332/Unprecedented-sex-harassment-in-Helsinki-at-New-Year-Finnish-police-report.html . Viewed 19 June 2017. **Rated B2.**

[39] For more on the statement of the Deputy Chief of Police of Helsinki, see the 11 January 2016 Finland Today article *Helsinki Deputy Police Chief: Sexual Assaults in the Streets Were Unknown Before Asylum Seekers Arrived in 2015.* The article can be seen online at: http://finlandtoday.fi/helsinki-deputy-police-chief-sexual-assaults-in-the-streets-were-unknown-before-asylum-seekers-arrived/ . Viewed 19 June 2017. **Rated B2.**

[40] For more on the attacks in these four cities, see http://www.sydsvenskan.se/malmo/gang-ofredade-kvinnor-pa-nyar-i-malmo/ , http://www.sydsvenskan.se/opinion/aktuella-fragor/det-var-som-om-djungelns-lag-radde-pa-knutpunkten/ , http://www.sydsvenskan.se/opinion/aktuella-fragor/det-var-som-om-djungelns-lag-radde-pa-knutpunkten/ and http://www.sydsvenskan.se/opinion/aktuella-fragor/det-var-som-om-djungelns-lag-radde-pa-knutpunkten/ . Viewed 19 June 2017. **Rated C2.**

[41] For more on the accusation that officials had been hiding the sexual assaults sine the year 2000, see the series of articles by the Swedish Dagens Nyheter paper which can be seen online at: http://www.dn.se/nyheter/sverige/stockholms-stad-kande-till-overgreppen-i-flera-ar/ . Viewed 19 June 2017. **Rated B2.**

[42] For more on the chain of events that led to claims about the non-reporting of events, see the 11 January 2016 article *Questions and answers on DN's handling of events in the Kungsträdgården.* The article can be seen online at: http://www.dn.se/nyheter/sverige/questions-and-answers-on-dns-handling-of-events-in-the-kungstradgarden/. Viewed 19 June 2017. **Rated B2.**

[43] See the Dagen Nyhetere 11 January 2016 article: *Questions and answers on DN's handling of events in the Kungsträdgården.* The article can be seen online at: http://www.dn.se/nyheter/sverige/questions-and-answers-on-dns-handling-of-events-in-the-kungstradgarden/ . Viewed 19 June 2017. **Rated B2.**

known to have been carried out by "migrant youths." The police, aware of the problems in the summer of 2014, appeared to have tried for greater enforcement in 2015. However, according to their own reports, widespread sexual assaults occurred anyway.[44]

The Jump from Social Media to the Mainstream

While difficult to assess with clarity, it is a reasonable to believe that the outcry on social media concerning the mass attacks in Cologne was responsible for bringing the attacks to the public's attention. A few politicians in Germany have accused the media of under-reporting events for fears that it could cause an anti-immigrant backlash. Both the police and the mainstream media appear complicit in hiding the organized and large-scale nature of issue. Germany's public broadcaster Zweites Deutsches Fernsehen (ZDF) admitted that they did have a "clear enough" view of the events and should have broadcast.[45]

Attempts to Mislead and Blame Women

It has been factually shown that even after the general details of the attacks in Cologne (and elsewhere) were known, a variety of media, political and religious figures attempted to mislead the public or blame the women as victims. In one rather ill-thought out piece of advice, Henriette Reker, the (female) Mayor of Cologne suggested that women should keep "at an arm's length" from strangers to avoid sexual harassment.[46] Sadly, this sort of advice suggests that women are somehow to blame or are at least partially responsible for the attack. How a woman is supposed to be able to fend off a group of two to twenty men attacking her was not made clear.[47]

It is also a fact that an Imam in Cologne also suggested that the women themselves were at fault. In his first statement to the press, Imam Abu Yusuf stated that "If they're half-naked and wearing perfume, it's not surprising that such things would happen." When asked by a second media outlet to confirm his statement, he stated that "There were scantily clad women who were wearing perfume as they walked through the drunken crowd. For some North Africans, this was reason to grope the women." In a third interview, he did state that he did not approve of such actions (i.e. attacking women) and "That doesn't mean that I think women shouldn't be allowed to dress like that."[48]

---

[44] The police attempt to respond to the sexual assaults is discussed in the 11 January 2016 Dagen Nyheter article *Assaults at the Stockholm festival have never been fully investigated.* The article can be seen online at: http://www.dn.se/nyheter/sverige/assaults-at-the-stockholm-festival-have-never-been-fully-investigated/ . Viewed 19 June 2017. **Rated B2.**

[45] Kate Connolly, *Tensions rise in Germany over handling of mass sexual assaults in Cologne*, The Guardian, 7 January 2016. The article is available online at: http://www.theguardian.com/world/2016/jan/06/tensions-rise-in-germany-over-handling-of-mass-sexual-assaults-in-cologne . Viewed 19 June 2017. **Rated B2.**

[46] Kate Connolly, *Cologne attacks: mayor lambasted for telling women to keep men at arm's length*, The Guardian, 6 January 2016. The article can be seen online at: http://www.theguardian.com/world/2016/jan/06/cologne-attacks-mayor-women-keep-men-arms-length-germany . Viewed 19 June 2017. **Rated B2.**

[47] According to Cologne Police, the size of the groups attacking women were from two to three to as many as twenty men in one group. For more on this see the police report at: http://www.presseportal.de/blaulicht/pm/12415/3215530 Viewed 19 June 2017. **Rated C2.**

[48] For more on the series of events and interviews, see Deutsche Welle press story by Kate Brandy of 21 January 2016 titled *Cologne imam: Women provoked sex attacks by 'wearing perfume' and being 'half-naked'.* The story is available online at: http://www.dw.com/en/cologne-imam-women-provoked-sex-attacks-by-wearing-perfume-and-being-half-naked/a-18997352 . Viewed 19 June 2017. **Rated B2.**

It is a known point that the blaming of women and the denial of reality is not unique to the Cologne case. In the Rotherham case above, a variety of girls had reported to the police about their abusers, sometimes with their fathers present. However, nothing was done. As one press article noted:

> Powerless white working-class girls were caught between a hateful, imported culture of vicious misogyny on the one hand, and on the other a culture of chauvinism among the police, who regarded them as worthless slags. Officials trained up in diversity and political correctness failed to acknowledge what was effectively white slavery on their doorstep. Much too embarrassing to concede that it wasn't white people who were committing racist hate crimes in this instance.[49]

Conclusions

It can be concluded from the above facts that Canada, the USA and Europe are facing a series of social, economic and political challenges in which the role of Islamists will play a prominent role. The challenges will come from front groups for the Muslim Brotherhood, Hizb ut-Tahrir, the Iranian Khomeneists, the Saudi funded Wahhabi movement, and the direct support of Qatar.

It is also reasonable to believe that the media and politicians in Canada cannot openly address issues such as the advocacy of wife beating,[50] sex with nine-year-old girls[51] and sexual assaults in public. If issues as blatant as the advocacy of wife beating cannot be discussed, how do we address Female Genital Mutilation, forced suicides and child marriages? Feminists, especially those who occupy positions of wealth, power or privilege should speak out – yet they are silent.

In the longer term, it is reasonable to suggest that we need to address political entryism, campus extremism and charities being used to fund extremism and terrorism overseas and here in Canada. The issues of freedom of thought, speech and expression are being corroded, but the very forces who should be at the forefront of such debates are silenced by their own self-censorship and political correctness. The media, and what one might loosely call the intelligentsia, are trapped by their delusions of their own competency and their self-imposed isolation from reality.

Implications

An opinion can be formed that if we do not have an intelligent and open discussion about the social and cultural future of Canada in a reasoned manner, then we will have the decisions made in a time of crisis by unreasoned voices and those in positions of power. It can also be concluded that political correctness, when wielded by Islamists and their apologists, is nothing more than a cudgel used to silence critics.

---

[49] Allison Person, *Rotherham: In the face of such evil, who is the racist now?*, The Telegraph, 27 August 2014. The story is available online at http://www.telegraph.co.uk/news/uknews/crime/11059138/Rotherham-In-the-face-of-such-evil-who-is-the-racist-now.html . Viewed 19 June 2017. **Rated B2.**

[50] A variety of Imams and student organizations in Canada advocate violence against women and wife beating. For more on this see *A Tale of the Handmaidens – Violence Against Women in Canada.* The article can be seen in Annex J.

[51] The Imam and Alim (resident religious scholar) of the Jaffari Mosque in Toronto at 9000 Bathurst Street openly advocates that girls can be married after the age of nine and that qualified temporary marriages are permissible for them as well. For more on these beliefs see *The Jaffari Mosque in Toronto: Strange Events and Police Action.* The article can be seen in Annex J.

CHAPTER 6: EXTREMISM, VIOLENT EXTREMISM, AND TERRORISM

Thomas Quiggin

Key Points

- Compromise with the Islamists is impossible.
- The ideology of the Islamists is incompatible with Western values.
- Islamist groups are, by definition, extremist in that they are totalitarian, non-pluralist and anti-democratic and believe their ideology is superior to any man-made law such as the Constitution of Canada or the Charter of Rights and Freedoms.

It is reasonable to believe that no way can be found to resolve the differences between Western values and the Islamists. The idea that 'moderate Islamists' exist is a contradiction in terms – a seductive illusion. No compromise can exist with those who have the objective to dominate you and eliminate your belief systems.

Islamists are totalitarians who are strikingly intolerant of any other form of social or political organization.

> "Accommodating the political demands of Islamist extremists in the context of Western democracies as a quid pro quo for pacifying hotheads among their ranks runs the risk of degenerating into a never-ending appeasement policy."[52]

This is the view of Alex Schmid, a Swiss-born Dutch scholar in terrorism studies and a former Officer-in-Charge of the Terrorism Prevention Branch of the United Nations. He is a long-time scholar and observer of extremism and terrorism of all categories. He adds that short term tactical alliances might in the long run do more harm than good. These alliances tend to legitimize the Islamist ideological leaders and their groups while they are rejecting Western values and taking advantage of their host societies.

It is a reasonable opinion that Canada (and much of the West) has been plagued by a series of weak political leaders. As in the past, they choose the path of appeasement when faced with totalitarian ideologies.[53] They hope, against all evidence, that by cooperating with the "non-violent Islamists/extremists," the problem will go away. Additionally, we have leaders who may believe that "diversity" and "multiculturalism" means allowing barbaric practices to flourish under the guise of "tolerance."

For many observers and analysts, a distinction exists between the acceptable "non-violent extremists" and the unacceptable "violent extremists." This creates a false distinction, as non-violent extremists may be more effective at undermining our social fabric than their more violent cousins who employ terrorism.

---

[52] For more on violent and non-violent extremism, see: *Violent and Non-violent Extremism: Two Sides of the Same Coin*, by Alex P. Schmid. It is available online at http://www.icct.nl/download/file/ICCT-Schmid-Violent-Non-Violent-Extremism-May-2014.pdf . Viewed 19 June 2017. **Rated A1.**

[53] For an example, see Chapter 12 of this book on Prime Minister Trudeau's relationship with the Islamists.

Extremism in all forms needs to be challenged and confronted, rather than accommodated and tolerated by liberal democracies.

It is necessary to make a distinction between "non-violent" and "not-yet-violent." Groups such the Muslim Brotherhood have been violent in past circumstances, such as the assassination of Egyptian President Anwar Sadat. They have advocated death by martyrdom as a means of advancing their cause. The Muslim Brotherhood are currently listed as a terrorist entity in a variety of countries such as Saudi Arabia, Egypt and the United Arab Emirates.[54]

It is a fact that a recent United Kingdom report states that the Muslim Brotherhood is deliberately opaque, habitually secretive organization that has a highly ambiguous relationship with extremism. The report further adds that "Both as an ideology and as a network it has been a rite of passage for some individuals and groups who have gone on to engage in violence and terrorism."[55]

Yet a variety of Muslim Brotherhood front groups regularly claim that they are non-violent. It is reasonable to believe that adherents of the Muslim Brotherhood, (and others) justify the violence and coercion when it suits their cause, and oppose it when it does not. As such, it is fair to say they might be "not-violent" while operating through North American front groups, but it is cannot be said they are "non-violent."[56] Their claims to be "non-violent" are false as you cannot claim to be "non-violent" on one hand and then justify the actions of martyrs (suicide bombers) on the other.

Based on the facts, it is reasonable to believe that adherents of Islamist beliefs often use two voices when speaking. To the public, they claim to believe in democracy and pluralism. But when they talk among themselves, the voice is different. They are clear when they state that their version of Islam is incompatible with democracy. Take the Islamic Circle of North America (ICNA) as an example. It is an Islamist group which adheres to the beliefs of the Muslim Brotherhood and Jamaat-e-Islami. They maintain a public façade of moderation, yet their own writings state:

- The political system of Islam is totally incompatible with Western democracy.
- The concept of government party and the opposition is alien to Islam.
- All belong to one Ummah with only one goal and pursue the same aims and objects of Islamic guidelines![57]

---

[54] For the most recent listing of a variety of Muslim Brotherhood front organizations, see the UAE official list online at http://www.thenational.ae/uae/government/list-of-groups-designated-terrorist-organisations-by-the-uae . Viewed 11 April 2017. **Rated A1.**

[55] The Prime Minister's statement on the UK investigation into the Muslim Brotherhood can be seen at https://www.gov.uk/government/speeches/muslim-brotherhood-review-statement-by-the-prime-minister . Viewed 19 June 2017. **Rated A1**.

[56] For more on the issue of non-violent vs not-violent extremism, see the article by Alex Schmid titled *Violent and Non -Violent Extremism: Two Sides of the Same Coin?* It is available online at http://www.icct.nl/download/file/ICCT-Schmid-Violent-Non-Violent-Extremism-May-2014.pdf . Viewed 19 June 2017. **Rated A1**.

[57] For an explanation and more on this view see *ICNA Canada refutes Trudeau: "Islam is totally incompatible with Western democracy".* The article is available online at http://en.cijnews.com/?p=27451 . Viewed 19 June 2017. **Rated B2.**

he Muslim Brotherhood in North America also makes their view clear. In their 1991 Explanatory Memorandum on the General Strategic Goal for the Brotherhood in North America[58] the following statement was made:

> "The process of settlement is a 'Civilization-Jihadist Process' with all the word means. The Ikhwan [Muslim Brotherhood] must understand that their work in America is a kind of grand jihad in eliminating and destroying the Western civilization from within and 'sabotaging' its miserable house by their hands and the hands of the believers..."

What is missed by many observers, and those who believe in cooperating with "moderates" such as the Muslim Brotherhood, is the following statement which is on the same page:

> "We must possess a mastery of the art of 'coalitions', the art of 'absorption' and the principles of 'cooperation.'"

From this, a reasonable opinion can be formed that Islamist groups such as the Muslim Brotherhood have a long-term strategy for their work in the West. They appear to be willing to enter temporary coalitions and cooperate, if it suits their long-term goals.

Ironically, although groups such as the Muslim Brotherhood, al Qaeda and ISIS are aligned in both ideology and objectives (a totalitarian caliphate), they differ widely in strategy and approach. ISIS in their Dabiq magazine[59] targeted several Muslim Brotherhood adherents for death.[60] In the eyes of ISIS, any individual cooperating with the West, even for gain, is an apostate and should be rewarded with death.[61] This applies, even if those involved in the cooperation have similar long terms goals as ISIS. The same can be said of al Qaeda adherents such as Dr. Ayman al Zawahiri. Himself a former Muslim Brotherhood member, Dr. Zawahiri wrote extensively on his dislike for the (then) lack of overt violence in Muslim Brotherhood processes.[62]

It is a fact, however, that the Muslim Brotherhood has a clear position of supporting violence. On 28 January 2015, they said they would return to a general path of violence with the following statement:

> "It is incumbent upon everyone to be aware that we are in the process of a new phase, where we summon what is latent in our strength, where we recall the meaning of jihad and prepare

[58] A copy of the general memorandum and a translation as used the Holy Land Relief terrorism funding trial can be seen at https://www.investigativeproject.org/documents/misc/20.pdf . Viewed 19 June 2017. **Rated B2.**

[59] For more on DABIQ, see the Clarion Project report at http://www.clarionproject.org/category/tags/isis . Viewed 19 June 2017. **Rated C3.**

[60] Among those on the target lists with Muslim Brotherhood connections are Sayeeda Warsi (AKA Baroness Warsi of the UK), Huma Abedin, Hamza Yusuf, Abdullah Hakim Quick and Mohamed Elibiary. Nihad Awad of CAIR USA is not named on the list, yet his picture appears predominantly in the article. Viewed 19 June 2017. **Rated C3.**

[61] In the words of ISIS, *One must either take the journey to dār al-Islām, joining the ranks of the mujāhidīn therein, or wage jihād by himself with the resources available to him (knives, guns, explosives, etc.) to kill the crusaders and other disbelievers and apostates, including the imāms of kufr, to make an example of them, as all of them are valid – rather, obligatory – targets according to the Sharī'ah, except for those who openly repent from kufr before they are apprehended*." For more on this see the Clarion Project report at http://www.clarionproject.org/category/tags/isis . Viewed 19 June 2017. **Rated C2.**

[62] For more on Dr. Zawahiri's views on the Muslim Brotherhood, see his book *Bitter Harvest.* For an introduction to this book see https://ent.siteintelgroup.com/Jihadist-News/site-institute-2-15-07-intro-to-second-edition-zawahiri-bitter-harvest.html. Viewed 19 June 2017. **Rated C2.**

ourselves, our wives, our sons, our daughters, and whoever marched on our path to a long, uncompromising jihad, and during this stage we ask for martyrdom." [63]

Assessing Islamist Front Groups and Organizations

In police, intelligence, governmental and even civil organization circles, the question often arises: How do you tell the difference between the "good guys" and the "bad guys" when searching out reliable contacts within the larger Muslim community? How do you distinguish between reliable partners and those who may be front groups; wanting cooperation only for Entryism? Which are the Islamists?

Questions should be asked about the nature of the group in question. Using the work developed from Roger Eatwell and Matthew J. Goodwin[64] comes the idea that a group can be extremist in either its values or its actions. Therefore, individuals such as Ronald Wibtrope[65] have suggested distinguishing between the groups in the following manner:

- Extreme by method but not by goal;
- Extreme by goal and method; and
- Extreme by goal but not method.

It can be believed that Islamist groups fall into both categories '2' and '3' above in that their goals are extremist (totalitarian caliphate) and frequently employ extremist action to accomplish those goals. Therefore, groups which are Muslim Brotherhood or Khomeneist fronts will also have an extreme goal but will only apply violence in what they determine to be the proper context.

Frequently, the standard that is applied when questioning groups as potential partners in the Muslim community is "Do you reject the use of terrorism?" The question is meaningless. Firstly, even those that favour violence would not identify themselves as terroristic in nature. They would see themselves as Soldiers of Allah in a just cause. Secondly, they will frequently lie anyway.

A more detailed and incisive approach is required. The following is perhaps a better set of questions or research points to finding better partners in the Muslim community. Does the group in question have:

- Respect for the constitution and the laws of the democratic state of which they are citizens or residents;

---

[63] The MEMRI Project. For this quotation and other information see *Muslim Brotherhood Turn to Terrorism Against Al-Sisi Regime: Threats of Attacks Against Foreign Diplomats, Workers In Egypt On Turkey-Based MB TV, Calls For Jihad And For Assassination Of Al-Sisi, Regime Head*, 20 February 2015. The articles can be seen online at http://www.memri.org/report/en/0/0/0/0/0/0/8446.htm . Viewed 19 June 2017. **Rated B2.**

[64] *Violent and Non-Violent Extremism: Two Sides of the Same Coin?*, Alex P. Schmid, ICCT Research Paper, May 2014. The article is available online at http://www.icct.nl/download/file/ICCT-Schmid-Violent-Non-Violent-Extremism-May-2014.pdf . Viewed 19 June 2017. **Rated A1**. For more on the work of Eatwell and Goodwin, see Robert Eatwell and Matthew J. Goodwin, *Introduction: the 'new' extremism in twenty-first century Britain*, in Robert Eatwell and Matthew J. Goodwin, eds. The New Extremism in 21st Century Britain (London: Routledge, 2010), p. 11. **Rated B3**.

[65] Ronald Wibtrobe, *Extremism: The Political Economy of Radicalism*, (Cambridge: University Press, 2006), p. 84. **Rated B3**.

- Respect for universal human rights in general and equal rights for women in particular;
- The presence or absence of efforts to create a parallel society that is separate from the democratic society;
- The presence or absence of efforts to introduce and enforce Sharia-law in its own communities;
- Evidence of incitement to jihad or glorification of (suicide) terrorism;
- Evidence of financial support for jihad in Muslim-majority countries facing Islamist insurgencies; and
- Participation in armed struggles in conflict zones?[66]

By combining the above points with an assessment of the ideological figures that inspire the group, a reasonable determination can be made as to whether the group is an Islamist group or not.

Implications

It is a reasonable opinion that Islamist groups are extremist in that they are totalitarian, non-pluralist and anti-democratic. Additionally, and consistent with their belief in Sharia, they advocate systemic violations of human rights in their approaches to women, gays and other identifiable minorities. Knowing who these groups are and how they operate in Canada is critical to eliminating them.

[66] *Violent and Non-Violent Extremism: Two Sides of the Same Coin?*, Alex P. Schmid, ICCT Research Paper, May 2014. The article is available online at http://www.icct.nl/download/file/ICCT-Schmid-Violent-Non-Violent-Extremism-May-2014.pdf . Viewed 19 June 2017. **Rated A1**.

CHAPTER 7: CAN WE ELIMINATE THE DANGERS OF POLITICAL ISLAM?

Saied Shoaaib

Key Points:

- Political Islam can and must be confronted before it gains further momentum in Canada.
- Understanding the Mecca and Medina interpretations of Islam is key to understanding Islamist ideology and Islamist terrorism.

Is it possible to eliminate the dangers of political Islam in Canada?

The answer is yes. If the Islamist ideology is aggressively addressed, it can be defeated or minimized. But this requires informed work, moving from reaction to action. Canada should not wait for more terror strikes coming from political Islam – the Islamists. We need a more precise definition of political Islam and its related Islamist terrorism. This is the basis on which we build solutions. We also need to rethink the tools of confrontation because they have not achieved the results we wish. There are also obstacles which hamper success, most of which are incorrect concepts which are fixed in the public mind as well as the political and media elites.

Stated differently, we must not just pursue terrorists, we must shut down the factories of Islamist ideology. It is from those factories that the violent and non-violent extremists emerge. These individuals can also be thought of as "armed" and "not armed."

What is political Islam?

When I said to my neighbour that we need as Muslims to remove the political side of Islam, as it is the cause of all the problems, for us and the world, he answered decisively: But what will remain of Islam?!

This is precisely the person who can be described as an "Islamist" or a "non-violent extremist." This type of person does not accept any other form of Islam. He refuses to deal with any others and will even kill someone who does not accept his version of Islam, even if he is a Muslim. He also believes that "Islam is both a religion and a state," and a Muslim is required to support the idea of a global "Islamic Caliphate." According to him, the Caliphate is the state of God, a state that implements the Sharia and is ruled by Islam.

Because of this widely held belief, it is difficult to separate Islam as a religion from political Islam. Sheikh Ahmed al-Tayeb (Grand Imam of al-Azhar, the largest Islamic Sunni university and institution in the world) believes that:

"Islam is the religion of the state, Arabic is its official language, and the principles of Islamic Sharia are the main source of laws."[67]

In an Islamic state such as this, the ruler is Muslim and other religious minorities have no rights. It also means applying Sharia, like cutting off the hand of the thief, stoning an adulteress to death, throwing homosexuals from a building, and killing a Muslim who leaves Islam, etc.

The Shiites, the largest Islamic group after the Sunnis, adopt the same ideology. The religious basis is the same, the difference is in some of the ritual details. Both Sunnis and Shiites have in the past established expansionary colonial empire; there is no substantial difference. Ironically, the Shiite Muslim state was persecuting the Sunnis, and the Sunni Muslim state was persecuting the Shiites.[68]

In 1979, Ayatollah Khomeini founded a religious and dictatorial state in Iran, like the states ruled by Sunni Islamists such as Sudan, the Taliban in Afghanistan, and ISIS in Syria and Iraq. The 1979 Iranian constitution said that the ruler must be a Shiite of the Twelver Jafariya doctrine, not only a Shiite but a Shiite of a specific sect. It also includes the "Wilayat al-Faqih" (who rule) on behalf of the absent imam whom Shiites await at the end of world. The function of this imam is understood as: "by order of God he sets the religion and application of the Sharia of Islam, (and he) has absolute rule over the Muslims."[69]

In Canada, there is Sunni influence through Saudi and Gulf funding. There is Khomeneist influence by Iranian funding and support, such as Imam As'ad Jafri, who believes in the Islamization of Canada, America and the West. He told his followers: "We must not work for anything else and anyone else, we must work to establish the government of God." He also believes that "Islam is not a regional religion for the Middle East, but for every place in the world." He further added "When Islamic values collide with the values of Canada, you have to choose the path of Islam."[70]

Therefore, there is no fundamental difference between Shiite and Sunni ideology in political Islam. There is also no fundamental difference between the Muslim Brotherhood and Sunni Islamic religious institutions; they are adopting the same ideology. The Sheikh of Al-Azhar is proud when he meets with some of the leaders of the Muslim Brotherhood, including the General Guide Muhammad Badi. The Sheikh has pointed out that half of the members of the Brotherhood studied in Al-Azhar.[71]

This same set of political beliefs can be seen in other leading Islamist figures. They believe that there is "only Islam" and there is no possible division of Islam as a religion and Islam as a political force. They believe that the very concept of "political Islam" is a Western creation designed to attack them. Among those who advance this belief are:

- Sheikh Yusuf Qaradawi, one of the great fathers of the Muslim Brotherhood, who states: "Political Islam" is an application of a plan devised by Islam's opponents, based on the division of Islam. It is not Islam as send by God, it is not as we believe.

---

[67] *Al-Azhar: Islamic sharia red line*, Islam Online, 31 January 2012. The article can be seen on line at https://islamonline.net/782 . Viewed 15 June 2017.

[68] https://www.sasapost.com/shia-states/

[69] http://www.irfaasawtak.com/a/separation-religion-from-state-3/327965.html

[70] Book "Lovers of Death" by Thomas Quiggin and Said Shoaaib.

[71] https://www.youtube.com/watch?v=0szh-o9yLlU and http://www.youm7.com/story/2011/5/3//الإمام-الأكبر-يستقبل-مرشد-الإخوان-وأعضاء-مكتب-الإرشاد-ويؤكد-الإخوان403917

- As the president of the World Union of Muslim Scholars, Yusuf Qaradawi also adds: Islam is as God has decreed, it can only be political. If Islam is stripped of politics, it must be another religion, which can be Buddhist, Christian or otherwise.[72]

- Dr. Sajid al-Abdali, former head of the Political Bureau of the Salafist Movement in Kuwait, asserts that the term political Islam carries great distortions.[73]

- Dr. Jaafar Sheikh Idris, a professor at some Saudi universities, says that the term "political Islam" is a Western industry and has made it a trick to discredit and repudiate religion.[74]

- The Sheikh of Egypt Abdul Rahman Abdul Khaliq steps to the true, saying: Fragmentation of Islam and take part of it and leave the other part, is a disbelief of God.[75]

The idea of political Islam is existing in Canada, widespread among Muslims. For example, the Muslim Foundation put an ad on its website that it is following method of Hassan al-Banna, who founded the Muslim Brotherhood in 1928. As is well known, his group founded the "State of Islam" and then "the world's professor," i.e. the Islamic caliphate.[76]

Another model of Islamic political Islam advocates is the Canadian-Egyptian Dr. Tarek Abdel Halim, the founder of Dar Al-Arqam schools and Dar Al-Arqam Mosque. He believes in an Islamic state which is governed by Sharia. And he says: There is no way to achieve it except through jihad. It is a complete demolition and building process, demolition of an existing system, from its roots, with all its institutions and perceptions, building an alternative system based on Islamic perception.[77]

This ideology has been adopted by different Islamic countries in the Middle East and even the League of Arab States. In 1996, the Council of Arab Ministers of Justice of the Arab League unanimously approved the unified Arab penal law.[78] This law provides for the killing of the apostate, killing the adulterer and the adulteress and cutting off the hand of the thief.[79]

Islamic countries outside the Middle East are pursuing the same method. The Constitution of Pakistan say: "All laws must comply with the teachings of Islam, which are mentioned in the Quran and the Sunna. It is not permissible to enact a law that contradicts these teachings." (Article 227).[80]

We do not need to point the Islamic countries that espouse this ideology; those who cannot catch up with modernity. Nor to the terrible violations against religious minorities and human rights in these countries. Sunni states oppress the Shiites on their soil and fight them out of their territory, and Shiite states are persecuting the Sunnis on their land and fighting them outside. It is not allowed to exist any different

[72] http://www.qaradawi.net/new/Articles-10353
[73] http://islamport.com/w/amm/Web/135/5002.htm
[74] http://islamport.com/w/amm/Web/135/5002.htm
[75] http://ar.islamway.net/fatwa/22581/ ما-مفهوم-الإسلام-السياسي
[76] http://ar.islamway.net/fatwa/22581/ ما-مفهوم-الإسلام-السياسي
[77] http://tariq-abdelhaleem.net/new/Article-72693
[78] Http://www.carjj.org/node/237 and http://goo.gl/kl7J5W
[79] http://www.ahewar.org/debat/show.art.asp?aid=488149
[80] https://www.constituteproject.org/constitution/Pakistan_2012.pdf?lang=ar

Islamic doctrine and any Muslim innovators, let alone non-Muslims. This happens even in Islamic countries that adopt a light version of this ideology such as Egypt.

How Did Political Islam Spread Throughout the World?

Islam began to spread over 1,400 years ago. It was the ideological basis of a colonial empire and it was this ideology that made it possible for the empire to exist. At the outset, the "Quraysh" (the tribe of the Prophet Muhammad) led the unification of the tribes of the Arabian Peninsula (by consent or by force) under the banner of "Islamic monotheism." The difficult task of political unification between warring tribes allowed the "Quraysh" to lead the other tribes as they invaded their surrounding world with under the "banner of Islam."

This religious banner was based on one the more violent political aspects of Islam, and developed it with what can be called a "colonial imperial jurisprudence". The Islam of that day allowed no other form of jurisprudence to grow. Any that tried were crushed, as was the case with many of them: Al-Hallaj, Mu'tazilah, Ibn Rushd, and others.

An empire is not built on the love and respect of those occupied or conquered. If an empire is going to invade and occupy a country and plunder its wealth, the occupier must believe that their system is the best. This requires an ideology to support it. There is, perhaps, no stronger ideology than religion, and after the occupation, the ideology of submission must be forced onto the occupied people. The rapid expansion of the Islamic Empire over several hundred years was no exception. It was much the same a that of the Roman Empire, the Persians, and others. Much the same can be said for the more recent colonial empires of France, Spain, England, and others.

Christianity often went hand in hand with the conquest of what France, Spain and England called the "new lands" they had "discovered." Christianity was used as one of the colonial tools to consolidate the new ideology and spread its culture, language, and religion.

There is, however, a difference between Christianity and Islam. Christ did not govern by himself, nor did his apostles, who conveyed his message, rule. In Islam, the Prophet Muhammad (PBUH) and his companions ruled by themselves without a secular or national leadership. They fought to establish the Islamic ideology in both armed and unarmed campaigns.

Another difficulty, reflected in today's problems, is that the Muslim rulers throughout the history of the various Islamic empires did not allow the existence of a religious institution (such as the Vatican). There was no Islamic jurisprudence that existed outside of their control. That is, the ruler was himself the representative of religion, through imams, and they were used as the ruler wanted. Of course, there were exceptions among the clerics and thinkers, but they were often met with severe repression.

Unlike the current day Islamists, no one else is demanding the return of their old empires. No call exists for the return of the Roman or Byzantine Empire, nor even the newer empires such as the French, Spanish, British or others. It is also hard to find anyone demanding the return of the form of government of these empires. It is even more difficult to find anyone who now demands that the Vatican return to power or even impose its religious authority on Western societies. The Vatican itself has ruled this out.

The West has fought long battles for religious reform. Instead of religion becoming an obstacle to progress, Christianity and Judaism in one way or another became supportive of human progress. But in the Islamist case, the prevailing religious culture is entrenched in the ideology of conflict and the expansion of empire as interpreted though the writings of Mohammed when he was in his Medina phase.

Unfortunately, many Muslims did not derive the human values that are in Islam and Islamic history. Therefore, consciously or unconsciously, they regularly support political Islam as well as both violent and non-violent extremist ideology. This may explain many of today's behaviours. Many Muslims will stand up in millions and protest should someone criticize the Prophet Muhammad. Some of them carry arms and kill, as in the case of Charles Hebdo. But they rarely move, not even in dozens, to reject the crimes of terrorist organizations. Maybe they feel like Muslims like them are "unstoppable" and are not outside fold of Islam.

After the collapse of the Ottoman Turkish Islamic Caliphate early in the last century, there was a chance. At that point, the rulers believed they could dismantle this colonial religious ideology and establish an alternative ideology that supported the liberation and prosperity of their peoples. Unfortunately, the current rulers in Turkey have become part of the problem, not the solution. President Erdogan of Turkey has become an absolutist ruler such as the Saudi royal family in Saudi Arabia. Islamic institutions subject to these rulers adopted the most violent ideology and hatred, and published them. There is no significant difference between Al-Azhar, Dar Al-Uloom University in India, Islamic University of Pakistan and Umm Al-Qura University in Saudi Arabia. They have left the Muslims captive to this ideology, even when they fought a conflict with the Islamists. Perhaps they did not realize that the Islamists are the product of this ideology in the here and now. They are the greatest threat to their regimes. Some may know and fear the loss of their religious legitimacy.[81]

The Islamist ideology is believed by Muslims around the world and most of them are not even aware of other ideologies. Many Muslims are ready to accept political Islam and are moving easily from religious to non-violent Islamists beliefs and then onwards to Islamist violence. The ideology for all of them is the same one. Therefore, as an example, the Muslim Brotherhood has spread to more than 81 countries, from the Philippines to China, Chechnya and Russia. The Islamists have access to power in some countries, such as Sudan and Turkey as well as having indirect access in other countries such as Morocco, Jordan, Pakistan, and others. Political Islam did not invest this ideology, but maintained and befitted from it to implement their political project.

Now, it can also be seen that Islamists have spread their reach into Canada, the USA, the UK, France, and Germany to name but a few Western countries. Their future is growing well, as these countries have already adopted a submissive posture to this new colonial invader.

Is this a Threat to Canada, America, and the West?

Yes, because this ideology is not limited to believers as individuals, not even its role is limited to the establishment of an Islamic state, but a fundamental part of the faith is the spread of this ideology everywhere. It is a religious duty, part of the faithful. So, the Gulf states, Turkey and Iran spend billions of dollars to spread the ideology of political Islam in the West.

It is true that all religions include advocacy, but in this Islamic situation is linked to violence and coercion, it is inspired by the "Islamic imperialist empire", which was founded on an occupying power and

[81] More details in the upcoming book "Islamization of Canada and America"

subjugation of other people. So, political Islam is a part of Islam, and this part believes that Islam is not about "Peace," but rather is about the "Submission" of others to their will.

These types of Islamist follower include many organizations. Among them are:

- Islamist groups such as the Muslim Brotherhood, ISIS, al Qaeda, the Renaissance movement in Tunisia, and the Justice and Development Party in Turkey;
- Islamic institutions and universities such as Al-Azhar in Egypt and the University of Median in Saudi Arabia;
- International institutions such as the International Union of Muslim Scholars and the Organization of the Islamic Conference; and
- Countries such as Saudi Arabia, Pakistan, and others.

The Islamists believe they have divine orders which were delivered to them more than 1,400 years ago. But they read them and implement them as if the Prophet Muhammad (PBUH) had received them now. They believe these divine orders must be applied always and in all places.

Mecca and Medina – Two Interpretations

The life of the Prophet Muhammad has two different aspects. This is reflected in both the Quran and in the various Hadiths (sayings of the Prophet). The first aspect is that of the life of the Prophet in Mecca, the city in which he was born and began his calling. The second aspect is that of his life after he moved to Medina following his persecution and the attacks upon his followers in Mecca.

The differences between these two aspects is quite stark. When Muslims refer to Islam as a religion of peace and they call upon the faithful to accept the beliefs of others, they are generally reliant upon Quranic quotations and Hadith from the Meccan period. When the Islamists call for death to the infidels and the killing of polytheists, they are reliant upon quotations from the Medina period.

The struggle for the soul of Islam can be seen through this dichotomy. Modernist and humanist Muslims wish to add science and democracy to move Islam ahead into modernity. They follow the Meccan traditions of the Prophet. When the Islamist want to drive Islam back into the 6th Century while imposing their interpretation of a caliphate on all others, they follow the traditions of Medina period.

Some of the quotations from the Meccan period include:

- Invite (all) to the Way of thy Lord with wisdom and beautiful preaching; and argue with them in ways that are best and most gracious: for thy Lord knoweth best, who have strayed from His Path, and who receive guidance. (Sura An-Nahl/The Bees 125)
- And the servants of (Allah) Most Gracious are those who walk on the earth in humility, and when the ignorant address them, they say, "Peace!"; (Sura al Furqan, 63)
- To you be your Way, and to me mine. (Sura al Kafirun, The Unbelievers: 6)
- If it had been thy Lord's will, they would all have believed, all who are on earth! Wilt thou then

compel mankind, against their will, to believe! (Sura Yunus: 99)

- If Allah had so willed, He would have made you a single people, but (His plan is) to test you in what He hath given you: so strive as in a race in all virtues. The goal of you all is to Allah; it is He that will show you the truth of the matters in which ye dispute; (Sura al Maaida 48)
- We sent thee not, but as a Mercy for all creatures. (Sura al Anbaya/Prophets: 107].
- Let there be no compulsion in religion: Truth stands out clear from Error: whoever rejects evil and believes in Allah hath grasped the most trustworthy hand-hold, that never breaks. And Allah heareth and knoweth all things. (Sura Al-Baqarah: 256)
- Say: "It is Allah; and certain it is that either we or ye are on right guidance or in manifest error!" (Sura Saba: 24)

It also includes many of the hadiths, which calls for tolerance, such as:

- "A woman entered Hell because of a cat which she tied up and did not feed, nor did she let it loose to feed upon the vermin of the earth." (Narrated by al-Bukhaari, 3140; Muslim, 2242).
- "I have been sent just to perfect the noble manners (ethics)." (Corrected by Al Albani)
- "Those closest to me in the hereafter (Day of Resurrection) are those who invoked blessings upon me the most (in dunya) (Narrated by Ahmad and Tirmidhi and Ibn Hibban)
- "Whoever killed a Mu'ahid (a person who is granted the pledge of protection by the Muslims) shall not smell the fragrance of Paradise." (Sahih Bukhari)

You will notice here that these Quranic verses contain "total values" and express the tolerance of others. The call to Islam does not include any violence or coercion. Islam is an invitation to "peace" with self and with others, not "surrender" or "submission" to the other.

These verses and Hadiths are not the problem. They do not form the religious basis for the armed terrorists and the Islamist extremists.

But what of the Quranic verses quoted by the terrorists and Islamist extremists? They are from the Medina period and convey an entirely different side of Islam:

- Fight those who believe not in Allah nor the Last Day, nor hold that forbidden which hath been forbidden by Allah and His Messenger, nor acknowledge the religion of Truth, (even if they are) of the People of the Book, until they pay the Jizya with willing submission, and feel themselves subdued. (Al-Tawba 29)
- They do blaspheme who say: "Allah is Christ the son of Mary." But said Christ: "O Children of Israel! worship Allah, my Lord and your Lord." Whoever joins other gods with Allah, - Allah will forbid him the garden, and the Fire will be his abode. There will for the wrong-doers be no one to help. (Al Maaida 72)
- They do blaspheme who say: Allah is one of three in a Trinity: for there is no god except One Allah.

> If they desist not from their word (of blasphemy), verily a grievous penalty will befall the blasphemers among them. (Al Maaida 73)

Much the same can be said for the Hadiths which quote the Prophet in the Medina period. Among them are:

- Who's my soul is in his hand (God), no one a Jew, nor a Christian, die and did not believe in my message, he will be in hell. (Saheeh Muslim)
- Get out the infidels from the Arabian Peninsula. (Bukhari and Muslim)
- I ordered that I fight people until they testify that there is one God and that Muhammad is the Messenger of God. They establish prayer and pay zakat. If they do that, they will protect their blood and money from me. (Bukhari and Muslim)
- "If a Muslim discards his religion, kill him." - Prophet Muhammad (Sahih Bukhari 4:52:60).
- I sent the sword in my hand to worship God alone without partner, God make my livelihood under the shadow of my spear and God make humiliation to who contradicts my order." (Narrated by Imam Ahmad.)

This second aspect in Islam is the one that was attained after the Prophet Muhammad emigrated from his city Mecca to Media (Yathrib). It began with his companions in protecting his call and publishing it, with the tools of that time, including the armed and unarmed armed struggle. Therefore, it was normal for the "enemies" to be non-Muslims, the "infidels" and the owners of the competing Abrahamic religions, the Jews and the Christians. You can say that religion at that time was the national identity in terms of our time, that is, the Muslims were not only a religious gathering, but they were also an armed political gathering, as a state within the concepts of that time. He who was non-Muslim was outside this political gathering, often an enemy, including Christians and Jews living at the time in the Arabian Peninsula.

After death of the Prophet, this aspect was expanded and consolidated by the caliphs, companions close to the Prophet: Abu Bakr al-Siddiq, Umar ibn al-Khattab, Uthman ibn Affan and Ali ibn Abi Talib. The caliphs who came after them continued to expand by arms and defeated the old Persian and Roman Empires.

This side of Islam (alongside the establishment of the state and the Islamic empire) became sacred, and became part of religion in the prevailing Islamic culture, which came from it what we call political Islam in our time. The essence of this ideology is the restoration of the state of the Prophet and the Companions, the Islamic pure state; the Islamic Caliphate that God wanted for all humanity.

This ideology was also based on the Prophet Muhammad is holy, what was transmitted to us from his deeds and his words is also sacred; we must follow all of them. The General Presidency for Research and Issuing Fatwas in Saudi Arabia said that there are Quranic verses that confirm this: Obey God and the Messenger, if you turn, God does not love the unbelievers" and "what the messenger gave you take it, and what asked you to prevent it, you should refrain it". And "who disobeys God and His messenger and transgresses his limits, enter him hell forever.[82]

---

[82] http://www.alifta.net/fatawa/FatawaDetails.aspx?

If we add the Prophet's Hadith (whoever obeys me, he obeys God and disobeys me, he disobeys God). This means that whoever denies and lies the Quran or the Prophet's hadeeth and his actions is an infidel.[83]

This means that consolidation of the political aspect of Islam, it is based only on the Quranic verses that protected and supported the new religion, but also on the Hadiths of the Prophet, which was written into a book one hundred years after his death. Both strongly support the political side of Islam.

There are Islamic trends, such as the Quranians (Who believe in the Quran only), that Muhammad has two aspects. The first is the messenger who came with a message from God. The second is the prophet with his life and his talks and his actions. This side as the leader of the Quranians Sobhi Mansour is sacred and non-binding for the Muslims. This opinion also relied on Quranic verses, such as: "I am only a mortal like you"(110- The Cave). And based on a prophetic hadith: "Do not write about me, whoever writes about me other than the Quran, he must cancel it." (Narrated by Muslim).

However, despite the importance of such jurisprudence, it is unfortunately not widespread and does not represent the prevailing culture that Islamic terrorism comes from.[84]

There is a problem facing the supporters of political Islam throughout history; the existence of two sides that appear to be contradictory in religion, but most of them came out of this impasse, that the verses of jihad copied (abolished) the verses of tolerance. For example, what many of the jurists call the sword verse: "If the holy months are gone, you must kill the polytheists where you found them ...". (Repentance: 5). The Islamists use verses and Hadiths of tolerance here in Canada, America, the West and everywhere, as a mask to hide their ideology that emanates from the other side of Islam.

This explains many of the speeches of the supporters of political Islam. For example, they are hostile to Jews, all Jews; it is an extension of the battle fought by the Prophet Muhammad against the tribe of Jews of "Bani Quraizah". As the Islamic history said they have allied with his enemies, he killed the adult prisoners (600 to 900) and took women and children as slaves and confiscated their money and property.[85]

So, the Islamists are hostile to Israel, because it occupies what they believe is Arab land. They are not hostile to Iran, which also occupies the land of the Arabs of Ahwaz and the islands of Amartia, nor are they hostile to Turkey which occupies the Syrian Alexandrian Brigade. The reason is that these countries are Muslim.

In the prevailing Islamic history, the Prophet Muhammad married Aisha, age 9. For that, the Islamists have invited others to marry young girls, including many imams in the West, in Canada and America.[86]

This also explains why unarmed terrorists spread hatred against infidels and why armed terrorists kill them. Although the battle of the Prophet Mohammed with them ended more than 1,400 years ago.

---

[83] Http://www.binbaz.org.sa/article/27

[84] Http://www.ahl-alquran.com/arabic/chapter.php?main_id=258

[85] http://www.alifta.net/Search/ResultDetails.aspx?languagename=ar&lang=ar&view=result&fatwaNum=&FatwaNumID=&ID=59&searchScope=2&SearchScopeLevels1=&SearchScopeLevels2=&highLight=1&SearchType=exact&SearchMoesar=false&bookID=&LeftVal=0&RightVal=0&simple=&SearchCriteria=allwords&PagePath=&siteSection=1&searchkeyword=216168217134217138032217130216177217138216184216169#firstKeyWordFound

[86] For more on this see Lovers of Death" Thomas Quiggin - Saied Shoaaib

Can we Differentiate between Islam and Islamists?

In the West, there is much discussion about Islam and political Islam (the Islamists). For example, the researcher Soner Chagatai says:

> Islam is not a political Islam; Islam is the faith; political Islam is an extremist, violent sometimes, non-historical ideology that seeks to gain legitimacy through Islam and focuses it efforts to recruit from Muslims. "Political Islam aims to create a new non-liberal world order that takes its justification from the imagined and severe past of the 7th century AD.

Chagatai is not the only one ones who believe in this separation. As Dr. Daniel Pipes, director of the Middle East Centre, says politicians have fallen into the same trap. This includes former Prime Minister David Cameron, who depicts the organization of the Islamic state in Iraq and Syria as an organization of "extremists who exploit Islam and harm to it" and "distort the Islamic faith and blasphemes it." He describes Islam as a "religion of peace" and calls out ISIS by saying they are "not Muslims, but monsters." His Immigration Secretary James Brokenshire claims that with respect to terrorism and extremism "there is no relationship between them and Islam".

"Islam has nothing to do with ISIS," said France's former president Francois Hollande. "The criminals who carried out the attack on Charlie Hebdo have no relationship between them and Islam."

Dutch Prime Minister Mark Roth echoed the same words: "ISIS abuses Islam and exploits it." Daniel Cohn-Bendit, a left-wing German politician, describes the Paris's killers as fascists not Muslims. From Japan, Prime Minister Shinzo Abe agrees: "Extremism and Islam are completely different."

Of course, former US President Barack Obama, and the two former US presidents Bill Clinton and George W. Bush, have already disseminated their understanding and views on what is Islam and what is not Islam. But they were less decisive.[87]

In addition, Canadian Prime Minister Justin Trudeau, leader of the Liberal Party, has ordered the government not to use the term ISIS, so that there is no link between it and Islam.[88]

Towards a New Definition of Political Islam:

We need a new definition of Islamists. I think the broader definition of Islamist Islamists, armed and unarmed, is to include everyone who believes in restoring this aspect of Islam and its history. Those who believe that Islam "is not only a religion but a political, social, legal and economic system, which is suitable for building state institutions. Like Iran, Saudi Arabia and the former Taliban regime in Afghanistan, Sudan and Somalia, they are examples of this project. Sometimes they reject the term "political Islam" and instead use "rule by Sharia" or "divine rule."[89]

Accordingly, it is better to include "fundamentalism" with political Islam. It is meant to return to the origin of the religion, the state of the Prophet and the state of the "caliphs" Omar ibn al-Khattab, Abu Bakr al-Siddiq, Uthman ibn Affan and Ali ibn Abi Talib. This term expresses a method of understanding and thinking that elevates itself to the level of ideology. It is based on a set of principles and ideas which they

[87] http://danielpipes.org/article/17523

[88] http://www.rcinet.ca/en/2016/08/30/63531

[89] https://pulpit.alwatanvoice.com/articles/2013/07/12/299806.html

present as the absolute truth. They reject any interpretation of the religious text and are limited to the literal understanding of the religious text without the realization of the mind. They attempt to explain the religious texts without any efforts or examples to put them in their historical context, or deal with them as historical texts.

Religious fundamentalism is characterized by its rejection of the distinction between religion and politics, and politics is a religion. They believe that religious principles are not limited to personal life or private life, but are the principles governing public life, including law, social behavior, economy and politics.[90]

They want to return Islam to its pure first image.[91] They are not based on the first picture, which includes the side of the total values that I have already been explained, but to the political aspect that was established in the state of the Prophet and what they came after him. They believe that the political party does not include the aspects that are tolerant or do not include violence and terrorism.

These Salafists divide it into a "Salafist science" that tries to spread "pure Islam" without violence and a Salafi Jihadist, which came out of terrorist organizations such as Al Qaeda and ISIS. The difference between the two is whether they take up weapons to apply "pure Islam," or not. Therefore, you will find many of those who recruited them were non-armed Salafis, when the Islamic state was founded by ISIS.

As for the "jihadist Salafist", the believers of it are those who decided to impose the Islamic state with weapons immediately. Therefore, the difference between two types is this: There is an unarmed terrorist, and an armed terrorist.

Before the "Arab spring revolutions" in the Middle East, perhaps in many Islamic countries, the impression was that they were not working in politics. They were Muslims interested only in "purifying Islam" from of the innovations that have occurred to it throughout history. But this is changed a lot, they now have political parties, such as the party of "Al-Nour" in Egypt.

You can say that they are more explicit and firm in expressing their ideology, than the Muslim Brotherhood, for example.

"Extremist Islam" or "hardliner" is prevalent term, that refers more to kinetic behavior more than to the ideology, to avoid a clash with Islam as a religion. In 2014 the British government defined "Extremist Islam" or "hardliner" as "an opposition to the basic British values, democracy, the rule of law, individual freedom, mutual respect and tolerance of different religions and beliefs." Adding to that was that Islamic extremism was an ideology that accuses the West of waging war on Islam. Prime Minister Tony Blair said he would ban Hizb ut-Tahrir, which supports the idea of a unified Islamic state.[92]

These British definitions are approaching the truth, but it also needed to get closer to the religious ideology that produces all of this. The fundamentalist, extremist or militant has the same substance, namely the restoration of the original Islamic state and the three centuries that followed it. Of course, the basis is the political aspect, the establishment of the caliphate. The same "radical Islam" believes in full adherence to Sharia, which covers all aspects of life, even those that were not there before.[93]

---

[90] http://www.aljazeera.net/programs/religionandlife/2004/6/3/مفهوم-الأصولية

[91] http://www.washingtoninstitute.org/ar/policy-analysis/view/what-is-salafism

[92] http://www.bbc.com/arabic/worldnews/2014/06/140610_islamist_extremism

[93] http://ar.danielpipes.org/article/4295

All belong to the political side of Islam, the procedural aspect of establishing a new state and a new society from A to Z. There is a difference in some details, not in the goals, nor in the general framework of the "Islamic caliphate" of which they dream. The difference, for example, is that ISIS rejects the elections in the framework of Islam, while the Muslim Brotherhood and the Shiite regime in Iran do it, but governed by Islam. Some of them totally reject the work of women, others agree with women working within "Islamic" conditions.

Most of the Salafists wear a sort of "uniform" using a style of dress close to the Afghan dress, with the moustache shaved and a full beard. In their view the Prophet Muhammad did this. Others like the Muslim Brotherhood are dressed in modern fashion. They are all differences in detail, not in the general theory, such as the application of the Sharia whereby the leader of a state is not allowed to be non-Muslim.

So, what is Islamic terrorism?

As you know many politicians in the West do not call it as "Islamic terrorism". So, Trump's use of this expression is quite true, even if it differs with some of what he does. This escape from this expression is done by many Muslims because they do not want to face the fact that this terrorism has a religious basis. And this is certainly what Islamic institutions and universities do, such as Al-Azhar. This university refused to preach against ISIS, while it simply disbelieved non-Muslims. Among others are Muslim rulers who prefer to use an unrealistic expression, such as "deviances" or "misguided", "Kharijites" (which were an armed group that fought Ali bin Abi Talib).

Perhaps deviation, extremism or other expressions can be understood on that basis, that there is an interpretation of the sacred texts, carries meaning that does not exist in them. But this is not true in the Islamic case, because the prevailing view is in reading the sacred texts, as if its events are here and now. And the Prophet Muhammad ruled by himself using the tools of his time, it was natural that reflected in the Qur'an, and reflected in his words and actions. Therefore, the foundations on which political Islam is based are explicit and do not require broad interpretation. Therefore, I think that the definition of Islamic terrorism is "One who kills on a religious basis to achieve and implement the political side of Islam."

The Spread of Islamism

Daniel Pipes says that with the spread of violent Islamism, politicians such as those above have increased their fear and sensitivity on such issues. They state that they do not want to offend Muslims, fearing that Muslims will become more violent if they see non-Muslims seeking a "war on Islam." Second, they worry that the focus on Muslims will necessarily lead to radical changes in the secular system, because they will have to take measures that they believe are against the foundations of secularism.[94]

But this separation will cause a problem, because it means that there is an inaccurate description of Islamist terrorism, and therefore leads to serious mistakes that disrupt its elimination, or at least mitigate it. The "non-linkage" between Islam and terrorism means that a lack attention to the real sources of political Islam, which is where the armed terrorists and extremists come from. In this case, for example, it is difficult to review the curricula most of Islamic schools, because they would view this as an unnecessary violation against the Islam as a religion.

---

[94] https://pulpit.alwatanvoice.com/articles/2013/07/12/299806.htm

Maybe they do not realize that Islam is different from Christianity because the Prophet Muhammad ruled by himself and entered political and armed conflicts to protect and spread his call. He founded a state with concepts and tools of his age, whereas Christ never ruled a political entity.

Linking Islam to Islamic terrorism is not enough, because it may turn some Muslims into "potential enemies." But if this is done with the publication and support of many Islamic jurisprudence that dismantle and destroy political Islam, many Muslims, especially in the West, will be transferred from "potential enemies" to supporters, because they are liberated from a nonhuman ideology of Political Islam and at the same time do not lose their religion. That is, you can cancel or ignore the political aspect of Islam without leaving Islam, but remain a believing Muslim.

The separation between Islam and Islamic terrorism is not meant to condemn or insult Islam. I am a Muslim, but to understand where the ideology of political Islam comes from, it comes from the political aspect of Islam itself. For many reasons, this aspect and history have become a religious sacred, prevalent among Muslims everywhere in the world. Without confronting these religious foundations of Islamic terrorism, it is difficult to defeat it.

The Myth of the Moderate Islamist

This leads us to the need to revisit definitions such as "moderate Islam", because it does not apply to "real moderates", but to those who say that about themselves. Anyone from the Islamist factions who says that he agrees with tolerance and liberties, becomes a "moderate". Anyone who does not use directly weapons is considered "moderate". This is also the first trick, because it is never enough to use the tolerant side of Islam, but more importantly, its religious position on the political side of Islam, the side of violence and terrorism.

The problem is that the definition of this "moderation" is not related to the basic ideology, but it is linked to performance, the latter can easily be a liar who issues a false statement that claims tolerance, love, etc. Therefore, it can not be considered that the Islamists who does not carry a weapon is "moderate". The terrorist who carries the weapon carries the same ideology as the Islamist. They support each other. The unarmed Islamist is an ideological extremist who creates a political and social space to prepare the "soldiers" and awaits the opportunity. Both are believers in the same ideology, this one calls for it and the other implements it.

Can a mosque in mosque in Canada that incites young people to "jihad" and wants the to become "lovers of death be considered "moderate?" Or are they unarmed Islamist extremists?[95]

In real terms, a moderate Muslim is "who does not believe in the political aspect of Islam (armed and not armed), believes in the other side only, and has a religious and historical foundation for this understanding". Therefore, expressions such as "extremist", "fundamentalist", "radical", etc., can be shortened to more precise terms, namely "unarmed Islamic terrorist" and "armed Islamic terrorist". All those who believe, spread and support this Islamist ideology put them under "unarmed Islamic terrorist", but for one reason or another they do not adopt the armed path. This is (sometimes) the situation with the Muslim Brotherhood and many other Islamists in the West. This same position is also seen with Islamic

[95] Book "Lovers of Death", Thomas Quiggin and Saied Shoaaib

religious and university institutions such as Al-Azhar and the Union of Muslim Scholars, as well as governments such as Saudi Arabia.

Certainly, the degrees are different, especially in Muslim-majority countries. There are extenuating versions such as Egypt and the United Arab Emirates. These regimes allow, for example, churches. In the UAE a Hindu temple was established. There are more explicit and clear versions such as Saudi Arabia, Iran and Sudan. Performance varies according to the nature of the ruling elite, the necessities of politics such as in Saudi Arabia, the rulers of the Gulf, Pakistan and Bangladesh, etc.

But the problem in Muslim countries, such as Egypt and the UAE, is that they propagate and support the ideology of political Islam through education, religious institutions, media and others. It is not permissible to have Islamic jurisprudence to break up this ideology. They suffice to fight the end products of such ideology, such as terrorist organizations and those who compete with them for power, but they do not close the factory from which they come.

They are committing the same mistake as Mustafa Kemal Ataturk, a modernist crust imposed by force, while maintaining the ideology of political Islam, which remains under the skin of society, until they have a power to appear publicly, as did Erdogan in Turkey.

How Can We Eliminate Islamist Extremism and Terrorism in Canada?

The tools needed in confronting this Islamist terrorism must be rethought because they are not achieving the results we need. Among these tools are some of the concepts that are stable among most of the political and non-political elites in the West, and I think they have become obstructive and need to be reconsidered.

Is Islam is owned by Muslims Only?

It is not true, because it is not only longer a religion in which a human group communicates with God, but for many reasons it has become a political project to control the world. For many reasons, this version of Islam spreading hatred, violence, and terrorism throughout the world. This political project has terrorist manifestations here and there, killing, destroying, terrorizing, and spreading horror. This project, wherever it is, is a dynamic manifestation that is corrupting the values of civilization, which had previously settled on humanity.

Therefore, it is difficult to deal with mainstream Islam as a religion like other religions, as it includes extremists and terrorists. Muslims are the only ones who kill others on a religious basis. Islam spread in our time, the political and terrorist aspect is part of its structure and not an outsider to it. It is not an added part for external reasons, or a part added by a group of religiously obsessed, but Islam structure and expansion, must produce all forms of political Islam, including terrorism. This is not the fault of Islam, but the disadvantage is the lack of "Islamic religious reform", that reconciles between Muslims and human civilization.

I believe that extremism is to deviate from the far right or the far left; to twist the neck of the sacred text, and saying something that is not in it. You cannot say that this applies to the prevailing Islamic situation, as I explained there are clear texts that incite hatred and terrorism. The prevailing ideology, as I have explained, is to read these texts as if they were occurring now. It is not to have dreams to restore the state of the prophet and the Islamic caliphate. It is not a history, but divine orders of God.

I wish as a Muslim if Islam was only a way to God, this is the first goal of any religion. It is your individual path to God. But the prevailing ideology of Islam does not believe this. It believes that your only way to God is to achieve his state and Islamic Caliphate on earth, all the earth if you can. It is a road full of blood and bodies of victims.

All religions undoubtedly have their missionary goals, and some believers in these religions have tried to force others to believe in their religion. But Humanity has renounced all these crimes. Many peoples and religious institutions have apologized. It is hard to find anyone in our time calling for the use of religious violence.

The exception in the case of Islam is that the Prophet Muhammad, as explained, by himself, fought an armed and unarmed armed struggle. It is precisely this aspect that needs new Islamic jurisprudence.

I hoped that all Muslims would adopt the humanitarian versions of Islam; its cultural manifestations would enrich human diversity, but it is no longer the case. For many reasons, most Muslims have failed miserably to make Islam humane. It is no longer logical to leave a factory dedicated to making human machines to kill and destroy, under the pretext to preserve the privacy of minorities in the West or because of the sensitivity of approaching religions because they are sacred.

Or perhaps because of criticism will push a large sector of Muslims to be terrorists, they will consider it a battle against their religion and civilizational conflict against Muslims, etc. This is possible, but it should not prevent us from this path. We have tried many ways and failed; the cost of survival of these terror factories is much higher than trying to close them.

I think that the time has come to cooperate seriously with Muslim innovators and Muslims who want to avoid the dangers of Islamic terrorism. Some Muslims and all Islamists repeat that all religions have terrorists and that "terrorism has no religion". First this does not justify Islamic terrorism. You do not have the right to steal because there are others steal and you do not have the right to kill because there are others kill. In the end, it is terrorism. Second, other religions ceased to produce terrorism (Abrahamic and non-Abrahamic) after a bitter bloody conflict in which Europe sank it and was rid of it by Christian and Jewish religious reform. Now there is almost no religion in the world that kills others because they are different in ideology. If this happens is a rare exception.

It is not true what some Muslims repeat "terrorism has no religion", because the most widespread terrorism now is Islamist terrorism. The adoption of this statement prevents Muslim access to the truth, namely that Islamist terrorism has a religious and historical basis belonged to Islam and Muslims only. There is no any kind of terrorism without an ideology that stems from it, it does not start from the vacuum.

It is not true that the "marginalization" of some Muslims in the West is the reason for their becoming terrorists. First, there are other minorities that suffer more than Muslims, however they did not commit terrorist crimes on religious or ethnic ideologies. In a census released by Statistics Canada in 2015[96], blacks constituted the most vulnerable group of hate crimes followed by Jews and then Muslims at 11.67%. Those who were targeted due to their sexual orientation were last. You should note that Muslims are in the third ranking of hate crimes, not the first as the Islamists are saying. The second observation is that no one person who was persecuted did not came out carrying his gun to kill the people who were different with him religiously, ethnically, or sexually.

---

[96] See the Stats Canada report at http://www.statcan.gc.ca/daily-quotidien/170613/dq170613b-eng.htm .

Add to that those who joined ISIS and other terrorist organizations were Westerners, not poor and had no sexual problem, so that they would blow themselves up just for the virgins in paradise." They do not suffer from any tyranny and dictatorship in their Western societies, until they become terrorists.

This ideology that threatens Western civilization and humanity is prevalent in all the countries where Muslims live. It is now also inside the West, here in Canada. It has become a threat to the normal life of ordinary citizens. Millions of Muslims live in the West as citizens; their leaders have failed to dry up the religious foundation of terrorism, on the contrary, many of them have supported the terrorism. The bets of some Western governments have failed on what they call "moderate Islam". The harvest now is terrorism and more terrorism, and it is time that "we do not leave Islam alone".

Therefore, Western societies cannot be left the Islam's reform to Islamists and Muslims alone, but it is primarily responsible of the Western, Muslim innovators and ordinary natural Muslims.

Do Muslims in the West owe their Religious Loyalty to Islamic Countries (such as Saudi Arabia) and Islamic institutions (such as the Union of Muslim Scholars or Al-Azhar)?

The spread of this idea that causes leniency and tolerance with the ideological and financial support coming from Islamic countries and Islamic institutions occurs as if it as natural. Even though these countries failed to provide an advanced model, Canada and the West welcomed that the allegiance of some of its citizens to countries, many of them support directly or indirectly inflicting terrorism, that is loyalty to the destructive ideology of Western civilization and humanity. These countries embrace and publish political Islam; their problem with the armed terrorists is competition for authority, so they make no significant effort to dismantle this ideology.

These countries have differences, including those reasonably tolerant to religious freedoms, such as the Emirates, where there is a Hindu temple and church. But they have not dismantled the religious basis of Muslim hatred of non-Muslims. They are still teaching this ideology in many schools and publish it in their media.

It is important to emphasize that Saudi Arabia is not a "Vatican Muslim" because it contains the holy Islamic symbols (the Kaaba, the tomb of the Prophet, etc.). The reason is that in the religious history of Muslims there is no such institution as the Vatican, with its influence and religious and non-religious authority throughout history. Islam is a different case. You can say that the Muslim ruler (throughout the caliphate) is at the same time a religious symbol or represents the religious legitimacy of Islam.

The loyalty of Catholics to the Vatican is different, as it does not include political allegiance, because the mainstream Catholic ideology has no political aspect, such as the prevailing Islamic ideology.

Secondly, among the Sunni Muslims, there is love for the Kaaba and for the holy symbols, but there is no sanctification for Saudi Arabia on whose land these holy sites are located. There is no reverence for any religious institution. Al-Azhar, for example, is the most important religious institution in the Sunni Muslim world, but it has no religious authority like the Vatican.

The Shiite situation is a little different, they are waiting "the absent Imam" for him at the end of time, to achieve justice for them and establish the state of Islam. This imam has representatives or deputies. The Shiite chooses an Imam; they must follow him in everything, pay him a percentage of his income, if he does not he is an infidel, because the imam is part of the religious faith.

Whatever, the ideological subordination of Muslims outside of Canada and the West is dangerous, because these states and institutions propagate a form of political Islam. So, it is important to think that there are alternative Canadian institutions, that we have a "Canadian Islam" that conforms to the standards agreed upon by humanity.

Islamists and Imams are the only Representatives of Islam and Muslims

No one has the right to has a monopoly on speaking in the name of Islam. All Muslims are representatives of their religion. Muslims did not elect Islamists and their imams. The Imam of the mosque is not elected whether the Muslim is Sunni, Shiite, or otherwise. It is therefore necessary to stop giving them political power in shaping the relationship between the Muslims to their communities and governments in Canada and the West. Most of them have proved to be part of the problem, not the solution. They have failed to confront the ideology of Islamic terrorism and they often support it or deflect criticism away from it. They also increase the fear among Muslims of planting the idea that their Western societies are hostile and hateful, by insisting on exaggerating what they call "Islamophobia". It is necessary to expand the circle of representation of Muslims from different groups, and to introduce Muslim and Muslim reformers who reject the ideology of political Islam and want to live in peace.

And even if we assume that Islamists and imams are good, and they fight Islamic terrorism and believe in Canadian values, this does not give them the right to be Muslim representatives, because this hinders the integration of Muslims in their societies.

Islamophobia

Perhaps the best model for understanding the myth of "Islamophobia" is the political investment made by Islamists based on the blood of Muslims following the murderous attack at the CCIQ mosque in Quebec City. This January 2017 attack resulted in six persons killed. Islamists were, however, quick to capitalize on their deaths by claiming “Islamophobia.” Not discussed by them, media or the government “elites” was the fact that that mosque was run by the Muslim Brotherhood (see Chapter 20).

This is a case of how unarmed Islamists can turn themselves into victims, even though they are a major cause of Islamic terrorism on a near global basis.

The head of one of the Islamic organizations was grateful and proud, when he told the Canadian Broadcasting Corporation that he received a phone call from Prime Minister Justin Trudeau, leader of the Liberal Party, after the terrorist incident in the mosque, describing it as was filled with noble sentiments.

The man is right in his pride. The prime minister gave him the honor of representing the Muslims in Canada and an honor receive solace of the victims of the massacre. This president and other heads of Islamic organizations were not chosen by anyone to represent Muslims, nor to speak for themselves. They are just civil society organizations that represent only their founders, even if their role is important in stopping any violations against Muslims, it does not give them the right to speak for Muslims.

Islamists benefited from sympathy towards the victims, pressed most of the Canadian parliament to denouncing "Islamophobia" and they refused to condemn any violation of Muslims within the "religious and ethnic minorities," and insisted on mentioning Muslims by name. Muslims are number three in exposure to hate crimes after blacks and Jews. The pressure also resulted, in part, in that parliament formed a committee to investigate the fact the hate crimes against Muslims. They depend on their penetration into the ruling Liberal Party and in the presence of many members of parliament from the

Muslim Brotherhood and the Islamists. All of this is done to realize their dream that no one will be allowed to criticize their Islamic ideology.[97]

This is the hidden reason, which of course contradicts the right to freedom of opinion and expression. They do not define the meaning of "Islamophobia" publicly, but on the ground, they use it as a weapon against anyone who criticizes Islamists and they consider it an incitement against Muslims. As example, a school principal in Canada who did nothing but criticize terrorism, had her work stopped, she was investigated and finally apologized for a crime she did not commit.[98]

If additional laws are needed, it is should be in the interests of all minorities and should not contradict Canadian values. It is therefore difficult to find claims to additional laws from any other religions or races living in the West. They know that they are protected by existing laws. In the West, you will not find terms such as "Buddhism phobias," "phobic Hinduism," or "Baha'i phobia," but you will find only "Islamophobia" adopted by the Islamists. They have succeeded to varying degrees in imposing it on **submissive** Western leaders.

The truth is there is no hostility to Islam and Muslims and I, as a Muslim, testify to the contrary. A Muslim in Canada, for example, enjoys more freedom than any Muslim country. Whatever your Islamic doctrine, you have the right to establish a mosque, religious school and institution, like the majority Catholics. You'll find Sunni mosques that are hard to find in Iran, for example. You'll find Shiite mosques that are hard to find in Saudi Arabia. And you'll find Islamic sects are taboo in most Muslim countries such as Baha'i, Ahmadiyya and others. Here Muslims have the same rights as Canadian citizens, and more rights than Muslims in "Muslim lands."

Many Muslims prefer to emigrate to the West from rich Islamic countries. Some of them risk their lives to live in the West, and die drowning, as with Syrian refugees.

The Muslims in Canada face no discrimination against them because they are Muslim. The Secretary of State for Foreign Affairs, for example, is MP Omar Alghabra, a Muslim of Syrian/Saudi origin and Minister of Immigration, MP Ahmed Hussen, is a Somali Muslim.

I will give you another example. When the terrorist attack against the Canadian parliament and two soldiers were killed, the federal police issued a statement confirming that its work is professional, is not subject to any outside influence and its function is to protect all Canadians, including Muslims. Provincial police also held workshops for Muslims to explain to them what to do if they were subjected to any violation.

This does not mean there are no violations, but they are criminalized by law. It also occurs for many minorities, such as indigenous people, blacks, Jews and homosexuals, as I have explained previously. But there is no systematic hostility against Muslims. After the terrorist attack on the Canadian parliament, a Christian or non-Muslim did not carry his gun or drive a car to beat Muslims in retaliation for what a Muslim terrorist did. The only incident that occurred was the attack on the Quebec Mosque (which may

---

[97] https://www.nccm.ca/canadian-muslim-leaders-call-for-government-action-on-islamophobia-lettre-ouverte-des-leaders-et-des-representants-des-communautes-musulmanes-du-canada/

[98] https://www.thestar.com/news/gta/2016/11/10/markham-principal-apologizes-for-discriminatory-facebook-posts.html?utm_source=Media+Watch+-+November+11th+2016&utm_campaign=MW_19-08-2016&utm_medium=email

have complicating factors. See Chapter 20). It is very likely that these attacks will increase in response to Islamic terrorism and they can not be described as Christian terrorism because they did not come from a Christian religious ideology.

The expression of Islamophobia was invented by the Islamists, including Tariq Ramadan, his father Saeed Ramadan, who was the husband of sister of Hassan al-Banna, the founder of the Muslim Brotherhood. Tariq Ramadan[99], one of the most prominent Islamists in the West, is one of the most important founders of the international organization of the Muslim Brotherhood in the West.

Perhaps this is what many politicians miss, makes them subject to blackmail, and may even feel that they are being more humane when they advocate for the "victims." For example, the Quebec MP Alexander Cloutier said that Quebec's parliament did not do enough to stand up to Islamophobia.[100]

As already stated, the concept of Islamophobia is not specific, as well as the concept of "hateful messages", which opens the way for violations of the freedom of opinion and expression. For example, a seminar for writer and activist Djamila Ben Habib on "Secularism and the Integration of Muslims" was canceled.[101] Writer Hassan Jamali stated that there was a chance in the wake of a bloody incident exploited by the Islamists, therefore he expects that the coming period will increase the restrictions on freedom of opinion and expression, will be to create a climate conducive to self-censorship, or to pass laws that limit these freedoms. And freedom is undoubtedly a Canadian and Western value founded on Western civilization.

There is racism in the extreme right that poses a great danger to Western civilization. Without a doubt, we must stand against it decisively, therefore we are required, as writer Richard Martino said, working on two fronts: one against the Islamists and the other against the extreme right. These bloodthirsty vermin feed on each other and are two sides of the same coin.

How Dangerous Is the Accusation of Islamophobia?

The charge of "hostility" means that you have decided to harm the Muslims, that is, become their enemy. The traditional Islamic culture prevailing in the West and in Islamic societies, considers that those who oppose Muslims are hostile to Islam as a religion, which means hostility to God and His Messenger. What is the duty of the ordinary Muslim in this case?

According to the prevalent interpretation of God's words in the Holy Quran:

> Against them make ready your strength to the utmost of your power, including steeds of war, to strike terror into (the hearts of) the enemies, of Allah and your enemies, and others besides, whom ye may not know, but whom Allah doth know. Whatever ye shall spend in the cause of Allah, shall be repaid unto you, and ye shall not be treated unjustly. (Anfal 60)

---

[99] Editorial note. Tariq Ramadan is currently facing claims of rape and sexual harassment from at least two women. Supporters of Ramadan claim that the charges are part of a Zionist plot. For more on this see https://www.nytimes.com/2017/10/29/world/europe/france-tariq-ramadan.html and http://en.rfi.fr/france/20171029-islamic-intellectual-tariq-ramadan-faces-second-rape-accusation .

[100] https://www.pressreader.com/canada/montreal-gazette/20170203/281608125166508

[101] http://ici.radio-canada.ca/nouvelle/1015733/maison-litterature-discussion-diaspora-arabe-djemila-benhabib

The force here according to the prevailing religious interpretations is weapons.

We also have the statement:

> O ye who believe! Take not my enemies and yours as friends (or protectors), - offering them (your) love, even though they have rejected the Truth that has come to you, and have (on the contrary) driven out the Prophet and yourselves (from your homes), (simply) because ye believe in Allah your Lord! If ye have come out to strive in My Way and to seek My Good Pleasure, (take them not as friends), holding secret converse of love (and friendship) with them: for I know full well all that ye conceal and all that ye reveal. And any of you that does this has strayed from the Straight Path. (Al-Mumtahana 1)

And:

> Fight those who believe not in Allah nor the Last Day, nor hold that forbidden which hath been forbidden by Allah and His Messenger, nor acknowledge the religion of Truth, (even if they are) of the People of the Book, until they pay the Jizya with willing submission, and feel themselves subdued. (At-Tawba 29)

The Islamists read the Quran as if it had come down from God now, and as if it is "valid for all times and all places." The orders of God at some fleeting time in the past must be implemented now. This suggests that the ordinary Muslim must prepare himself to fight the infidels and enemies of God at the right moment when he is the strongest.

Dialogue, the Islamists interpret, is not allowed as there is no dialogue with the enemies of God. There is no freedom of opinion and expression. But it is a war either to win or to be killed and enter paradise, where the virgins await in paradise

It is certain that Islamists who have inflated Islamophobia, know this and know these Quranic verses as well:

> Those who reject our Signs, we shall soon cast into the Fire: as often as their skins are roasted through, we shall change them for fresh skins, that they may taste the penalty: for Allah is Exalted in Power, Wise. (An-Nisaa 5)

This also must know:

> Therefore, when ye meet the Unbelievers (in fight), smite at their necks; At length, when ye have thoroughly subdued them, bind a bond firmly (on them): thereafter (is the time for) either generosity or ransom: Until the war lays down its burdens. Thus (are ye commanded): but if it had been Allah's Will, He could certainly have exacted retribution from them (Himself); but (He lets you fight) in order to test you, some with others. But those who are slain in the Way of Allah, he will never let their deeds be lost. (Mohammad 4)

And finally:

> And as the Prophet said: "I have been commanded to fight against the people till they testify La ilaha illAllah (There is no true god except Allah) and that Muhamma is His slave and Messenger, and to establish As-Salat (Iqamat-as-Salat), and to pay Zakat; and if they do this, then their blood

and property are secured except by the rights of Islam, and their accountability is left to Allah." [Al- Bukhari and Muslim]

Therefore, the use of this weapon, "Islamophobia" or hostility to Muslims and Islam is a license to kill. It must be stopped here in Canada.

Do Islamists Harm Muslims?

Islamists in Canada (and the USA) spread a religious ideology that does not have a big difference from the religious basis of ISIS and other terrorist organizations. This is done through many mosques and Islamic schools and this is of course a factory for producing armed terrorists and Islamist extremists. This is especially critical as the Islamic jurisprudence that fights this ideology is not available to Muslims in Canada and the West. The Islamists are fighting with all their might to stop the publishing of any humanitarian versions of Islam.

Secondly, the Islamists are also spreading a climate of intimidation to influence politicians, the media, and others from approaching their institutions, schools and mosques that spread terrorism. If one criticizes them, they will be accused of "Islamophobia."

Third, the Islamist want to increase the fear and hatred of Muslims towards "the other" by asserting that there are those in the West who hate Islam. The West, they say, has wanted to destroy Muslims since the time of the Prophet Muhammad, who fought the infidels, Jews and Christians. It is the West, they say, that destroyed the Islamic caliphate(s). This makes the Muslim in the West separate and hate the societies in which he lives. He lives the contradiction between his religion and his country. His country is a home of war and not peace, because the country he is living in does not apply Islam.

What Islamists are doing deliberately increases the fears of Canadian society. Some observers ask the questions "Why do Muslims want to destroy the liberties that have brought them to our country? We have welcomed them, granted them freedom like us, given them the nationality of our country and all equal rights with us. Why do they want us to reduce our freedom? Why they want to give a preference to themselves? Why do they want to destroy our country, which enjoys such wealth?"

The problem is that most ordinary citizens in the West do not differentiate between Islamist and Muslim and therefore the average Muslim who wants a normal life suffers from the mistakes of the Islamists. This is precisely the inhumane investment of the blood of ordinary Muslims in a battle they are not involved in. This is exactly what the Islamists are doing to sabotage the lives of Muslims in the West.

Non-Criticism of Islam and Muslims

There is a widespread belief that criticizing Islam and Muslims is unwelcome and dangerous. Many in the West fell that criticizing Islam is "off limits" because it is a religion and not a political system. The second reason is that others believe that this criticism will anger Muslims and push even more of them into extremism and terrorism.

With regard to the first reason, it is not possible to fight Islamist ideology and terrorism, as explained earlier, without first examining its religious foundations. Therefore, this is an essential part of the solution, not a part of the problem. The West has no problem criticizing Christianity and Judaism, why exclude Islam?

Of course, the criticism will provoke the anger of the Islamists, because that means fighting the hard-religious foundation they are promoting. It may anger some Muslims, but at the same time it will attract large segments of ordinary Muslims who want to live normally.

Proposed Mechanisms to Counter Islamist Terrorism and Extremism

A variety of mechanisms and policies could be put into place immediately to undercut the power of the Islamists in Canada. Among them are

- Stop Foreign Financial and Ideological Support: Most of the financial support for Islamists comes from the Gulf States, especially Saudi Arabia and Qatar. This can be from governments, individuals, and institutions. The problem is that these countries adopt the ideology of political Islam, some of them are implemented literally, such as Saudi Arabia and some of them carry out watered down versions of it. But they all support this ideology in the West financially, ideologically, and politically. Some of these countries are now fighting the Muslim Brotherhood and the other factions of political Islam in their country, because they do not accept competition for power and governance, but here in Canada, America and the West they support them and support all spectrums of political Islam.

- Iran's support for Khomeinism is also dangerous. Its ideological basis, as explained earlier, is little different from the Sunni ideological bases. Turkey increasingly supports political Islam as well, especially the Muslim Brotherhood in the West. Erdogan and his party are ideologically aligned with the Muslim Brotherhood, which explains their embrace of the opposition Brotherhood in government of Egypt and their hostility to Bashar Assad's regime.

- The main supporter is Saudi Arabia, followed by countries such as Qatar, Kuwait, and Pakistan. The support they offer is not just books and publications, but direct financial support to build mosques and Islamic centres, and support them to continue to work.

Examples of Saudi Support

- The Kingdom donated 500,000 riyals to establish the Islamic Center in Toronto and 880,000 riyals for the establishment of the Islamic Center in Quebec.

- One of the most important centres and mosques that the Kingdom of Saudi Arabia contributed to establishment of the mosque of Calgary.

- The mosque of the Islamic Society of Toronto, where an old church was purchased and converted into a mosque. A dispute broke out between the ancient immigrants of the Muslim minority and the new immigrants. King Faysal bin Abdul Aziz Al Saud intervened and paid $120,000 to buy the mosque In Toronto.

- In Ottawa, there was a modest prayer center set up by the Ottawa Islamic Society. The association began to build a mosque a school for the education of Muslim children. King Faisal donated $ 54,000 in 1974.

- There is a branch of the Muslim World League in Canada, an institution controlled by Saudi Arabia, with branches and activities throughout the world that support the propagation of the Wahhabism (a kind of political Islam) through the construction of mosques and Islamic institutions.

- King Fahd bin Abdul Aziz presented to the Islamic Center in the Canadian city of Toronto support of more than $500,000.

- In July 2014, the Saudi journalist and physician Dr. Hussein Qasti, decided to build the first mosque in the capital city of Iqaluit, the capital of the territory of Nunavut, with a population of only 8,000, mostly from the original Innu, including 80 Muslims, 30 Arabs, and the rest from India and Somalia. The mosque costs $750,000, the Saudi founder says, all donations from within Canada.

- As noted in Chapter 13, the Islamic Society of North America (ISNA) received millions of dollars from Saudi Arabia, despite attempts to deny this.

Examples of Those Who Seek Gulf Financial and Ideological Support

Dr. Mohamed Ibrahim Al-Masri, President of the Islamic Congress of Canada, praised Saudi Arabia's efforts to serve Islam and Muslims and to take care of Muslim minorities in the world. And he said: "We have good relations with many Arab and Islamic governments, through our meetings with their ambassadors twice a year. We ask them to support and send the children of Muslims born in Canada to some Islamic countries so that they can create an impression about Islam, thus take a correct picture of Islam in these countries, and from time to time as the President of the Canadian Islamic Congress visits to these countries and meet with some officials."

You will notice here that the President of the Islamic Congress considers that the model of "true Islam" exists in Saudi Arabia and the Gulf States. And he is keen to link Canadian Muslim youth with this .

Dr. Muhammad Aabid, the head of the Muslim Centre for Social Support and Integration, called for the establishment of an Islamic radio station to interpret the Holy Quran and the Sunna. Dr. Munir Al Qasim, Imam of the Islamic Centre of Southwest Ontario, called on Gulf charities to support Islamic media in Canada.

You will notice that the ideological support includes all the details of the life of the Canadian Muslim, and the attempt to apply the Saudi and Gulf model, assuming that it is a successful model and that it is the true Islam.

These are examples of financial and ideological support, you will also notice the urgency of the Islamists in Canada for financial and religious support.[102]

Work Permits for Imams

Most imams in Canada and the West are faithful sons of the ideology of political Islam. Like the imam who calls on Muslims to kill Jews.[103] And another imam called for the marriage of young girls at the age of nine.[104]

---

[102] The Book of "Death Lovers" Thomas Quiggin - Saied Shoaaib

[103] http://www.cbc.ca/news/canada/montreal/imam-sermon-montreal-mosque-1.4037397

[104] http://en.cijnews.com/?p=52750

Yet another Imam demanded the rape of wives, because the woman who refuses to invite her husband to sex, is curse by angels.[105]

And others sanctify what they call the "Islamic Caliphate" which was based on the occupation of other people's, plundering their wealth, changing their religion and language by force. And others see that God ordered the man to beat his wife and that this is an expression of his love for her![106]

They also believe in the "state of Islam" which applies the law of God, and then want to fight the whole world to impose their religion, language, and laws under the banner of "Islamic Caliphate." These are the imams from which the ordinary Muslim takes religious teachings. And in the prevailing Islamic culture, they are viewed as almost sacred.

Most of them have a religious background that comes from Islamic universities in India, the most famous of which is the Islamic University "Dar Al Uloom", as well as the Islamic University of Pakistan and the Umm Al-Qura Universities in Saudi Arabia. The mother university of the Islamic Sunni world is Al-Azhar in Egypt, the origin of all these branches.

Many imams put the name of one of these universities proudly in their personal profile. The head of a mosque in the Canadian capital Ottawa stated that "We demand that the imam be graduated from Al-Azhar University, until we make sure that he is not an extremist. Because he believes Al-Azhar in represents" Islamic moderation.

Dr. Mohamed Ibrahim al-Masri, head of the Canadian Islamic Congress said: the city of Vancouver, for example, studied at Al-Azhar in Egypt, the Islamic University of Saudi Arabia and the Islamic University of Pakistan.

Is It True That Al-Azhar Represents the Middle and Moderation?

The Sheikh of Al-Azhar University refused to religiously criticize the ideology of ISIS because they are Muslims. He did criticize their methods with respect to the over use of violence.[107] One of the most inhumane fatwas come from Dr. Soad Saleh, a professor at Al-Azhar University. It was he who said that it is the Muslim's duty to enjoy the female prisoners (rape) with the aim of humiliating them.[108]

Lessons from Al Azhar

- "Take the tribute from the Christians and the Jews and they are bad, and say to them - Give tribute, you are the enemy of God".
- Jihad against the infidels is a duty for everyone healthy, sane, free, capable man."
- It is forbidden to build churches in Dar al-Islam (Islamic state), Christians wear a different garment and are forbidden to ride horses and Christian women are distinguished by wearing the iron collar around their necks).

---

105 https://vid.me/pxAE
106 The Book of "Death Lovers" Thomas Quiggin - Saied Shoaaib
107 http://www.coptstoday.com/Archive/Detail.php?Id=11780
108 https://www.youtube.com/watch?v=dGD1SJ_V6Pg

Not everyone who graduates from Al-Azhar becomes a terrorist carrying arms, but most of them believe in this ideology. In this case he is an unarmed terrorist, an Islamist, and he can be moved to armed terrorism easily.

Examples of Al-Azhar Graduates

- One of the leaders of the terrorist organization Boko Haram Abu Bakr Shikawa graduated from the Faculty of Sharia and Law in Al-Azhar University in Egypt.

- The founder of the Moro Islamic Liberation Front in the Philippines "Salamat Hashim" is a graduate of the faculty of the origins of religion at Al-Azhar University. He transformed the liberation movement into an Islamic movement.

- Abdullah Azzam, a Palestinian who founded the terrorist organizations in Afghanistan, is called the “father of modern jihad." He received his master's and doctorate from al-Azhar.

- Dr. Omar Abdul Rahman (The Blind Sheik), was a professor at the faculty of the origins of religion at Al-Azhar University and founder of the Islamic Group, which carried out terrorist acts in the eighties of the last century in Egypt. He was sentenced to life in prison by a US court for complicity in terrorist acts. His doctoral dissertation, "The Opponents of the Quran," was the former Sheikh of Al-Azhar, Sayyed Tantawi, and his ideas were founded on terrorist organizations such as al-Qaeda.

If all professions in Canada are licensed, it is perhaps even more important that the imam obtains a license to practice this dangerous profession, which can easily produce terrorism and terrorists. It's not just Muslim imams, it should apply to all clergy in Canada. A public debate should be conducted about the specifications and qualifications that must be available in the Muslim imam. Muslims innovators and Muslims from different groups should participate if possible. Mosque libraries should also include books for all kinds of jurisprudence, not just as it is now, only of books that incite armed and unarmed terrorism, including the books of one of the founding father of the Islamists, Sayed Qutb.

Islamic Schools

Islamic schools must have curricula that conforms to Canadian and Western standards. For example, schools that impose the wearing of hijab on female students should be disallowed.

The books that are used for teaching come mostly come from Gulf countries, which means that they support in one way or another the ideology of the Islamists. There are other books printed by some centres in North America (Canada and the United States of America) which are no different from this trend, in the sense that they adopt the same approach.

Not all of these books are evil. Some of them, for example, talk about the value of truthfulness, that theft is a bad act that infuriates God, the importance of humility and the importance of treating the servant well (Gulf societies rely on servants from other countries). Or caring for children's personal hygiene.

All the books that have been examined in Canada to date by the authors do not speak of the value of living with those who differ with us in religion, race, or sex, even thought this can be found in some verses of the Quran, Hadith and the Prophet's biography. The books also include violent verses against infidels (non-Muslims), they say infidels will go to hell after death, while the Muslims will go to heaven. This means a kind of discrimination that produces hatred of course, even while there are Islamic views asserting that paradise is not exclusive to Muslims.

The sanctification of all that the Prophet said and did means that the Muslim student is required to imitate the Prophet in everything. However, there are Islamic views, for example, that the wars and battles fought were linked to their time and are not required now, such as the destruction of the Prophet Muhammad of the religious symbols of all religions, except Islam, when he entered the city of Mecca with his army. This type of destruction is not required of the Muslim now.

Umar ibn al-Khattab sent armies to invade another country like Egypt. Is this required of the Muslim today? Is it required of every Muslim mother to push her children to participate in armies occupying other countries? Or is it best to adopt a teaching curriculum to respect good deeds by the standard of our time, rather than to sanctify all that a person does?

The call to Islam is a religious duty to every Muslim as the book said. But it does not teach children in the context of the freedom of all other religions to call, nor in the framework of freedom of opinion and expression, which must be guaranteed to Muslims and non-Muslims.

There is no talk about belonging to the homeland or humanity, but only belonging to Islam and Muslims. This is dangerous, as it makes individuals isolated from their society, perhaps hostile to it and perhaps at another stage belonging to the ideas in the history and ended, such as the Islamic caliphate and which is founded by a preacher.

There is no reference to the renunciation of terrorism based on the verses of the Quran and the Prophet's Hadith. This means that Islamic teaching content and curricula here in Canada are incompatible with modern human civilization and are contrary to the human values that humanity has recognized in its long journey The value of human freedom, the value of peaceful coexistence, the renunciation of violence and terrorism. It is the values of human rights that have been adopted by international conventions. Therefore, these curricula must be re-examined and alternative approaches compatible with Canadian values. We need new approaches, involving Muslim innovators and education experts under the supervision of the Canadian and provincial governments.

The Support Muslim Innovators and Their ideology

The ordinary Muslim in Canada and the West is a prisoner of the ideology of political Islam as frequently there are no others. The Islamists' ideology has besieged them in the mosque, the school, the home and the Islamic institution that allegedly speaks on their behalf. The supporters of this ideology portray to the ordinary Muslim that their ideology is the only Islam. They are deliberately obscured from the jurisprudence of the old and new Muslim innovators. And if Muslim discover them by himself, they will disbelieve them and disbelieve the Muslim who follows them (Takfir means a decision to kill in the ideology of political Islam).

In religious history, there are many Muslim innovators, such as Mu'tazilah, Sufi schools and philosophers such as Ibn Rushd, Farabi, and Abu Bakr al-Razi. In modern times, there are many new innovators who address the problem of Islamic terrorism from its roots. Among them are:

- Dr. Nasr Hamed Abu Zaid explains the interpretation of the Koranic text, the prophetic Hadith in their historical context, so that they correspond to our time. Is not required of the Muslim now to implement it literally. For example, the battle between the Prophet and the tribe of Bani Quraiza

Judaism was linked to a political conflict that ended. There is no eternal hostility with the Jews as promoted by Islamists and a Muslim is not required to dislike any Jew because he is a Jew.

- Sheikh Ali Abdul Razek believes that there is no state in Islam, and God did not send the Prophet as a politician, but a messenger carrying a divine message to all people. And therefore, must abandon the political aspect of Islam.

- Said al-Ashmawi sees that the Islamic caliphate is not a religious project and was not ordered by God, but a political project that was colonial like all ancient empires and should not be followed by the Muslim now.

- Islam Bahiri sees the need to review the Hadiths attributed to the Prophet, as well as the prophetic biography attributed to him, many of which is doubtful, and many of them contradict with the Quran. For example, it is common among Muslim circles that God is commanded to marry young girls, because the Prophet married Aisha, she was a 9-year-old girl. While Bahiri proved that the Prophet married Aisha, age 18, and confirms that what the Islamists call it is a crime of rape of children. The second modern example attributed to the Prophet "who instead of his religion, kill him" is a dubious and we should not follow it now. Bahiri has made a great effort to reinterpret many of the verses on which the Islamists use it to spread hatred and terrorism.

- Dr. Muhammad Shahrour, for example, introduces new interpretations through the linguistic aspect of the Quran, such as the equality of men and women in inheritance, and the marriage of a man from one woman, not four.

- The German orientalist Christoph Luxemburg in his book "Syriac Aramaic reading of the Quran" made a big discovery that about 40% of his words of Quran are Aramaic Syriac, misunderstood by Muslim interpreters and translators. For example, "hoor al-ayn" in Paradise according to the prevailing interpretation is the virgins who wait in heaven for those who blows themselves up to kill the enemies of God. Its real meaning is "white grapes".

- The Quran did not order a Muslim to marry four or to have sex with any number of slave women. The Syriac translation of the verse: If ye fear that ye shall not be able to deal justly with the orphans, marry women of your choice, two or three or four; but if ye fear that ye shall not be able to deal justly (with them), then only one, or (a captive) that your right hands possess, that will be more suitable, to prevent you from doing injustice. (Women 6). It is mean marrying a woman who has a contract with you.

- Mohamed Mahmoud Taha believes that the Quran consists of origins and branches. The assets are received by the Prophet from God in city "Mecca", but the branches are received after his migration to the city Medina and the building of his state. The assets do not change, the branches are linked to the nature of the mentality of believers at the time and not for all time. Branches do not cancel assets. What the Muslim should follow today is assets. Based on this view, all the verses that include violence, jihad and hatred against each other have been stopped. They also abolish Sharia, such as cutting the hand of the thief, stoning the adulterer, etc.

There are many other innovators, who are important to support and disseminate their ideas. They can destroy the ideology of political Islam, that is, the closure of Islamist ideology and terror factories in Canada and the world.

As a closing note, the Constitution of the Muslim Student Association at York University specifically states that "innovations in religious matters or "modernisation" will not be acceptable, as Islam is a way of life for all times and places and hence is not subject to being outdated or needing reform."[109] This tells you what you need to know about the MSA and its leadership.[110]

---

[109] The constitution of the York University Muslim Students Association can be seen at their own website at http://yorkmsa.ca/wp-content/uploads/2016/04/final_constitution-2.pdf .

[110] According to Member of Parliament Iqra Khalid, she wrote the constitution of the MSA at York University. For more on this see John Steward, *This millennial not only votes, she's running for MP*, Inside Toronto Magazine, January 16, 2015. The article is available online at http://www.insidetoronto.com/blogs/post/5262154-this-millennial-not-only-votes-she-s-running-for-mp/ . Viewed 19 June 2017. **Rated B2**.

CHAPTER 8: THE FALSE NARRATIVE OF ISLAMOPHOBIA, RACISM, AND VICTIMIZATION

Thomas Quiggin

Key Points

- Islamophobia is a required element of the Islamist narrative in non-Muslim countries.
- Islamists depend on the appearance of a constant state of victimization. They then use fear mongering to advance their agenda.
- Whenever some cries "Islamophobia," a close examination of the events and individuals involved should be examined to see if connections exist to extremist groups or if the event occurred.

A reasonable opinion can be formed that Islamophobia is a required element of the Islamist narrative in non-Muslim countries. Islamist proponents, such as the Muslim Brotherhood, Hizb ut-Tahrir and the Khomeneists, use Islamophobia because they have a significant problem. The ideology of the Islamists is so abhorrent that it would not survive any open debate in a country with basic human rights. Therefore, an informed belief could be that Islamophobia is required to silence the critics of the Islamists.

It has been factually shown that the Islamist ideology supports, among other ideas, the absolute submission of women to servile positions, female genital mutilation, honor killings, the dissolution of the Westphalian state replaced by a single caliphate, a Salafist/regressive interpretation of Sharia Law, the stoning of gays and the killing of adulterous women. It is also exclusionary to all other forms of religious and/or political beliefs and anti-democratic. (Chapters Ten, Thirteen and Twenty-One).

It can be believed that Islamists also depend on the constant state of victimization and fear mongering to survive and advance their agenda. Islamophobia, and the fear of being offended, are both artificial concepts designed to advance their cause. Islamists are utterly ruthless when in power and cry total victimhood when not in power. Consequently, accusations of racism and 'Islamophobia' have become the sword and shield of Islamists in the West. Even when faced with evidence of honor killings, groups such as CAIR USA and CAIR CAN/NCCM will claim that they are the victims of cultural prejudice, racism and Islamophobia. (See example of Shaima Alawadi below).

It is not just the adherents of extremist Islam that use racism and Islamophobia to attack critics. Many who might self-identify as 'progressives' or 'social justice warriors' also use the terms. Ignorance aside, their use of the term is heavily laden with irony. When extremist Islam comes to power, the first political group they slaughter is the leftists, quickly followed the press. During the Iranian Revolution in 1979, leftist groups and leftist/Islamists such as the Fedayeen and the People's Mojahedin supported the Ayatollah Khomeini believing he was better than the Shah. Unfortunately for them, Ayatollah Khomeini rewarded their loyalty with mass killings and jailing which began during the consolidation of the revolution.

A Brief History

The origin of the term Islamophobia is obscure. Etienne Dinet, a French convert who lived in Algeria, may have used the term in French as early as 1916.[111] The earliest common users of the term were Iranian mullahs, starting with the 1979 Iranian revolution. It was a term used to disparage women who would not wear the hijab as directed by the new regime of the Ayatollah Khomeini.[112]

Richard Stone was one of the authors of a letter to The Guardian in 1994 that used the term and he was on the Runnymede Trust that put the term into broad circulation in 1996.[113] The term became increasingly popular when the Runnymede Trust began its study Commission on British Muslims and Islamophobia.[114]

The contested view of what the term means became evident on April 1, 1996 in a Guardian article. The article was titled "Muslim leader says Zionists orchestrating 'Islamophobia'" and it covered a speech by "Muslim Parliament" leader Dr. Kalim Siddiqui. The tension in the article highlights the issue. Dr. Siddiqui accuses "Zionists" and the Government of the United Kingdom of orchestrating a wave of Islamophobia. Yet in the same article, Dr. Siddiqui claims that jihad is an obligation for all Muslims around the world and that the fatwa calling for the killing of Salman Rushdie should be supported (i.e. killing Rushdie).

It was also recently made public that Trevor Phillips, the former chair of the Equality and Human Rights Commission, had played a role in popularizing the term Islamophobia. He was quoted as saying:

> 'Twenty years ago, when, as chair of the Runnymede Trust, I published the report titled Islamophobia: A Challenge for Us All, we thought that the real risk of the arrival of new communities was discrimination against Muslims.'[115]

Now, however, he has changed his beliefs and stated that:

> "In my view, we have to adopt a far more muscular approach to integration than ever, replacing the failed policy of multiculturalism."[116]

According to Abdur-Rahman Muhammad, a former radical Imam, the term Islamophobia came into popular usage in North America when the International Institute for Islamic Thought (IIIT) in Northern

---

[111] Vakil, Abdoolkarim (2008), *'Is the Islam in Islamophobia the same as the Islam in anti-islam; or, when is it Islamophobia time?'* in Sayyid, Bobby S. and Abdoolkarim Vakil, eds, Thinking thru Islamophobia, University of Leeds, http://www.ces.uc.pt/e-cadernos/media/ecadernos3/Vakil.pdf . Viewed 19 June 2017. **Rated C3.**

[112] See, among many others, the article *Islamophobie?* by Caroline Fourest & Fiammetta Venner from edition N°26-27 (Automne-Hiver 2003) of Prochoix. It is available online at: http://www.prochoix.org/frameset/26/islamophobie26.html . Viewed 19 June 2017. **Rated C3.**

[113] Cheradenine Zakalwe, *The Origins of the Term Islamophobia in English-Language Discourse*, 28 December 2011. The article can be seen online at hehttp://islamversuseurope.blogspot.com.es/2011/12/origins-of-term-islamophobia-in-english.htmlre. **Viewed 19 June 2017. Rated C3.**

[114] *Commission on British Muslims and Islamophobia.* The website of this organization can be seen at http://www.runnymedetrust.org/projects-and-publications/past-projects/commissionOnBritishMuslims.html . Viewed 19 June 2017. **Not rated.**

[115] Douglas Murray, *Trevor Phillips is finally discovering the pitfalls of the term 'Islamophobia,'* The Spectator, 11 April 2016. The article can be seen online at https://blogs.spectator.co.uk/2016/04/trevor-phillips-is-finally-discovering-the-pitfalls-of-the-term-islamophobia/# . Viewed 17 May 2017. **Rated B2.**

[116] David Barrett, *British Muslims becoming a nation within a nation, Trevor Phillips warns*, The Telegraph, 11 April 2016. The article can be seen online at http://www.telegraph.co.uk/news/2016/04/10/uk-muslim-ghettoes-warning/ . Viewed 17 May 2017. **Rated B2.**

Virginia decided to start using the term to silence their critics. According to Mr. Muhammad, the Islamists at the IIIT "decided to emulate the homosexual activists who used the term homophobia to silence critics. He said the group meeting at IIIT saw Islamophobia as a way to beat up their critics."[117] The IIIT is a Muslim Brotherhood front organization, according to the FBI and a variety of other sources.[118]

Additionally, a British report released in December 2015, has identified the Muslim Brotherhood as an extremist group which has a highly ambiguous relationship with violent extremism. It believes that the Muslim Brotherhood comprises both a transnational network, with links in the UK, and national organizations in and outside the Islamic world. The movement is deliberately opaque, and habitually secretive. The UK government also believes that that membership of, association with, or influence by the Muslim Brotherhood should be considered as a possible indicator of extremism (Emphasis added). Individuals closely associated with the Muslim Brotherhood in the UK have supported suicide bombing.

It is reasonable to believe that Islamophobia and accusations of racism should be seen for what they are in the case of the Islamists. The terms are used narrowly to silence women and those Muslims who have a modernist, humanist or secular view and used broadly to attack all other critics. Islamophobia is nothing more than a politically correct tool to disqualify criticism and defend their abhorrent beliefs from public view. Those using the terms should be regarded as either believers in the ideology of extremist Islam or ignorant supporters who have little real knowledge. They might have been called useful idiots or fellow travelers in other circumstances.

Advocates of Islamophobia

CAIR USA (Council on American-Islamic Relations USA) purports itself to be a leading advocate for justice and mutual understanding and a grassroots civil rights and advocacy group.[119] It has, however, been identified as a terrorist entity and a Muslim Brotherhood front group by the United Arab Emirates.[120] CAIR USA had also been indemnified as an unindicted co-conspirator in the Holy Land Relief terrorism funding case, but their name was removed from the list of co-conspirators. The judge ruled, however, that "the government has produced ample evidence to establish the associations of CAIR, ISNA, NAIT, with the Islamic Association for Palestine, and with (terrorist group) Hamas."[121]

It can be seen that CAIR USA regularly exploits attacks against Muslims and frequently creates false stories in the media to create fake outrage. They blame Islamophobia and the inherent racism against Muslims, even when there is no case to be made.

---

[117] *Moderate Muslims Speak Out on Capitol Hill*, IPT News, October 1, 2010. The report is available online at: http://www.investigativeproject.org/2217/moderate-muslim-speak-out-on-capitol-hill# . Viewed 19 June 2017. **Rated C3.**

[118] See the FBI memo concerning this at http://www.investigativeproject.org/documents/misc/159.pdf . Viewed 19 June 2017. **Rated B2.** For more on the IIIT, see http://www.investigativeproject.org/737/forgotten-investigation-emails-offer-insight-into-iiit-probe . Viewed 19 June 2017. **Rated B3.**

[119] For more, see the CAIR USA website at http://www.cair.com/about-us/vision-mission-core-principles.html . Viewed 19 June 2017. **Rated E5.**

[120] A list of the designated terrorist entities can be seen in the article *List of groups designated terrorist organisations by the UAE*, 16 November 2014. http://www.wam.ae/en/news/emirates-international/1395272478814.html . Viewed 19 June 2017. **Rated B2.**

[121] The decision of the court on this issue is available online at http://www.scribd.com/doc/43380629/2009-order-on-Holy-Land-Foundation-unindicted-coconspirator-list . Viewed 19 June 2017. **Rated B3.**

The murder of Shaima Alawadi is one such fake case. According to a police affidavit, Shaima Alawadi's daughter 17-year-old Fatima Alawadi of El Cajon Californian jumped out of her mother's car going approximately 35 miles per hour (56 kilometres per hour). They were having a discussion concerning her upcoming forced marriage to her cousin living in Iraq. According to the affidavit based on police, paramedic and hospital staff, she told her mother "I love you Mom" and jumped out of the car as she did not want the forced marriage.[122]

On 21 March 2012, Fatima's mother Shaima Alawadi, while at home, was hit six times in the head and suffered four skull fractures. According to police, was beaten with a large object.[123] On 24 March 2012, Shaima Alawadi was taken off life support and she died in hospital from her beating injuries. Her body was flown back to Iraq for burial. She and her husband had initially left Iraq to escape persecution suffered under President Saddam Hussein.

On 25 March 2012, police state that whatever the motive, the attack appeared to have been "an isolated event," not part of an overall pattern of violence toward immigrants. Concerns about a hate crime were raised as it was also reported that a note had been left next to her body with the statement: "Go back to your country, you terrorist."

On 8 November 2012, her husband Kassim Alhimidi was arrested for her murder. It turns out that his wife was planning a divorce and the 17-year-old daughter of the family was refusing to marry her cousin who lived in Iraq.

On 31 January 2014, the CAIR USA (Chicago Chapter) Monitor ran a story that blamed the death of Shaima Alawadi on the "America's inherent racism and prejudice."[124] This was 13 months after the arrest of Kassim Alhimidi for what appears to be an honour killing and some 21 months after police stated that the attack was an isolated event.

The paragraph stating that the killing of Shaima Alawadi was the fault of America reads as follows:

> "On February 26, 2012, George Zimmerman shot and killed Trayvon Martin in self-defense as Martin was on his way home in Sanford, FL, armed with a bag of skittles and iced tea. He was 17-year-old, an African-American student at Michael Krop High School. One month later on March 21st, Shaima Alawadi was beaten to death inside her home and a note left next to body that read, "This is my country. Go back to yours, terrorist." She was a 32-year-old mother of five who had left her country, Iraq, with her family following the Shiite uprisings, in hopes of finding peace in El Cajon, CA. **These two now-lifeless Americans represent the true victims of America's inherent racism and prejudice.** We must then think to ourselves: what was their crime—the color of their

---

[122] See, among many others, Tony Perry, *Don't talk to cops, said text to daughter of slain Iraqi woman*, Los Angeles Time, 06 April 2015. The article can be seen online at http://latimesblogs.latimes.com/lanow/2012/04/slain-iraqi-immigrant-search-warrant.html . Viewed 19 June 2017. **Rated B3.**

[123] Tony Perry, *El Cajon police ask public's help to solve Iraqi woman's beating death*, Los Angeles Time, 25 March 2015. The article can be seen online at http://articles.latimes.com/2012/mar/25/local/la-me-iraqi-woman-20120326 Viewed 19 June 2017. **Rated B3.**

[124] Samia Shameem*, Hello, May I Call you a Terrorist?,* Chicago Monitor*, 31 January 2014.* The article can be seen online at http://chicagomonitor.com/2014/01/hello-khan-may-i-call-you-terrorist/ . Viewed 19 June 2017. **Rated B3.**

skin (i.e. their darker than white complexions), their ethnicity, their beliefs? —and when will the hate end." (Emphasis added)

As seen from the above case, it can be believed that CAIR USA tried to blame the murder of Shaima Alawadi on America's inherent racism and prejudice, even after it had been made clear that she was murdered in her own home for disobeying the will of her husband. A reasonable person could believe this was an honour killing related to the families own belief structures, not that of America or the West.

This murder of Shaima Alawadi is not a unique case. In Houston Texas, a fire with multiple points of origin broke out at the Islamic Society of Greater Houston on 25 December 2015. The Houston chapter of CAIR immediately called for authorities to investigate the arson as a hate crime. As it turns out, the fire was set by a Muslim who was a regular attendee at the mosque.[125] The call for a hate crime investigation by CAIR USA remains on their website, even though they are aware of the facts of the case.[126]

Islamophobia and the Law: A Special Class of Defendants for Muslims?

In April of 2015, Sabrine Djaermane and El-Mahdi Jamali were arrested in Montreal. The terrorism-related charges included possession of an explosive substance, attempting to leave Canada to commit a terrorist act abroad, facilitating a terrorist act, and committing an act under the direction or for the profit of a terrorist organization.[127] During the searches at the time of the arrests, the police also allegedly found materials necessary to make a pressure cooker bomb similar to that used in the Boston Marathon bombing.[128]

In the follow-on legal proceedings, defence lawyers attempted to have a publication ban maintained for all materials found in the search warrants. This is irregular, as such material is normally released to the press and the public as part of the legal process.

In January 2016, the defence introduced into the proceedings an expert's report which had the title La publication des informations visées par la requête amendée pose--t--elle un risque sérieux pour l'administration de lajustice?[129] (The publication of information covered by the amended motion – does it pose a serious risk to the administration of justice?)

The argument of the report was that further disclosure of information in the press concerning the judicial process surrounding Sabrine Djaermane would pose a serious risk to the administration of justice. The report appears to suggest that Islamophobia is such a wide spread problem in Quebec that the basic right

---

[125] Carol Christian and Leah Binkovitz , *Man charged with setting Houston mosque fire says he was a devout attendee*, , Houston Chronicle. Updated 3:59 pm, Wednesday, December 30, 2015. The article can be seen online at http://www.chron.com/houston/article/Federal-officials-arrest-man-in-connection-with-6727623.php . Viewed 19 June 2017. **Rated B3**.

[126] The CAIR USA call for an investigation can be seen at https://www.cair.com/press-center/press-releases/13323-cair-seeks-probe-of-possible-bias-motive-for-fire-at-houston-mosque.html . Viewed 19 June 2017. **Rated E5**.

[127] *Teens charged with terror-related offences*, CTVNews.ca, Published Monday, April 20, 2015 12:52PM EDT. The article is available online at http://www.ctvnews.ca/canada/teens-charged-with-terror-related-offences-1.2335813 . Viewed 19 June 2017. **Rated B3**.

[128] *New evidence presented for accused terrorists*, CTV Montreal. Friday, April 24, 2015 12:40PM. The article is available online at http://montreal.ctvnews.ca/new-evidence-presented-for-accused-terrorists-1.2343362 .

[129] The expert report of Professor Valerie Amiraux was titled: *La publication des informations visées par la requête amendée pose--t--elle unrisque sérieux pour l'administration de lajustice* ? Valérie Amiraux, Chaire de recherché du Canada en étude du pluralisme religieux, Université de Montréal. Remise le 9 octobre 2015.

to a fair trial would be compromised. The report did not address the related case of El-Mahdi Jamali who was arrested with her.

An informed reading of the report suggests problems in four areas, not least of which is that Islamophobia is a contested concept. The report also appears to infer that a special class of legal consideration be given to those who are Muslim and charged with the offences related to terrorism. No such consideration exists for any other group of defendants. The research depends (directly and indirectly) on input from well-known Islamist organizations whose credibility is questionable. This includes CAIR CAN/NCCM and CAIR USA (and others). CAIR USA is a listed terrorist organization in the United Arab Emirates.[130]Additionally, there seems to be little in the search warrants that is not already in the public realm which would contribute to a substantive change of view in the overall situation.

Furthermore, a random sampling of the other sources used in the report also shows that those sources in turn use CAIR CAN material (and others). For example, the 'Bibliographie' of the report shows: CAIR CAN. 2004. "Presumption of Guilt: A National Survey on Security Visitations of Canadian Muslims." Ottawa: Canadian Council on American---Islamic Relations.

The use of CAIR CAN material is highlighted at the start of the main body of the report in the first section and it is used in the formative stages of the report:

> I. Le contexte québécois: radicalisation, islamophobie et commérages

The example reads:

> "À l'intersection des discours médiatiques et des discours politiques, l'image publique des musulmans s'est considérablement altérée depuis le 11 septembre, le ton négatif et l'accentuation des stéréotypes s'accroissant notamment par effet du traitement médiatique des informations" (Helly, 2004; CAIR CAN, 2004 ; Canadian Islamic Congress, 2005 ; Perry, 2015). (Page 2 of 22 in the PDF version of the report).

This example also notes the works of Denise Helly. It should be noted that when the sources attributed to Helly in this report are examined, they in turn rely on information provided by CAIR CAN. In the article Le traitement de l'islam au Canada. Tendances actuelles[131] CAIR CAN is identified 12 times. These occur once in the Biliographie and 11 times in footnotes. These footnotes where CAIR CAN is noted are (13, 14, 15, 17, 31, 49, 54, 67, & 69). (67 and 69 have two mentions of CAIR CAN each).

As is evident, the article depends extensively on the use of material provided by CAIR CAN.

In another article quoted by the author and written by Helly, the same problem occurs. In the article Flux migratoires des pays musulmans et discrimination de la communauté islamique[132] CAIR CAN is quoted

---

[130] A list of the UAE designated terrorist entities can be seen in the article *List of groups designated terrorist organisations by the UAE*, 16 November 2014. http://www.wam.ae/en/news/emirates-international/1395272478814.html Viewed 19 June 2017. **Rated B2.**

[131] Denise Helly, *Le traitement de l'islam au Canada. Tendances actuelles.* This article is available online at http://remi.revues.org/274 . Viewed 19 June 2017. **Rated D4.**

[132] Denise Helly, *Flux migratoires des pays musulmans et discrimination de la communauté islamique* . This article is available online at: http://classiques.uqac.ca/contemporains/helly_denise/flux_migratoire_musulmans/flux_migratoire_musulmans.html Viewed 19 June 2017. **Rated D4.**

twice. Furthermore, another source used by Helly is the report noted as Nimer M. (2001), Report, The Council on American-Islamic Relations. The report by Helly does not specify it, but further research suggests that 'Nimer" is in fact Mohamed Nimer, Director of Research at CAIR USA, the parent organization of CAIR CAN.

In another example, the author of the expert report quotes Barbara Perry in the article All of a Sudden, There Are Muslims: Visibilities and Islamophobic Violence in Canada. In this article, Perry includes CAIR CAN as a reference twice. Furthermore, Perry also quotes Helly twice and as well as Mohamed Nimer. As already identified above, Helly's work is informed by CAIR CAN and CAIR USA.

The author of the expert report also uses the Maclean's Magazine article of John Geddes of October 3, 2013, Canadian anti-Muslim sentiment is rising, disturbing new poll reveals.[133] The article begins with information and quotations from Sallah Hamdani, the former head of Islamic Relief Canada and Ishaan Gardee of the National Council of Canadian Muslims (formerly known as CAIR CAN). The inclusion of these two individuals in an article used as an academic source is problematic, given their own connections to Islamist organizations.

In addition to this report, it should be noted that the author of the expert's report was one of the organizers[134] of a symposium on Islamophobia held in Montreal from October 29 to November 1, 2015. The conference title was Combatting Islamophobia: Issues and challenges for a pluralistic Quebec. The conference had speakers from CAIR CAN and CAIR USA.

As can be seen, the work of CAIR CAN appears in both the experts report and repeatedly in the sources used by the authors. As such, it is a fair opinion to state that a significant portion of the material depends on input from CAIR CAN and CAIR USA.

Credibility

It can be reasonable said that CAIR USA suffers from several credibility issues. Among others, CAIR USA was listed as a terrorist entity by the United Arab Emirates[135] when the UAE was listing proxy and front groups related to the Muslim Brotherhood and others.

CAIR USA has also been identified as an unindicted co-conspirator in the Holy Land Relief Foundation terrorism funding trials. CAIR USA attempted to have its name removed from the list of unindicted co-

[133] John Geddes, *Canadian anti-Muslim Sentiment is Rising, Disturbing New Poll Reveals*, Macleans Magazine. 03 October 2013. The article can be seen online at http://www.macleans.ca/politics/land-of-intolerance/ . Viewed 19 Jue 2017. **Rated C3.**

[134] Du 29 octobre au 1er novembre 2015, Denise Helly (INRS), Michael Nafi (John Abbott College), Valérie Amiraux et Patrice Brodeur (Université de Montréal) vous invitent à participer au symposium international « Islamophobie. Race, religion, libéralisme. http://www.uquebec.ca/reseau/fr/contenu/symposium-international-islamophobie . Viewed 19 June 2017. Not rated.

[135] A full list of the terrorist entities can be seen in the article of *UAE publishes list of terrorist organisations: Cabinet decision includes Al Qaida, Daesh and the Muslim Brotherhood,* 14 November 2014. Viewed 19 June 2017. **Rated B2.**

conspirators, but its request was refused.[136] The FBI has also stated that CAIR USA is not an appropriate partner for the FBI and that it has suspended all formal contacts.

The parent organization of CAIR CAN is CAIR USA. CAIR CAN was formed to support and fund the activities of CAIR USA. CAIR CAN is now known as the NCCM or the National Council of Canadian Muslims. The current head of the CAIR CAN/NCCM is Ishaan Gardee. He has given press interviews[137] and testified to Parliament[138] that CAIR CAN has no relation to CAIR USA, despite the commonality of their nomenclature. It is reasonable to believe this is false, and more than 20 examples can be seen where CAIR USA and CAIR CAN each claim to be a partner of the other. (Chapter 13)

Ironically, Mr. Gardee attended a 19 February 2016 conference organized by the Office for Democratic Institutions and Human Rights (ODIHR) of the OSCE. The conference was to address A Holistic Approach to Addressing Intolerance and Discrimination against Muslims in the OSCE Region.[139] Sending the head of a group with direct and longstanding ties to Islamist ideology to a conference on intolerance against Muslims does seem a bit strange.

Given the contested nature of the existence of Islamophobia and the fact that the expert's report was based on information from organizations which have a vested self-interest in promoting the concept, doubts can be raised. Islamists, when arrested, should probably not have special protection above any other class or group of individuals in Canada.

Furthermore, this example raises the question about how some of the academic work in Canada on the issue of Islamophobia is "informed" by polling and information which itself is highly doubtful, given its sources.

The Rotherham Example

As noted elsewhere in this book, it is a proven fact that 1,400 girls aged 11 to 14 were groomed, raped, and forced into sexual slavery. The victims were primarily white girls and the rapists and pimps were primarily Pakistani Muslim men. After the Jay Report came out showing how this had happened, the victimhood and Islamophobia narrative kicked in again. The "Muslim Community of Rotherham" called for a boycott of any cooperation with the police, trying to blame the police for what happened. Furthermore, they claim that Islamophobia is now rampant in the town.[140] Rather than address the issue within their own community, which was well known for years, the narrative is to blame "Islamophobia" and the police after the rape of 1,400 girls.

---

[136] Josh Gerstein, *Judge snubbed U.S. Islamic groups in secret ruling*, Political, 11/01/09. The article can be seen online at http://www.politico.com/blogs/under-the-radar/2009/11/judge-snubbed-us-islamic-groups-in-secret-ruling-022503. Viewed 19 June 2017. **Rated C3.**

[137] The 9:58 interview is embedded on the CBC website at: http://www.cbc.ca/news/muslim-group-demands-apology-from-harper-chief-spokesman-1.2514099 . Viewed 19 June 2017. **Not rated**.

[138] See, among many others, the CBC report at: http://www.cbc.ca/news/politics/bill-c-51-hearings-committee-testimony-ends-as-opposition-readies-amendments-1.3010134. Viewed 19 June 2017. **Rated B3**.

[139] More information on this can be seen at the OSCE website at http://www.osce.org/odihr/223491 .

[140] *Rotherham Muslims call for boycott of South Yorkshire Police over 'demonization' since Jay report*, Alexandra Sims, The Independent, Monday 26 October 2015. The article can be seen online at http://www.independent.co.uk/news/uk/home-news/rotherham-muslims-call-for-boycott-of-south-yorkshire-police-over-demonization-since-jay-report-a6709356.html . Viewed 19 June 2017. **Rated B3**.

Implications

As noted above, it is reasonable to believe that Islamophobia and perpetual victimhood are a necessary part of the Islamist narrative. Islamists have created it and nurtured it as a means of distracting attention away from their own barbaric ideology and objectives. Whenever some one cries "Islamophobia" a close examination of the events and individuals involved should be examined to see if connections exist to extremist groups. All too often, they do.

CHAPTER 9: A HELPFUL GUIDE ON BEING ISLAMOPHOBIC IN CANADA

Thomas Quiggin

Key Points

- Does your wife enjoy being beaten when she steps out of line?
- Does being beaten make her smarter?
- These are important questions to know as you could be accused of being Islamophobic if you get the answers wrong.

Some Women Enjoy Being Beaten

In Toronto Ontario, the Muslim Student Association of York University handed out free books for its annual Islam Awareness Week (2015).[141] One of the books had the relatively innocuous title of Women in Islam & Refutation of some Common Misconceptions. Besides York University, this book was distributed free at the portable Dawah booth at Dundas Square in downtown Toronto. It is also available at the Walk-in Islamic Info Centre (WIIC), a Toronto-based not-for-profit Muslim organization dedicated to propagating Islam through Dawah.[142] It also sells it online.[143,144,145]

The book was written by Dr. Abdul-Rahman al-Sheha, a Saudi scholar and printed by the Saudi Dawah organization known as the Muslim World League (MWL). The MWL, as a Dawah organization, has a somewhat complicated history and has funded doubtful Dawah efforts around the world.[146] As of April 2017, the Muslim World League is among those being sued for $UD 4.2 billion by two dozen U.S. insurers over the 911 attacks on New York.[147]

---

[141] For sourcing and more information on this event see *A Tale of the Handmaidens – Violence Against Women in Canada.* The article is available online at http://tsecnetwork.ca/a-tale-of-the-handmaidens-violence-against-women-in-canada/ . Viewed 19 June 2017. **Rated A1.**

[142] *Why does the Ontario Government ignore the free distribution of an Islamic book that legalizes wife-beating?*, CIJ News, 22 September 2015. The article is available online at http://en.cijnews.com/?p=8301 . Viewed 10 April 2017. **Rated A1.**

[143] See https://www.amazon.co.uk/Women-Islam-Common-Misconceptions-Project-ebook/dp/B00JZANQ2K . Viewed 17 May 2017. **Rated A1.**

[144] See https://www.amazon.ca/Women-Islam-Common-Misconceptions-Project-ebook/dp/B00JZANQ2K Viewed 17 May 2017. **Rated A1.**

[145] See https://www.amazon.com/Women-Islam-Common-Misconceptions-Project-ebook/dp/B00JZANQ2K Viewed 17 May 2017. **Rated A1.**

[146] For more on the Muslim World League and its Dawah mission, see the Pew Research Centre article *Muslim World League and World Assembly of Muslim Youth*. It is available online at http://www.pewforum.org/2010/09/15/muslim-networks-and-movements-in-western-europe-muslim-world-league-and-world-assembly-of-muslim-youth/. Viewed 15 April 2017. **Rated A1**

[147] Jonathan Stempel and Katie Paul, *Saudi banks, bin Laden companies face $4.2 billion U.S. lawsuit by 9/11 insurers,* Reuters News, 13 April 207. The article is available online at http://www.reuters.com/article/us-usa-saudi-sept-idUSKBN17F2FX . Viewed 15 April 2017. **Rated A1.**

Given the title, it might be expected that the book will help dispel the perception that woman in Islam, are treated as second class individuals. However, the book has a chapter titled *Wife Disciplining*. This chapter suggests that wives should only be beaten as part of a three-stage correctional process. The chapter starts with a set of contradictory statements. It first says that "Islam forbids beating women and forbids strictly against it." However, it immediately reverses this position and states that "Islam permits the beating of wives in a restricted manner and limited sense only as a final solution and acceptable valid reason when all else fails." It also notes that there are different kinds of women, including the view that:

- "Submissive or subdued women; these women may even enjoy being beaten at times as a sign of **love and concern**."[148] (Emphasis added)

It is reasonable to believe that the question must arise when discussing Islamophobia. If you point out that wife beating is not allowed in Canada and that the advice in this book runs against the values of the Constitution and the Charter of Rights, are you denying the rights of Islamist men to beat their wives? Are you saying that women do not enjoy being beaten and are you therefore Islamophobic for raising these issues? If you asked a Muslim woman if she enjoys being beaten, are you committing an act of Islamophobia?

Beating Women Makes Them Smarter?

If you beat a woman, does it make her smarter? According to Sheik Houssein Muhammad Amer of Montreal, it does. As he notes:

- "Beating in Islam is a type of education. The beating is used after exhausting all effective and successful [possible] solutions and [it turned out that] there is no treatment without it... This is the case regarding the wife if you are right... if the estrangement fails the beating [of the wife] is permitted."[149]

This raises another question on Islamophobia. If you argue that there is no evidence to support the idea that beating women is a form of education for them and that the beatings are intended merely to force women in submission, are you Islamophobic?

Is the Man in Charge of the Family?

Dr. Jamal Badawi is a long-time NCCM/CAIR CAN board member, a co-founder of the Muslim American Society and a well-known North American Muslim Brotherhood figure. The MAS has been listed as a terrorist entity by the United Arab Emirates.[150] Badawi has written extensively on many Islamist issues.

---

[148] *Women in Islam & Refutation of some Common Misconceptions."* See the chapter on Wife Disciplining.
[149] *Canada's top Imam explains Quranic verse on wife beating,* CIJ News, 16 December 2016. http://en.cijnews.com/?p=77680 . Viewed 10 April 2017. **Rated A1**.
[150] The official list is online at http://www.thenational.ae/uae/government/list-of-groups-designated-terrorist-organisations-by-the-uae . Viewed 11 April 2017. **Rated A1.**

Among them has been the question of wife beating.[151] He approves of the practice and falls back on the belief that men oversee women because they spend their resources to support them. The verse in the Quran that he refers to is Surat An-Nisā' (The Women) 4:34.[152]

- "Men are in charge of women by [right of] what Allah has given one over the other and what they spend [for maintenance] from their wealth. So righteous women are devoutly obedient, guarding in [the husband's] absence what Allah would have them guard. But those [wives] from whom you fear arrogance - [first] advise them; [then if they persist], forsake them in bed; and [finally], strike them. But if they obey you [once more], seek no means against them. Indeed, Allah is ever Exalted and Grand."[153]

Dr. Badawi has made his views clear and he has a separate website[154] just to address these issues. His introductory paragraph is worth reading in full:[155]

> "In the event of a family dispute, the Quran exhorts the husband to treat his wife kindly and not overlook her POSITIVE ASPECTS (see Quran 4:19). If the problem relates to the wife's behavior, her husband may exhort her and appeal for reason. In most cases, this measure is likely to be sufficient. In cases where the problem continues, the husband may express his displeasure in another peaceful manner, by sleeping in a separate bed from hers. There are cases, however, in which a wife persists in deliberate mistreatment and expresses contempt of her husband and disregard for her marital obligations. Instead of divorce, the husband may resort to another measure that may save the marriage, at least in some cases. Such a measure is more accurately described as a gentle tap on the body, but NEVER ON THE FACE, making it more of a symbolic measure then a punitive one."

Dr. Badawi also thinks women are unfit to fill leadership roles simply because they are female. According to him:

> "According Islam women unfit by nature to lead because they undergo various physiological and psychological changes during their monthly periods and pregnancies."[156]

The issues on this website raise more questions about Islamophobia. For instance, are men placed in charge of women by divine right? Are you Islamophobic is you raise the issue of whether women can think for themselves in a family situation and that beating them is perhaps not the answer? Is it OK to beat a woman, if you do not hit her in the face?

---

[151] Dr. Jamal Badawi, *Is wife beating allowed in Islam?* See the website at http://www.themodernreligion.com/women/w_abuse_badawi.htm . Viewed 10 April 2017. **Rated A1**.

[152] See http://quran.com/4/34 . Viewed 10 April 2017. **Rated A1**.

[153] There are multiple interpretations of what it means to beat or strike a woman as noted at the end of the third last sentence. For seven different English language translations, see http://corpus.quran.com/translation.jsp?chapter=4&verse=34 . Viewed 10 April 2017. **Rated A1**.

[154] Dr. Jamal Badawi, *Is wife beating allowed in Islam?* The website is at http://www.themodernreligion.com/women/w_abuse_badawi.htm . Viewed 10 April 2017. **Rated A1**.

[155] *Is wife beating allowed in Islam?* By Dr. Jamal Badawi: http://www.themodernreligion.com/women/w_abuse_badawi.htm Viewed 10 April 2017. **Rated A1**.

[156] Canadian Imam: *"You have to choose either Allah or Canada"; wife must obey and serve her husband*, CIJ News, 1 December 2015. The article is available online at http://en.cijnews.com/?p=15654 . Viewed 10 April 2017. **Rated A1**.

How Does a Man Handle a Rebellious Wife? Does Beating Her Bring Her Back to Her Senses?

If the man is head of the family, how should he handle a rebellious and disobedient wife? According to Abu Ameenah Bilal Philips of Ontario[157]:

> "Men are considered the head of the family and the final decisions are in his hand... her responsibility is to obey him as long as his requests are permissible according to Islamic law... [In] Islam, a woman is obliged to give herself to her husband and he may not be charged with rape... It is true that the Sharee'ah does permit a husband to hit his wife... The Quranic verse outlines the procedures which should be followed in the case of a rebellious and unjustly disobedient wife... the intent of this beating is not inflicting pain and punishment but merely to bring the woman back to her senses and re-establish authority in the family."

From the point of view of Islamophobia, the following question should be raised. Is it OK to beat your wife to bring her "back to her senses" or are you Islamophobic if you suggest that beating your wife has more to do with forcing her into submission than helping her?[158]

Is Canada a Feminine Country? Should Women Quit Feminism?

According to Abdi Hersy, who was the Imam of Abu Bakr Musallah in Calgary, women must obey men. For instance, if a man tells his wife to cook food, she must obey the husband. A wife cannot bring anyone into the house without first seeking permission from the husband and she cannot leave the house without his permission. As Abdi Hersy states:

> "You have to choose either Allah, the most glorified, the most high, or Canada. Canada is a feminine country. So ladies, the other thing that I want you to quit from your life is feminism. Sometimes they ask you questions that you cannot even answer."[159]

Sheikh Musleh Khan of Ontario makes the same general observations when he states:

> "The husband is the only leader of the family; "the wife should be obedient to her husband at all times" including when he calls her to bed; she should "ask her husband permission before leaving the home" and "is obliged to serve her husband."[160]

These ideas do not exist in isolation. Yusuf Al Qaradawi is the most quoted and revered inspirational cleric of the Muslim Brotherhood. He wrote a book with the title The Lawful and the Prohibited in Islam. In this book, Qaradawi makes the position of a women clear. She is to be obedient and subservient. This is, of course, due to the nature ability of the man over the woman as he says:

---

[157] Possibly living in Qatar as of the time of writing. Qatar provides shelter to many of the worst Islamists.

[158] *Canada's top Imam explains Quranic verse on wife beating,* CIJ News, 16 December 2016. http://en.cijnews.com/?p=77680 . Viewed 10 April 2017. **Rated A1**.

[159] *Canadian Imam: "You have to choose either Allah or Canada"; wife must obey and serve her husband,* CIJ News, 1 December 2015. The article is available online at http://en.cijnews.com/?p=15654 . Viewed 10 April 2017. **Rated A1**.

[160] *Canada's top Imam explains Quranic verse on wife beating,* CIJ News, 16 December 2016. http://en.cijnews.com/?p=77680 . Viewed 10 April 2017. **Rated A1**.

> "Because of his natural ability and his responsibility for providing for his family, the man is the head of the house and of the family. He is entitled to the obedience and cooperation of his wife, and accordingly it is not permissible for her to rebel against his authority, causing disruption… "If the husband senses that feelings of disobedience and rebelliousness are rising against him in his wife… If this approach fails, it is permissible for him to beat her lightly with his hands… To be specific, one may beat only to safeguard Islamic behavior and if he (the husband) sees deviation only in what she must do or obey in relation to him."

Is it Islamophobic to say that it is wrong to beat your wife even if she is being beaten to safeguard the Islamic (Islamist) behavior? Is it Islamophobic to think that a wife can leave a house without seeking permission from her husband? Can she invite her friends in without his permission? What about feminism? Can a woman describe herself as a feminist without being accused of being Islamophobic?

Are you Islamophobic to Question a Minister of the Canadian Government?

In April of 2016, the Minister of Immigration, Refugees and Citizenship attended an awards dinner hosted Canadian Council of Imams at their annual dinner.[161] The Minister at the time, John McCallum, received an award for his "outstanding service to "the community." No mention was made as to what these outstanding services were that so pleased the ICNA or the Canadian Council of Imans. Dr. Iqbal Al-Nadvi is the Chairperson of Canadian Council of Imams[162] as well as being the Amir or head of Islamic Circle of North America (ICNA). The ICNA openly advocates violence against women and backs a variety of policies which are openly misogynistic. The syllabus of learning from the ICNA promotes, among others, that women are inferior to men,[163] wife beating is permissible[164] and that Western civilization is the enemy.[165] Islam, they argue, is totally incompatible with democracy.[166]

If you were to criticize the Minister for accepting an award on behalf of the Government of Canada from an organization that advocates wife beating and is openly anti-democratic, are you an Islamophobe? Does questioning the Minister's judgement in attending such a dinner become an act of Islamophobia or is it an act of free speech?

Are all Canadian Soldiers War Criminals?

---

[161] Canadian Council of Imams, *Our First Annual Dinner on April 11 celebrating 26 years of Service was a success*, 14 April 2016. The article can be seen online at http://www.canadiancouncilofimams.com/2016/04/our-first-annual-dinner-on-april-11-celebrating-26-years-of-service-was-a-success/ . Viewed 31 March 2017. **Rated A1.**

[162] *Dr. Iqbal Al-Nadvi-New Amir of ICNA Canada for 2016-2017,* http://icnacanada.net/dr-iqbal-al-nadvi-new-amir-of-icna-canada-for-2016-2017/ . Viewed 31 March 2017. **Rated A2.**

[163] CIJ News, *ICNA Canada's online syllabus: women are inferior to men, Western civilization "enemy"*, 23 February 2016. The article is available online at http://en.cijnews.com/?p=27294 . Viewed 31 March 2017. **Rated A1.**

[164] CIN News, *ICNA Canada's online syllabus on wife beating*, 18 February 2017. The article is available online at http://en.cijnews.com/?p=26599 . Viewed 31 March 2017. **Rated A1.**

[165] CIJ News, *ICNA Canada's online syllabus: women are inferior to men, Western civilization "enemy"*, 23 February 2016. The article is available online at http://en.cijnews.com/?p=27294 . Viewed 31 March 2017. **Rated A1.**

[166] CIJ News, *ICNA Canada contradicts Trudeau: "Islam is totally incompatible with Western democracy"*, 25 February 2017. The article can be seen online at http://en.cijnews.com/?p=27451 . Viewed 31 March 2017. **Rated A1.**

Hizb ut-Tahrir is an Islamist organization that operates in a variety of countries, including Canada. It is a spinoff of the Muslim Brotherhood and was founded in 1952.[167] Hizb ut-Tahrir states that their end goal is the Islamization of Canada as part of this global caliphate.[168] It appears that the head of Hizb ut-Tahrir in Canada is Mazin Abdul-Adhim. He is a Canadian citizen but was born in Iraq and now lives in London, Ontario. Abdul-Adhim openly stated that:

> "No Muslim should honour the memory of those war criminals by wearing a poppy, just as no one would honour a criminal that killed his or her mother and father."[169]

As a Canadian citizen, are you allowed to disagree with Abdul-Adhim and state that Canadian soldiers are not war criminals? Or is that being Islamophobic?

The Islamic Circle of North America (ICNA)

According to its own website, ICNA Canada's vision is to build an "Exemplary Canadian Muslim Community." It is intended to be "A community that sets path towards personal excellence in faith, worship and morality and shares basis for the moral, social, and economic development of the Canadian Society." It will do this by a "total submission to Him [Allah] and through the propagation of true and universal message of Islam." Its head office is at 391 Burnhamthorpe Rd., East, Oakville, Ontario.[170]

On its official website ICNA Canada shares with its members, followers, and supporters the book "Riyad as Saliheen" (The Gardens of the Righteous) compiled by Imam Zakaruya Yahya Bin Sharaf An-Nawawi, a Sunni Shafi'ite jurist and hadith scholar who lived in 13th Century. The Gardens of the Righteous (Arabic: Riyadh as-Salihin), is a compilation of verses from the Quran and Hadith by Al-Nawawi. It contains a total of 1,905 hadith divided across 372 chapters, many of which are introduced by verses of the Quran. The book "Riyad as Saliheen" appears on ICNA Canada site, which adds modern commentary to the verses from the Quran and hadith.[171]

This book forms the syllabus for the ICNA education program for its members. Included in the syllabus are the following observations:

- The majority of the dwellers of Hell are women.
- Pregnant adulteresses are to be stoned after giving birth.
- Adulterers should be stoned, and hands chopped off thieves.

---

[167] See more on Hizb ut-Tahrir at their own site which is available online at http://english.hizbuttahrir.org/index.php/about/about-us . Viewed 10 April 2017. **Rated A1.**

[168] For more on this see http://jonathanhalevi.blogspot.ca/2013/08/the-endgoal-is-islamization-of-canadian.html . Viewed 10 April 2017. **Rated A1.**

[169] Mr. Tahir Gora (Director General, Canadian Thinkers' Forum) at the Public Safety and National Security Committee. This statement can be seen online at https://openparliament.ca/committees/public-safety/41-2/58/tahir-gora-1/only/ . Viewed 10 April 2017. **Rated A1.**

[170] The vision statement for ICNA can be seen on their website at http://icnacanada.net/about-2/ . Viewed 10 April 2017. **Rated A1.**

[171] This entire paragraph was taken from *ICNA Canada's online syllabus: jihad against "infidels" strives for Islamic global dominance,* CIJ News, 24 February 2016. The entire article can be seen online at http://en.cijnews.com/?p=27398 . Viewed 10 April 2017. **Rated A1.**

- Honour killing is acceptable in Islam.
- Slave-girls are conditionally legal.
- Muslims will dominate the Jews and kill them,
- Islam will be victorious over the disbelieving people.
- Every human being is born as a Muslim.

This raises some more interesting questions about Islamists and Islamophobia. If you raise a question about whether Muslims should be able to kill all the Jews or if most persons in Hell are women, are you being Islamophobic? If, during a theological debate you question the idea of whether all persons are born Muslim, are you being Islamophobic?

Muslims Only

Imagine if you ran an advertisement on a social media platform looking to rent out an apartment. In the ad, you state that you do not want any Muslims to apply. Would that make you guilty of Islamophobia? Should someone act against that?

This is not a two-way street. According to CIJ News[172], they tracked ads on Kijiji for a two-week period in the Greater Toronto Area. In just two weeks, they found the following ads:

- "We have 1 private room immediately available... We are looking for 1 lady preferably Muslim & urdu/hindi speaking."
- "I am offering my... 1 bedroom... apartment to share with preferably a Muslim brother."
- "Room on rent muslim male neede[d]."
- "Looking for a Male Muslim Roomate."
- "2 bed room apartment... looking for male student from india . Preferring muslim."
- "Room (s) for rent for muslim girls... You would be living with a paki family."
- "A share or Single Person room available with Muslim, Pakistani, Bangladeshi, Indian."
- "Private room with HALAL MEALS for Muslim Lady."
- "Apt for sharing w/ Muslim brother."
- "Den (room) for rent MUSLIM."

---

172 *Rental ads only for "racialized" people*, CIJ News, 8 April 2017. The article can be seen online at http://en.cijnews.com/?p=215092 . Viewed 10 April 2017. **Rated A1**.

- "SHARED ACCOMODATION for Muslim male(s)."
- "Roommate required... (Muslim and Male only)... Only MUSLIMS and MALES are welcome."
- "Room... muslim male needed."
- "Master bedroom available... Male Pakistani or Muslim preferred."
- "Room for Rent – Muslim Female Only."

Are you Islamophobic if you point out that announced discrimination in renting property might be a violation of the Human Rights Code section on "Freedoms from Discrimination"?

Implications

It is a reasonable opinion to hold that such questions are becoming serious. With the Parliament of Canada having passed the Islamophobia motion (M-103) and with the hearings around it being pushed ahead, free speech may be at stake.

If the Islamophobia motion passes into law after the hearings, Canadians will have to self-monitor their own speech to ensure they are not offending the sensitives of the Islamists and the Government of Canada. At that point, Canadians will have to decide whether some women truly enjoy being beaten, or if you are Islamophobic for simply asking the question.

CHAPTER 10: BEING BEATEN IS A SIGN OF LOVE AND CONCERN - WOMEN AND ISLAMIST IDEOLOGY

Thomas Quiggin

Key Points

- The greatest single group of victims of Islamist is likely women.
- Islamists regularly call for women to be beaten for a variety of reasons – not the least of which is that they enjoy a good beating now and again.
- Feminists in Canada are as silent as beaten wives on the issue of violence against women advocated by extremist Islam.

As the Islamists gradually spread their influence, the position of women degenerates. It may be difficult to believe, but it is now acceptable in Canada to openly advocate that women should be beaten or killed in the name of Islam (Islamists).

The willingness to become predators of women is perhaps the most visible in ISIS but it is common wherever the Islamist ideology is growing. Women are stoned to death for being victims of rape. Their crime? The rape must have been their fault as they tempted the men through their dress or activities. ISIS, in their Dabiq magazine[173] says that non-Muslim women can be forced into sexual slavery while the lack of a sexual slavery stands at the root of male misbehaviour. This is similar to calls made in Canada by the ICNA. (Chapter Nine)

Canadian Examples

As noted above, the Muslim Student Association at York University in Toronto, thinks that beating wives is not only acceptable, but some women enjoy being beaten.[174] How is it that a university funded association at a taxpayer funded public institution can openly advocate wife beating? Member of Parliament Iqra Khalid was elected to represent the riding of Mississauga-Erin Mills in 2015. She was formerly the head of the Muslim Student Association at York University.[175] Her views on this subject are not clear, but she has not condemned the Muslim Student Association for its views. This is interesting, given that Iqra Khalid claims to have written the constitution for the York University Muslim Student Association.[176]

---

[173] For an overview of Dabiq Magazine, see *The Islamic State's (ISIS, ISIL) Magazine*, Wed, September 10, 2014. The article is available online at http://www.clarionproject.org/news/islamic-state-isis-isil-propaganda-magazine-dabiq . Viewed 19 June 2017. **Rated B2**.

[174] For sourcing and more information on this event see *A Tale of the Handmaidens – Violence Against Women in Canada.* This article is available in Annex J.

[175] John Steward, *This millennial not only votes, she's running for MP*, Inside Toronto Magazine, January 16, 2015. The article is available online at http://www.insidetoronto.com/blogs/post/5262154-this-millennial-not-only-votes-she-s-running-for-mp/ . Viewed 19 June 2017. **Rated B2**.

[176] According to Member of Parliament Iqra Khalid, she wrote the constitution of the MSA at York University. For more on this see John Steward, *This millennial not only votes, she's running for MP*, Inside Toronto Magazine,

Another example is Imam Shazim Khan of Ontario, who has said:

> "So the Prophet, peace be upon him (PBUH he said): 'Even in that situation she should not refuse.' And to refuse, and to refuse to obey her husband in this respect [to respond to his call to have sex] is a major sin in Islam. It is a major sin... If a man calls on his wife to satisfy his desire with her and she refuses for no genuine reason... the angels curse her till the morning... One of the rights of the husband over his wife also is that she should serve him... wife should protect his honour... she stays away from everything that her husband doesn't like in order to please him..."

Imam Abdi Hersy of Alberta, who is wanted in the USA on sexual assault charges, says that:

> "The husband has many rights on his wife... first and foremost, she has to obey you. She has to obey you, ok. He comes with the orders. You have to give orders and she has to obey you... That's one of the rights of the husband for his wife. So she is going to cook and clean and prepare food... So she has to obey you... And the biggest thing when it comes to obeying your husband, ladies, is when he calls you in the bed stop what you are doing, quit... Obey your husband... The other thing that is a right upon the wife for her husband is she cannot leave the house without his permission... "First and foremost, ladies obey husbands... First and foremost, if you order her to pray or to obey Allah... she has no choice but to obey him... if husband calls his wife to his bed and she refuses without any valid excuse... the angels curse her until morning... She has to listen if he orders to restrain herself or refrain from haram [forbidden action]. She wants to do haram [forbidden action], and he says no, she has to obey him with that... if you order to do prayer, do prayers... she has to obey you, she cannot say no."

Abu Ameenah Bilal Philips of Ontario continues with the similar line of thought and says that:

> "Men are considered the head of the family and the final decisions are in his hand... her responsibility is to obey him as long as his requests are permissible according to Islamic law... [In] Islam, a woman is obliged to give herself to her husband and he may not be charged with rape... It is true that the Sharee'ah does permit a husband to hit his wife... The Quranic verse outlines the procedures which should be followed in the case of a rebellious and unjustly disobedient wife... the intent of this beating is not inflicting pain and punishment but merely to bring the woman back to her senses and re-establish authority in the family."

"Shaykh" Said Rageah adds a somewhat different perspective and says you should assault someone who looks at your wife or sister. He has told his followers:

> "Also something that we are not doing it is [that] we no longer have the ghirah [protective jealousy] that is needed... when a man looks at your sister or your wife and her brother passes by what should you [her brother] do? Knocking him out. Right?"

January 16, 2015. The article is available online at http://www.insidetoronto.com/blogs/post/5262154-this-millennial-not-only-votes-she-s-running-for-mp/ . Viewed 19 June 2017. **Rated B2**.

In Mississauga, the annual Halal Food Fest in 2014 had a bookstore with a book titled *Rulings Pertaining to Muslim Women*.[177] This book has some interesting views including "It is obligatory upon the Muslim woman to obey her husband in that which is halal." The book also states that:

> "Among the rights of a husband upon his wife is that she looks after his house and does not go outside unless she has his permission. She does the housework and does not force him to employ a maid."

The book also says that women are not allowed to look at men and points out that:

> "So it is upon the Muslim woman to lower and avert her gaze from men, and not look at the provocative pictures which are found in various media, magazines, TV and video, in order to protect herself from evil consequences..."

Furthermore, women are not allowed to travel outside the house alone without an escort to preserve their chastity. The book advises that:

> "Among the means of preserving chastity is to prevent the woman from travelling unless she has a mahram [an unmarriageable kin with whom sexual intercourse would be considered incestuous] to protect her from the desires of the licentious and the sinful."

The Jaffari Mosque in Thornhill, Toronto

The Iman of the Jaffari Mosque is Moulana[178] Sayyid Muhhamad Rizvi. He is known by the short title of Imam Rizvi. In addition to filling the role of Imam, he is also an "Alim" or a resident scholar at the mosque, which is located at 9000 Bathurst Street in the City of Vaughan.

Educated in the city of Qom, he is an open supporter of the (Shia) Iranian Khomeneists and is believed to be operating in sympathy with the Government of Iran and the Khomeneists (arguably one and the same).[179]

Imam Rizvi believes that the Khomeneist interpretation of Shia Islam is to take precedence over all matters including those which are personal, social, economic and political. He is, in short, an Islamist supremacist.[180]

---

[177] *Book sold in Mississauga guides the Muslim woman to obey and serve her husband including when he calls her to bed*. The article is available online at http://jonathanhalevi.blogspot.ca/2015/03/book-sold-in-mississauga-guides-muslim.html . Viewed 19 June 222017. **Rated B2**.

[178] The title or honorific Moulana is given to one who has completed a course of studies on Islamic education at the tertiary level. This program of studies is normally referred to as an Alim Course, and takes between 5-8 years to complete. For more on this see: http://islamqa.org/hanafi/darululoomtt/52300 Viewed 19 June 2017. **Rated B2.**

[179] For more on Jaffari Mosque see Annex J.

[180] Michael Petrou, *Carleton University teams up with Iranian embassy to honour Ayatollah Khomeini*, Macleans Magazine, June 6, 2012. The article is available online at http://www.macleans.ca/authors/michael-petrou/carleton-university-teams-up-with-iranian-embassy-to-honour-ayatollah-khomeini/ . Viewed 19 June 2017. **Rated B2**.

Based on the facts in his own book, it is reasonable to believe that Imam Rizvi has misogynist views on women and girls. For instance, he makes it clear in his book[181] that he believes in "muta" (temporary) marriages. He has stated that if an individual "finds it difficult to control his or her sexual desire, then the only way to fulfill the sexual desire is muta." He continues this by saying: "I cannot overemphasize the temporary nature of muta. The message of Islam is quite clear: marry on a permanent basis; if that is not possible, then adopt temporary abstinence; if that is not possible, only then use the muta marriage."

The practice of muta marriages in widespread in Shia Islam. Under the 'new' interpretation of the Shia mullahs under Ayatollah Khomeini following the 1979 Iranian revolution, the practice of muta re-emerged and gained a considerable following. In Iran, claims were made no prostitution existed under the Khomeneist government. However, even the government of Iran eventually gave up on the claims as it was obvious that prostitution was becoming a larger problem on Iran as the practice of muta spread and was seen to be managed and approved by Imams operating out of Shia mosques. The religious cities of Qom and Mashad are (in)famous for their role in these practices.[182]

The practice also appears to be spreading into Sunni Islam, even though all four main schools of Sunni jurisprudence had earlier banned it. The practice is still seen among some Sunnis in Jordan and it may be gaining wider acceptance now in Saudi Arabia as a more theocratic and Islamist view grows. While muta was banned by President Saddam Hussein of Iraq, it appears to be making a comeback there as well, mainly, but not exclusively, in Shia communities.[183]

According to his own book, Imam Rizvi also believes and openly advocates that sex with nine-year-old girls is acceptable, if it occurs within muta (temporary) or da'im (permanent) marriage. Permanent marriage is preferred, but sex with girls within the concept of a temporary marriage is permissible. This would appear to be sanctioning pedophilia and statutory rape, despite Canadian laws against under age marriages and forcing underage females to have sex.[184]

The muta marriage is performed for a fee by an Imam. The fee appears to go the Imam and the mosque, in much the same way as any other funeral or marriage ceremony would do. There is no minimum or maximum time involved for a muta marriage. [185] The payment or mahr goes to the woman involved. The fact that a fee is charged for a "temporary marriage" also raised the question of whether the Imams involved can be considered to be living off the avails of prostitution (i.e. pimping).

To be clear, Imam Rizvi's view of sex with nine-year-old girls being permissible and muta marriage is not an exception nor is he an outlier in his field. His views, from his own book, are in line with the view of the

---

[181] Sayyid Muhammad Rizvi, *Marriage and Morals in Islam, Islamic Education & Information Center.* A version of this book can be seen online at https://www.al-islam.org/marriage-and-morals-islam-sayyid-muhammad-rizvi . Viewed 19 June 2017. **Not rated.**

[182] *Iran Permits Brothels Through Temporary Marriages*, Published June 7th, 2010 - 09:04 GMT http://www.albawaba.com/behind-news/iran-permits-brothels-through-temporary-marriages. Viewed 19 June 2017. **Rated C2.**

[183] *Abuse of Temporary Marriages Flourishes in Iraq*, National Public Radio report of October 19, 20108:18 PM ET http://www.npr.org/templates/story/story.php?storyId=130350678 . Viewed 19 June 2017. **Rated C2.**

[184] Sayyid Muhammad Rizvi, *Marriage and Morals in Islam, Islamic Education & Information Center.* A version of this book can be seen online at https://www.al-islam.org/marriage-and-morals-islam-sayyid-muhammad-rizvi . Viewed 19 June 2017. **Not rated.**

[185] See question 27 at: http://www.alulbayt.com/rulings/11.htm Fatwa rulings of Grand Ayatollah Sistani on Marriage. Viewed 19 June 2017. **Rated C2.**

Khomeneists in Iran and wherever Khomeneist beliefs exist around the world. As an aside, Imam Rizvi also approves of consanguineous marriages between first cousins as he states in his book.

The Department of Foreign Affairs and International Trade Canada

On February 26, 2015, the Department of Foreign Affairs and International Trade Canada (DFAIT) hosted a conference in Ottawa with the title: Conference on Tackling Early and Forced Marriage and 'Honour' Based Violence in Canada. The conference featured a rather notable list of guest speakers from countries such as the UK. A variety of individuals spoke about Female Genital Mutilation (FGM), forced marriages and wife/daughter killing. The conference noted that young girls are being taught how to avoid being sent overseas to become victims of FGM or being forced into underage arranged marriages.[186] These young girls in the UK are being taught to put a spoon in their underwear when going through security at the airport. When the metal detector trips, the girls are taught to ask for a private pat down and then tell the security official they are being forced overseas.[187] This is rather depressing stuff for conference discussions, but it is clear evidence as to how women and girls are abused.

Three Canadian women, who were invited to the conference and have considerable profile on the issues of violence against women, were contacted ahead of the conference. They were less-than-subtlety warned that they were not to raise questions about violence against women in Canada and how it related to "culturally embedded practices." This term is, of course, a politically correct way to describe violence against women as described by Islamists in Canada. They were told that if such issues were raised, they would not be invited to any further events or discussions. DFAIT bureaucrats, like many others, were more worried about political correctness than they were women being killed and mutilated in Canada. The bureaucrat responsible these statements was Fiona Jarvis, Senior Policy Officer, Vulnerable Children's Consular Policy Consular, Policy and Programs (JPP). When questioned at the conference by this author on the issue, she was evasive.

Aruna Papp was one of those Canadians who attended the conference. She is a Canadian who is nationally and internationally recognized as an educator and advocate of human rights. Her focus is on women's rights in cross-cultural perspectives. She believes that the conference and the Government of Canada wish to sweep the entire issue of hour based violence under the carpet. The position of the government appears to be that all cultures have domestic violence and therefore there is no difference between them. As Ms. Papp notes, violence in cultures manifests itself differently. For instance, girls in Canada are typically allowed to date, become educated, rent their own apartments, or chose their own husbands. However, many girls and young women in Canada are subjected to violence in the household and are victimized by honour killings and forced suicides.

Ms. Papp also believes that the violence against these girls and women is not the result of domestic disputes such as a husband and wife fighting over money. Rather, this violence used to control the lives of women based on honour codes found in Islamist beliefs and ancient cultural practices.

---

[186] *Spoon in underwear saving some British youths from forced marriage*, The Journal IE, 15 August 2013. The article can be viewed online at http://www.thejournal.ie/spoon-security-alert-airport-forced-marriage-1038549-Aug2013/ . Viewed 24 May 2017. **Rated B2**.

[187] Mel Hattie, *U.K. girls learn about female genital mutilation before danger of 'cutting season'*, CBC News in London, 15 May 15 2016. The article can be viewed online at http://www.cbc.ca/news/world/fgm-london-education-1.3577240 . Viewed 24 May 2017. **Rated B2**.

As with many others, she identifies the political correctness of the Government of Canada as part of the problem. How can you identify a problem, train people, and hopefully solve the problem is you cannot even name it?

Honour Killings

According to court documents, on 30 June 2009 in Kingston, Ontario, multimillionaire Mohammad Shafia murdered his four daughters Zainab, 19, Sahar, 17, and Geeti, 13, along with his first wife Rona Amir Mohammed, 50. He was assisted by his son Hamed. The victims were found dead in the Rideau Canal lock at Kingston Mills. Mohammad Shafia's second wife in their polygynous marriage, Tooba, was also arrested for her role in the murders. The four females had been placed in a Nissan Sentra, bought the day before, and the Nissan was then run into the canal where it overturned in the water. All three were convicted of murder in 2012.

Much debate has occurred in Canada and around the world as to whether the murders amounted to that of an honour killing. Whatever the beliefs of others, it is a fact that Mohammad Shafia was clear on the issue. The murders occurred due to his perception of lost honour. During the investigation, it came out that he had called his daughters "whores," "filthy" and "rotten children." He said they had betrayed the family as well as betraying Islam.[188] By contrast, Mohammad Anwar Yaqubi, a half brother to Mohammad Shafia, said he had never heard of the concept of honour killing and that the deaths were the result of a "traffic accident."[189]

The most damning evidence suggesting it was an honour killing may have come from Mohammad Shafia himself. While the investigation was ongoing, his conversations with his second wife Tooba and their son Hamed were caught on police intercepts. He stated[190]:

> "Whatever she threw in our way, she did. **We lost our honour**. Even if they come back to life a hundred times, if I have a cleaver in my hand, I will cut (her) in pieces ... If we remain alive one night or one year, we have no tensions in our hearts, (thinking that) our daughter is in the arms of this or that boy, in the arms of this or that man. May the Devil s--- on their graves! Is that what a daughter should be? Would (a daughter) be such a whore?... Honourless girl!"
>
> "I say to myself, 'you did well. Would they come back to life a hundred times, for you to do the same again.' That is how hurt I am, Tooba, they betrayed us immensely. They violated us immensely. There can be no betrayal, no treachery, no violation more than this. By God! It was

---

[188] *'Cut someone in pieces with a cleaver' just a childhood expression, Shafia witness tells jury,* Postmedia News | January 17, 2012 3:25 PM ET. The article is available online at http://news.nationalpost.com/news/canada/cut-someone-in-pieces-with-a-cleaver-just-a-childhood-expression-shafia-witness-tells-jury . Viewed 19 June 2017. **Rated B2.**

[189] *'Cut someone in pieces with a cleaver' just a childhood expression, Shafia witness tells jury,* Postmedia News | January 17, 2012 3:25 PM ET. The article is available online at http://news.nationalpost.com/news/canada/cut-someone-in-pieces-with-a-cleaver-just-a-childhood-expression-shafia-witness-tells-jury . Viewed 19 June 2017. **Rated B2**.

[190] For the contents of the intercepts, see among many others, http://www.macleans.ca/news/canada/the-hunt-for-the-truth/ . See also http://www.macleans.ca/news/canada/inside-the-shafia-killings-that-shocked-a-nation/ and http://www.thestar.com/news/gta/2016/03/02/by-any-definition-shafia-murders-were-honour-killings-dimanno.html . All the articles are available online. All viewed on 19 June 2017 and all rated **B2**.

> all treason from beginning to end. They betrayed kindness, they betrayed our tradition, they betrayed everything."
>
> "There is nothing more valuable than our honour. I am telling your mother that be like a man as you have always been. I know it hurts. Don't worry at all. Don't regret or wish that this would have happened or that would have happened. I am telling you now and I was telling you before that whoever plays with my honour, my words are the same. There is no value of life without honour."
>
> "Even if they hoist me up onto the gallows... **nothing is more dear to me than my honour**. Let's leave our destiny to God and may God never make me, you or your mother honourless. **I don't accept this dishonour**." (Emphasis added).

With no trace of irony, Mohammad Shafia, his son Hamad and his second wife Tooba Yahya tried in early 2016 for a retrial. Lawyers for the three claims that the trial was 'tainted by cultural prejudice.'[191]

It should be made clear in Canada that there is indeed a 'cultural prejudice' towards the practice of honour killing. It should also be made clear that it is both immoral and illegal in Canada to murder your wife and three daughters if they embarrass you.

Implications

It is a fact that women in Canada have the right to exist as persons before the law along with all the rights that come with that. It is a reasonable opinion to believe that the quasi-religious and cultural practices of Islamists and their followers have no place in Canada or its future.

It is also reasonable to hold the opinion that brown feminists in Canada appear to have been beaten into silence by the coercive discourse of political Islamists and, a times, by the Government of Canada.

White Canadian so-called "feminists" seem to adhere to the culture of political correctness. For the most part, they remain silent on these issues.

---

[191] Michael Friscolanti, *Shafia family 'honour killers' fight for new trial: Lawyers for the imprisoned trio argue that 2012 guilty verdicts may have been 'tainted by cultural prejudice.'*, Macleans Magazine, 03 March 2016. The article is available online at http://www.macleans.ca/news/canada/shafia-family-honour-killers-fight-for-new-trial/ . Viewed 19 June 2017. **Rated B2**.

CHAPTER 11: M-103 – HOW ISLAMIST STYLE BLASPHEMY LAWS MAY BE COMING TO CANADA

Thomas Quiggin

Key Points

- The purpose of M-103 is to silence critics of the Islamists and to expand the narrative of perpetual victimhood. The victimhood narrative is required to justify Islamist activities.

- The Parliamentary Motion M-103 on Islamophobia and the Ministry of Heritage hearings are an attempt to move Islamist style blasphemy laws into Canada.

- Member of Parliament Iqra Khalid was the sponsor of Motion 103 titled "Systemic racism and religious discrimination".[192] As someone who has multiple direct and family links to Islamist ideology, her motivations for sponsoring the motion must be questioned.

M-103 – the Parliamentary Motion on "Islamophobia"

The Parliament of Canada passed a Motion on Islamophobia on 23 March 2017 by a vote of 201–91. The motion had been presented to Parliament on 05 December 2016 by Iqra Khalid, the Liberal Member of Parliament for Mississauga-Erin Mills. The motion was seconded by Liberal MP Frank Baylis. The motion calls for: "Commons heritage committee to study how the government could develop a government-wide approach to reducing or eliminating systemic racism and religious discrimination, including Islamophobia, and collect data to provide context for hate crime reports and to conduct needs assessments for impacted communities. Findings are to be presented within eight months."

The full text of the motion reads:

> "Ms. Khalid (Mississauga- Erin Mills), seconded by Mr. Baylis (Pierrefonds—Dollard), moved, — That, in the opinion of the House, the government should: (a) recognize the need to quell the increasing public climate of hate and fear; (b) condemn Islamophobia and all forms of systemic racism and religious discrimination and take note of House of Commons' petition e-411 and the issues raised by it; and (c) request that the Standing Committee on Canadian Heritage undertake a study on how the government could
>
> (i) develop a whole-of-government approach to reducing or eliminating systemic racism and religious discrimination including Islamophobia, in Canada, while ensuring a community-centered focus with a holistic response through evidence-based policy-making, (ii) collect data to contextualize hate crime reports and to conduct needs assessments for impacted communities, and that the Committee should present its findings and recommendations to the House no later than 240 calendar days from the adoption of this motion, provided that in its report, the Committee should make recommendations that the government may use to better reflect the

---

[192] House of Commons, IQRA KHALID - PRIVATE MEMBERS' MOTIONS - CURRENT SESSION, 23 March 2017. The article can be seen online at http://www.ourcommons.ca/Parliamentarians/en/members/Iqra-Khalid(88849)/Motions?sessionId=152 Viewed 17 May 2017. **Rated A1.**

enshrined rights and freedoms in the Constitution Acts, including the Canadian Charter of Rights and Freedoms. (Private Members' Business M-103)"[193]

Victimhood

The motion has caused considerable upset, as it creates two distinct standards in its wording, one for Muslims and one for everyone else. It is a reasonable opinion to believe this perception has grounds, given that the motion privileges Islamophobia while refusing to define it.[194] The motion also clearly states that it would "condemn Islamophobia and all forms of systemic racism and religious discrimination." Why, many ask, could it simply not say it would "condemn all forms of systemic racism and religious discrimination." As MP Maxime Bernier put it: "Is this motion a first step towards restricting our right to criticize Islam? Given the international situation, and the fact that jihadi terrorism is today the most important threat to our security, I think this is a serious concern we have to take into account."[195]

The purpose of the motion and the following hearings is primarily two-fold. The first is a blatant attempt to silence the critics of the Islamists. As noted earlier, the political agenda of the Islamists is abhorrent to Canadian values, so Islamists want a pre-emptive strike on the criticism to silence it.

More worrying, however, is the subtext. By combining Islamophobia with the narrative on perpetual victimhood, a potentially explosive combination is created. For instance, Hamas, a Muslim Brotherhood front group in Gaza, justifies the use of violence as a divinely sanctioned jihad. It is easy to see how the narrative of victimhood and the justification of violence can potentially represent the first "building block" of radicalization and militancy.[196]

The Process in Canada

How is it that the Islamophobia motion can be presented to the people of Canada? Is this motion and its follow-on committee studies leading Canada towards blasphemy laws which are common in Islamist countries such as Saudi Arabia and Pakistan?

Pakistan is a useful example. According to the Immigration and Refugee Board (IRB) of Canada, Pakistan has strict blasphemy laws which result in a prison sentences, extrajudicial killings and false accusations.[197]

---

[193] For more on this motion and its progress in the House of Commons, see the official parliamentary website at http://www.ourcommons.ca/Parliamentarians/en/members/Iqra-Khalid(88849)/Motions?documentId=8661986%2520&sessionId=152 . Viewed 28 July 2017. **Not rated.**

[194] Kathleen Harris, *Conservatives wrestle over Liberal MP's anti-Islamophobia motion,* CBC News, 14 February 2017. The article can be seen online at http://www.cbc.ca/news/politics/islamophobia-M-103-khalid-motion-1.3982013 . Viewed 28 April 2017. **Rated C3.**

[195] Kathleen Harris, *Conservatives wrestle over Liberal MP's anti-Islamophobia motion,* CBC News, 14 February 2017. The article can be seen online at http://www.cbc.ca/news/politics/islamophobia-M-103-khalid-motion-1.3982013 . Viewed 28 April 2017. **Rated C3.**

[196] For a larger discussion on the linkages between Islamophobia, victimhood, and violence, see Dr. Lorenzo Vidino, *The Muslim Brotherhood in Austria*, Program on Extremism at George Washington University and the University of Vienna, August 2017. The article can be seen online at https://extremism.gwu.edu/sites/extremism.gwu.edu/files/MB%20in%20Austria-%20Print.pdf . Viewed 03 October 2017. **Rated B2.**

[197] IRB Canada, *Blasphemy laws, including legislation, implementation, related violence, reform, and state response,* The document can be seen online at

The IRB also refers to a climate of vigilantism that exists. As has been noted about such laws, "An analysis of 361 cases of blasphemy offences registered by the police between 1986 and 2007 shows that as many as 49 per cent were registered against non-Muslims. The high rate of cases against non-Muslims should be contrasted with the fact that religious minorities comprise less than four per cent of the country's population."[198]

Facebook has recently (2017) caved into Pakistani pressure and is removing content that the Government of Pakistan deems blasphemous in Facebook postings.[199] An individual in Pakistan was sentenced to death for a Facebook posting deemed by the Government of Pakistan to be blasphemous.[200]

It can be reasonably assessed that the Islamists in Canada need this motion and the false concept of Islamophobia for one reason. Their belief systems and practices are so abhorrent that they cannot withstand public discussion. Therefore, all discussions about their Islamist ideology needs to be silenced.

The best tools for silencing these discussions now are political correctness combined with charges of racism/Islamophobia, libel lawsuits and legislation. As noted above, the M-103 Islamophobia motion does not even define Islamophobia. The reason for this lack of a definition is also rather simple. If Islamophobia simply meant anti-Muslim bigotry, then virtually everyone in Canada could agree that this is an unacceptable form of behaviour. Instead, the vagueness of the Islamophobia concept will be used to silence legitimate questions based on free speech.

It can be believed that the policy of silencing critics is consistent with that of Hassan al-Banna, the founder of the Muslim Brotherhood when he stated:

> "It is the nature of Islam to dominate, not to be dominated, to impose its law on all nations and to extend its power to the entire planet."

To understand how this motion came into being and what it represents, it is useful to look at the Member of Parliament who presented it: Iqra Khalid. It is also worth looking at the Islamist group Jamaat-e-Islami, and the Islamic Society of North America (among others).

Jamaat-e-Islami

The Jamaat-e-Islami was founded in 1941 in "British India" by Sayed Abul A'la Maududi. It is widely regarded as the sister group to the Muslim Brotherhood in South Asia. The Jamaat-e-Islami is now centred in Pakistan, but with branches in India, Bangladesh, Afghanistan, the Jammu/Kashmir territory and other countries around the world.

---

https://www.justice.gov/sites/default/files/eoir/legacy/2014/03/04/PAK104260.E.pdf . Viewed 21 August 2017. **Not rated**.

[198] Mansoo Raza, *Blasphemy laws: a fact sheet*, Dawn, 15 April 2010. The article can be seen online at https://www.dawn.com/news/845129 . Viewed 21 August 2017. **Rated C3**.

[199] *Facebook meets Pakistan government after blasphemy death sentence*, Asian Correspondent, 08 July 2017. The article can be seen online at https://asiancorrespondent.com/2017/07/facebook-meets-pakistan-government-blasphemy-death-sentence/#2bbXLuZmSiBfaaZy.99 . Viewed 21 August 2017. **Rated C3**.

[200] *Pakistan: Man gets death sentence for blaspheming on Facebook,* Asian Correspondent, 12 June 2017. The article can be seen online at https://asiancorrespondent.com/2017/06/pakistan-man-gets-death-sentence-blaspheming-facebook/#A5ObCA5uJT9VGcAF.99 . Viewed 7 April 2017. **Rated C3.**

Abul A'la Maududi has said in his book, Jihad in Islam (pp. 6 and 22)[201] that:

> "**Islam wishes to destroy all states and governments anywhere on the face of the earth** which are opposed to the ideology and programme of Islam regardless of the country or the Nation which rules it. (...) Islam does not intend to confine this revolution to a single State or a few countries; the aim of Islam is to bring about a universal revolution." (Emphasis added).

Abul A'la Maududi also believed that because Islam is all-encompassing, the Islamic state was for all the world and should not be limited to just the "homeland of Islam." Furthermore, Abul A'la Maududi also stated that "Islam, speaking from the viewpoint of political philosophy, is the very antithesis of secular Western democracy.[202]

Pakistan

A variety of Islamist groups are thriving in Pakistan, often with the cooperation or tacit approval of government. The Islamists such as Jamaat-e-Islami appear to be at the forefront. Along with Qatar and Saudi Arabia, Pakistan is increasingly seen as a major export centre for Islamist ideology.[203] As noted by the CATO Institute:

> "Without the active support of the government in Islamabad, it is doubtful whether the Taliban could ever have come to power in Afghanistan. Pakistani authorities helped fund the militia and equip it with military hardware during the mid-1990s when the Taliban was merely one of several competing factions in Afghanistan's civil war. Only when the United States exerted enormous diplomatic pressure after the Sept. 11 attacks did Islamabad begin to sever its political and financial ties with the Taliban. Even now it is not certain that key members of Pakistan's intelligence service have repudiated their Taliban clients." [204]

Iqra Khalid – Background

Iqra Khalid was born in Rukanpur in the Rahim Yar Khan District of Pakistan. She moved with her family to Canada in the 1990s. Her father, Hafiz Khalid was an open and vocal supported of the Jamaat-e-Islami, although he appears to have become less outspoken on this issue as his daughter has entered politics.

---

[201] *Jihad in Islam* by Maulana Abul A'la Maududi. The full book can be seen online at: http://www.muhammadanism.org/Terrorism/jihah_in_islam/jihad_in_islam.pdf . Viewed 7 April 2017. **Rated A1.**

[202] *Islamic Law and Constitution* by Maulana Abul A'la Maududi. The full book can be seen online at http://www.muslim-library.com/dl/books/English_Islamic_Law_and_Constitution.pdf . Viewed 7 April 2017. **Rated A1.**

[203] Rob Crilly, *Mike Mullen: Pakistan is 'exporting' terror: America's top military officer Admiral Mike Mullen offered the sternest rebuke yet to Pakistan, claiming it was exporting violence through the Haqqani network*, The Telegraph, 22 September 2011. The article can be seen online at http://www.telegraph.co.uk/news/worldnews/asia/pakistan/8783139/Mike-Mullen-Pakistan-is-exporting-terror.html . Viewed 28 July 2017. **Rated B3.**

[204] Ted Galen Carpenter, *Terrorist Sponsors: Saudi Arabia, Pakistan, China*, November 16, 2001. The article is available online at https://www.cato.org/publications/commentary/terrorist-sponsors-saudi-arabia-pakistan-china Viewed 7 April 2017. **Rated B2**. See also Bill Roggio, *Pakistan: Friend or Foe in the Fight Against Terrorism?,* 12 July 2016. The article can be seen online at http://www.longwarjournal.org/archives/2016/07/pakistan-friend-or-foe-in-the-fight-against-terrorism.php . Viewed 7 April 2017. **Rated B2.**

Iqra Khalid has a close association to the ISNA. For instance, she chose to announce her Liberal Party candidacy there. The charitable status for the ISNA development fund was revoked by CRA for funding terrorism in 2013.[205] Two other charities connected to the ISNA also had their charitable status revoked with cause by CRA.[206] The ultimate recipient of the money involved was the Jamaat-e-Islami.

The ISNA also tried to host the head of Jamaat-e-Islami as a speaker at a 2008 convention[207], despite his having been listed as head of a terrorist organization in multiple countries.[208] The ISNA was also an unindicted co-conspirator in the Holy Land Relief terrorism funding trials in the USA.[209]

Iqra Khalid joined the Liberal Party approximately seven months before she was nominated on December 13th, 2014.[210] Rule 2.5 [E] of the National Selection Rules[211] of the Liberal Party of Canada requires that the candidate has a demonstrated history of commitment to the party. A seven-month membership does seem short, but the Green Light Committee of the Liberal Party apparently overlooked this despite a written complaint. Ms. Khalid's own website and biographical material do not make mention of any previous experience with Liberal youth organizations prior to this decision to run.

The National Selection Rules also requires that the candidate subscribes to the policies and values of the Party (Rule 2.5 [F]). While this is clearly a subjective question, it remains unclear if Ms. Khalid's work with Islamist organizations represents the "policies and values" of the Liberal Party.

During the election campaign, Ms. Khalid told the press she was the president of the Muslim Student Association (MSA) while at York University.[212] In the same press interview, she also stated that she wrote the constitution for the MSA when it was combined with the Pakistani Student Association.

The constitution of the Muslim Student Association of York University is interesting for its views on Sharia, Salafism, and modernity. Among other interesting observations, it states:

---

[205] For more on this situation see the press release online at http://www.marketwired.com/press-release/canada-revenue-agency-revokes-registration-isna-development-foundation-as-charity-1833203.htm . Viewed 28 July 2017. **Not rated**.

[206] Stewart Bell and Sean Craig, *Government revokes group's charity status, audit cites possible funding of Pakistani militants*, Global News, 19 July 2017. The article can be seen online at http://globalnews.ca/news/3606224/government-revokes-groups-charity-status-audit-cites-pakistani-militants/ . Viewed 28 July 2017. **Rated B2**.

[207] *North American Islamist Group (ISNA) planned to host Pakistani Terror Leader -invited Al Qaeda supporter to speak in Toronto*, June 23, 2008. The article can be seen online at http://www.militantislammonitor.org/article/id/3515 . Viewed 19 April 2017. **Rated B2.**

[208] *North American Islamic Group Hosts Pakistani Terror Leader*, Patrick Poole June 21, 2008. The article can be seen online at http://pjmedia.com/blog/north-american-islamic-group-hosts-pakistani-terror-leader/ . Viewed 19 April 2017. **Rated B2.**

[209] For a list of the Unindicted Co-conspirators and/or Joint Venturers see https://www.investigativeproject.org/documents/case_docs/423.pdf . Viewed 27 February 2017. **Rated A1**.

[210] The YouTube video can be seen at https://www.youtube.com/watch?v=NbWaxNFtxww . Viewed 28 July 2017. **Not rated**.

[211] The rules can be seen at https://www.liberal.ca/files/2014/01/national-nomination-rules.pdf . Viewed 28 July 2017. **Not rated**.

[212] *This millennial not only votes, she's running for MP*, Jan 16, 2015. The article is available online at http://www.mississauga.com/blogs/post/5262154-this-millennial-not-only-votes-she-s-running-for-mp/ . Viewed 28 July 2017. **Rated B2**

- 2.01 The MSA is a mainstream Sunni Islamic Association that follows and adheres to the Quran and Sunnah upon the understanding of the Salaf. (The Constitution describes Salaf as referring to righteous and pious predecessors or the first three generations of Muslims.)

- 8.03 The Executive shall strive to adhere to the Shariah.

- 15.03 Directors shall strive to adhere to the Shariah.

- 20.01 The MSA will organize events in accordance with the Shariah. Any **innovations** in religious matters or "**modernization**" will not be acceptable, as Islam is a way of life for all times and places and hence is not subject to being outdated or needing reform. (Emphasis added)

In other words, it is reasonable to believe that the constitution of the Muslim Student Association is Salafist in orientation and supports the application of Sharia principles. It rejects modernity and progress.[213] Its views on Sharia, Salafism and "innovations" appear consistent with that of the Muslim Brotherhood itself.

The Muslim Student Association of York University handed out free books at its annual Islam Awareness Week in February of 2015 (after Khalid was no longer there). One of the books has a section on Wife Disciplining and advises that wives should only be beaten as part of a three-stage correctional process. It also notes that there are different kinds of women, including the view that:

> "Submissive or subdued women. These women may even enjoy being beaten at times as a sign of **love and concern**..." (Women in Islam & Refutation of some Common Misconceptions)[214]

It is worth noting that this sort of advice is common in the Islamist world. Yousef Qaradawi, one of the leading clerics of the Muslim Brotherhood, also believes that some women enjoy being beaten. On an Al Jazeera TV program, he stated "There is a woman who cannot agree to being beaten, and sees this as humiliation, while **some women enjoy the beating** and for them, only beating to cause them sorrow is suitable..."[215] (Emphasis added)

As for the nomination, Ms. Khalid became the candidate rather late in the process as noted above. Mr. Shafqat Ali is/was a long time Liberal Party member in the Mississauga area and he was thought to have a front running position for the nomination. For reasons that have not publicly made clear, he withdrew his nomination[216] at an ISNA hosted event. On Sunday 16 November 2014, he asked that his followers support Iqra Khalid. At the community dinner hosted jointly by himself and Iqra Khalid at the ISNA he

---

[213] The constitution of the York University MSA can be seen on their website at http://yorkmsa.ca/wp-content/uploads/2016/04/final_constitution-2.pdf . Viewed 19 April 2017. **Rated A1.**

[214] For more on the advocating of violence against women in Canada by the Muslim Student Association (and others) see *A Tale of the Handmaidens – Violence Against Women in Canada.* The article is available in Annex J.

[215] Steven Stalinsky and Y. Yehoshua, "Muslim Clerics on the Religious Rulings Regarding Wife-Beating," MEMRI, Special Report #27, March 22, 2004 http://memri.org/bin/articles.cgi?Page=archives&Area=sr&ID=SR2704 . Viewed 20 April 2017. **Rated A2.**

[216] For more on this see the Facebook posting at https://www.facebook.com/permalink.php?id=1416396095257204&story_fbid=1562609463969199 . Viewed 28 July 2017. **Not rated.**

stated: "I am making this sacrifice today so that tomorrow we have one voice that will be our voice in the House of Commons." He made no mention of why he felt the need to step done so suddenly or whether he received any compensation for his decision.

Iqra Khalid is/was a member of CAMP – the Council for the Advancement of Muslim Professionals.[217] She was the Communications Coordinator under (then) President and CEO Najamuddin Mohammed.[218] Despite claiming to be a networking organization, CAMP's own website says it was created to:

> "educate and activate the community on issues of political significance at home and abroad. CAMP organizes activities and lectures, seminars and discussions on political activism to get the membership and the community involved in the political process to better ourselves and our communities at home or abroad."[219]

CAMP appears to have multiple ties to the North American Muslim Brotherhood. At one-point, a former head of the ISNA was listed by CAMP as an adviser and Zeba Iqbal, the Vice-Chair of CAMP International, was also on the board of the Muslim Public Affairs Council (MPAC-NY). At least one of the CAMP chapters, CAMP Toronto, has joined with other Muslim Brotherhood organizations such as the Council on American Islamic Relations (CAIR), ISNA, and the Islamic Circle of North America (ICNA)[220] to issue protests at Israeli actions in Gaza and against the Niqab ban. As noted in one of its own announcements:

> "The Council for the Advancement of Muslim Professionals (CAMP) has announced that it second keynote speaker for its July 2010 annual dinner, held during the Islamic Society of North America (ISNA)_weekend, will be Obama administration faith advisor Dahlia Mogahed."[221]

As a Member of Parliament, Iqra Khalid spoke at an event organized by ICNA (Sisters) and said she thought there was a lot of power and influence in the room and that it was great.[222] It is worth noting the Islamic Circle of North America believes that democracy is incompatible with Islam. On its own website, the ICNA recommends to its members and followers that they read the book "Riyad us Saliheen."[223] The ICNA has chosen to refer its readers to the modern commentary on this ancient book and states that:

---

[217] See the Yahoo Groups information at https://groups.yahoo.com/neo/groups/CAMP-Toronto/search/messages?advance=true&am=CONTAINS&at=email:iqra.khalid1@&dm=IS_ANY&fs=false&count=10 . Viewed 19 April 2017. **Rated B2.**

[218] See the Yahoo groups information at https://groups.yahoo.com/neo/groups/CAMP-Toronto/conversations/messages/561 . See also http://www.naseeb.com/journals/camp-toronto-2010-2012-team-180586 and xa.yimg.com/kq/groups/11043774/120763514/.../newsletterMARCH.pdf

[219] http://web.archive.org/web/20010802055058/campnet.net/home.htm Viewed 28 July 2017. **Not rated.**

[220] *ANALYSIS: Some Reflections on The Rashad Hussain Affair*, By gmbwatch on February 28, 2010. The article is available online at http://www.globalmbwatch.com/2010/02/28/analysis-reflections-rashad-hussain-affair/ Viewed 28 July 2017. **Rated B3.**

[221] *Obama Faith Advisor to Speak at Council for the Advancement of Muslim Professionals Dinner*, By gmbwatch on May 16, 2010. The article is available online at http://www.globalmbwatch.com/2010/05/16/obama-faith-advisor-to-speak-at-council-for-the-advancement-of-muslim-professionals-dinner/ Viewed 28 July 2017. **Rated C3.**

[222] A portion of the speech can be seen on YouTube at https://www.youtube.com/watch?v=KdMMjClASsY&nohtml5=False . Viewed 19 April 2017. **Rated A1.**

[223] For more on this see the *article ICNA Canada refutes Trudeau: "Islam is totally incompatible with Western democracy."* The article is available online at http://en.cijnews.com/?p=27451#prettyPhoto . Viewed 28 July 2017. **Rated B2.**

"673. Abu Bakrah (May Allah be pleased with him) reported: I heard Messenger of Allah (PBUH) saying, "He who insults the rulers Allah will insult him." [At-Tirmidhi].

Commentary: To affront and degrade the ruler means to disobey him and to by-pass his orders. This impairs his power, honour and dignity. Believers have been told to obey and support rulers for the sake of national interest and welfare, understanding that they desist from committing an overt disbelief and maintain congregation Salat and other duties of religion. **The political system of Islam is totally incompatible with Western democracy. The concept of government party and the opposition is alien to Islam.** All belong to one Ummah with only one goal and pursue the same aims and objects of Islamic guidelines!" (Emphasis added)

As noted in Chapter 9, the ICNA also holds a series of abhorrent views which favourably view wife beating, sexual slavery, honour killings and forcing women to remain in the home.

Interestingly, one of Ms. Khalid's first visits to a community organisation after her election was to Palestine House. This organization had been earlier defunded by the federal government due to a pattern of support for Islamist extremism.[224]

Implications

With Ms. Khalid's membership and/or participation with such groups, it is not clear what her value systems represent. What she advocates within the M-103 Islamophobia motion is not compatible with the Constitution of Canada and the Charter of Rights. They are consistent, however, with the Jamaat-e-Islami, the Muslim Brotherhood, the ISNA and the ICNA. It is a reasonable opinion that Canadians should be fearful of her Parliamentary Motion 103.

[224] Chris Clay, *Government ends funding for Palestine House*, Mississauga News, February 14, 2012. The article is available online at http://www.mississauga.com/news-story/3123915-government-ends-funding-for-palestine-house/ . Viewed 19 April 2017. **Rated A2**.

CHAPTER 12: THE TRUDEAU PARTY, ENTRYISM AND EXTREMIST ISLAM

Thomas Quiggin

"Their blind quest for uniformity will never eradicate conflict. Globalism will only replace wars between nations with wars within former nations. It takes battles that formerly took place on borders and spreads them from street to street. Rather than global harmony, endless and irrevocable conflict is globalism's true end game."[225]

Key Points

- Prime Minister Justin Trudeau's cooperation with Islamist groups in Canada is an integral part of his globalist belief system.

- Prime Minister Trudeau has used the weight of government offices to silence press criticism of his support for Islamist causes.

- In both word and deed, Prime Minister Trudeau has gone out of his way to support Islamist groups and their ideology in Canada.

The title of this chapter is deliberate. It could have read the "Islamist Wing of the Liberal Party" but it does not. Many Liberals party members are sincerely worried about the direction of their party is taking with respect to the ongoing Islamist cancer growing in its inner circles. Liberal Party members have provided ideas, inspiration and suggestions on where to look for information for this chapter. They are aware that that the Islamist intrusion into their party continues, often aided and abetted by senior leadership figures. Of note, while the Liberal Party is currently the party in power, all three mainstream parties have an Islamist infiltration problem at the federal and provincial level.

The Liberal Party Green Light Committee did try to screen out some of the problems in advance of the 2015 election. However, it appears they lacked a data base or the research skills to dig into the background of some of their candidates. Or perhaps they lacked the will.

The influx of Islamists into the Liberal Party is the partially the construct of Prime Minister Justin Trudeau himself, along with a few close friends and advisors such as Omar Alghabra,[226] currently the Parliamentary Secretary for Foreign Affairs (i.e. Junior Foreign Minister).

Prime Minister Trudeau and His Global/Islamist Belief System

Prime Minister Justin Trudeau's cooperation with Islamist groups and individuals in Canada is an integral part of a larger belief system. This is not to say he is an Islamist, but rather to say he sees defending

---

[225] Jim Goad, *What's So Bad About Globalism*? 27 February 2017. The article can be seen online at http://takimag.com/article/whats_so_bad_about_globalism_jim_goad/print#axzz4a1G8mpSb Viewed on 30 March 2017. **Rated A1**.

[226] *Sharia Law Supporter Omar Alghabra is the new Parliamentary Secretary for Foreign Affairs.* The article can be seen in Annex J.

Islamists and cooperating with them as useful as he reshapes Canadian political, cultural and value systems in his own image.

According to Prime Minister Trudeau, Canada has "no core identity" and there is "no mainstream in Canada." He believes, that Canada is the "first post-national state" and that the nation is longer shaped by its European national origins but by a "pan cultural heritage."[227] This is obviously false. Canada is not different from many other Westphalian states. It is not "post national."

However, based on the totality of Prime Minister Trudeau's statements and actions, it appears to be a goal for him, rather than a statement of the current reality. Prime Minister Trudeau's statement on Multiculturalism Day on 27 June 2016 clearly echoed this when he stated: "We are from far and wide, and speak over 200 languages. Our national fabric is vibrant and varied, woven together by many cultures and heritages…"[228]

His views, like those of his friend George Soros, include the belief that only the so-called globalist "elites" can be trusted to shape the future of the world and the "population" cannot be trusted with such things as referendums or a direct role in governance.

Prime Minister Trudeau believes that a variety of current values must be devalued. Among these are national sovereignty, national identify, and freedom of speech. This same set of globalist beliefs also supports funding and supporting massive migration programs as a means of watering down national identity and value systems.

Trudeau's Statement on Twitter about Soros made that clear: Thanks to @georgesoros for sharing your insights on the global economic outlook and climate change. #Davos2016 #WEF[229]

Prime Minister Trudeau's beliefs in a "post national state" do not occur in isolation from that of other political leaders. While many European leaders were considering tightening border controls following a mass influx of refugees in 2015 and 2016, European Commission president Jean-Claude Juncker stated that borders were the "worst invention ever."[230] Mr. Juncker followed this statement by telling European nations that they must to more to more to express solidarity with refugees and their children.

Prime Minister Trudeau's overt affection for Cuban dictator Fidel Castro is a strong indicator of his views. He publicly mourned the passing of Cuban President Fidel Castro in an official government statement

---

[227] Douglas Todd, *The dangers of Trudeau's 'postnational' Canada*, Vancouver Sun, 13 March 2016. The article can be seen online at http://vancouversun.com/news/staff-blogs/the-dangers-of-trudeaus-postnational-canada . Viewed 31 March 2017. **Rated B2.**

[228] *Statement by the Prime Minister of Canada on Multiculturalism Day*, 27 June 2016. The statement is available online at http://pm.gc.ca/eng/news/2016/06/27/statement-prime-minister-canada-multiculturalism-day . Viewed 25 March 2017. **Rated A1.**

[229] @CanadianPM, "Thanks to @georgesoros for sharing your insights on the global economic outlook and climate change #Davos2016 #WEF", www.twitter.com, 20 January 2016. Viewed 17 May 2017. The Tweet can be seen at https://twitter.com/CanadianPM/status/689906363003191297

[230] David Hughes and Kate Ferguson, *National borders are 'the worst invention ever', says EC chief Jean-Claude Juncker,* The Independent, 22 August 2016. The article is available online at http://www.independent.co.uk/news/world/europe/national-borders-are-the-worst-invention-ever-says-ec-chief-jean-claude-juncker-a7204006.html . Viewed 13 April 2017. **Rated A2.**

describing him as a "larger than life leader who served his people for almost half a century."[231] He also stated that the Cuban people had a deep and lasting affection for "el Comandante". The statement made no note of the sixty plus years of absolute dictatorship, Cuba's brutal suppression of human rights nor its systemic persecution of gays and democratic opponents.

China also plays heavily in Trudeau's mind. When asked at a $250 a plate "Ladies Night with Liberal Leader Justin Trudeau" he was asked a rather straightforward question: "Which nation, besides Canada, which nation's administration do you most admire, and why?"

The answer was rather stunning, both for its choice of country and the justification of that choice. Trudeau stated that he admired the "basic dictatorship" of China and their ability to move quickly on issues. His answer was reported as:

> "You know, there's a level of admiration I actually have for China because their basic dictatorship is allowing them to actually turn their economy around on a dime and say 'we need to go green fastest...we need to start investing in solar."[232]

Trudeau's admiration did not seem to be towards China looking for "greener" energy sources, but rather than they have a "basic dictatorship" that enables the government of China to act quickly.

Prime Minister Trudeau has appointed his brother Sacha as an advisor.[233] This is worrying as Sacha cooperated with the Iranian state-owned PressTV to co-produce a fawning documentary titled "The New Great Game." This documentary stated that Iran's nuclear program is for "defensive" purposes only, serving as an effective "deterrent" against Israeli aggression and belligerence. While not announced at the time of airing, it became clear later that Al Jazeera Arabic was also a contributor to the project.[234] Al Jazeera is the media mouth piece of the State of Qatar and under heavy influence of the Hamas and Muslim Brotherhood.[235] Al Jazeera's support for the Muslim Brotherhood[236] has resulted in internal

---

[231] *Statement by the Prime Minister of Canada on the death of former Cuban President Fidel Castro.* This statement can be seen online at http://pm.gc.ca/eng/news/2016/11/26/statement-prime-minister-canada-death-former-cuban-president-fidel-castro . Viewed 31 March 2017. **Rated A1.**

[232] David Akin, *Trudeau admires China's 'basic dictatorship',* Post Media Network, 08 November 2012. The article can be seen online at http://www.torontosun.com/2013/11/08/trudeau-admires-chinas-basic-dictatorship . Viewed 31 March 2017. **Rated A2.**

[233] Christopher Curtis, *The other brother: Sacha, the 'apolitical' one, joins Justin Trudeau's campaign team,* Post Media News, 12 October 2012. The article can be seen online at http://news.nationalpost.com/news/canada/the-other-brother-sacha-the-apolitical-one-joins-justin-trudeaus-campaign-team . Viewed 31 March 2017. **Rated A2.**

[234] Mike Fegelman, *When it Comes to Israel, Alexandre Trudeau's Got it Wrong,* Huffington Post, 25 October 2012. The article can be seen online at http://webcache.googleusercontent.com/search?q=cache:pwn2a_NZQnwJ:www.huffingtonpost.ca/mike-fegelman/alexandre-trudeau_b_2018038.html+&cd=1&hl=en&ct=clnk&gl=ca . Viewed 31 March 2012. **Rated B2.**

[235] David Andrew Weinberg, Oren Adaki and Grant Rumley, *The Problem with Al Jazeera*, The National Interest, 10 September 2014. The article can be seen online at http://nationalinterest.org/feature/the-problem-al-jazeera-11239 . Viewed 31 March 2017. **Rated B2.**

[236] Nicholas Noe and Walid Raad, *Al-Jazeera Gets Rap as Qatar Mouthpiece*, Bloomberg News, 10 April 2012. The article can be seen online at https://www.bloomberg.com/view/articles/2012-04-09/al-jazeera-gets-rap-as-qatar-mouthpiece . Viewed 31 March 2017. **Rated C2.**

problems for them when some of their reporters quit[237] rather than support the biased reporting towards the Muslim Brotherhood. Ironically, Qatar's support for the Islamist ideology is so great that even the Government of Saudi Arabia complained about this after Saudi Arabia had declared the Muslim Brotherhood to be a terrorist group[238] and threatened to isolate Qatar[239] if they did not crackdown on them.

In an earlier documentary (The Fence), Sacha Trudeau profiled Zakaria Zubeidi, then leader of the terrorist group Al Aqsa Martyrs Brigades, portraying him as a Robin Hood-like "leader of the resistance."[240] Al Aqsa is the military arm of Hamas, which describes itself as the Muslim Brotherhood in Palestine in its own charter. This support for the Muslim Brotherhood appears to be a consistent theme throughout the belief systems of the two brothers, even though the Muslim Brotherhood are listed as a terrorist entity by a variety of states, including Saudi Arabia and the United Arab Emirates. The United Kingdom report on the Muslim Brotherhood noted that affiliation with the Muslim Brotherhood was an indicator of extremism.[241]

In Word and Deed

While politicians have been known to make broad statements with little indication that they support them, Prime Minister Trudeau's actions suggest something different. In both word and deed, Prime Minister Trudeau has gone out of his way to support Islamist groups and their ideology in Canada. He has consistently attended mosques and conferences of an Islamist nature while avoiding contact with Muslim reformist groups such as Muslims Facing Tomorrow, the Muslim Reform Movement, or the Canadian Thinkers' Forum.

Islamist Conference: "Shared Beliefs, Shared Values and Shared Vision"

In December of 2015, newly elected Prime Minister Trudeau sent a video message to the Toronto based "Reviving the Islamic Spirit" conference. Long term observers of this conference will know that the conference has morphed into a "who is who" in the world of Islamists in Canada and the USA. The list of speakers has included Tariq Ramadan, the grandson of the Muslim Brotherhood founder and Imam Siraj

---

[237] Bob Dreyfuss, *Al Jazeera's Muslim Brotherhood Problem, Staff quits en masse over Qatar-imposed favoritism for the Brothers*, The Nation, 10 July 2013. The article can be seen online at https://www.thenation.com/article/al-jazeeras-muslim-brotherhood-problem/ . Viewed 31 March 2017. **Rated B2.**

[238] BBC News, *Saudi Arabia declares Muslim Brotherhood 'terrorist group'* 7 March 2014. The article can be seen online at http://www.bbc.com/news/world-middle-east-26487092 . Viewed 31 March 2017. **Rated B2.**

[239] BBC News, *How the Middle East has gone cool towards Qatar*, 10 March 2014. The article can be seen online at http://www.bbc.com/news/world-middle-east-26517134 . Viewed 31 March 2017. Rated **B2.**

[240] Mike Fegelman, *When it Comes to Israel, Alexandre Trudeau's Got it Wrong,* Huffington Post, 25 October 2012. The article can be seen online at http://webcache.googleusercontent.com/search?q=cache:pwn2a_NZQnwJ:www.huffingtonpost.ca/mike-fegelman/alexandre-trudeau_b_2018038.html+&cd=1&hl=en&ct=clnk&gl=ca . Viewed 31 March 2012. **Rated B2.**

[241] The statement of the Prime Minister of the United Kingdom concerning the report on the Muslim Brotherhood can be seen at https://www.gov.uk/government/speeches/muslim-brotherhood-review-statement-by-the-prime-minister . The full report can be seen online at https://www.gov.uk/government/uploads/system/uploads/attachment_data/file/486932/Muslim_Brotherhood_Review_Main_Findings.pdf . Viewed 31 March 2017. **Rated A1.**

Wahhaj[242], a US unindicted co-conspirator in the 1993 World Trade Center bombing. The conference was also sponsored by IRFAN Canada – until that charity lost is charitable status for funding terrorism.[243] Many conference speakers have also come from ISNA Canada which lost the charitable statues for its "Development Fund" which was caught funding the terrorist organization Jamaat-e-Islami.[244]

Prime Minister Trudeau had the option of not sending any message at all, or he could have sent a message of integration. Instead, he chose to signal that he would submit to the demands of Islamist groups such as ISNA, CAIR CAN/NCCM, ICNA and the Muslim Association of Canada. The message he sent included repeated and direct references to how he shared the views of the conference attendees. Specially, he referenced his:

- "Shared beliefs,"
- "Shared set of values," and
- "Shared vision."

These groups represent Islamists beliefs that run contrary to Canadian values as expressed in the Constitution, the Charter of Rights and the Criminal Code of Canada.

What exactly does Prime Minister Trudeau have on common with a series of groups and individuals who have multiple connections to Islamist groups? Does he believe that it is the nature of the Islamists to dominate rather than be dominated such as the Muslim Brotherhood's founder believed? Do the shared set of values include the idea that women are inferior to men,[245] wife beating is permissible,[246] and owning slave girls should be legal?[247]

"A Special Immigration Program More Open to Muslims and Arabs"

Many Canadians were shocked by the sudden "need" of the Government of Canada to import some 40,000 Syrian refugees who were almost exclusively Sunni Muslim. This, even though it was clearly the Yazidis and other minorities that were the most vulnerable groups in the Syrian/IISIS conflict.

---

[242] David B. Harris, *Trudeau's Bad Company at the Islamic Convention*, Huffington Post. Posted: 12/21/2012 5:30 pm EST. Viewed 30 March 2017. Available online at http://www.huffingtonpost.ca/david-b-harris/ris-convention_b_2344566.html . **Rated A2**.

[243] *Revoked Canadian charity listed under the Criminal Code as terrorist entity*. The CRA announcement is available online at http://www.cra-arc.gc.ca/chrts-gvng/chrts/whtsnw/trrrst-ntty-eng.html . Viewed on 27 February 2017. **Rated A1.**

[244] For more on this charitable status revocation, see http://news.gc.ca/web/article-en.do?nid=773409 . Viewed 5 February 2017. **Rated A1**.

[245] CIJ News, *ICNA Canada's online syllabus: women are inferior to men, Western civilization "enemy"*, 23 February 2016. The article is available online at http://en.cijnews.com/?p=27294 . Viewed 31 March 2017. **Rated A1**.

[246] CIN News, *ICNA Canada's online syllabus on wife beating*, 18 February 2017. The article is available online at http://en.cijnews.com/?p=26599 . Viewed 31 March 2017. **Rated A1**.

[247] CIJ News, *ICNA Canada's online syllabus legalizes "slave-girls"*, 15 February 2016. The article can be seen online at http://en.cijnews.com/?p=26432 . Viewed 31 March 2017. **Rated A1**.

In 2014, while a Member of Parliament, Justin Trudeau gave an interview to the Montreal-based newspaper Sada al-Mashrek.[248] This paper is openly known to be Khomeneist in nature and supports Iran (as well as Hezbollah). During this interview, Trudeau also told the paper that he would have a special immigration program that was more open to "Muslims and Arabs."

Terrorists and Citizenship

In July of 2105, then Prime Ministerial candidate Justin Trudeau attended a town hall style meeting. An audio recording of the meeting revealed that Trudeau commented on Bill C-24, a bill which would remove Canadian citizenship from dual citizens if they took up arms against Canada, or were convicted of terrorism or treason. In his comments, Trudeau stated:

> "The Liberal Party believes that terrorists should get to keep their Canadian citizenship... because I do. And I'm willing to take on anyone who disagrees with that. As soon as you make citizenship for some Canadians conditional on good behaviour, you devalue citizenship for everyone." [249]

This support for maintaining the citizenship of terrorists was not hyperbole. Then Minister of Immigration, Refugees and Citizenship John McCallum introduced Bill C-6 in the House of Commons intended to undo the earlier Bill C-24. While introducing the Bill that would allow convicted dual citizen terrorists to maintain their Canadian citizenship, McCallum stated: "A Canadian is a Canadian is a Canadian."[250]

Current Minister of Immigration, Refugees and Citizenship Ahmed Hussen repeated the "A Canadian is a Canadian is a Canadian" statement as part of his testimony to a Senate's social affairs committee in early March of 2017.[251]

Zakaria Amara, one of the terrorists convicted as part of the Toronto 18 plot will likely have his citizenship restored under the new legislation, after having it revoked in 2015.

Ironically, the current Trudeau government is revoking citizenship now (2016-2017) at a higher rate than under the government of former Prime Minister Stephen Harper. Those having their citizenship revoked now largely fall into the categories of fraud and misrepresentation.

---

[248] A copy of this article can be seen online at http://www.postedeveille.ca/2014/07/le-npd-et-le-parti-lib%C3%A9ral-commanditent-un-%C3%A9v%C3%A9nement-des-fr%C3%A8res-musulmans.html . Viewed 4 April 2017. **Rated B3.**

[249] *In audio recording, Trudeau says Bill C-24 makes citizenship conditional upon 'good behaviour*, CTV News, 27 September 2015. The article is available online at http://www.ctvnews.ca/politics/in-audio-recording-trudeau-says-bill-c-24-makes-citizenship-conditional-upon-good-behaviour-1.2583849?hootPostID=929e90cc6e3b7446d374d578c323b7be . Viewed 4 April 2017. **Rated B2.**

[250] Chris Hall, *As a 'matter of principle,' convicted terrorists are fellow citizens*, CBC News, 26 February 2017. The article can be seen online at http://www.cbc.ca/news/politics/citizenship-terrorism-chris-hall-1.3464668 . Viewed 4 April 2017. **Rated A2.**

[251] Marie-Danielle Smith, *Immigration minister defends legislation that prevents convicted dual nationals from losing citizenship*, CBC News, 01 March 2017. The article is available online at http://news.nationalpost.com/news/canada/canadian-politics/immigration-minister-defends-legislation-to-prevents-convicted-dual-nationals-from-losing-citizenship . Viewed 4 April 2017. **Rated A2.**

Clearly, the standard of "A Canadian is a Canadian is a Canadian" is not being applied. Terrorists will get to remain in Canada as citizens, but those who misrepresent themselves on immigration application forms will have their citizenship revoked. Terrorists, it seems, are to be held to a lower standard.

Visit to Montreal Mosque Al Sunnah Al-Nabawiah – "You must kill any Muslim who does not practice his religion"

Then Member of Parliament Justin Trudeau visited the Al Sunnah Al-Nabawiah mosque in his Quebec riding of Papineau in 2014. The mosque has been identified as a having a strong Wahhabist orientation and according to documents from the Pentagon, it was a place where "al-Qaida members were recruited, facilitated or trained." [252]

Mr. Trudeau responded to criticism of his visit by saying:

> "We in Canada have our own determinations for those sorts of things because the U.S. is known to make mistakes from time to time."[253]

The reality is that the mosque had previously been exposed in Canada as a major centre of jihadist oriented Islamists.

In 2006, a journalist of Algerian origin, Mohamed Sifaoui, spent three weeks living undercover in Montreal's Muslim community.[254] Mr. Sifaoui is a specialist in Islamic groups and had previously written a book, Mes "frères" assassins, recounting his time spent infiltrating Islamist terrorist cells in Paris. In Montreal, he discovered in a small shop in Côte-des-Neiges a compact disc that glorified terrorism, holy war and suicide bombings. Upon attending the Al Sunnah Mosque on Friday, 21 July 2006, Mr. Sifaoui listened to the sermon of Sheikh Omar Soufyane. The sermon discussed the Middle East crisis at the time and the Imam called for God to kill all the enemies of Islam to the last.

Upon visiting the mosque library, the next day, Mr. Sifaoui also found writings by Ibnoun Baz, known for his highly ideological views on Islamic fundamentalism. Mr. Sifaoui stated that "My attention was drawn to this one. I knew it as a book banned in some Muslim countries because it incites violence and murder." As an example, when Ibnoun Baz was asked a question, he replied that "you must kill any Muslim who does not practice his religion." Also, available in the mosque library was a magazine on jihad.[255]

---

[252] *U.S. lists Montreal mosque as al-Qaeda 'recruiting' place; Detainee who lived in Montreal disputes U.S. claims of links to millennium bomb plot, 9/11*, CBC News Posted: Apr 25, 2011 9:17 PM ET. The article can be seen online at http://www.cbc.ca/news/world/u-s-lists-montreal-mosque-as-al-qaeda-recruiting-place-1.1124571 . Viewed on 31 March 2017. **Rated B2**. See also the New York Times article with the ordinal information at: http://www.nytimes.com/interactive/2011/04/24/world/guantanamo-guide-to-assessing-prisoners.html?_r=0#doc2 Viewed on 31 March 2017. **Rated B2**.

[253] Jessica Hume, *Trudeau lambasted for visiting mosque linked to al-Qaida recruitment,* 5 August 2014. The article can be viewed online at http://www.torontosun.com/2014/08/05/trudeau-lambasted-for-visiting-mosque-linked-to-al-qaida-recruitment . Viewed on 31 March 2017. **Rated B2.**

[254] Parts of this section have already been published in *"The Lovers of Death"? Islamist Extremism in Our Mosques, Schools and Libraries.*

[255] Ici.radio-canada.ca, *"Inside the mosques"* (original in French), Radio Canada (Greater Montreal Edition), 08 September 2006. The article can be seen online at . http://ici.radio-canada.ca/nouvelle/320706/zl-islam-mosquees . Viewed 17 May 2017. **Rated A2.**

On Friday, August 11, 2006 Mr. Sifaoui again attended the Al Sunnah Mosque. This time the Imam (a replacement) told they youth that they should mobilize prepare to fight a Holy War. Referring to the youth, he told them that they were the "ammunition of our community."[256]

As such, it can be said that the mosque has a dismal reputation that has been publicly known since at least 2006. Despites its reputation as an al Qaeda recruiting centre, its call for killing all enemies of Islam and its desire to recruit youth for jihad, Prime Minister Trudeau has seen fit to defend the mosque and participate in its activities.

The Regularization of Misogyny and the Ottawa Mosque Visit of September 2016

Prime Minister Trudeau has declared himself to be a "feminist"[257] and says he is committed to increasing the role of women in society.[258] However, he recently visited a gender-segregated mosque in Ottawa. Female Members of Parliament who attended with him had to enter by a side door and sit in the segregated area.[259] The Imam of the mosque is part of the International Union for Muslim Scholars (IUMS), according to the mosque's own website. This organization is part of the overall Muslim Brotherhood network and was placed on a list of designated terrorist organizations by the United Arab Emirates in 2014.[260] More interestingly, a first-hand review of the teaching and reading material of the mosque in early 2016 revealed a disturbing fact. The study noted that "It is not the presence of extremist literature in the mosque libraries that is worrisome. The problem is that there was nothing but extremist literature in the mosque libraries."[261]

The most appalling event however, was a statement by the Prime Minister. While speaking, he stated:

> "...as I look at this beautiful room — sisters upstairs — everyone here, (I see) the diversity we have just within this mosque, within the Islamic community, within the Muslim community in Canada."[262]

This is an ongoing part of the normalization of the oppression of women. Why would the Prime Minister of Canada, alleged to be a country which respects human rights, acknowledge that women where being

---

[256] *À l'intérieur des mosques*, Publié le vendredi 8 septembre 2006. The article is available online at http://ici.radio-canada.ca/nouvelles/national/2006/09/08/004-zl_islam_mosquees.shtml . Viewed on 31 March 2017. **Rated A1.**

[257] *Justin Trudeau Teaches Men How To Be Better Feminists In 10 Seconds*, The Huffington Post Canada, by Andree Lau, Posted: 04/30/2016 8:36 pm EDT. http://www.huffingtonpost.ca/2016/04/30/justin-trudeau-feminist-advice-snapchat_n_9815126.html . Viewed on 31 March 2017. **Rated B2.**

[258] Parts of this section were previously published at the Gatestone Institute in an article titled *Guess Who Is Helping Islamists to Oppress Women?* The article from which some of this material is drawn can be seen at https://www.gatestoneinstitute.org/9064/canada-islamists-women . Viewed on 31 March 2017. **Rated B2.**

[259] David Akin ,*'Feminist' Trudeau under attack for attending gender-segregated event at Ottawa mosque,* September 13, 2016 10:01 PM ET. The article can be seen online at http://news.nationalpost.com/news/canada/canadian-politics/feminist-pm-defends-attendance-at-gender-segregated-event Viewed on 31 March 2017. **Rated B2.**

[260] Anthony Furey, *Trudeau visits mosque with terror connections*, Postmedia Network, 12 September 2016, The article can be seen online at http://www.torontosun.com/2016/09/12/trudeau-visits-mosque-with-terror-connections . Viewed 17 May 2017. **Rated A2.**

[261] Thomas Quiggin, *"Lovers of the Death?" – Islamist Extremism in Mosques and Schools*, August 2016.

[262] Anthony Furey, *Mosque calls Sun story 'categorically false,'* Postmedia Network, 13 September 2016. The article can be seen online at http://www.torontosun.com/2016/09/13/mosque-calls-sun-story-categorically-false Viewed 17 May 2017. **Rated A2.**

subjugated and forced into segregated seating? Additionally, his own female MPs were not allowed to se the front door.

This could have been a moment for the Prime Minister to insist that female MPs be allowed to use the front door or that females be allowed to sit in the main hall. Instead, he chose to cast a positive spin on the segregation and subjugation.

Anthony Furey and the Prime Minister's Office – Attempting to Silence the Facts

On 12 September 2016, Anthony Furey of Post Media News wrote an article concerning the visit of Prime Minister Trudeau to the Ottawa Main Mosque.[263] The article began noting that Prime Minister Justin Trudeau had "visited a gender-segregated mosque Monday morning whose imam is a member of a group considered a terrorist organization abroad." The story had been sent to the PMO (Prime Minister's Office) before publication but did not receive a response. The lawyers at Post Media, recognizing most of the information in the story concerning the Imam and his connection came from the mosque's own website, approved the story.

Following publication, however, the Prime Minister's Office contacted Anthony Furey that evening while he was at home. The call, which lasted approximately ten minutes, was hostile in its tone. The PMO spokesman attempted to make several main points to Furey during the call. They were:

- "This is not the story";
- Furey was "irresponsible" for writing the story;
- The PMO spokesman attempt to suggest that the story was Islamophobia, and
- The headline has word terrorism in it and associated the mosque and its followers to terrorism.

At several points during the story, Furey asked the PMO spokesman if there were any errors of fact in his story. If so, they could be immediately corrected. The spokesman repeatedly refused to address the issue during the conversation and was not able to point out any factual errors in the story. Furey followed up the story the following day. The mosque claimed that the story about them was "categorically false" although they could not point to any errors in the story.[264] Furey publicly revealed the pressure from PMO in a story four months later.[265] The Imam is, in fact, a member of the International Union for Muslim Scholars (IUMS). This organization was placed on a list of terrorist entities by the United Arab Emirates[266]

---

[263] Anthony Furey, *Trudeau visits mosque with terror connections*, Post Media News, 12 September 2016. The article is available online at http://www.torontosun.com/2016/09/12/trudeau-visits-mosque-with-terror-connections . Viewed 10 April 2016. **Rated A1**.

[264] Anthony Furey, *Mosque calls Sun story 'categorically false'*, Post Media News, 13 September 2017. The article is available online at http://www.torontosun.com/2016/09/13/mosque-calls-sun-story-categorically-false. Viewed 10 April 2016. **Rated A2**.

[265] Anthony Furey, *Canadians want a light shone on radical Islam*, Post Media News, 21 February 2017. The article can be seen online at http://www.torontosun.com/2017/02/21/canadians-want-a-light-shone-on-radical-islam . Viewed 17 May 207. **Rated A2**.

[266] The National, UAE, *List of groups designated terrorist organisations by the UAE*, 16 November 2014. The article can be seen online at http://www.thenational.ae/uae/government/list-of-groups-designated-terrorist-organisations-by-the-uae . Viewed 17 May 2017. **Rated A1**.

in 2014. The IUMS was founded by Yusuf al-Qaradawi, the Muslim Brotherhood's leading ideologue. Qaradawi himself was wanted on an Interpol Red Notice.

The call from the PMO to the press is stunning for several reasons. First, the PMO was complaining about the story, but was not able to show a single error of fact in the story. Secondly, the call was hostile in in tone. Thirdly, it is highly unlikely that the PMO spokesman was calling on his own behalf, despite saying so in the call. He was using a PMO phone and a decision to call the press and attempt to silence a story would not be taken lightly. Lastly, the PMO spokesman attempted to say the story was Islamophobic, despite the lack of any errors in the story.

This attack on the freedom of the press is, however, consistent with the words and deeds of Prime Minster Trudeau. He has made it repeatedly clear that he supports the Islamist cause and will continue to do so, despite their obvious and repeated connections to extremism and terrorism. This kind of attempt to instil fear in the press does not bode well for the future.

The Peterborough Mosque, Hijab Attacks and Fake Hate Crimes

The Government of Canada has been making false or unverifiable claims about Islamophobia and hate crimes. In an area with enough problems already, false reports by senior officials do not help.

London Ontario Attack

In June of 2016, a woman wearing a hijab was approached by another woman, "unknown to her" who "began yelling at her for no apparent reason ... spat on the victim, then punched her several times" creating "minor injuries" before grabbing "onto the victim's hijab and attempted to pull it off of her head before pulling the victim's hair."[267]

The media began spinning this as an "Islamophobic" attack almost immediately. Public Safety Minister Ralph Goodale said he was "Saddened to hear about the recent attack on a Muslim woman in London, Ont. This deplorable act has no place in Canada."[268]

The Minister and the media went silent shortly thereafter. The reason? It appears that it was a case of one Muslim woman attacking another, and therefore difficult to assess how such an attack could be defined as Islamophobic.

Peterborough Mosque Burning – No Evidence of a Hate Crime

In November of 2015, a mosque in Peterborough suffered an internal fire that caused approximately $90,000 in damages. According to local fire officials, the fire was deliberately set.[269]

---

[267] Joe Warmington, *Remember there are two sides to a story,* London Free Press, 27 June 2016. The article can be seen online at http://www.lfpress.com/2016/06/27/remember-theres-two-sides-to-a-story . Viewed 31 March 2017. **Rated A2**.

[268] Joe Warmington, *Remember there are two sides to a story,* London Free Press, 27 June 2016. The article can be seen online at http://www.lfpress.com/2016/06/27/remember-theres-two-sides-to-a-story . Viewed 31 March 2017. **Rated A2**.

[269] Jessica Nyznik, *Peterborough mosque fire deliberately set, say police,* The Peterborough Examiner, 16 November 2015. The article can be seen online at http://www.thepeterboroughexaminer.com/2015/11/15/peterborough-mosque-fire-under-investigation . Viewed 31 March 2017. **Rated A2**.

Immediate claims of a hate crime were made. Following the attack, Prime Minister Trudeau urged Canadians to avoid "acts of hatred and racism."[270]

Following repairs to the mosque, Prime Minister Trudeau appeared at the re-opening ceremony and stated "What happened to this place of worship just one day after the brutal terrorist attacks in Paris is reprehensible. I have not met a single Canadian who was not as profoundly disturbed as I was to see this kind of hate crime taking place."[271]

The problem, of course, is that there is no evidence of a hate crime having been committed at the Peterborough Mosque. No one has been arrested, no one charged and there have been no publicly known interviews with suspects. This is more than a year after the event.

The mosque is run by Shazim Khan, a well-known Islamist misogynist. In YouTube videos posted in 2009, entitled Marriage: Are You Ready?[272] Shazim Khan gave a lecture explaining why it's "a major sin" for a wife to not have sex whenever her husband wants and that "there is no need for her to go out" if her husband provides for her, along with other sexist musings.

The Prime Minister and his Public Safety Minister (who is both the chief law enforcement and intelligence officer) have both made unsupported claims of hate crimes against Canadian citizens, even though there is no evidence to support them. Unfortunately, these kinds of fake hate crime complaints are common in the world of Islamists. These kinds of false claims against Canadian citizens in an area where too many fake claims are already made is damaging. From very senior officials, we expect better.

Prime Minister Trudeau appears willing to make such unfounded claims when they support his agenda of supporting Islamist belief systems.

Barbaric Practices, Wife Beating and the Need for Responsible Neutrality

In 2011, the Government of Canada was updating its Discover Canada guide, a handout which is intended to assist immigrants to understand life in Canada and prepare for the citizenship test. The guide included the following lines:

> "Canada's openness and generosity do not extend to barbaric cultural practices that tolerate spousal abuse, 'honour killings,' female genital mutilation, forced marriage or other gender-based violence. Those guilty of these crimes are severely punished under Canada's criminal laws."[273]

Then Liberal MP Justin Trudeau attacked the Conservative Government for the use of term barbaric, even though the term had been in the guide since 2009. Trudeau claimed to be shocked at the use of the term

---

[270] Emily Chan, Trudeau *condemns 'highly disturbing' hate crimes*, CTV News, 18 November 2015. The article can be seen online at http://www.ctvnews.ca/canada/trudeau-condemns-highly-disturbing-hate-crimes-1.2664070 . Viewed 31 March 2017. **Rated A2**.

[271] *Trudeau visits Peterborough, Ont., mosque repaired after arson*, CBC News, 17 January 2016. The article can be seen online at http://www.cbc.ca/news/canada/trudeau-mosque-peterborough-1.3407697 . Viewed 31 March 2017. **Rated A2**.

[272] See the YouTube video at https://www.youtube.com/watch?v=8y34jEDDUS4 . Viewed 31 March 2017. **Rated A1**.

[273] Bryn Weese, *Honour killings term angers Trudeau*, Toronto Sun, 14 March 2011. The article can be seen online at http://www.torontosun.com/news/canada/2011/03/14/17610021.html . Viewed 9 April 2017. **Rated A2.**

barbaric in a government document and said the term was unacceptable. Rather bizarrely, he was widely reported to have stated that: "There needs to be a little bit of an attempt at responsible neutrality."

The response was revealing for its globalist view. In the mind of MP Trudeau, the Government of Canada needs to take a position of "responsible neutrality" on the issues of wife beating and female genital mutilation. This is cultural relativism at its worst. If Canada (and any other country) has a value system in place, it needs to be able to identify and fully condemn the mutilation of women and the abuse of children.

Canada does not need, nor should it ever be seen, to have a position of "responsible neutrality" on the issues of gender based violence.

Only following a series of critical press article and public discussion[274], did MP Trudeau issue a clarifying statement which included the line: We accept that these acts are absolutely unacceptable[275].

State Sponsor of Funding Islamic Relief Funding

Ahmed D. Hussen, Minister of Immigration, Refugees and Citizenship, on behalf of Marie-Claude Bibeau, Minister of International Development and La Francophonie, announced on 17 March 2017 that Canada will provide $119.25 million in humanitarian funding to respond to needs of crisis-affected people in Nigeria, Somalia, South Sudan and Yemen. According to Hussen's statement, Canada's support includes Islamic Relief Canada, which will receive some $1.5 million.[276] It is hard to understand why the Government of Canada would see fit to fund Islamic Relief Canada when it has been repeatedly identified as funding terrorism, and a variety of banks and organizations have distanced themselves from it for this reason.

Islamic Relief was one of four groups identified in Senate testimony as being a front group for the Muslim Brotherhood in Canada. The parent organization of Islamic Relief Canada is Islamic Relief Worldwide, which was formed in Birmingham, UK as a front group for the Muslim Brotherhood and operates on their behalf. While the charity does some legitimate work, it has been repeatedly identified that it provides funding directly and indirectly to Muslim Brotherhood front groups such as Hamas. The Muslim Brotherhood itself has been declared to be a terrorist group by several countries including Saudi Arabia, Egypt, the United Arab Emirates and Russia. Islamic Relief Worldwide operates in more than 40 countries[277] beyond its home base of the United Kingdom. One of those countries is Canada.

Here in Canada, Islamic Relief Canada has had a significant series of connections to the Muslim Brotherhood through its senior staff and board members. Dr. El-Tantawy Attia (Vice President) has openly

---

[274] Bryn Weese, *Trudeau tweets a retreat on 'barbaric' comments,* Canoe News, 11 March 2011. The article can be seen online at http://cnews.canoe.com/CNEWS/Politics/2011/03/15/17622291.html . Viewed 9 April 2017. **Rated A2.**

[275] Bryn Weese, *Honour killings term angers Trudeau*, Toronto Sun, 14 March 2011. The article can be seen online at http://www.torontosun.com/news/canada/2011/03/14/17610021.html . Viewed 9 April 2017. **Rated A2.**

[276] CIJ News, *Canada's foreign aid surpasses $10 billion*, 17 March 2017. The article can be seen online at http://en.cijnews.com/?p=214223. Viewed 31 March 2017. **Rated A1**.

[277] For more information on this see the Islamic Relief website at http://www.islamic-relief.org.uk/news/independent-investigation-of-islamic-relief-operations/ . Viewed 03 October 2017. **Not rated**.

stated to the press that at his mosque (Dundas Street Mosque, Toronto Ontario, Muslim Association of Canada) that they are followers of the Muslim Brotherhood.[278]

In 2014, the United Arab Emirates released a list of some 85 entities that it believes are terrorist organizations or front groups.[279] The list included major terror groups such as Al Qaida, Daesh and the Muslim Brotherhood, as well as the regional and local affiliates. Dr. Ebtisam Al Ketbi, chairwoman of Emirates Policy Centre explained that:

> "The expanded list of designated terror groups shows the UAE addresses the root causes of the threat of terrorism, which requires the pursuit of a comprehensive international strategy that prevents recruitment."

She further added that:

> "The banned groups also include proxy terror actors and front organisations that give others the funding, training, and weapons to carry out terrorist acts."[280]

The UAE list included the Islamic Relief Worldwide, which it describes as "an affiliate of the International Organisation of the Muslim Brotherhood" and its offshoot the Islamic Relief in London.

In June 2014, Israel "banned a British-based charity from operating in the occupied West Bank, accusing Islamic Relief Worldwide (IRW) of being a source of funding for the Palestinian Hamas Islamist movement."[281] In issuing the ban, Israel stated that charity's chapters, including those in the West Bank and Gaza Strip, were run by Hamas members. "The IRW is one of the sources of Hamas's funding and a means for raising funds from various countries in the world," he said. "We do not intend to allow it to function and abet terrorist activity against Israel."[282]

The parent organization of Islamic Relief Canada has had its bank accounts closed by Swiss bank UBS. Islamic Relief Canada itself was removed from the "Financial Post 25 Top Charities of the Year" list for perceived improprieties.

---

278 National Post Staff, *Cancelled debate highlights tension among Canadian Muslims*, February 7, 2011, http://life.nationalpost.com/2011/02/07/cancelled-debate-highlights-tension-among-canadian-muslims/ . Viewed 20 June 2017. **Rated B2**.

279 The official list is online at http://www.thenational.ae/uae/government/list-of-groups-designated-terrorist-organisations-by-the-uae . Viewed 11 April 2017. **Rated A1.**

280 Samir Salama, Associate Editor, *UAE addresses root causes of terror,* Gulf News, 16 November 2017. The article is available online at http://m.gulfnews.com/news/uae/uae-addresses-root-causes-of-terror-1.1413289 . Viewed 20 June 2017. **Rated B2**.

281 *Israel bans UK-based Muslim charity accused of funding Hamas*, Reuters, 19 June 2014. The article is available online at http://uk.reuters.com/article/2014/06/19/uk-palestinians-israel-charities-idUKKBN0EU1FE20140619 . Viewed 20 June 2017. **Rated B2.**

282 *Israel bans UK-based Muslim charity accused of funding Hamas*, Reuters, 19 June 2014. The article is available online at http://uk.reuters.com/article/2014/06/19/uk-palestinians-israel-charities-idUKKBN0EU1FE20140619 . Viewed 20 June 2017. **Rated B2.**

In 2012, Islamic Relief in the UK has had its account closed while at the same time any further zakat (charitable/religious) donations to its account were blocked by the Swiss bank UBS.[283] This was done due to counter-terror concerns.[284]

In 2014, Islamic Relief's donation page was removed from Charities Aid Foundation website. The CAF would not comment directly as to why it ceased to have an affiliation with Islamic Relief, but it did release a statement which said:

> "It would be wrong for us to discuss our processes, but like any financial intermediary, we have robust systems in place to ensure we comply with our UK and international obligations to protect against fraud, money laundering, bribery and corruption and terrorism financing while working with charitable organisations to support their work in conflict zones and elsewhere."[285]

The Financial Post of Canada removed Islamic Relief Canada from its "25 Charities of the Year" list stating that it was "pulled from this year's list, due to the fact that its international arm has been banned elsewhere (though not in Canada) for allegedly funneling funds to the terrorist organization Hamas."[286]

Funding Mosques that are Muslim Brotherhood Fronts

The Government of Canada announced that the Kitchener Masjid, which is part of the Muslim Association of Canada,[287] would receive a federal grant. The money is coming from a community infrastructure program celebrating Canada's 150th birthday. The $197,000 will be used towards renovation of the mosque.[288]

---

[283] An archived version of this article ca be seen at https://web.archive.org/web/20121124044239/http://www.civilsociety.co.uk/finance/news/content/13757/banking_sector_nerves_blocking_international_relief_says_islamic_relief_finance_director . Viewed 03 October 2017. **Not rated**.

[284] *UBS closes Islamic Relief account over terror risk*, Money Jihad, 08 November 2012. The article is available online at https://moneyjihad.wordpress.com/2012/11/09/ubs-closes-islamic-relief-account-over-terror-risk/ . Viewed 20 June 2017. **Rated C3**. See also the very last line in the article *HSBC to close bank account of Muslim charity working Gaza,* Civil Society News, 25 July 2014. The article is available online at http://www.civilsociety.co.uk/finance/news/content/17903/hsbc_to_close_bank_account_of_muslim_charity_working_in_gaza . Viewed 20 June 2017. **Rated C2**. See also the very last line in the article at: http://www.civilsociety.co.uk/finance/news/content/17903/hsbc_to_close_bank_account_of_muslim_charity_working_in_gaza. Viewed 20 June 2017. **Rated C2.**

[285] *Islamic Relief's donation page is removed from CAF website*, Civil Society News, 03 September 2014. The article is available online at http://www.civilsociety.co.uk/fundraising/news/content/18091/islamic_reliefs_donation_page_is_removed_from_caf_website . Viewed 20 June 2017. **Rated B3**.

[286] Claire Brownell, *Financial Post's Charities of the Year: Why these 25 are worth your donations (and which ones we're cautious about),* The Financial Post, 12 December 2014. The article can be seen online at http://business.financialpost.com/news/financial-post-charities-of-the-year-2014 . Viewed 24 July 2017. **Rated B2**.

[287] *Federal government announces funding for Kitchener Masjid*, CTV Kitchener, published Sunday, May 15, 2016 7:20PM EDT. The article can be seen online at http://kitchener.ctvnews.ca/federal-government-announces-funding-for-kitchener-masjid-1.2903310 . Viewed 31 March 2017. **Rated A1**.

[288] *Kitchener Masjid receives $,* CBC News Posted: May 16, 2016 10:35 AM ET. The article can be seen online at http://www.cbc.ca/news/canada/kitchener-waterloo/kitchener-masjid-federal-funding-renovations-1.3583977

The Kitchener Mosque self-identifies as a part of the Muslim Association of Canada (MAC).

The Muslim Association of Canada has presented the following on its own website:

> "We believe that the efforts of Al-Banna and subsequent generations of the Muslim Brotherhood remain the truest reflection of Islamic practice in the modern era." [289]

The Muslim Association of Canada also says:

> "Much of the philosophy and vision of the Muslim Association of Canada derives from the heritage of the Muslim Brotherhood." [290]

The Senate of Canada heard in May 2015[291] that the Muslim Brotherhood, listed as a terrorist organization in several countries[292], has a series of some eight to ten front organizations in Canada. Among them were the Muslim Association of Canada; the National Council of Canadian Muslims; (formerly known as Council of American Muslim Relations – Canada or CAIR-CAN); Islamic Relief Canada, and the International Relief Fund for the Afflicted and Needy – Canada, IRFAN. IRFAN no longer exists, as it lost it Canada Revenue Agency charitable status for funding terrorism and was later declared to be a terrorist entity.[293]

The testimony[294] to the Senate was given by Dr. Lorenzo Vidino,[295] one of the world's leading experts on the Muslim Brotherhood. He is currently the Director of the Program on Extremism at the Center for Cyber and Homeland Security, George Washington University. He has also held positions at the Centre for Security Studies, the Rand Corporation, the Kennedy School of Government, Harvard University, and the U.S. Institute of Peace.

The Government of the United Kingdom released a report in late 2015 that stated the Muslim Brotherhood, "which can be seen primarily as a political project," had a "highly ambiguous relationship with violent extremism." The Muslim Brotherhood is "deliberately opaque, and habitually secretive" and

---

[289] This statement can be seen on the MAC website at https://www.macnet.ca/English/Pages/FAQ.aspx Viewed 31 March 2017. **Rated A1.**

[290] This statement can be seen on the MAC website at https://www.macnet.ca/English/Pages/FAQ.aspx Viewed 31 March 2017. **Rated A1.**

[291] THE STANDING SENATE COMMITTEE ON NATIONAL SECURITY AND DEFENCE EVIDENCE, OTTAWA, Monday, May 11, 2015, SECD 52124, 1640- 1, http://www.parl.gc.ca/content/sen/committee/412/SECD/52124-E.HTM . Viewed 31 March 2017. **Rated A1.**

[292] Among the countries which list the Muslim Brotherhood as a terrorist organization are Egypt, Saudi Arabia, the United Arab Emirates, Kazakhstan and Russia. The United Kingdom stated in 2015 that the Muslim Brotherhood had a "highly ambiguous relationship with violent extremism."

[293] Government of Canada news release, *Government of Canada Lists IRFAN-Canada as terrorist entity*. 29 April 2014. This release can be seen online at http://news.gc.ca/web/article-en.do?nid=843809 . Viewed 17 May 2017. **Rated A1**.

[294] Ian MacLeod, *Beware of the Muslim Brotherhood, expert warns*. The Ottawa Citizen, 16 May 2015. The article can be seen online at http://ottawacitizen.com/news/politics/beware-of-the-muslim-brotherhood-expert-warns . Viewed 17 March 2017. **Rated A2**. The article was based on the Senate of Canada testimony by Dr. Lorenzo Vidino. For a full transcript of Dr. Vidino's testimony on the Muslim Brotherhood in Canada see: http://www.parl.gc.ca/content/sen/committee/412/SECD/52124-E.HTM Viewed 31 March 2017. **Rated A2.**

[295] See, among many others: https://cchs.gwu.edu/dr-lorenzo-vidino . Viewed 27 February 2017. **Rated B2.**

that both as "an ideology and as a network it has been a rite of passage for some individuals and groups who have gone on to engage in violence and terrorism."[296]

Dr. El-Tantawy Attia[297] is the executive director of the Masjid Toronto[298] which has been identified as being part of the Muslim Association of Canada. The Masjid and the Toronto chapter office of Muslim Association of Canada are in the same building. Dr. Attia made his views clear with respect to the Masjid when he stated: "Here, we follow the teachings of the Muslim Brotherhood."[299]

The question must be asked: Why is the Government of Canada using tax payer funds to support a Muslim Brotherhood front organization in Canada? The Muslim Brotherhood, with its Islamist supremacist ideology, is determined to destroy Western values and impose its form of political Islam on Canada. Of note, this just one some example of the Government of Canada funding extremism. A variety of Islamist organizations have charitable status or receive similar grants.

Minister of Immigration, Refugees, and Citizenship Gets Award from Misogynists

Prime Minister Trudeau and the (former) Minister of Immigration, Refugees and Citizenship John McCallum regularly interact with organizations that openly advocate misogynistic polices. In April of 2016, for instance, Prime Minister Justin Trudeau sent greetings to the Canadian Council of Imams at their annual dinner and commended the Imams of their many years of service to the country.[300] At this meeting, Minister John McCallum received an award for his outstanding service from the same organization.[301] No indication was given in the article as to what "outstanding service" he gave to the "community."

Dr. Iqbal Al-Nadvi is the Chairperson of Canadian Council of Imams.[302] He was also recently elected as the Amir (President) of Islamic Circle of North America (ICNA). The ICNA openly advocates violence against

---

[296] The statement of the Prime Minister of the United Kingdom concerning the report on the Muslim Brotherhood can be seen at https://www.gov.uk/government/speeches/muslim-brotherhood-review-statement-by-the-prime-minister . The full report can be seen online at https://www.gov.uk/government/uploads/system/uploads/attachment_data/file/486932/Muslim_Brotherhood_Review_Main_Findings.pdf . Viewed 31 March 2017. **Rated A1**.

[297] The Muslim Association of Canada describes Dr. Attia in the following manner: *Dr. El-Tantawy Attia, Executive Director of MAC's Masjid Toronto. https://www.macnet.ca/English/Winnipeg/Pages/Home.aspx see also: https://www.macnet.ca/English/Toronto/Pages/Home.aspx* . Viewed 31 March 2017. **Rated A2**.

[298] For more on this see http://muslimsforwhiteribbon.com/category/portfolio/page/2/ Viewed 31 March 2017. **Rated B2.**

[299] National Post Staff, *Cancelled debate highlights tension among Canadian Muslims*, February 7, 2011, http://life.nationalpost.com/2011/02/07/cancelled-debate-highlights-tension-among-canadian-muslims/ . Viewed 20 June 2017. **Rated B2**.

[300] Canadian Council of Imams, *Our First Annual Dinner on April 11 celebrating 26 years of Service was a success*, 14 April 2016. The article can be seen online at http://www.canadiancouncilofimams.com/2016/04/our-first-annual-dinner-on-april-11-celebrating-26-years-of-service-was-a-success/ . Viewed 31 March 2017. **Rated A1**.

[301] Canadian Council of Imams, *Our First Annual Dinner on April 11 celebrating 26 years of Service was a success*, 14 April 2016. The article can be seen online at http://www.canadiancouncilofimams.com/2016/04/our-first-annual-dinner-on-april-11-celebrating-26-years-of-service-was-a-success/ . Viewed 31 March 2017. **Rated A1**.

[302] *Dr. Iqbal Al-Nadvi-New Amir of ICNA Canada for 2016-2017,* http://icnacanada.net/dr-iqbal-al-nadvi-new-amir-of-icna-canada-for-2016-2017/ . Viewed 31 March 2017. **Rated A2**.

women and advocates a variety of policy which are overtly misogynistic. The syllabus of learning from the ICNA, advocates, among other that:

- Women are inferior to men; [303]
- Wife beating is permissible; [304]
- Owning slave girls should be legal; [305]
- A Muslim wife must obey her husband when he calls her to bed; [306]
- Sex slaves are permissible in certain circumstance; [307]
- Pregnant adulteress to be stoned after giving birth; [308]
- Western civilization is the enemy, [309] and
- Islam is totally incompatible with democracy. [310]

A letter of complaint was sent to Patty Hajdu in her role as Minister for the Status of Women in Canada. Despite a direct email and an internet article, she remained silent on the issue of senior cabinet ministers accepting awards from Islamist groups that advocate violence against women and women as sex slaves.[311]

Minister Hajdu's position appears to be consistent with that of Prime Minister Trudeau and most White privileged feminists. The rights of women in Canada do not apply to brown women if it means contesting the values of the Islamists whom Prime Minister Trudeau supports.

The Islamophobia Hearings in Canada

---

[303] CIJ News, *ICNA Canada's online syllabus: women are inferior to men, Western civilization "enemy"*, 23 February 2016. The article is available online at http://en.cijnews.com/?p=27294 . Viewed 31 March 2017. **Rated A1**.

[304] CIN News, *ICNA Canada's online syllabus on wife beating*, 18 February 2017. The article is available online at http://en.cijnews.com/?p=26599 . Viewed 31 March 2017. **Rated A1**.

[305] CIJ News, *ICNA Canada's online syllabus legalizes "slave-girls"*, 15 February 2016. The article can be seen online at http://en.cijnews.com/?p=26432 . Viewed 31 March 2017. **Rated A1**.

[306] CIJ News, *ICNA Canada's online syllabus: Muslim wife must obey her husband when he calls her to bed,* 21 February 2016. The article can be viewed online at http://en.cijnews.com/?p=27059 . Viewed 31 March 2017. **Rated A1**.

[307] CIJ News, *ICNA Canada's syllabus explains ruling on 'sex slaves' in Islam*, 10 January 2016. The article can be seen online at http://en.cijnews.com/?p=19009 . Viewed 31 March 2017. **Rated A1**.

[308] CIJ News, *ICNA Canada's online syllabus: pregnant adulteress to be stoned after giving birth,* 19 February 2016. The article can be seen online at http://en.cijnews.com/?p=26659 . Viewed 31 March 2017. **Rated A1**.

[309] CIJ News, *ICNA Canada's online syllabus: women are inferior to men, Western civilization "enemy",* 23 February 2016. The article is available online at http://en.cijnews.com/?p=27294 . Viewed 31 March 2017. **Rated A1**.

[310] CIJ News, *ICNA Canada contradicts Trudeau: "Islam is totally incompatible with Western democracy"*, 25 February 2017. The article can be seen online at http://en.cijnews.com/?p=27451 . Viewed 31 March 2017. **Rated A1**.

[311] *Open Letter to the Minister of the Status of Women – Are Women Inferior to Men? Can They Be Sex Slaves?* This article can be seen in Annex J. An email was also sent directly to the office of Minister Hajdu on 28 August 2016. No response was received

The chair of the House of Commons committee that will be studying Islamophobia in Canada will be Heritage Minister Hedy Fry. This raises several questions. The first is why such a set of hearings is not being conducted by the Department of Justice, which would be the natural fit. The question then becomes why the Heritage Ministry is handling this file. Is the issue of "Islamophobia" seen as a legal or social issue? Or, is the reason that a Department of Justice hearing would tend to raise more legal issues surrounding freedom of thought, speech, and conscience, thus discounting the entire process?

Additionally, there would be the legal question of whether the Government of Canada could or should rule on a "phobia." A phobia can be defined as an excessive and irrational fear reaction to a given object, activity, or situation. Is it Islamophobic to complain about the Muslim Student Association when they hand out a book saying you can beat your wife and she may see it as a sign of "love and concern." Is it Islamophobic to say you think adulterous women should not be stoned to death, although the Islamic Circle of North America advocates this? If you are Jew or Christian living in Canada, are you Islamophobic when you react to calls in mosques to kill the Jews and the non-believers or kuffars? Are you Islamophobic to argue that the National War Memorial should have extra protection following the murder of a ceremonial guardsman by an individual claiming to act on behalf of an Islamist ideology?

Having Minister Hedy Fry in charge of these hearing is itself a doubtful proposition, given her history of race baiting and fake accusations of hate crimes done for political reasons. This was done when she was the Secretary of State for Multiculturalism.

In March of 2001, then Secretary of State for Multiculturalism Hedy Fry stated the situation in the interior of British Columbia was comparable to the apartheid regime in South Africa and the religious warfare in the Balkans of the 1990s. On the International Day for the Elimination of Racism, she stated:

> "We can just go to British Columbia in Prince George, where crosses are being burned on lawns as we speak. I know of this because I was contacted immediately that these incidents occurred by the mayor of Prince George."

The problem, of course, was that there were no cross burnings in Prince George and the mayor of Prince George stated that he had never heard of such a problem. The riding of Prince George was held, at that time, by the Canadian Alliance Party. The unfounded hated based racial based slurs on Prince George called into question whether the comments were politically motivated.[312]

POLITICAL ENTRYISM

The first public article that suggested the Liberal Party of Canada was the victim of infiltration or "political entryism" was in April 2014.[313] This article suggested that the Muslim Brotherhood and Jamaat-e-Islami would attempt to run multiple candidates in the 2015 federal election using the Liberal Party of Canada as its political entry point. The question must arise as to whether any candidates in represent extremist

---

[312] Daniel Leblanc and Robert Matas, *Cross-burning' furor hits Liberal,* Globe and Mail, 23 March 2001. The article can be seen online at http://www.theglobeandmail.com/news/national/cross-burning-furor-hits-liberal/article4145631/ . Viewed 30 April 2017. **Rated B2.**

[313] *Brotherhood Front Groups Target Canadian Parliament; The promotion of certain Muslim candidates by Islamist organizations is not a good sign for Canadian politics.* BY Tahir Gora Thursday, April 3, 2014. The article is available online at http://www.clarionproject.org/analysis/brotherhood-front-groups-target-canadian-parliament Viewed 20 June 2017. **Rated B2**

views brought into Canada by the Muslim Brotherhood, its proxies, or its front groups. With some 700(+) dues paying Muslim Brotherhood members in Canada[314], the question is increasingly relevant.

According to the 2014 article:

> "The Islamic Society of North America (ISNA), the Islamic Circle of North America (ICNA), the National Council of Canadian-Muslims - formerly the Canadian affiliate of the Council on American-Islamic Relations (CAIR) - and others are full of members linked to the Muslim Brotherhood, its Jamaat-e-Islami sister group and their ideology."

The article also states that the author had a long conversation with a staunch member of the Jamaat-e-Islami. He reports the conversation in the following manner:

> "We want Muslims' representation in our parliament so that our members can watch our interests in the government. By Muslims, he meant Jamaat-e-Islami and Muslim Brotherhood followers."

In addition to Islamist infiltration, the Liberal Party also has several "useful idiots." Despite its seemingly glib nature, the term "useful idiot" is a proper political term. The term is frequently applied to an individual who supports one side of an ideological debate, but who is manipulated and held in contempt by the leaders of their faction or is unaware of the ultimate agenda driving the ideology to which they subscribe. "Useful idiots" are also perceived as naive and susceptible to manipulation for propaganda or other purposes or as any person similarly pliable for political purposes.[315]

Political Entryism can be defined as the "policy or practice of members of a particular political group joining an existing political party with the intention of changing its principles and policies, instead of forming a new party."[316] Sourcewatch added to this definition and says Entryism is "a political tactic in which an organisation or group enters a larger organisation in an attempt to gain recruits, gain influence or to take control of the larger organisations' structure."[317]

The term Entryism may have first been popularized by the entry of French Trotskyists into the party Section Française de l'International Ouvrière (SFIO). This effort, which began 1934, was discussed by Trotsky in his work The French Turn.[318] Other examples have been the efforts of the British Militant Tendency to enter the Labour Party of the UK in the 1950s and the 1930s Entryism of Adolph Hitler and Ernst Rohm into German Workers' Party (DAP) which would eventually become the Nazi Party (NSDAP). In August of 2015, it was reported that more than "100 Green Party candidates have tried to join Labour

---

[314] Tharwat Kherbawi is a former leadership figure of the Egyptian Muslim Brotherhood and the international organization of the Muslim Brotherhood. He has three books on the Muslim Brotherhood, which are "From the Heart of the Muslim Brotherhood" and "The Mystery of the Temple" and the "Imams of Evil." He has hundreds of articles and press and television appearances on this subject. In early 2015, he was interviewed about the Muslim Brotherhood in Canada. In this interview, he notes that there are some 700 dues paying members of the Muslim Brotherhood in Canada. He regards this figure as low, because many Muslim Brotherhood members have left Egypt following the ouster of the Muslim Brotherhood's President Morsi in 2013. **Rated C2**

[315] For more on useful idiots see https://en.oxforddictionaries.com/definition/useful_idiot , http://rationalwiki.org/wiki/Useful_idiot or https://en.wikipedia.org/wiki/Useful_idiot .

[316] http://www.thefreedictionary.com/entryism Viewed 20 June 2017. **Not rated.**

[317] The Sourcewatch definition can be seen online at http://www.sourcewatch.org/index.php/Entryism .

[318] See, among many other articles, *Lessons from the Struggle for the Fourth International*, The 'French Turn' which is available online at http://www.bolshevik.org/1917/no9/no09frnt.html . Viewed 20 June 2017. **Rated C3.**

in the latest evidence of Entryism by people who want to vote for Jeremy Corbyn in the party's leadership contest."[319]

The entryists will do their level best to help the party gain power, but their intent is to then use that party for efforts or effects which had little to do with the original intent of the party. In the case of the Islamists in the West, their Entryism will mean a direct attack on the most fundamental of human rights. This has already begun, with Islamist groups calling for exceptions to be made so that Western society can 'respect' their 'culture'.

The process of Islamist Entryism is well established. In the UK for example, Labour Party Minister Jim Fitzpatrick stated in 2010 that the Islamic Forum of Europe (IFE) had infiltrated and corrupted the Labour Party. He stated specifically that:

> "They are acting almost as an entryist organisation, placing people within the political parties, recruiting members to those political parties, trying to get individuals selected and elected so they can exercise political influence and power, whether it's at local government level or national level. They are completely at odds with Labour's programme, with our support for secularism." [320]

A 2015 British report, drawn up by the Home Office with a foreword by (then) Conservative Home Secretary (now Prime Minister) Theresa May, also refers to the problem of Entryism when it states:

> "We have seen evidence of extremist 'Entryism' where extremists have consciously sought to gain positions of influence to better enable them to promote their own values." [321]

Entryist Omar Alghabra

Elected in 2015, the current Member of Parliament for Mississauga-Centre is Omar Alghabra[322], previously a Member of Parliament from 2006 to 2008 in Mississauga-Erindale. The electoral boundaries from his previous riding were redrawn prior to the 2015 election.

---

[319] Andrew Grice, *Labour leadership: 100 Green Party candidates have joined party in latest evidence of 'entryism', Labour already suspects infiltration by members of hard left groups,* The Independent, Wednesday, 5 August 2015. The article can be seen online at http://www.independent.co.uk/news/uk/politics/labour-leadership-100-green-party-candidates-have-joined-party-in-latest-evidence-of-entryism-10441692.html . Viewed 20 June 2017. **Rated B2.**

[320] *Islamic radicals 'infiltrate' the Labour Party; A Labour minister says his party has been infiltrated by a fundamentalist Muslim group that wants to create an "Islamic social and political order" in Britain*, Andrew Gilligan, The Telegraph, 10:00PM GMT 27 Feb 2010. The article can be seen online at http://www.telegraph.co.uk/news/politics/labour/7333420/Islamic-radicals-infiltrate-the-Labour-Party.html . Viewed 20 June 2017. **Rated B2.**

[321] Andrew Gilligan and Robert Mendick, *Extremism in Britain: Now the crackdown is launched; Ministers are planning a raft of new measures to help stem the tide of Islamic extremism and radicalisation*, The Telegraph, 10:00PM GMT 07 Mar 2015. The report can be seen online at http://www.telegraph.co.uk/news/uknews/terrorism-in-the-uk/11457174/Extremism-in-Britain-Now-the-crackdown-is-launched.html . Viewed 20 June 2017. **Rated B2.**

[322] House of Commons, *Members of Parliament - Omar Alghabra, (Mississauga Centre).* http://www.ourcommons.ca/Parliamentarians/en/members/Omar-Alghabra(89535) Viewed 17 May 2017. **Rated A2.**

Mr. Alghabra was born in 1969 in Khobar Saudi Arabia to Syrian parents. He left Saudi Arabia and arrived in Canada as the age of 19. He is the only member of his family to migrate to Canada.[323] He is also, according to Prime Minister Trudeau's website, "a mechanical engineer by trade and an MBA graduate from York University. He has served in a variety of positions with General Electric Canada, Enbala Power, and the Ontario Energy Board. He was recently a Distinguished Visiting Fellow within the Faculty of Engineering and Architectural Science at Ryerson University."[324]

Mr. Alghabra has also been member of the community editorial board of the Toronto Star.[325]

In 2002, Mr. Alghabra stated that he did not believe that Hamas (Muslim Brotherhood proxy group) or Islamic Jihad were terrorist groups.[326] After being elected in 2016, he offered a slightly more nuanced version when he stated that the Government of Canada has listed Hamas as a terrorist organization.[327] Although supporting the government position, he did not expand on what his personal views were on the issue at that time.

Mr. Alghabra has openly stated that he favors Sharia Law for Ontario and that he was disappointed when he did not happen in Ontario after the 2003/2006 debate in Ontario. In a 14 December 2006 interview with the Al-Mughtarib newspaper, he stated:

> "Unfortunately, the majority of Muslims remained silent during the research of this law and abandoned the field to a dissenting minority [of Muslims] which had a louder voice. As a result, this plan ended in failure. The problem was not a stand taken [by non-Muslims] against Muslims, but it was we [Muslims] who were divided among ourselves and disunited in our ranks." [328]

Upon being nominated for the 2006 election, Mr. Alghabra thanked the Islamic Society of North America (ISNA) for their support, as was noted by attendee Galal Abdelmessih.[329] The ISNA still runs three federally registered charities, despite have lost one (Development Fund) after a CRA audit discovered that ISNA was funding a terrorist group: the Jamaat-e-Islami. As noted elsewhere, Jamaat-e-Islami is the ideological sister of the Muslim Brotherhood. The issue of the ISNA, ostensibly a religious charity, offering its support and use of its premises to political campaign raises question about legality.

---

[323] San Grewal, *Mississauga mayor leads charge to raise $5M for Syrian refugees; Bonnie Crombie brings together business, faith and community leaders to sponsor 32 families*, Toronto Star, Published on Thursday September 17 2015. The article is available online at http://www.thestar.com/news/gta/2015/09/17/mississauga-mayor-will-help-raise-5m-for-syrian-refugees.html . Viewed 29 September 2017. **Rated B3.**

[324] See more at: http://pm.gc.ca/eng/parliamentary-secretaries/omar-alghabra#sthash.zAgpt7c1.dpuf . Viewed 20 June 2017. **Not Rated.**

[325] See more at: http://pm.gc.ca/eng/parliamentary-secretaries/omar-alghabra#sthash.zAgpt7c1.dpuf .

[326] *Courting the extremist vote*. The article is available online at http://www.torontosun.com/2014/08/22/courting-the-extremist-vote . Viewed 20 June 2017. **Not Rated.**

[327] CIJ News, *Omar Alghabra: We believe that Hamas is a terrorist organization*, 18 March 2016. The article can be viewed online at http://en.cijnews.com/?p=30131 . Viewed 4 April 2017. **Rated A1**.

[328] See the original article at http://www.danielpipes.org/rr/blog_553.php . For more background on this issue see http://pointdebasculecanada.ca/the-rebel-video-hamas-supporter-omar-alghabra-appointed-parliamentary-secretary-to-the-minister-of-foreign-affairs/ . Viewed 20 June 2017. **Rated B2.**

[329] Charlotte West, *Canada's Islamist Seat*, Tuesday, January 31, 2006. The article is available online at http://archive.frontpagemag.com/Printable.aspx?ArtId=5747 . Viewed 20 June 2017. **Not Rated.**
For more on Galal Abdelmessih, see http://www.peo.on.ca/index.php/ci_id/29427/la_id/1.htm . Viewed 20 June 2017. **Not Rated.**

Omar Alghabra was also speaker at the 2007 ISNA 33rd Annual conference which was held in conjunction with the Muslim Student Association (founded by the Muslim Brotherhood)[330] and Muslim Youth of North America conferences. That conference was headlined by Tariq Ramadan, grandson of the founder of the Muslim Brotherhood.[331]

The ISNA had also made the news in 2008 when they tried to invite the head of Jamaat-e-Islami (Qazi Hussein Ahmad) to speak at an ISNA conference in Canada in 2008.[332] Mr. Ahmad has been previously banned some 25 countries, yet the ISNA sought to have him in Canada.[333] His visa to Canada was pulled at the last minute. Mr. Ahmad had spoken at a previous ISNA conference in St Louis in 1998. The ISNA-Canada conference was run jointly with the Muslim Students Association and Muslim Youth of North America, and endorsed by the Canadian Council on American-Islamic Relations (now NCCM), the Islamic Circle of North America, and the Muslim Association of Canada. These organization have been identified repeatedly as Muslim Brotherhood front groups.

Of note, the ISNA was involved in a series of scandals whereby charity money for the poor was squandered on other projects.[334] As well, the ISNA High School received Saudi money, despite several initial denials from the ISNA[335] and the ISNA High School Principal was a guest speaker at the annual conference of Hizb-ut-Tahrir[336], perhaps the fastest growing extremist group in Canada. The ISNA high school also made the news when its soccer team refused to play another high school team that had girls on it.[337]

---

[330] *Is the Muslim Student Association of Canada/USA a Recruiting Point for Extremism?* See Chapter 14.

[331] The web archive version of the speakers list for the 33rd Annual ISNA conference can be seen at http://web.archive.org/web/20070701222024/http:/www.isnacanada.com/Convention/Toronto/33/speakers.html . Viewed 20 June 2017. **Not Rated.**

[332] *North American Islamist Group (ISNA) planned to host Pakistani Terror Leader -invited Al Qaeda supporter to speak in Toronto*. The article can be seen online at http://www.militantislammonitor.org/article/id/3515 or at https://pjmedia.com/blog/north-american-islamic-group-hosts-pakistani-terror-leader/ . Viewed 20 June 2017. **Not Rated.**

[333] Patrick Poole, *North American Islamic Group Hosts Pakistani Terror Leader*. 21 June 2008, PJ Media. The article can be seen online at https://pjmedia.com/blog/north-american-islamic-group-hosts-pakistani-terror-leader/ . Viewed 03 October 2017. **Rated C3.**

[334] Jesse Mclean, *Muslim charity squandered money for poor.* 20 January 2011, The Toronto Star. This article is available online at: http://www.thestar.com/news/gta/2011/01/20/muslim_charity_squandered_money_for_poor.html . Viewed 24 July 2017. **Rated B2**.

[335] Marina Jiménez and Omar El Akkad, *Values at heart of Islamic tensions*, 08 November 2005, The Globe and Mail. The article can be seen online at http://www.theglobeandmail.com/news/national/values-at-heart-of-islamic-tensions/article989709/?page=all Viewed 24 July 2017. **Rated B2**.

[336] *Operating with Impunity – Extremism in Mississauga*. The article is available online in Annex J.

[337] Diana Mehta, *Muslim school which objected to girls on boy's soccer team told to abide by rules*, The Canadian Press, Published Friday, May 29, 2015 5:25PM EDT. The article is available online at http://www.ctvnews.ca/canada/muslim-school-which-objected-to-girls-on-boys-soccer-team-told-to-abide-by-rules-1.2397987 . Viewed 20 June 2017. **Rated B2**.

According to the Muslim Brotherhood[338] friendly[339] Al Jazeera News Service of Qatar, Omar Alghabra is a "long-time personal friend" to Prime Minister Trudeau. Additionally, Mr. Alghabra is stated to have been able to "recruit more than 12,000 volunteers across the country to work for Trudeau's campaign."[340]

When (then) Liberal leader Justin Trudeau spoke at the ISNA in 2013, he noted the following:

> "In particular, I would like to thank the organizers of this event: Yasmin Ratansi, our Liberal candidate for Don Valley East; Omar Alghabra, who will represent the Liberal Party in Mississauga Centre; and Salma Zahid, the Liberal candidate for Scarborough Centre."

Human Rights and Political Entryism

Human rights are an important weapon in challenging the rise of Islamist ideology, especially on the issues of women and arbitrary killings. In Canada and other Western societies, we have seen pressure put on government officials to accept 'differences' when migrant populations arise. For instance, government officials in Norway, Sweden and Denmark have reacted to migrant men bring in their multiple wives, especially when those 'wives' happen to be in the age range of eleven to fourteen years old. Norway alone had some 61 reported cases. However, Islamists immediately criticized the government and stated that this is an attack on Islamist family values:

> "These couples are married. Even if the man is twice as old, they have built a family and we cannot destroy family life."[341]

Not surprisingly, the Danish Imam and mosque president who made this statement, Oussama El-Saadi, also stated that he wants to see an Islamic Caliphate, he does not believe in democracy and that a Danish convert who became a suicide bomber is a hero.[342]

The issue of human rights and Entryism is of interest with the non-violent extremists, but the problem runs right across the entire spectrum of Islamist. As Jonathon Russel noted:

> While strategies of Islamist organisations may differ significantly between ISIL jihadists, who use violence or the threat of violence to pursue political change illegally, and Muslim Brotherhood

---

[338] Bob Dreyfuss, *Al Jazeera's Muslim Brotherhood Problem, Staff quits en masse over Qatar-imposed favoritism for the Brothers*, The Nation, 10 July 2013. The article can be seen online at https://www.thenation.com/article/al-jazeeras-muslim-brotherhood-problem/ . Viewed 31 March 2017. **Rated B2**.

[339] Nicholas Noe & Walid Raad, *Al-Jazeera Gets Rap as Qatar Mouthpiece*, Bloomberg News, 10 April 2012. The article can be seen online at https://www.bloomberg.com/view/articles/2012-04-09/al-jazeera-gets-rap-as-qatar-mouthpiece . Viewed 31 March 2017. **Rated B2.**

[340] Shenaz Kermalli , *Justin Trudeau: Canada's agent for change? Supporters pin their hopes on Trudeau's inclusive approach following his election as the Liberal Party leader*, 16 Apr 2013 06:44 GMT, Al Jazeera. The article can be seen online at http://www.aljazeera.com/indepth/features/2013/04/20134157922367832.html . Viewed 31 March 2017. **Rated C3**.

[341] *Danish imam says government should accept child marriages among refugees; Aarhus cleric says child brides should be looked at from a "different perspective"*, February 15th, 2016 11:57. The article is available online at http://cphpost.dk/news/danish-imam-says-government-should-accept-child-marriages-among-refugees.html . Viewed 31 March 2017. **Rated B2**.

[342] *Danish mosque doubles down on Isis support*, The Local, Published: 06 Jan 2015 20:59 GMT+01:00. The article is available online at http://www.thelocal.dk/20150106/danish-mosque-doubles-down-on-isis-support . Viewed 31 March 2017. **Rated B2**.

> entryists, who aim to expand influence and their ideas by infiltrating institutions or using mainstream platforms legally, groups and individuals across the Islamist spectrum tend to share a disparaging attitude towards human rights.[343]

The issue of human rights is also key to addressing the idea of an Islamist Caliphate, especially for those who come from Islamist groups such as the Muslim Brotherhood and Hizb ut-Tahrir. In their idealized version of a Caliphate, everyone must submit to Islam. Those who do not can be killed for reasons of being an apostate. Killing someone simply for their religious beliefs (or lack thereof) is about the most fundamental violation of human rights possible.

Sidetracked Cases

A series of judicial cases involving Islamists have been sidetracked or derailed since Justin Trudeau became Prime Minister. Each case can individually be perceived as controversial on its own. But collectively, the following cases suggest interference based not on the evidence of the cases, but on how they were dismissed or consigned into obscurity.

The four cases are:

- The payment of 10.5 million dollars to Omar Khadr.
- The sudden reversal, by the Minister of Justice, on the long running case against Abdullah Almalki, Ahmad El Maati and Muayyed Nureddin.
- The criminal investigation against the International Relief Fund for the Afflicted and Needy (IRFAN) was dropped without public announcement or reasons given.
- The massacre at the Quebec City mosque of January 2017 has not been pursued as a terrorism case, despite multiple events and indications that the attacks (plural) are nearly a text book case of terrorism.

Elevated suspicion exists as Prime Minister Trudeau has demonstrated consistency on his handling of events related to the Islamist cause. The Prime Minister has been (politely put) "inconsistent" on many files such as electoral reform, energy and pipelines, and the economy. However, the Prime Minster has been resolute on events related to the Islamist cause. He has, on every occasion, supported Islamists, deflected criticism from them or funded them. As noted, he has never met or contacted any Muslim reform group in Canada.

Combined with this consistency was the Prime Minister's rather startling statements to the Reviving the Islamic Spirit conference. The message, as noted earlier, was that with the most extreme of Islamist groups in Canada that he shared their beliefs, values and vison. Among the public beliefs of the groups represented at the Reviving the Islamic Spirit conference are that Islam is not compatible with democracy (ICNA), sexual slavery for women is permissible under certain circumstances (ICNA), and that it is nature of Islam to dominate all others (MAC).

THE CASES

Omar Khadr

---

[343] *Subordinating to Entryism is Detrimental to Human Rights*, By Jonathan Russell, March 18, 2015 at 16:29, HTTP://WWW.QUILLIAMFOUNDATION.ORG/BLOG/SUBORDINATING-TO-ENTRYISM-IS-DETRIMENTAL-TO-HUMAN-RIGHTS-BY-JONATHAN-RUSSELL/ Viewed 29 September 2017. **Rated B2**.

The Government of Canada paid Omar Khadr $10.5 million for reasons which were never made clear. Omar Khadr's case is complex, long lasting and involved multiple mistakes and questionable actions on the part of many individuals and agencies. It has been a highly emotive with all sides using frequently false and misleading information to advance their own political or ideological agendas. Complicating everything is that Omar Khadr's father was one of the 120 "lions" or martyrs of al Qaeda and his son was specifically noted for "tossing his little child (Omar) in the furnace of the battle."

The Government of Canada did make the argument that the payment was a cost saving measure as Khadr was suing the government for 20 million dollars and a loss was possible. However, running from a possible loss did not seem a reasonable argument, or as one journalist put it, the whole affair had a "hush-money feel to it."[344]

Almalki, El Maati and Nureddin- The 100 Million Dollar Lawsuit

Abdullah Almalki, Ahmad El Maati and Muayyed Nureddin had a 100-million-dollar lawsuit against the government of Canada. The proceedings began in 2006 when Abdullah Almalki and his family sued for compensation after he was arrested at the American border.[345]

The RCMP had a special project in place for years to prepare for the trail which was due to begin in January of 2017. The proceedings appear to have been approved by the Commission of the RCMP and the Minister of Public Safety.

Yet suddenly, the Government of Canada dropped the 100-million-dollar lawsuit over the advice of the RCMP Commissioner and the Public Safety Minister. Why? Each of the three will likely get paid out 10.5 million dollars in addition to all the other costs of running the RCMP project for more than ten years.

The trial would likely have exposed the evidence collected by the RCMP and would have shown why the RCMP was determined to bring this long-standing lawsuit to court. Did the Government of Canada fear that the evidence in the case would have been embarrassing? Would the evidence involved have exposed the names of individuals currently holding public office?

Project Sapphire and IRFAN

The RCMP has dropped their criminal investigation into IRFAN without an announcement or explanation (See Chapter 13 for more on IRFAN). Project Sapphire was aimed at IRFAN, which had its charitable status revoked for funding terrorism (Hamas) and was declared a terrorist entity after they continued to fund terrorism even after they lost their charitable status. The operation was publicly announced after the execution of search warrants against IRFAN on 4 April 2014. The announcement stated "Yesterday, the RCMP's Integrated National Security Enforcement Teams (INSETs) in Ontario and Quebec executed search warrants as part of a terrorist financing investigation on the International Relief Fund for Afflicted and Needy-Canada (IRFAN-Canada), which is linked to the terrorist entity Hamas. The operation named Project Sapphire led INSETs to execute search warrants in two locations: IRFAN's head office in

---

[344] Terry Glavin, *Why the Khadr payout has a hush-money feel to it*, 11 July 2017, the Ottawa Citizen. The article can be seen online at http://ottawacitizen.com/opinion/columnists/glavin-why-the-khadr-payout-has-a-hush-money-feel-to-it . Viewed 26 September 2017. **Rated B3.**

[345] Andre Duffy, *Almalki torture case will be unlike any in Canadian history,* 11 March 2016, The Ottawa Citizen The article can be seen online at http://ottawacitizen.com/news/local-news/almalki-case-would-be-unlike-any-in-canadian-history . Viewed 29 September 2017. **Rated B3.**

Mississauga, Ontario, and a residence in Montreal, Quebec. An extensive amount of documentary evidence along with stored media, money and other records were seized."[346]

The RCMP, as is typical in criminal investigations, has made little other public information available.

But why was the operation suddenly dropped? As with the two previous cases, any trial into IRFAN would have involved exposing the complex networks of personalities who willfully and directly raised tens of millions of dollars for a listed terrorist group. Many of the original founders of IRFAN have gone on to have very public and high profiles careers with connections that reach into the Canadian government, foreign governments, academia, federal agencies and federal charities.

Quebec City Mosque

As noted in Chapter 20, a mosque in Quebec City was the scene of a mass murder. The same mosque has also been the scene of several other events such as a pig's head dropped on its front entryway and a pamphlet distributed around the neighbourhood which targeted the political leanings of the mosque. Since the mass murder at the mosque, the car of the president of the mosque was burned. In short, it appears that a campaign of violence and intimidation has been aimed at the mosque based on its Muslim Brotherhood affiliations.

This appears to be a near text book case of violence used for political aims – terrorism. Yet no terrorism charges have been laid and neither the government nor the main stream press are raising the issue. As with the other cases, a terrorism investigation would require examining the motive. Such an examination would expose at the mosque is part of a larger community of Muslim Brotherhood sympathizers and front groups. The mosque, for instance, had repeatedly funded IRFAN over a period of years.

Assessment of the Sidetracked Cases

In a perfect world, the forces of politics on one side and law enforcement/intelligence on the other side would not intersect. Political agendas would not be able to interfere with due process. In the real world, however, the firewalls are often breached, and political agendas are deeply interwoven with appointments and decisions.

In these cases, it is reasonable to assess that politics may be playing a role in the decision to not follow through on legal options. A variety of forms of analysis was applied to the information flows, and each process produced its own incongruities.

Any one case might get dropped for reasons that are not clear to the outside observer. However, when several cases which are closely linked in nature are suddenly dropped, questions must be asked as to why this is happening. Another form of intelligence and political analysis (black box analysis) allows the observer to posit a series of possible reasons as to why decisions are being made. In this case, one possible analysis, which fits, suggests that the government of day does not want these cases to go ahead as the evidence exposed would embarrass a variety of individuals who have close ties to the Liberal Party.

---

[346] A copy of the announcement can be seen at https://www.ontariosecuritytraining.com/safety_alerts.php?author=&page_num=6522&find= . Viewed 27 February 2017. **Rated A1**.

Prime Minister Trudeau, Canadian Values, and the Liberal Party

Human rights, once regarded as one of the peak accomplishments of Western civilization, have been degraded significantly. Countries such as Canada, the United Kingdom, France and now Germany have led the downward spiral, especially where the rights of women are concerned.

Violence against women and gays has been normalized in Canada, where the Prime Minister of Canada points out in a positive manner that women are segregated. Neither Prime Minister Trudeau nor any senior official of the Liberal Party has challenged the statements of Islamist who call for the stoning of gays and wife beating. Prime Minister Trudeau attends and supports organization that call for wife beating and sexual slavery. Islamist terrorists have been elevated to the point where being a convicted terrorist is not cause for the revocation of citizenship. Calling for the killing of all non-Muslims is apparently not an issue and government funding and tax dollars are regularly provided to Muslim Brotherhood front groups. Advocating sex with nine-year-old girls is not pedophilia, if it is done within the Islamist context.

Prime Minister Trudeau is perceived to have performed policy reversals on several issues. First among these was the promise that the 2015 election would be the last[347] to be fought under the first-past-the-post rules.[348] Other perceived policy reversals have included pipelines/National Energy Board review[349] and veteran's affairs.[350] Prime Minister Trudeau's positions on government spending and increasing debt to GCP rations are, to say the least, ambiguous.[351] However, he has remained consistent in his support for the Islamist cause while ignoring input from reformist Muslim groups.

A Straight Line from 2008 to 2017

---

[347] *Electoral reform: Moving beyond first-past-the-post voting system*, CBC News - The Current with Anna Maria Tremonti, Friday 26 August 2016. The article can be seen online at http://www.cbc.ca/radio/thecurrent/the-current-for-august-26-2016-1.3736686/electoral-reform-moving-beyond-first-past-the-post-voting-system-1.3736704 . Viewed 8 April 2017. **Rated A2.**
Electoral reform: Moving beyond first-past-the-post voting system

[348] Tania Kohut, *What Trudeau said: A look back at Liberal promises on electoral reform,* Global News, 1 February 2017. The article can be viewed online at: http://globalnews.ca/news/3102270/justin-trudeau-liberals-electoral-reform-changing-promises/ . Viewed 8 April 2017. **Rated A2.**

[349] See, among many others, Mark Hislop, *How the Trudeau government tore up the rulebook on pipelines,* Canadian Business, 21 July 2016. The article is available online at http://www.canadianbusiness.com/economy/how-the-trudeau-government-tore-up-the-rulebook-on-pipelines/ . Viewed 8 April 2017. **Rated B2.**

[350] John Paul Tasker, *Ottawa's legal manoeuvre on veteran's benefits called 'a betrayal'*, CBC News, 17 May 2016. The article can be seen online at http://www.cbc.ca/news/politics/kent-hehr-veterans-court-benefits-1.3586013 . Viewed8 April 2017. **Rated B2.** See also Gloria Galloway, *Veterans say government is breaking election promises by taking them back to court*, The Globe and Mail, 13 June 2016. The article is available online at http://www.theglobeandmail.com/news/politics/liberal-government-breaking-pension-pledge-to-injured-veterans-lawyer/article30438822/ . Viewed 8 April 2017. **Rated B2.** See also Tasha Kheirddin, *Why is Trudeau kicking veterans to the curb?,* iPolitics, 19 May 2016. The article can be seen online at http://ipolitics.ca/2016/05/19/why-is-trudeau-kicking-veterans-to-the-curb/ . Viewed 8 April 2017. **Rated B2.**

[351] Financial Post Comment, *The Federal Government is ditching its fiscal pledge, adding another thing to the list of broken promise,* Financial Post, 9 April 2017. The article can be seen online at http://business.financialpost.com/fp-comment/the-federal-government-is-ditching-its-fiscal-pledge-adding-another-thing-to-the-list-of-broken-promises . Viewed 9 April 2017. **Rated B2.**

Prime Minister Trudeau has not only not opposed the Islamists and their barbaric ideology, he has made a multi-year long effort to support them both in word and in deed. His vision for the future includes the Islamist, progressive and globalist ideology which is clearly the opposite of the Canadian values found in the Constitution and the Charter of Rights.

Defending the Islamist Views

Consider the views of the Muslim Brotherhood's most respected and followed Imam, Yusuf Qaradawi, who was wanted on an INTERPOL Red Notice.[352] He is regularly cited as the leading clerical figure in the Muslim Brotherhood.[353]

> "Conquest through da'awa, that is what we hope for. We will conquer Europe, we will conquer America! Not through sword but through da'awa."

In 2007, Qaradawi repeated this same view by stating:

> "The peaceful conquest has foundations in this religion, and therefore, I expect that Islam will conquer Europe without resorting to the sword or fighting. It will do so by means of da'wa and ideology. Europe is miserable with materialism, with the philosophy of promiscuity, and with the immoral considerations that rule the world "considerations of self-interest and self-indulgence".[354]

Prime Minister Trudeau, and many like minded globalists/progressives feel that can simply reach their goals by flooding Western states with refugees and economic migrants. They have no plans – or intent – to achieve integration in the face of ideologies such as those advocated by Qaradawi. They have no plans or ideas on how to confront the poisonous and barbaric belief systems imported and spread from street to street. They have no idea or are willfully ignoring the warning signs of terrorism and societal conflict developing. Islamists, on the other hand, clearly understand the situation and are exploiting it.

Whether the Liberal Party choses to purge itself of these problems remains a key question for the future of Canada. Canada's two other leading parties face the same challenge.

---

352 See the INTERPOL Red Notice at http://www.interpol.int/notice/search/wanted/2014-58772 . The notice says he is wanted for "Agreement, incitement and assistance to commit intentional murder, helping the prisoners to escape, arson, vandalism and theft." Viewed 9 April 2017. **Rated A1.**

353 *Yusuf Qaradawi Profile*. The profile can be seen online at http://www.investigativeproject.org/profile/167/yusuf-al-qaradawi . Viewed 9 April 2017. **Rated A2.**

354 Sheik Yousuf Qaradawi: *Islam's "Conquest of Rome" Will Save Europe from Its Subjugation to Materialism and Promiscuity*, Qatar TV, 28 July 2007. The material can be seen online at http://www.memritv.org/clip/en/1592.htm . Viewed 9 April 2017. **Rated A1.**

CHAPTER 13: A PARTIAL OVERVIEW OF FRONT ORGANIZATIONS IN CANADA

Thomas Quiggin

Key Points

- The Muslim Brotherhood operates in at least 81 different countries, including Canada, but rarely uses the name. Hamas and the Muslim Association of Canada are two exceptions.

- Islamist groups depend on front groups for their operations in most countries. The number of front groups per country can range from one to more than a dozen.

- Muslim Brotherhood front groups have operated in Canada for years.

In May 2015, Muslim Brotherhood expert Dr. Lorenzo Vidino testified to the Standing Senate Committee on National Security and Defence in Ottawa.[355] He stated that the number of major Muslim Brotherhood front groups in Canada was from eight to ten. The four front groups he identified by name were:

- The Muslim Association of Canada,

- The National Council of Canadian Muslims (formerly CAIR CAN),

- Islamic Relief Canada, and

- IRFAN Canada (now defunct and listed as a terrorist entity).

In his testimony, he referred to the Muslim Brotherhood front groups and stated:

> "If you are the gatekeeper, the self-appointed representative, you might at some point actually become the representative. If the government sees you as a reliable partner, and, for example, it's a big thing in a lot of European countries to teach Islam in schools, then the government will appoint you to teach Islam in public schools. Then you have the ability to shape the education system. So becoming a gatekeeper is a very important thing for them ... They want to be the ones telling you that's what Muslims think."[356]

Dr Vidino explained to the Senate Standing Committee that while the Muslim Brotherhood organisations do fund terrorist organisations such as Hamas, the greater threat comes from spreading a revivalist

---

[355] For a transcript of the testimony of Dr. Vidino before the Standing Senate Committee on National Security and Defence, see https://sencanada.ca/en/Content/Sen/committee/412/secd/52124-e . Viewed 11 April 2017. **Rated A2.**

[356] For a transcript of the testimony of Dr. Vidino before the Standing Senate Committee on National Security and Defence, see https://sencanada.ca/en/Content/Sen/committee/412/secd/52124-e . Viewed 11 April 2017. **Rated A2.**

interpretation of Islam among Muslims which is conducive to radicalisation, and which harms social cohesion and integration.

The warnings of Dr. Vidino are clear and highlight real world issues. Consider the beliefs of Zeid al-Noman, one of the most senior leadership figures of the Muslim Brotherhood in North America. In a 1981 speech al-Noman was introduced as a Masul (leader) of the Executive Office of the Muslim Brotherhood in America.[357] In a 1992 document, he was identified as being on the Shura Council (board of directors) of the same organization as well as holding a position as a Masul in the domestic work department. In his now infamous 1981 speech in Kansas City, he was asked questions about front organizations and he offered the following views on the use of fronts, their existence and the issue of secrecy in organizations:

> "By God, fronts are one method ...., one method for grouping and are one method to communicate the Ikhwan's (Muslim Brotherhood) thought. They are one method to communicate the Ikhwan's point of view. A front is not formed until after a study and after an exhaustive study. I mean, the last front formed by the Group is the Islamic Association for Palestine."[358]
>
> "And so on, we can now ..., speak about the fronts, for instance. **For instance, the brothers in Egypt don't have fronts in the same broad way we have in America and the fronts are one of the means and so on**." (Emphasis added)

With respect to carrying out military and security training at Muslim Brotherhood camps, Zeid al-Noman makes the following observations in response to an audience question:

> Question from Unidentified Male: By "Securing the Group", do you mean military securing? And, if it is that, would you explain to us a little bit the means to achieve it.
>
> Zeid al-Noman: No. Military work is listed under "Special work". "Special work" means military work. "Securing the Group" is the Groups' security, the Group's security against outside dangers. For instance, to monitor the suspicious movements on the...., which exist on the American front such as Zionism, Masonry .... etc. Monitoring the suspicious movements or the sides, the government bodies such as the CIA, FBI...etc., so that we find out if they are monitoring us, are we not being monitored, how can we get rid of them. That's what is meant by "Securing the Group".

In the same speech, Zeid al-Noman also addressed the issue of weapons training in camps run by the Muslim Brotherhood. He stated: "...here in America, there is **weapons training** in many of the Ikhwans' camps."

The Major Islamist Front Groups in Canada

---

[357] *The Ikhwan in America: Zeid al-Noman*. For a transcript of this speech as presented in the US v HLF terrorism funding trial, see http://www.investigativeproject.org/redirect/Ikhwan_in_American-Zeid_Al-Nomann.pdf . It was entered as Government Exhibit 003-0089. Viewed 11 April 2017. **Rated A1.**

[358] *The Ikhwan in America: Zeid al-Noman*. For a transcript of this speech as presented in the US v HLF terrorism funding trial, see http://www.investigativeproject.org/redirect/Ikhwan_in_American-Zeid_Al-Nomann.pdf . It was entered as Government Exhibit 003-0089. Viewed 11 April 2017. **Rated A1.**

It is reasonable to believe that Islamists have been setting up front groups to advance their cause in Canada for almost 60 years. The first well-known Islamist figure to arrive in Canada with the intent of spreading the Islamist ideology was likely Dr. Ismail al-Faruqi. He was a governor/mayor in the British Palestinian Mandate – district of Galilee- and left the area after the founding of Israel. He eventually moved to Montreal Canada in 1958. After ten years in Canada, he moved to the USA. Dr. al-Faruqui is deceased, having been murdered in his own home by a convert member of the Muslim community in Philadelphia in 1987.[359]

Dr. al-Faruqi would later become known for his books and for co-founding of the International Institute for Islamic Thought (IIIT) in 1980-81. His major intellectual contribution was the concept of the Islamization of Knowledge. The IIIT bears the motto: Towards Islamization of Knowledge and Reform of Islamic Thought.[360] According to a variety of reports, the IIIT was initially set up with money from Saudi sources as well as Muslim Brotherhood money.[361]

Since then, several large and small Islamist organizations have been set up. As noted by Dr. Lorenzo Vidino in his Senate testimony, the Muslim Brotherhood alone has some eight to ten large front groups in Canada. One of those he noted, the Muslim Association of Canada, has a variety of properties across the country.

Muslim Association of Canada

The Muslim Association of Canada (MAC) was established in 1997 with a stated vision: a desire to help foster a Muslim presence within Canada that adopts a balanced, moderate understanding of Islam and that is actively and beneficially engaged within society.[362]

The MAC is also one of only two organizations that openly claim they are followers of the Muslim Brotherhood, the other being Hamas. The MAC has made such claims on their website since at least 2004. The following shows their belief in the Muslim Brotherhood and its founder Hassan al-Banna.

> "It is now 75 years since Al-Banna initiated that blessed effort. The efforts of the Muslim Association of Canada are separate from the writings and organization of Al-Banna by time and space. The assertion that much of our philosophy and vision derive from the efforts of Al-Banna should not be taken to mean that we adopt in wholesale fashion all of the ideas developed and put forward by Al-Banna or the Muslim Brotherhood. However, **we believe that the efforts of Al-Banna and subsequent generations of the Muslim Brotherhood remain the truest reflection of Islamic practice in the modern era**.[363]

---

[359] Ruth O'Bryan, *Confession Details Stalking, Slaying of Islamic Scholars,* The Morning Call, 08 July 1987. The article can be seen online at http://articles.mcall.com/1987-07-08/news/2595065_1_confession-young-knife Viewed 20 June 217. **Rated C2**.

[360] The IIIT website can be seen at http://iiit.org/ . Viewed 20 June 2017. **Not rated**.

[361] John Mintz and Douglas Farah, *In Search of Friends Among the Foes: U.S. Hopes to Work With Diverse Group*, Washington Post, Saturday, September 11, 2004; Page A01. The article is available online at http://www.washingtonpost.com/wp-dyn/articles/A12823-2004Sep10.html . Viewed 20 June 2017. **Rated B2**.

[362] For this statement and more information on the MAC see their website at http://www.macnet.ca/English/Pages/Our%20Story.aspx . Viewed 11 April 2017. **Not Rated.**

[363] This statement can be seen at http://www.macnet.ca/english/pages/about%20mac.aspx . Viewed 20 June 2017. **Not rated**.

> MAC's roots are deeply enshrined in the message of Prophet Mohammad. Its modern roots can be traced to the vigorous intellectual revivalist effort that took hold in Muslim societies starting in the early twentieth century. This revival aimed at reconciling faith with the challenges of modernity and providing a clear articulation of balance and moderation in understanding Islam. In the Arab world, this revival culminated in the writings of the late Imam Hassan al-Banna and the movement of the **Society of Muslim Brothers (commonly known as the Muslim Brotherhood).** Al-Banna's core messages of constructive engagement in society, focus on personal and communal empowerment, and organizational development had a deep impact on much of the Muslim world." [364] (Emphasis added)

One of the mosques of the Muslim Association of Canada is the Dundas Street mosque in Toronto. A leading figure at this mosque Dr. El-Tantawi Attia[365] He is the executive director of the Masjid, as well as a long-time member of MAC. Dr. Attia made his views clear with respect to the mosque when he stated: "Here, we follow the teachings of the Muslim Brotherhood."[366]

A new full-time resident Imam was hired in 2014 for the Dundas Street mosque and its affiliated location at 84 Adelaide St. East. Dr. Wael Shehab holds a PhD in Islamic Studies from Al-Azhar University and was the Head of the Sharia and Fatwa sections at the English website, OnIslam.net. Dr. Shehab is also a member of the International Union for Muslim Scholars (IUMS).[367] Sheikh Yusuf Qaradawi is the head of the IUMS. The IUMS is listed as a terrorist entity by the United Arab Emirates.[368]

According to the official English language website[369] of the Muslim Brotherhood, Sheikh Yusuf Qaradawi played a major role in the pioneering initiative of launching the new Islamonline.net website. Qaradawi, who was wanted on an INTERPOL Red Notice,[370] is regularly cited as the leading clerical figure in the Muslim Brotherhood. Among others, he is famous for his statements on how the Muslim Brotherhood and the Islamist ideology will take over Europe and North America from the inside.

---

[364] This statement can be seen at http://www.macnet.ca/english/pages/about%20mac.aspx . Viewed 20 June 2017. **Not rated**.

[365] The MAC describes Dr. Attia as: *Dr. El-Tantawy Attia, Executive Director of MAC's Masjid Toronto.* This statement can be seen online at http://www.macnet.ca/English/Toronto/Pages/Home.aspx . Viewed 20 June 2017. **Not rated**.

[366] National Post Staff, *Cancelled debate highlights tension among Canadian Muslims*, February 7, 2011, http://life.nationalpost.com/2011/02/07/cancelled-debate-highlights-tension-among-canadian-muslims/ . Viewed 20 June 2017. **Rated B2**.

[367] *Masjid Toronto welcomes new Imam and resident scholar*, posted by iqradotca, Apr 20, 2015. The article is available online at http://iqra.ca/2015/masjid-toronto-welcomes-new-imam-and-resident-scholar/ . Viewed 20 June 2017. **Rated C3.**

[368] For the most recent listing of a variety of Muslim Brotherhood front organizations, see the UAE official list online at http://www.thenational.ae/uae/government/list-of-groups-designated-terrorist-organisations-by-the-uae . Viewed 11 April 2017. **Rated A1.**

[369] "Ikhwanweb, The Muslim Brotherhood Official English website", *www.ikhwanweb.com* Viewed 19 May 2017. **Rated B2.**

[370] INTERPOL issued a Red Notice for Qaradawi. The Red Notice stated he was wanted for "Agreement, incitement and assistance to commit intentional murder, helping the prisoners to escape, arson, vandalism and theft." The Red Notice caused a considerable stir at the time. For more on this see *Islamist group criticizes Egypt over arrest warrant for cleric,* Reuters Canada, 15 December 2014. The article can be seen online at http://ca.reuters.com/article/topNews/idCAKBN0JT14X20141215 . Viewed 20 June 2017. **Rated B2**.

"Conquest through dawah; that is what we hope for…. We will conquer Europe, we will conquer America, not through the sword but through dawah." [371]

Consistent with the general views of the Muslim Brotherhood, the new Imam believes that homosexuality is a sin, Muslims should avoid gays as homosexuality is evil, transgender people should return to their original gender and seek counselling. Additionally, Dr. Shehab believes Muslims should read the book by Qaradawi titled Fiqh of Jihad and follow its teachings. This book has concepts such as "Muslims do not fight to achieve material or worldly goals. On the contrary, the objective of fighting is only to make the Word of Allah (Exalted and Glorified be He) the uppermost."[372] In other words, fighting can make Islam the only religion in the world. This is a statement in support of offensive jihad.

The MAC also owns many mosques, schools, and cultural centres across Canada. The following image provides an overview:

The rate of expansion of the MAC is rapid and high value. The chart on real estate expansion shows some recent acquisitions.

The MAC has also been accused in the press of sending money to IRFAN after it had lost its charitable status for funding terrorism in 2011. According to press reports based on an RCMP probe, IRFAN had received some $300,000 from the MAC. The money would eventually find its way to Hamas according to the press reports.[373]

Council on American Islamic Relations Canada/National Council of Canadian Muslims

The Council on American Islamic Relations Canada (CAIR CAN) was originally founded as CAIR Montreal before becoming CAIR Ottawa and later CAIR CAN. It changed its name in 2013 to become the National Council of Canadian Muslims or NCCM.

According to CAIR CAN/NCCM's website, NCCM "is an independent, non-partisan and non-profit organization dedicated to protecting the human rights & civil liberties of Canadian Muslims (and by extension of all Canadians), promoting their public interests and challenging Islamophobia and other forms of xenophobia."

CAIR CAN/NCCM was also identified as a Muslim Brotherhood front organization in testimony in the Canadian Senate in May 2015.[374]

---

[371] Qaradawi speaking to the Muslim Arab Youth Association, MAYA Conference, Toledo, OH, 1995. See more on this at http://www.investigativeproject.org/profile/167/yusuf-al-qaradawi . Viewed 20 June 2017. **Rated C2**.

[372] For more on the book by Qaradawi, see https://web.archive.org/web/20150116071426/http:/www.onislam.net/english/shariah/contemporary-issues/interviews-reviews-and-events/412153-al-qaradawis-fiqh-of-jihad-book-review-811.html?Events . Viewed 17 November 2017. **Not rated**. See also http://jonathanhalevi.blogspot.ca/2015/05/downtown-torontoimam-transsexuals.html . Viewed 20 June 2017. **Rated B2**.

[373] Brian Daly, *Canadian Muslim group linked to terror financing denies wrongdoing,* QMI Sun News, 15 January 2015. The article is available online at http://www.ottawasun.com/2015/01/29/canadian-muslim-group-linked-to-terror-financing-denies-wrongdoing . Viewed 18 April 2017. **Rated A1**.

[374] Ian MacLeod, *Beware of the Muslim Brotherhood, expert warns*, Ottawa Citizen, May 16, 2015 http://ottawacitizen.com/news/national/beware-of-the-muslim-brotherhood-expert-warns . Viewed 18 April 2017. **Rated A2**.

The parent organization of CAIR CAN/NCCM is CAIR USA and CAIR CAN/NCCM was formed to support and fund the activities of CAIR USA, according to the founder.

CAIR USA has a troubled history. CAIR USA was incorporated in 1994 by three members of the Islamic Association for Palestine (IAP). They were Nihad Awad, Omar Ahmad[375] and Refeeq Jaber.[376] The incentive to create this organization derived from the Oslo Peace Accords which envisaged a peace settlement between the Palestinians and Israel. The IAP was fundamentally opposed to a peaceful settlement as it conflicted with their views that no peace was acceptable with Israel and that conflict must continue. This view was consistent with that of Hamas, which is the Palestinian arm of the Muslim Brotherhood.

The Islamic Association for Palestine (IAP) is a self-described Muslim Brotherhood (Ikhwan) front organization. In a 1991 document with the title A Historical outline and the main issues,[377] it was noted that:

> "In 1981, the Ikhwan founded the Islamic Association of Palestine to serve the cause of Palestine on the political and the media fronts. The Association has absorbed most of the Ikhwan's Palestinian energy at the leadership and the grassroots levels in addition to some of the brothers from the other countries. Attention was given to the Arab new arrivals, immigrants and citizens in general, while focusing on the Palestinians in particular. The Association's work had developed a great deal since its inception, particularly with the formation of the Palestine Committee, the beginning of the Intifada at the end of 1987 and the proclamation of the Hamas movement. The Association has organizations affiliated with it such as (The United Association for Studies & Research, The Occupied Land Fund and The Media Office), dedicated main personnel, several periodicals, research, studies and field branches in all the regions."

CAIR USA was also listed as an unindicted co conspirator in the Holy Land Foundation terrorism funding trials. CAIR USA has been directly tied Hamas (though organization and funding) according to an American federal judge in 2009.[378]

CAIR USA was also listed as a terrorist entity by the United Arab Emirates in 2014.[379] This was done as part of an overall effort by the UAE to identify proxies, front groups, and funders of the Muslim Brotherhood.

The current head of the CAIR CAN/NCCM is Ishaan Gardee. He has been "with CAIR-CAN since 2006 where he first served as CAIR CAN's Community Relations & Operations Director before being promoted as CAIR

---

375 Omar Ahmad would be with CAIR from its founding until 2005.

376 *"Articles of Incorporation, Council on American-Islamic Relations"* 15 September 1994. For more on this see https://www.investigativeproject.org/documents/misc/109.pdf . Viewed 20 June 2017. **Rated C2**.

377 See Government Exhibit 003-0003; 3:04-CR-240-G; U.S. v. HLF, et al. See also: http://www.investigativeproject.org/documents/case_docs/439.pdf Viewed 18 April 2017. **Rated A1**.

378 The court rulings can be seen at http://www.investigativeproject.org/documents/case_docs/1425.pdf and http://www.investigativeproject.org/documents/case_docs/1424.pdf . Viewed 18 April 2017. **Rated A1**.

379 A full list of the terrorist entities can be seen in the article of 14 November 2014 *UAE publishes list of terrorist organizations: Cabinet decision includes Al Qaida, Daesh and the Muslim Brotherhood.* The article can be seen at http://www.thenational.ae/uae/government/list-of-groups-designated-terrorist-organisations-by-the-uae . Viewed 15 April 2017. **Rated A1**.

CAN's fourth executive director in October of 2008." Prior to his employment with CAIR-CAN, he was "involved with CAIR CAN as an occasional volunteer from its early years."[380]

Mr. Gardee has given press interviews[381] and testified in Parliament[382] that CAIR CAN has no relation to CAIR USA, despite the commonality of their nomenclature.

In a CBC interview, the following exchange occurred between the interviewer and Mr. Gardee:

> (Begins at 4:20) Interviewer: "Some say they consider the Canadian version a branch plant.
>
> (Begins at 4:28) Gardee: "Well Evan, what I can tell you is that we have never had any funding relationship with them, **we never had an operational relationship** with them, we have always had two separate boards of directors, constitutions, bylaws, employees" (interviewer interrupts) (Emphasis added)
>
> (Begins at 4:46) Interviewer: "There are no links, but you chose the same name?"
>
> (Begins at 4:49) Gardee: "The organization as I mentioned and as I just told you went with that name as it was a well-recognized name within the Muslim civil liberties movement."

Shahina Siddiqui, a former board member and spokesperson for CAIR CAN, also told Senators in testimony at the Senate of Canada that CAIR USA and CAIR CAN/NCCM are not related.[383]

However, this does seem to be incorrect, according to CAIR CAN/NCCM itself, as well as its parent CAIR USA and the United States State Department.

It is a reasonable opinion to believe there are direct connections between CAIR CAN and CAIR USA, based on the following factual reports:

- The US Department of State refers to CAIR CAN as the Canadian Chapter of CAIR USA. The US State Department stated that "Expressions of anti-Muslim sentiment continued during the reporting period, according to the Canadian chapter of the Council on American Islamic Relations (CAIR CAN)."[384]

- CAIR CAN was set up to support CAIR USA:

    - According to a sworn court affidavit of the founder of CAIR CAN, the organization was set up to support CAIR USA. It began as CAIR Montreal, then CAIR Ottawa and finally CAIR

---

[380] See the biographic information at https://www.nccm.ca/wp-content/uploads/2014/03/NCCM-Annual-Report-2013-online.pdf . Viewed 20 June 2017. **Not rated.**

[381] The 9:58 interview is embedded on the CBC website at: http://www.cbc.ca/news/muslim-group-demands-apology-from-harper-chief-spokesman-1.2514099 . Viewed 20 June 2017. **Rated B3.**

[382] See, among many others, the CBC report at: http://www.cbc.ca/news/politics/bill-c-51-hearings-committee-testimony-ends-as-opposition-readies-amendments-1.3010134 . Viewed 18 April 2017. **Rated A2.**

[383] See more on this at: http://www.torontosun.com/2015/02/24/senate-questions-muslim-leader-over-alleged-ties-to-radicals Viewed 18 April 2017. **Rated A2.**

[384] The State Department view on this issue can be seen at http://www.state.gov/j/drl/rls/irf/2003/24482.htm Viewed 15 April 2017. **Rated A1.**

CAN. The founder of CAIR CAN says she (Dr. Sheema Khan) joined CAIR USA while living in Montreal.[385]

- According to Dr. Khan, the first Canadian chapter of CAIR was formed in Montreal. The Quebec Registry of Enterprises (File 3346439360) showed the Council on American-Islamic Relations as CAIR-Montreal. CAIR-Montreal was registered in January 1997, struck off the Registry in May 1999, replaced by CAIR-Ottawa, and by CAIR CAN in 2000.[386] The stated purpose of the Montreal chapter was to promote awareness of CAIR (USA) in Montreal. That was in 1996 and Dr. Khan states that she was director of this chapter until 1998.[387] She added that at that time CAIR USA had control over the character and quality of the activities of the Canadian chapter.

- Note the last sentence in paragraph 6 from the affidavit: Paragraph 6: "In 1996 a Canadian chapter of CAIR UNITED STATES was established in Montreal. The purpose of the chapter was to promote CAIR UNITED STATES awareness in Montreal. One of the means of promoting awareness was through the distribution in Canada of CAIR UNITED STATES' newsletters, publicity kits, brochures and handbooks. CAIR UNITED STATES had direct control over the character and quality of the activities of the Canadian chapter in Montreal." (Emphasis added)

- According to the affidavit, the founder goes on to state that CAIR USA has direct control over the character and quality of all activities of CAIR CAN as well.

- Paragraph 8: "That CIRC used the trademarks CAIR and CAIR CAN and the name Council on American-Islamic Relations Canada under licenses from CAIR UNITED STATES. Under terms of the license CAIR UNITED STATES has direct control over the character and quality of all activities of CIRC including the use of its trade mark and trade name."

* CAIR CAN/NCCM says that its parent organization is CAIR USA:

  - According to CAIR CAN's website,[388] CAIR CAN/NCCM has a parent organization which is identified as CAIR USA based in Washington DC.

  - In this extract from a 2003 publication titled "A Journalist's Guide to Islam" on a website belonging to CAIR CAN/NCCM the following statement is made:

    > "CAIR (Council on American-Islamic Relations) This Washington-based organization is CAIR CAN's parent organization. It has an email newsletter for the news media, providing news releases and background materials about important

---

[385] This can be seen in paragraph 5 of the 16 December 2003 affidavit signed by Dr. Khan.

[386] This can be seen on the following website which is online at http://macrames4.rssing.com/chan-3726988/all_p7.html . Viewed 18 April 2017. **Rated B2.**

[387] Paragraph 6 of the 16 December 2003 affidavit signed by Dr. Khan.

[388] The website referred to here is www.caircan.ca. The site was caircan.ca was registered originally with a creation date of 2001/05/16 according to the WHOIS website using information from the Canadian Internet Registration Authority, (http://www.cira.ca/). When checked on 28 February 2016 the site showed as active with an expiry date of 2018/05/16 and a last update of 2013/06/25. The DMOZ Title (Directory Mozilla) for the site is: CAIR-CAN - Council on American -Islamic Relations Canada.

Islamic events. It is worth receiving. Tel: 202-488-8787 Fax: 202-488-0833 Email: webmaster@cair-net.org, Web site: www.caircan.org (A Journalist's Guide to Islam (version 2003) Conceived by the Council on American Islamic Relations Canada. Published by Islamic Social Services Association Canada." [389]

- CAIR in Canada was formed to work with CAIR USA:
  - According to CAIR CAN's website statements in 2005, CAIR in Canada was founded to work with CAIR USA which was "well known" to Canadian Muslims. On their website in 2005, CAIR CAN provided a graphic that contained the following information:

    "In 1996, a group of concerned Canadian Muslims started an informal network in Canada to work with the Washington-based CAIR, an organization well known among Canadian Muslims since 1994. In the spring of 1997, CAIR-Montreal was formed, and was soon after replaced by CAIR Ottawa. In 2000, CAIR CAN was incorporated as a Canadian organization speaking out for Canada's Muslim population." [390]

It is a fact that CAIR USA states in their communications that CAIR CAN/NCCM is their Canadian office. The main CAIR USA website (www.cair.com) has published many articles where its states that CAIR CAN is their Canadian office. Typical of these articles are statements such as:

- Libraries Get New Package to Study Islam. 16 July 2012:

  "The main branch of the Calgary Public Library was the site for the launch of the CAIR CAN -- the Canadian office of the Council on American-Islamic Relations -- national Islamic library project." [391]

- Canadian newspaper publishes apology for anti-Muslim article:

  "Dr. Sheema Khan, chair of CAIR's Canadian office (CAIR CAN)." [392]

- CAIR-CAN: Is Canada 'Subcontracting' Torture?

---

[389] Archived copies of the CAIR CAN website can be found by using the Internet archive website called "The Way Back Machine" which can be found at www.web.archive.org. For a copy of the see *http://web.archive.org/web/20030701034732/http://www.caircan.ca/* and the select "download the CAIR CAN Journalists Guide" which will then be found at: http://web.archive.org/web/20030617021214/http://www.caircan.ca/downloads/jgprint.pdf Viewed 18 April 2017. **Rated A1.**

[390] 2005, CAIR CAN Annual Review, History, page three. Viewed 15 April 2017. **Rated A2.**

[391] This reference can be seen at http://www.cair.com/press-center/cair-in-the-news/7025-libaries-get-new-package-to-study-islam.html . Viewed 15 April 2017. **Rated A2.**

[392] This reference can be seen at *https://www.cair.com/action-alerts/179-canadian-newspaper-publishes-apology-for-anti-muslim-article.html* . Viewed 15 April 2017. **Rated A2.**

"The Canadian office of the Council on American-Islamic Relations (CAIR CAN) questioned whether Canadian security agencies may be "subcontracting" torture against Canadian citizens." [393]

- CAIR CAN Cited in 2005 Human Rights Report:

"(OTTAWA, CANADA, 10/26/06) – The Canadian office of the Council on American-Islamic Relations' (CAIR CAN) survey, "Presumption of Guilt: A National Survey on Security Visitations of Canadian Muslims," was cited in the U.S. State Department's 2005 Human Rights Report." [394]

- CAIR CAN Meets with U.N. Rapporteur:

"The Canadian office of the Council of American-Islamic Relations (CAIR CAN) expressed its concern that Canada is not protecting the rights of Canadian Muslims and Arabs when they travel to the United States." [395]

- Her Comic Take:

"She's a trailblazer," said Sheema Khan, chairwoman of the Canadian office of the Council on American-Islamic Relations." [396]

- Canadian MP offers apology for assistant's remark:

"Dr. Sheema Khan, chair of CAIR's Canadian office (CAIR CAN) CONTACT: Riad Saloojee at 613-254-9704; E-mail: cnada@cair-net.org" [397]

- Canadian Muslims condemn firing of Publisher:

"The Canadian office of the Council on American-Islamic Relations (CAIR CAN) today condemned CanWest Global's firing of Russell Mills... CONTACT: Riad Saloojee at 613-798-0003; E-mail: Canada@cair-net.org" [398]

- Canadian Muslims condemn vandalism against Jewish institutions:

---

[393] This reference can be seen at http://www.cair.com/press-center/cair-in-the-news/7049-cair-can-is-canada-subcontracting-torture.html . Viewed 15 April 2017. **Rated A2.**

[394] This reference can be seen at http://www.cair.com/press-center/press-releases/2052-cair-can-survey-cited-in-state-department-rights-report.html . Viewed 15 April 2017. **Rated A2.**

[395] This reference can be seen at http://www.cair.com/press-center/cair-in-the-news/7008-cair-can-meets-with-u-n-rapporteur.html . Viewed 15 April 2017. **Rated A2.**

[396] This reference can be seen at http://www.cair.com/press-center/cair-in-the-news/6935-her-comic-take.html . Viewed 15 April 2017. **Rated A2.**

[397] This reference can be seen at http://www.cair.com/action-alerts/179-canadian-newspaper-publishes-apology-for-anti-muslim-article.htmll . Viewed 15 April 2017. **Rated A2.**

[398] This reference can be seen at http://www.cair.com/press-center/cair-in-the-news/6471-canadian-muslims-condemn-firing-of-publisher.html. Viewed 15 April 2017. **Rated A2.**

"The Canadian office of the Council on American-Islamic Relations (CAIR CAN)…" [399]

- Canadian group denied public funding to fight circumcision.

  "Alhamdulillah (Praise be to Allah.) The Canadian office of the Council on American-Islamic Relations (CAIR-CAN) has announced that the Court Challenges Program of Canada denied public funding for a legal challenge…" [400]

- Muslims urge denial of public funding for Anti-circumcision (sic) campaign:

  "The Canadian Office of the Council on American-Islamic Relations (CAIR CAN) today called on the Court Challenges Program of Canada**Error! Bookmark not defined.** to deny public funding for a campaign designed to ban male circumcision." [401]

- Vandals attack Canadian Islamic Center:

  "The Council on American-Islamic Relations' Canadian office (CAIR CAN) is calling on law enforcement officials to investigate vandalism at the Manitoba Islamic Center." [402]

- Suspicious fire destroys Canadian Mosque:

  "The Council on American-Islamic Relations (CAIR) is calling on Canadian law enforcement officials to investigate a suspicious fire at Surrey Masjid in Surrey, British Columbia…. …. The Washington-based Islamic advocacy group says tensions in the Middle East and recent stereotypical portrayals of Islam in the American and Canadian media point… … This anti-Muslim rhetoric can easily turn into the reality of physical attacks," said Dr. Sheema Khan, director of CAIR's Canadian Office (CAIR CAN).[403]

- CAIR USA chapters report on their websites that that CAIR CAN is one of CAIR USA chapters:

  As of early 2014, two CAIR chapters in the USA claim that CAIR CAN is a chapter of the same organization of which they are members. These are:

  http://cairhouston.org/chapters.htm [as of 28 February 2014]

  http://www.cairchicago.org/cair-chapters/ [as of 28 February 2014]

- CAIR USA Chicago's website lists CAIR CAN as a Canadian chapter:

---

[399] This reference can be seen at *http://www.cair.com/press-center/cair-in-the-news/6403-canadian-muslims-condemn-vandalism-against-jewish-institutions.html*. Viewed 15 April 2017. **Rated A2.**

[400] This reference can be seen at http://www.cair.com/action-alerts/184-canadian-group-denied-public-funding-to-fight-circumcision.html . Viewed 15 April 2017. **Rated A2.**

[401] This reference can be seen at *http://www.cair.com/press-center/press-releases/665-muslims-urge-denial-of-public-funding-for-anti-circumsion-campaign.html*. Viewed 15 April 2017. **Rated A2.**

[402] This reference can be seen at http://www.cair.com/press-center/press-releases/661-vandals-attack-canadian-islamic-center.html . Viewed 15 April 2017. **Rated A2.**

[403] This reference can be seen at http://www.cair.com/press-center/press-releases/648-suspicious-fire-destryos-canadian-mosque.html. Viewed 20 June 2017. **Rated A2.**

The website of the Chicago chapter of CAIR USA lists 32 chapters of CAIR and identifies CAIR CAN as being one them.[404] http://www.cairchicago.org/cair-chapters/

CAIR - Canada

P.O. Box 13219 K21 1x4

99 Kakulu Rd., Suite 100

Kanata, ONT K2L 3C8

Main Telephone: 866-524-0004 FREE

Alternate Telephone: 613-254-9704

Fax Number: 613-254-9810

Email: canada@cair-net.org

Website: http://www.caircan.ca - See more at: http://web.archive.org/web/20140413090415/http://www.cairchicago.org/cair-chapters/#sthash.kGWRZxsc.dpuf

- Technical Connections:

  CAIR CAN has used the email address of canada@cair-net.org . This is the same service used by other CAIR USA chapters such as CAIR San Antonio SanAntonio@cair-net.org , CAIR Cleveland http://ohio.cair.com and Care Ohio which also uses ohio@cair-net.org

  CAIR USA posted contact information for its Canadian chapter. Note the 613 Ottawa area calling code and the root of the email address: @ciar-net. QUOTE: CONTACT: Riad Saloojee at 613-254-9704; E-mail: cnada@cair-net.[405]

CORPORATE HISTORY - The corporate history of this organization[406] is:

Corporate Name History

- 2000-07-10 to 2013-06-24
  - COUNCIL ON AMERICAN ISLAMIC RELATIONS (CANADA)
- 2013-06-24 to Present

---

[404] This reference can be seen at http://www.cairchicago.org/cair-chapters/ Viewed 20 June 2017. **Rated A2**.

[405] This information can be seen at http://www.cair.com/press-center/cair-in-the-news/6703-canadian-mp-offers-apology-for-assistant-s-remark.html . Viewed 15 April 2017. **Rated A2.**

[406] https://www.ic.gc.ca/app/scr/cc/CorporationsCanada/fdrlCrpDtls.html?corpId=3784720 . Viewed 20 June 2017. **Rated A2**.

- NATIONAL COUNCIL OF CANADIAN MUSLIMS (NCCM)

The International Relief Fund for the Afflicted and Needy (IRFAN)

IRFAN was set up in the year 2000, ostensibly as a federally registered charity. It was warned by the Canada Revenue Agency (CRA) in 2004 that it appeared to be funding Hamas.

In 2011, the CRA revoked (for cause) the charitable status of IRFAN-Canada. This was due to a series of failures and for funding Hamas which has been listed in Canada as a terrorist group. The short form of the statement as it appears on the CRA website reads:

> "On the basis of our audit, we have concluded that IRFAN-Canada has: ceased to comply with the requirements of the Act for its continued registration; failed to comply with or contravened sections 230 to 231.5 of the Act; issued a receipt for a gift or donation otherwise than in accordance with the Act and the Regulations or that contains false information; and failed to file an information return as required under the Act-[o]ur analysis of the audit information has led the CRA to believe that **IRFAN-Canada provides support to Hamas**, a listed terrorist organization. Our findings indicate that IRFAN-Canada provided over $14.6 million in resources to operating partners that were run by officials of Hamas, openly supported and **provided funding to Hamas**, or have been listed by various jurisdictions because of their support for Hamas or other terrorist entities." (Emphasis added)

In addition to failing to comply and funding a terrorist group, the CRA also noted that IRFAN was raising money by appeals made to the public under misleading circumstances. Specifically, CRA notes that IRFAN requested pledges for money for the 2004 Tsunami disaster, the South-East Asia Earthquake Disaster of 2006, the Indonesian Earthquake of 2006, the Bangladesh Cyclone of 2007, the Burma Cyclone of 2007, the Pakistan Earthquake of 2008 and the Indonesian Earthquake of 2008. The CRA audit discovered that the money raised through these campaigns was not sent to assist those in need. Rather, the money was then mixed with the general monies of IRFAN and used for other activities such as funding terrorism. (Section 2.5 Public Breach Test/Deceptive Funding)[407]

It was also proven that the CRA audit revealed IRFAN was an integral part of the international fund-raising efforts to support Hamas. CRA stated that it is a strong possibility that IRFAN was created to circumvent the CRA's refusal to grant charitable status previously to the Povrel Jerusalem Fund for Human Services (JFHS). The CRA believes there are "strong indicators" that the JFHS acted in Canada on behalf of the American based Holy Land Foundation.[408] The Holy Land Foundation has been the subject of an extensive criminal investigation in the USA which resulted in convictions for funding terrorism.[409]

---

[407] For more information on the deceptive fund-raising efforts of IRFAN see Section 2.5 *Public Breech Test/Deceptive Funding,* (page 22/27) of the CRA report/letter dated 14 December 2010 (file number 3001490). The subject line of the letter was RE: Audit of Registered Charity: International Relief Fund for the Afflicted and Needy (Canada). Viewed 19 June 2017. **Rated A2**.

[408] Page 3/27 of the CRA report/letter dated 14 December 2010 (file number 3001490). *RE: Audit of Registered Charity: International Relief Fund for the Afflicted and Needy (Canada).* Viewed 19 June 2017. **Rated A2**.

[409] See the United States Department of Justice 2009 statement *Federal Judge Hands Downs Sentences in Holy Land Foundation Case, Holy Land Foundation and Leaders Convicted on Providing Material Support to Hamas*

The CRA also stated that clear evidence existed that at their earliest inception, the HLF and JFHS were in close communication, their identities overlapped, and they were part of the North American network established by the Muslim Brotherhood's Palestine Committees to support Hamas.[410] Furthermore, the CRA notes that JFHS and IRFAN had a past pattern (1992-2002) of funding organizations that have been recognized as having links to Hamas and despite its 2004 undertaking, IRFAN continued to do so.[411]

The CRA believes that IRFAN was set up in 2000 to circumvent the refusal of the Government of Canada to grant charitable status to the JFHS. The founding members of the board of directors of IRFAN were Nadeem Siddiqi, Mohamed Farhad Khadim, Reyad Hobba and Mohammad Ammak.[412]

As made clear by the Hamas Covenant itself, Hamas is part of the Muslim Brotherhood.[413] The CRA audit of IRFAN and the Holy Land Foundation trial in the USA make it clear that IRFAN, JFHS and others are part of the various Palestine Committees set up by the Muslim Brotherhood in North America.

It is also a proven point that this support of Hamas goes back to at least 1992. On 2-3 October 1993, five leading members of the US Palestine Committee met at the Marriott Courtyard Hotel in Philadelphia USA for a conference.[414] As it turns out, the meeting was monitored by the FBI, which was already deeply suspicious of the intent of the individuals involved in the meeting. Wiretap transcripts of this meeting were entered into evidence at the 2007 trial of the Holy Land Foundation (HLF) which resulted in convictions and heavy sentences for funding terrorism.[415] The recipient of the funding was Hamas. At the meeting, the role of the Canadian-based Jerusalem Fund for Human Services was discussed.

A Canadian present at this meeting, Rasem Abdel Majid (also known as Abou Basem) discussed the fund raising for Hamas in Canada, which had already been successful. It should be noted that Rasem Abdel Majid was the manager of the Jerusalem Fund for Human Services as well as being the manager for IRFAN throughout the life span of both organizations. The following conversation which concerned funding for Hamas was wiretapped and placed into evidence[416] at the HLF trial:

Terrorist Organization. It is available online at: http://www.justice.gov/opa/pr/2009/May/09-nsd-519.html . Viewed 20 June 2017. **Rated A2**.

[410] See page 15/27 of the CRA report/letter dated 14 December 2010 (file number 3001490). *RE: Audit of Registered Charity: International Relief Fund for the Afflicted and Needy (Canada).* Viewed 19 June 2017. **Rated A2**.

[411] See page 15/27 of the CRA report/letter dated 14 December 2010 (file number 3001490). *RE: Audit of Registered Charity: International Relief Fund for the Afflicted and Needy (Canada).* Viewed 19 June 2017. **Rated A2**.

[412] As listed on the T3010 form of IRFAN as submitted to the CRA for the year 2000. Available on the CRA website.

[413] Section Two of the Covenant begins with the line: *The Islamic Resistance Movement is a branch of the Muslim Brotherhood chapter in Palestine.* The entire Covenant of HAMAS can be seen at: http://www.palestine-studies.org/files/pdf/jps/1734.pdf . Viewed 15 April 2017. **Rated A2**.

[414] For more on this meeting see the IPT report *Omar Ahmad and the Palestine Committee*. It is available online at http://www.investigativeproject.org/documents/misc/635.pdf . Viewed 15 April 2017. **Rated A2.**

[415] For more on this see the FBI statement *Federal Judge Hands Downs Sentences in Holy Land Foundation Case Holy Land Foundation and Leaders Convicted on Providing Material Support to Hamas Terrorist Organization.* The statement is available online at https://archives.fbi.gov/archives/dallas/press-releases/2009/dl052709.htm . Viewed 15 April 2017. **Rated A1.**

[416] Audio file: MTGB 19931002 8.WAV, GOVERNMENT EXHIBIT, Philly Meeting – 15 3:04-CR-240-G U.S. v. HLF, et al. Page 5 of 16 in the written transcript. **Rated A2**.

> Abdel Halim Al Ashqar: "We heard about Jerusalem for Human Services but we didn't hear from our brothers at the (Islamic) Association (for Palestine) about what they do. So, I hope that media and public activism in Canada is mentioned if there is something prepared. It might be first opportunity for some of the brothers to meet people from Canada."
>
> Abdel Halim Al Ashqar "...Now, the second question, brother Abou Basem, is for Canada: how much do you raise annually?"
>
> Abou Basem: "... m. The first half of this year [we raised] 214,000."
>
> Abdel Halim Al Ashqar: "[How about] last year?"
>
> Abou Basem: "This is for '93. From now until June '93, we raised 214,000. In 1992 [we raised] 167 for the entire year."

In 2013, the Government of Canada designated IRFAN as a terrorist entity, effectively closing the operation. IRFAN had continued to operate after losing its charitable status in 2011.

Islamic Relief Canada

The parent organization of Islamic Relief Canada is Islamic Relief Worldwide[417] which was formed in Birmingham, UK. HSBC, the UK's largest bank, cut off Islamic Reliefs accounts due to terrorism funding concerns.[418] Islamic Relief UK was also listed as a terrorist entity by the United Arab Emirates.[419]

Islamic Relief Canada was identified as a Muslim Brotherhood front group in Senate Testimony in Canada.[420]

While the charity does some legitimate work, it has been repeatedly identified that it provides funding directly and indirectly to Muslim Brotherhood front groups such as Hamas.[421] The Muslim Brotherhood itself has been declared to be a terrorist group by several countries including Saudi Arabia, Egypt, the UAE

---

[417] Islamic Relief Canada itself makes this claim and says that the first Islamic Relief office was in Birmingham UK in 1984. For more on this see the photo and statement at http://islamicreliefcanada.org/about/history/ on the Islamic Relief Canada website. Viewed 22 August 2017. **Not rated**.

[418] Dipesh Gadher, *Terror fear makes HSBC cut ties to Muslim charity,* the Times of London, 3 January 2016. The article can be seen online at https://www.thetimes.co.uk/article/terror-fear-makes-hsbc-cut-ties-to-muslim-charity-fgm5d796mlr . Viewed 15 April 2017. **Rated A1.**

[419] The official list is online at http://www.thenational.ae/uae/government/list-of-groups-designated-terrorist-organisations-by-the-uae . Viewed 11 April 2017. **Rated A1.**

[420] See the Ottawa Citizen report by Ian MacLeod *Beware the Muslim Brotherhood, expert warns* at http://ottawacitizen.com/news/politics/beware-of-the-muslim-brotherhood-expert-warns. Viewed 25 July 2017. **Rated A2.** The full Senate Testimony can be seen at http://www.parl.gc.ca/content/sen/committee/412/SECD/52124-E.HTM . Viewed 25 July 2017. **Rated A2.**

[421] *Islamic Relief Worldwide's 2014 Internal Investigation*, NGO Monitor, 11 January 2015. The report can be seen online at http://www.ngo-monitor.org/reports/islamic_relief_worldwide_s_internal_investigation/ . Viewed 11 April 2017. **Rated B2.**

and Russia. Islamic Relief Worldwide operates in more than 40 countries[422] beyond its home base of the United Kingdom. One of those countries is Canada.

Here in Canada, Islamic Relief Canada has had a significant series of connections to the Muslim Brotherhood through its senior staff and board members. In 2014, the United Arab Emirates released a list of some 85 entities that it believes are terrorist organizations or front groups.[423] The list included major terror groups such as Al Qaida, Daesh and the Muslim Brotherhood, as well as the regional and local affiliates.

Dr. Ebtisam Al Ketbi, chairwoman of Emirates Policy Centre explained that:

> "the expanded list of designated terror groups shows the UAE addresses the root causes of the threat of terrorism, which requires the pursuit of a comprehensive international strategy that prevents recruitment."

She further added that:

> "The list includes terrorist groups and Islamist NGOs that are involved in fund raising and health-care operations in areas of contention. Some of these Islamic NGOs are deeply involved in Europe and **North America** and are seen as a source of **trouble specifically related to the Muslim Brotherhood.** Their activities, which also include conferences, **are pro-Muslim Brotherhood**, and the point here is to cast light on their role in acting as gateways to recruitment into terrorist and extremist groups. The UAE's designation of these known terrorist and extremist groups seeks to cast light on their illegal activities that not only threaten UAE interests but also the UAE homeland itself." (Emphasis added)
>
> "The banned groups also include proxy terror actors and front organisations that give others the funding, training, and weapons to carry out terrorist acts."[424]

The UAE list included the Islamic Relief Worldwide, which it describes as "an affiliate of the International Organisation of the Muslim Brotherhood" and its offshoot the Islamic Relief UK in London.[425]

Israel

In June of 2014, Israel "banned a British-based charity from operating in the occupied West Bank, accusing Islamic Relief Worldwide (IRW) of being a source of funding for the Palestinian Hamas Islamist movement."[426] In issuing the ban, Israel stated that charity's chapters, including those in the West Bank

---

[422] This statement can be seen at http://www.islamic-relief.org.uk/news/independent-investigation-of-islamic-relief-operations/ Viewed 20 June 2017. **Rated D4.**

[423] The official list is online at http://www.thenational.ae/uae/government/list-of-groups-designated-terrorist-organisations-by-the-uae . Viewed 11 April 2017. **Rated A1.**

[424] Samir Salama, Associate Editor, *UAE addresses root causes of terror,* Gulf News, 16 November 2017. The article is available online at http://m.gulfnews.com/news/uae/uae-addresses-root-causes-of-terror-1.1413289 . Viewed 20 June 2017. **Rated B2**.

[425] The official list is online at http://www.thenational.ae/uae/government/list-of-groups-designated-terrorist-organisations-by-the-uae . Viewed 11 April 2017. **Rated A1.**

[426] *Israel bans UK-based Muslim charity accused of funding Hamas*, Reuters, 19 June 2014. The article is available online at http://uk.reuters.com/article/2014/06/19/uk-palestinians-israel-charities-idUKKBN0EU1FE20140619 . Viewed 20 June 2017. **Rated B2**

and Gaza Strip, were run by Hamas members. "The IRW is one of the sources of Hamas's funding and a means for raising funds from various countries in the world. We do not intend to allow it to function and abet terrorist activity against Israel."[427]

Of note, Islamic Relief USA, the sister organization to Islamic Relief Canada, had its charity status lowered from 4 stars to 2 stars by Charity Navigator for fraudulent bookkeeping from 2001 to 2010. For instance, Islamic Relief USA gave the appearance of having received over $160 million in donations in 2010.[428] When it used corrected valuation techniques in 2011, IR-USA reported contributions of only $60 million.[429] Islamic Relief USA later explained that the variations may have been related to market-value purchase pries, its Gift in Kind program, handling and related costs and accounting practices.[430]

In 2014, Islamic Relief Worldwide's donation page was removed from Charities Aid Foundation website. The CAF would not comment directly as to why it ceased to have an affiliation with Islamic Relief, but it did release a statement which said:

> "It would be wrong for us to discuss our processes, but like any financial intermediary, we have robust systems in place to ensure we comply with our UK and international obligations to protect against fraud, money laundering, bribery and corruption and terrorism financing while working with charitable organisations to support their work in conflict zones and elsewhere."[431]

The Financial Post of Canada also removed Islamic Relief Canada from its "25 Charities of the Year" list stating that it was "pulled from this year's list since its international arm has been banned elsewhere (though not in Canada) for allegedly funneling funds to the terrorist organization Hamas."[432]

The CEO of Islamic Relief Canada, Sallah Hamdani, was suddenly removed in 2014 for unknown reasons. He is the brother of Hussein Hamdani who was removed from the Cross-Cultural Round Table, partly for his role in co-writing the Muslim Student Association manual on how to politicize university student politics and take financial control. No clear accounting has ever been made of either decision which saw

---

[427] *Israel bans UK-based Muslim charity accused of funding Hamas*, Reuters, 19 June 2014. The article is available online at http://uk.reuters.com/article/2014/06/19/uk-palestinians-israel-charities-idUKKBN0EU1FE20140619 . Viewed 20 June 2017. **Rated B2.**

[428] *Leadership shuffle at U.S. Islamic charities*, Money Jihad, 09 November 2017. The article is available online at https://moneyjihad.wordpress.com/2014/11/09/leadership-shuffle-at-u-s-islamic-charities/ . Viewed 20 June 2017. **Rated C2**.

[429] *Islamic Relief USA Replaces CEO; Charity Once Part Of A Michelle Obama Initiative*, The Global Muslim Brotherhood Daily Watch, 11 November 2014. The article is available online at http://www.globalmbwatch.com/2014/11/11/islamic-relief-usa-replaces-ceo-charity-part-michelle-obama-initiative/ . Viewed 20 June 2017. **Rated C3**.

[430] William Barrett, *Islamic Relief USA Says Drug Donations Fell 91%*, 14 September 2012, Forbes. The article is available online at https://www.forbes.com/sites/williampbarrett/2012/09/14/islamic-relief-usa-says-drug-donations-fell-91/#5ecf929e1493 . Viewed 17 November 2017. **Rated B2.**

[431] *Islamic Relief's donation page is removed from CAF website*, Civil Society News, 03 September 2014. The article is available online at http://www.civilsociety.co.uk/fundraising/news/content/18091/islamic_reliefs_donation_page_is_removed_from_caf_website . Viewed 20 June 2017. **Rated B3**.

[432] Claire Brownell, *Financial Post's Charities of the Year: Why these 25 are worth your donations (and which ones we're cautious about)*, The Financial Post, 12 December 2014. The article is available online at http://business.financialpost.com/news/financial-post-charities-of-the-year-2014 . Viewed 20 June 2017. **Rated B2**.

Mr. Hamdani removed from his position. In an interview, Sallah Hamdani noted that "All universities across Canada have Muslim Students' Associations or Islamic Relief chapters that raise funds, advocate, organize and support our projects."[433] The Muslim Student Association is a Muslim Brotherhood front organization that does education and recurring work for the Muslim Brotherhood.[434] (Chapter 14)

Dr. Essam al-Haddad

Dr. Essam al-Haddad was a co-founder and later the head of Islamic Relief in the United Kingdom. He figures prominently in the "who is who" in the world of the Muslim Brotherhood.[435] Essam al-Haddad is also the father of Gehad al-Haddad who is a spokesman for the Muslim Brotherhood.[436] He would become the advisor for security and international affairs for the Muslim Brotherhood's President of Egypt and a member of the Muslim Brotherhood's Guidance Bureau.[437] As of late 2017, he is in jail in Egypt.

According to a Washington Institute biography, he has held many key positions related to the Muslim Brotherhood.[438]

- Position: Head of the Office of the President; member of the Muslim Brotherhood Guidance Office,
- Occupation: Doctor, businessman in 2012, Islamic Relief in the UK has had its account closed while at the same time any further zakat (charitable/religious) donations to its account were blocked by Swiss bank UBS.[439] This was done due to terror funding concerns.[440]

---

433 *Islamic Relief Canada, Member Profile July-August 2013*. This article can be seen online at http://www.ccic.ca/members/profiles/IRC_2013-08_e.php . Viewed 20 June 2017. **Not rated.**

434 *Is the Muslim Student Association a Recruiting Point for Extremism?* See Chapter 14.

435 Kyle Shideler, *Funding terrorists: Giving money to groups tied to terror finance must end*, the Washington Times, 29 November 2017. The article is available online at http://www.washingtontimes.com/news/2015/nov/29/kyle-shideler-funding-terrorists-must-end/ . Viewed 20 June 2017. **Rated C2.**

436 *Brotherhood spokesman Gehad al-Haddad held in Egypt,* BBC News, 17 September 2017. The article can be seen online at http://www.bbc.com/news/world-middle-east-24132046 . Viewed 17 November 2017. **Rated B2.**

437 Eric Trager, Katie Kiraly, Cooper Klose, and Eliot Calhoun, *Who's Who in Egypt's Muslim Brotherhood,* The Washington Institute, September 2012. The article is available online at http://www.washingtoninstitute.org/policy-analysis/view/whos-who-in-the-muslim-brotherhood . Viewed 11 April 2017. **Rated A1.**

438 Eric Trager, Katie Kiraly, Cooper Klose, and Eliot Calhoun, *Who's Who in Egypt's Muslim Brotherhood,* The Washington Institute, September 2012. The article is available online at http://www.washingtoninstitute.org/policy-analysis/view/whos-who-in-the-muslim-brotherhood#EssamalHaddad. Viewed 20 June 2017. **Rated A1**.

439 Niki May Young, *Banking sector nerves blocking international relief, says Islamic Relief FD*, Civil Society Finance, 08 November 2012. The article is available online at https://web.archive.org/web/20121124044239/http://www.civilsociety.co.uk/finance/news/content/13757/banking_sector_nerves_blocking_international_relief_says_islamic_relief_finance_director . Viewed 20 June 2017. **Rated C2.**

440 *UBS closes Islamic Relief account over terror risk*, Money Jihad, 08 November 2012. The article is available online at https://moneyjihad.wordpress.com/2012/11/09/ubs-closes-islamic-relief-account-over-terror-risk/ . Viewed 20 June 2017. **Rated C3**. See also the very last line in the article *HSBC to close bank account of Muslim charity working Gaza,* Civil Society News, 25 July 2014. The article is available online at http://www.civilsociety.co.uk/finance/news/content/17903/hsbc_to_close_bank_account_of_muslim_charity_working_in_gaza . Viewed 20 June 2017. **Rated C2**.

The Islamic Society of North America

The Islamic Society of North America (ISNA) was incorporated in Indiana in 1981.[441] A number of the original members of the ISNA were adherents of the Muslim Brotherhood.[442] Dr. Jamal Badawi, who was one of the founders of the Muslim American Society (MAS) also served on ISNA's Shura Council. Jamal Badawi has been identified by the Muslim Brotherhood itself as one of its most important leaders in North America. Of note, the MAS has since been identified as a terrorist entity by the United Arab Emirates.[443]

The ISNA grew into a large organization with chapters in Canada and the USA. It can be seen that ISNA Canada is a chapter of ISNA USA, although ISNA Canada has tried to deny this with a series of confusing statements following ISNA Canada's loss of charitable status for its Development Fund in 2011.

Page four of the ISNA 1997 Annual Report makes the connections clear with this statement:

> "Since its inception as a student body in 1963 and its graduation to a national community organization, **ISNA has maintained a continental stance**, and the "American" in ISNA-sponsored activities relates to both the **United States and Canada**. Consequently, the various ISNA conferences, like the ISNA Annual Convention, **have due representation from both countries**." (Emphasis added).

The same 1997 Annual Report also included a statement from Ebrahim Lunat, the Certified Public Accountant who oversaw the financial aspects of the report. He stated that:

> "The accompanying financial statements show an amount of $434,682 due to ISNA Canada which is a Canadian tax-exempt organization closely affiliated with ISNA/USA."

The relationship between the two organizations was close as noted by an archived "ISNA Canada Membership Application" which includes as "Membership Benefits" a "Discount of ISNA Annual Convention (USA) Registration" and the "Right to vote during ISNA and ISNA Canada elections.[444]

The Canada Revenue Agency shows a June 2011 entry for the Islamic Society of North America and gives its Effective Date of Status as 1983-01-01. The address is listed as: 2200 South Sheridan Way, Mississauga, Ontario, CA L5J2M4. The BN/Registered Number is 118971886RR000118.[445]

The ISNA Canada mission statement uses the terms "ISNA" and "ISNA Canada" interchangeably. When viewed on 5 March 2017, it included this statement:

---

[441] Office of the Secretary of State of Indiana, *"Articles of Incorporation, Islamic Society of North America,"* filed July 14, 1981. **Rated A2**.

[442] USA v. Holy Land Foundation for Relief and Development, et al, 3:04-CR-240-G (TX ND), Government Exhibit Elbarasse Search 1. **Rated A2**.

[443] The official list is online at http://www.thenational.ae/uae/government/list-of-groups-designated-terrorist-organisations-by-the-uae . Viewed 11 April 2017. **Rated A1.**

[444] The membership benefits can be seen at: https://web.archive.org/web/20110430061022/http://www.isnacanada.com/isna/membership.html Viewed 5 March 2017. **Rated A2.** See also the membership form at https://web.archive.org/web/20091229192111/http://www.isnacanada.com/doc/isna_memform.pdf Viewed 20 June 2017. **Rated A2.**

[445] Canada Revenue Agency Listing for "Islamic Society of North America."

> "ISNA is dedicated to working on the national level to promote and protect the Muslims interests **in North America**." [446] (Emphasis added)

It is reasonable to believe that ISNA has close associations to funding operations for Hamas. ISNA and the North American Islamic Trust (NAIT) both appeared as unindicted co-conspirators in the Holy Land Relief terrorism funding trials. Despite their attempts to have their names removed from the process, U.S. District Court Judge Jorge Solis said in a 1 July 2009, ruling[447] that:

> "The government has produced ample evidence to establish the associations of CAIR, **ISNA**, NAIT, the Islamic Association for Palestine, and with Hamas." (Emphasis added)

It can also be seen that ISNA Canada has been repeatedly tied directly to issues of concern about the promotion of terrorist groups or the funding of terrorism. The most recent and well documented of these is the Canada Revenue Agency statement of September 2013 which revoked the charitable status of the ISNA Development Foundation.[448] Specifically, the CRA had concerns that the charity's money "may have been used to support the political efforts of Jamaat-e-Islami and/or its armed wing, Hizbul Mujahideen."[449]

ISNA Canada has a previous history with the Jamaat-e-Islami such as when they invited the head of Jamaat-e-Islami to be a speaker at the 2008 34th Annual Convention. The conference was called "Our Youth, Our Future: Path to Paradise." The conference was endorsed by CAIR CAN, the ICNA, the Muslim Association of Canada (MAC) and the event was sponsored by Human Concern International (HCI).

Invited to the conference was Zazi Hussain Hamad (also reported as Qazi Hussain Hamad). He was the head of Jamaat-e-Islami in Pakistan at that time. The group has been banned as a terrorist group in numerous countries. He was intended to have been a speaker on both the Saturday and Sunday dates (23 May/24 May 2008).[450] Mr. Hamad did not make it to the convention as the Canadian government pulled his visa shortly before the conference after a complaint from the NGO Canadian Coalition for Democracies (CCD).[451]

---

[446] The ISNA mission statement can be seen at http://www.isna.ca/1/about-us/our-mission . Viewed 5 February 2017. **Rated A1**.

[447] A copy of the ruling is available online at http://www.investigativeproject.org/documents/case_docs/1424.pdf . Viewed 15 April 2017. **Rated A1.**

[448] A PDF version of the 36-page letter from CRA is available online at: http://www.thestar.com/content/dam/thestar/static_images/IDF-complete-audit-letter.pdf . Viewed 15 April 2017. **Rated A2.**

[449] *The Canada Revenue Agency Revokes the Registration of the ISNA Development Foundation as a Charity*, Market Wired, 20 September 2013. The article can be seen online at http://www.marketwired.com/press-release/canada-revenue-agency-revokes-registration-isna-development-foundation-as-charity-1833203.htm . Viewed 20 June 2017. **Rated A2**.

[450] http://canadafreepress.com/article/ccd-urges-immediate-action-on-eligibility-of-qazi-hussain-ahmad-to-enter-ca Viewed 15 April 2017. **Rated B2.**

[451] *Canada Denies Visa for Leader of Jamaat-e-Islam To Attend ISNA Conference*, The Global Muslim Brotherhood Daily Watch, 22 June 2008. The article is available online at http://globalmbreport.org/?p=942 . Viewed 20 June 2017. **Rated B2**.

In July 2013, ISNA issued a press announcement to clarify its position on allegations that ISNA Canada was affiliated with ISNA HQ in the USA. The announcement stated that ISNA and its Islamic Development Foundation (IDF), a department of ISNA, were separate from ISNA Canada and its IDF.[452]

The statement read:

> "ISNA Canada and Islamic Development Foundation (IDF) in Canada are federally registered charities in Canada. It is important to note that the leadership and management of both of these organizations in Canada are separate from ISNA and its IDF (a department of ISNA), registered in the United States. There has been no links of authority or responsibility between the United States and Canadian organizations for a few decades, despite the similarity of names.
>
> The bylaws of the Islamic Society of North America (ISNA) do allow Canadians to become members and elect an officer designated as vice-president (Canada) who sits on the executive council of ISNA, headquartered in Plainfield, Indiana. However, these members are individuals and have direct relationship with the Indiana-based ISNA and its IDF. No communication or relationship with them flows through the Mississauga-based ISNA Canada or its IDF." [453]
>
> The announcement acknowledges that ISNA and ISNA Canada share officials but denies any "**communication or relationship with them flows through the Mississauga based ISNA Canada** or its IDF."[454]

The statement was somewhat less-than-clear. Below are some examples of ISNA and ISNA Canada sharing officials which shows a considerable overlap in the operations of these two closely related organizations.

- Dr. Syed Imitiaz Ahmad is President of ISNA Canada and serves on the ISNA Canada Board (Majlis-As-Shura). According to Ahmad's bio on the ISNA-CAN website, his past positions have included Vice President and President of ISNA.[455] ISNA's incorporation documents cited Ahmad as one of the founding board of directors of ISNA. The address listed for Ahmad is: 373 Randolph Ave., Windsor, Ont., Canada;[456]

- Pervez Nasim is secretary of ISNA Canada and serves on the ISNA Canada Board.[457] Nasim also serves on the ISNA's Board of Directors and Executive Council;[458]

---

[452] *"ISNA Clarifies its Position on ISNA Canada," ISNA Special Announcement*, July 26, 2013. **Not Rated**.

[453] *"ISNA Clarifies its Position on ISNA Canada," ISNA Special Announcement*, July 26, 2013. **Not Rated.**

[454] *"ISNA Clarifies its Position on ISNA Canada," ISNA Special Announcement*, July 26, 2013. **Not Rated.**

[455] See the *"ISNA-Canada Board of Directors 2015."* The list is available online at http://www.isna.ca/downloads/misc/ISNA_Majlis/20150608MergedMajlisBios.pdf . Viewed 20 June 2017. **Rated B2.**

[456] *ISNA's Articles of Incorporation*, July 14, 1981.

[457] See the *"ISNA-Canada Board of Directors 2015."* The list is available online at http://www.isna.ca/downloads/misc/ISNA_Majlis/20150608MergedMajlisBios.pdf . Viewed 20 June 2017. **Rated B2.**

[458] See the *"Islamic Society of North America Board of Directors & Executive Council."* The list is available online at http://www.isna.net/board-ofdirectors/ . Viewed 20 June 2017. **Rated B2.**

- Abdallah Idris Ali is the Executive Director of ISNA Canada.[459] Idris is also identified as a director of the ISNA-IDB Education Trust (Canada).[460] According to his online bio, "[Abdallah Idris Ali] was appointed to the Executive Council of the Islamic Society of North America (ISNA) then elected to its consultative body (Majlis Ash-Shura) and later served as President of ISNA for the two maximum terms (1992 – 1997)."[461] Idris is listed as a featured speaker at the 54th Annual ISNA Convention from June 30-July 3, 2017 in Chicago, IL;[462]

- ISNA's Executive Council for 1997-1998 comprised of: Syed Imtiaz Ahmad (Vice President-Canada), Anwarul Haque (Canada-West Zone Rep.), Abdullah Hamoud (Canada-East Zone Rep.);[463]ISNA's Majlis Ash-Shura for 2002-2003 comprised of Syed Imtiaz Ahmad, Vice President-Canada. ISNA's Executive Council for 2002-2003 consisted of Syed Imtiaz Ahmed, Vice President-Canada, Usama Al-Shiraida, West Zone Rep-Canada;[464]

- In 2010, Dr. Mohamed Bekkari, Vice President of ISNA Canada was elected to ISNA's Majlis Ash-Shura. Bekkari's online bio states that he "has been involved with ISNA (MSA, ISNA Continental, ISNA-Canada) since the late 1970s"[465], and

- ISNA's Majlis Ash-Shura (2002-2003) lists Syed Imtiaz Ahmad, Vice President—Canada. The ISNA Majlis Ash-Shura (1997-1998) included Syed Imtiaz Ahmad (Vice President—Canada).

ISNA Funding

When interviewed for a 2004 article on the Saudi funding of institutions in Canada, the centre denied receiving any Saudi funding.[466]

However, it was later revealed that in 2002 the Saudi Ministry of Culture and Information had noted that the late King Fahd of Saudi Arabia had given the centre a one-time grant of US$ 5.0 million, followed by an annual grant of US$ 1.5 million dollars.

---

[459] http://www.isna.ca/1/about-us/staff

[460] See the staff list for ISNA at *"Islamic Society of North America Board of Directors & Executive Council."* The list available on line at http://www.isna.net/board-ofdirectors/ . Viewed 20 June 2017. **Rated B2.**

[461] See the biography of Abdalla Idris Ali at http://www.manal.ca/sites/default/files/BIOGRAPHY%20OF%20ABDALLA%20IDRIS%20ALI%20-%202009.pdf . It is available online at 20 June 2017. **Not rated.**

[462] 54TH ANNUAL ISNA CONVENTION, HOPE AND GUIDANCE THROUGH THE QURAN. The convention outline can be seen at http://www.isna.net/54th-annual-isna-convention/ . Viewed 20 June 2017. **Rated B2.**

[463] 1997 Annual Report (Dec. 21, 1996-Dec. 31, 1997), Presented at ISNA's 35th Annual Convention, Sept. 4-7, 1998, St. Louis, Missouri. **Rated B2.**

[464] *"2002 Annual Report, Jan. 1, 2002-Dec. 31, 2002,"* Presented at ISNA's 40th Annual Convention, Aug. 30, 2003, Chicago, Illinois. **Rated B2.**

[465] ISNA – CANADA BOARD OF DIRECTORS 2015. The list can be seen at http://www.isna.ca/downloads/misc/ISNA_Majlis/20150608MergedMajlisBios.pdf. Viewed 20 June 2017. **Rated B2.**

[466] Friday, July 30, 2004, *Saudis fund radicals in Canada: Centre propagating Islamic extremism given millions: U.S.*, Robert Fife, Ottawa Citizen, http://tarekfatah.com/ottawa-citizen-saudis-fund-radicals-in-canada-1-5-million-annually-to-just-one-toronto-mosque/ . Viewed 15 April 2017. **Rated A2.**

Katherine Bullock, a convert to Islam, author/editor[467] and a spokesperson for the ISNA stated to a journalist that the centre had received funding from the Islamic Development Bank, and later denied this in an email to the same journalist. Ironically, the ISNA's own website stated that the funding had in fact occurred.[468] In 2005, ISNA also received a $275,000 grant for their co-located high school as well as money for a scholarship program.[469]

Katherine Bullock of ISNA is the same person who, as a Lecturer in the Department of Political Science, University of Toronto at Mississauga[470], stated in a speech that:

> "from an Islamic point of view this absolutely **nothing radical about wanting Caliphate or wanting Sharia**. These are completely normal traditional points of view." [471] (Emphasis added).

ISNA Legal Problems

It can be assessed as well that that the ISNA has a serious internal corruption problem that resulted in money collected for the poor being squandered.[472] An audit found that of the $810,777 collected over four years, only $196,460 went to aid the poor. The rest of the money was spent on non-charity matters, such as funding the health care programs of two daughters of an employee, even though they did not work there. The problems had been ongoing for several years, but culminated in an audit that was presented in 2010.

In May 2015, the ISNA Canada school made news when it objected to two girls on an opposing boy's soccer team. The girls had been allowed to play in the boy's league due to the small size of their school and the lack of a girl's team. The ISNA objected to the girls playing for "religious reasons" and the two girls were forced to sit out the second half of the game, contrary to league rules and the Charter of Rights and Freedoms of Canada.[473]

Islamic Circle of North America - Lovers of Death

---

[467] She is the editor of the book *Muslim Women Activists in North America: Speaking for Ourselves*. (2005)

[468] Marina Jiménez and Omar El Akkad, *Values at heart of Islamic tensions*, Globe and Mail, Published Tuesday, 08 November 2005, 12:00 AM EST. http://www.theglobeandmail.com/news/national/values-at-heart-of-islamic-tensions/article989709/?page=all . Viewed 15 April 2017. **Rated B2.**

[469] Marina Jiménez and Omar El Akkad, *Values at heart of Islamic tensions*, Globe and Mail, Published Tuesday, 08 November 08 2005, 12:00 AM EST. http://www.theglobeandmail.com/news/national/values-at-heart-of-islamic-tensions/article989709/?page=all . Viewed 15 April 2017. **Rated B2.**

[470] Katherine Bullock, "Katherine Bullock," *University of Toronto Mississauga*,. The article can be seen online at https://www.utm.utoronto.ca/political-science/katherine-bullock Viewed 22 May 2017. **Rated B1.**

[471] For the speech see *ISIS, Violence and the Politics of Deradicalization.* This is available online at http://digitalcommons.osgoode.yorku.ca/video_lectures/12/ . Viewed 15 April 2017. **Rated A1.**

[472] Jesse Mclean, *Muslim charity squandered money for poor.* 20 January 2011, The Toronto Star. This article is available online at: http://www.thestar.com/news/gta/2011/01/20/muslim_charity_squandered_money_for_poor.html . Viewed 24 July 2017. **Rated B2.**

[473] *Muslim school which objected to girls on boys soccer team told to abide by rules,* Diana Mehta, The Canadian Press, Published Friday, May 29, 2015 5:25PM EDT. The article can be seen online at http://www.ctvnews.ca/canada/muslim-school-which-objected-to-girls-on-boys-soccer-team-told-to-abide-by-rules-1.2397987 . Viewed 15 April 2017. **Rated A1.**

The Islamic Circle of North America operated in Canada and the USA and has a program to extend its Islamist influence into Mexico and Central America. Its conferences, often jointly run with the Muslim American Society, are well attended. 18,000 people attended the 2014 joint ICNA/MAS conference.[474] The relationship between the ICNA and the MAS has been described as a "particularly close relationship."[475] The MAS has been listed as a terrorist entity by the government of the United Arab Emirates.[476]

The ICNA (Islamic Circle of North America) has offices in Canada and the USA. Each of them also has a youth wing and a children's wing. The youth wing in Canada is called "Young Muslims in Canada." Its website (http://web.youngmuslims.ca/) provides reading and references to a long list of Muslim Brotherhood figures such as the founder of the Muslim Brotherhood Hassan al-Banna as well as Dr. Yusuf Qaradawi and Sayyid Qutb. Dr. Qaradawi holds a prominent intellectual role in the Muslim Brotherhood and stated himself that he grew up in its traditions.[477] Sayyid Qutb was a key figure of the Muslim Brotherhood in the 1950s and 1960s, and was executed for his role in the attempted overthrow of the government of the late President Nasser of Egypt. His written works such as In the Shade of the Quran and Milestones retain a high profile in Muslim Brotherhood circles to this day.

The ICNA Canada website says that it has three divisions which are the "ICNA Canada Sisters Wing, Young Muslims Sisters and Young Muslims Brothers." [478]

In 2007, the Young Muslims in Canada organization was described in the press as:

> "Mississauga-based Young Muslims of Canada is a grassroots organization that works towards outreach, education and development, and service was started in 1995. Syed Reza, 25, the national coordinator for the organization, said Muslim youths are at times at odds with their surroundings, and the problem has to be addressed by the community as a whole." [479]

When promoting itself to potential youth members, the Young Muslims in Canada website offers the following:

> "Who are we? An Islamic organization working for and through the Muslim youth in Canada. **Our aim is the establishment of Islam in North America in its entirety and comprehensiveness.** We work towards the spiritual, moral, intellectual, and social revival of Muslim youth through Dawah

---

[474] The 2014 convention report for the joint ICNA/MAS conference can be seen at http://messageinternational.org/38th-annual-icna-mas-convention-report/ . Viewed 15 April 2017. **Rated B2.**

[475] The report that made this description can be seen at https://www.globalmbwatch.com/2008/06/22/canada-denies-visa-for-leader-of-jamaat-e-islam-to-attend-isna-conference/ . Viewed 15 April 2017. **Rated B2.**

[476] A full list of the terrorist entities can be seen in the article of 14 November 2014 *UAE publishes list of terrorist organizations: Cabinet decision includes Al Qaida, Daesh and the Muslim Brotherhood.* The article can be seen at http://www.thenational.ae/uae/government/list-of-groups-designated-terrorist-organisations-by-the-uae . Viewed 15 April 2017. **Rated A1**.

[477] In an introduction to one of his books. Dr. Qaradawi states: However, in most examples I will be citing the Muslim Brotherhood, because that is the movement where I grew up; I experienced all its hardships and good times, and shared in many of the events it witnessed over almost a half-century. See the Islam Basics Online article at http://www.islambasics.com/view.php?bkID=48&chapter=1 . Viewed 20 June 2017. **Rated C3**.

[478] See the ICNA website at http://icnacanada.net/about-2/divisions/ Viewed 20 June 2017. **Rated B2**.

[479] Radhika Panjwani, Young Muslims divided over wearing the hijab, Mississauga Community, 13 December 2007. The article is available online at http://www.mississauga.com/community-story/3120558-young-muslims-divided-over-wearing-the-hijab/. Viewed 20 June 2017. **Rated C3.**

(invitation to Islam), Tarbiyah (education & training), Tazkiyah (personal development), and community involvement and activism." [480] (Emphasis added)

A variety of articles in their online library of books provides insight into what is being presented to the youths involved. The article written by Hassan al-Banna with the simple title of "Jihad" has a preface written by Dr. A. M. A. Fahmy of the International Islamic Forum. In the preface[481] Dr. Fahmy notes the following:

> "Though jihad may be a part of the answer to the problems of the ummah, it is an extremely important part. Jihad is to offer ourselves to Allah for His Cause. **Indeed, every person should according to Islam prepare himself/herself for jihad and every person should eagerly and patiently wait for the day when Allah will call them to show their willingness to sacrifice their lives.** We should all ask ourselves if there is a quicker way to heaven? It is with this in mind that this booklet is being published." [482] (Emphasis added).

In the paper views worthy of note by Hassan al-Banna are presented on the Young Muslims in Canada website:

> "My brothers! The ummah that knows how to die a noble and honourable death is granted an exalted life in this world and eternal felicity in the next. Degradation and dishonour are the results of the love of this world and the fear of death.
>
> Therefore, prepare for jihad and be the **lovers of death**. Life itself shall come searching after you. (Emphasis added).
>
> You should yearn for an honourable death and you will gain perfect happiness. May Allah grant myself and yours the honour of martyrdom in His way!"

As one observer notes about the overall indoctrination of young Muslims living in Canada:

> "Young minds are encouraged to feel hostility for their Canadian homeland in Sayyid Qutb's Milestones which propounds that "any place where the Islamic Shariah is not enforced and where Islam is not dominant becomes the home of Hostility [Dar-ul-Harb, more precisely translated as the House of War] for both the Muslim and the Dhimmi [religious minorities tolerated by Muslims in exchange of a special tax]" and that "A Muslim will remain prepared to fight against it…".[483]

---

[480] This statement has been archived on the World Wide Web and can be seen online at http://web.archive.org/web/20041230155029/http://www.youngmuslims.org/about/ . Viewed 22Augusst 2017. **Rated B3**.

[481] This same preface also shows up on a Facebook site with the title "Return of The Khilafa before 1445 A.H. In sha Allaah." The Facebook site appears to be calling for the return of a caliphate before 1445 A.H. which means 2024 C.E. This statement can be seen at https://www.facebook.com/ReturnOfTheKhilafaBefore1445AhInShaAllaah . Viewed 20 June 2017. **Rated C3**.

[482] See a reference to this online at https://openparliament.ca/committees/public-safety/41-2/59/thomas-quiggin-1/only/. Viewed 20 June 2017. **Rated B2**.

[483] For more on this subject see *The Radical Indoctrination of Canadian Muslim Youth* which is available online at http://davidouellette.net/2005/04/06/the-radical-indoctrination-of-canadian-muslim-youth/ . Viewed 22Augusst 2017. **Rated B2**.

Iranian Khomeneists

The Iranian theocracy remains listed as one of three global state sponsors of terrorism, along with Syria and Sudan, according to the US State Department.[484] Canada also lists the Iranian Quds Force as a terrorist entity[485] and states that:

> "[the Quds Force] is [the] clandestine branch of Iran's Islamic Revolutionary Guard Corps (IRGC) responsible for extraterritorial operations, and for exporting the Iranian Revolution through activities such as facilitating terrorist operations."

In addition, Iran also has one of the most dismal human rights records of any country. Human Rights Watch and others say that the human rights situation in Iran is "dire."[486] Women, gays and minorities are the most cruelly persecuted.

It can be assessed that the Khomeneist Iranian (Shia) theocracy has worked diligently since 1979 to export its form of politicized Islam to the rest of the world. The first efforts were in Pakistan, even as the 1979 revolution was unfolding. The violence that gripped the country during the 1980s and 1990s was largely a result of the radicalization of the Shia by the Iranian Khomeneist movement. With the formation of Pakistan as a country in 1947, the Shia were a minority, but there are no indications of any widespread or systemic persecution or violence against the Shia until the late 1970s and early 1980s.[487]

In Canada, an informed opinion would suggest that the influence of the Iranian government can be seen in many ways. One glaring example was the Iranian government opening the Iranian Cultural Centre on Sheppard Avenue, Toronto. The centre had its incorporation papers filed on 16 January 2008. One of the three directors listed was Fazel Larijani, at the time cultural attaché at the Iranian embassy in Ottawa. Fazel Larijani is one of the (in)famous Larijani brothers of Iran.[488] His father was Grand Ayatollah Hashem Amoli. His brother Sadeq is married to Grand Ayatollah Vahid Khorasami, while his brother Ali is married to the daughter of Ayatollah Mortaza Motehari, said to be Grand Ayatollah Ruhollah Khomeini's most revered student.

Fazel is also the brother of Ali Larijani, speaker of the Iranian parliament, and Ayatollah Sadegh Larijani, head of the country's judiciary.[489] As noted in TIME Magazine, Mohammad Javad Larijani, a Berkeley-

---

[484] The US State Department 2016 report on terrorism can be seen at https://www.state.gov/documents/organization/258249.pdf . Viewed 16 April 2017. **Rated A1.**

[485] The Canadian Government's full listing of terrorist entities can be seen at https://www.publicsafety.gc.ca/cnt/ntnl-scrt/cntr-trrrsm/lstd-ntts/crrnt-lstd-ntts-en.aspx . Viewed 16 April 2017. **Rated A1.**

[486] A 2015 Human Rights Watch report on women's rights on Iran can be seen at https://www.hrw.org/news/2015/10/28/womens-rights-iran . Viewed 16 April 2017. **Rated B2.**

[487] For more on the issue of sectarian violence in Pakistan see Muhammad Qasim Zaman, *Sectarianism in Pakistan: The Radicalization of Shi'i and Sunni Identities,* Modern Asian Studies 32, 3 (1998) pp. 689-716, Cambridge University Press, UK. **Rated C3**.

[488] Nour Samaha, *The Brothers Larijani: A sphere of power, As the country gears up for the elections, Al Jazeera takes a look at one of Iran's most influential political families*, Last Modified: 09 Jun 2013 12:04. The article can be seen online at http://www.aljazeera.com/indepth/spotlight/2013/06/2013628374847373.html . Viewed 20 June 2017. **Rated C3**.

[489] Sam Grewal, *Is Iranian government tied to Toronto cultural centre?* 14 April 2010, the Toronto Star. The article can be viewed online at

educated mathematician, has been a member of parliament, Deputy Foreign Minister and adviser to Supreme Leader Ali Khamenei. Bagher Larijani, a physician, has served as Deputy Minister of Health.[490]

Another example was the Iranian "Cultural Center" located in Ottawa. It was owned by the Mobin Foundation which is an arm of the Iranian Revolutionary Guards Council. Its ownership had been transferred from the Fatima Cultural Activities to the Mobin Foundation in 2001.[491] The property was later seized as part of a list of Iranian Government assets[492] under the C-CAT[493] sponsored Justice for Victims of Terrorism Act as part of a terrorism case where the government of Iran had been funding a terrorist group (Hamas in this case).[494]

It is reasonable to assess that a further example is the Iranian Cultural Association of Carleton University, which helped sponsor the conference attended by Imam Rizvi of the Jaffari Mosque in Toronto. The conference was run by Ehsan Mohammadi. Mohammadi is the son of the Iranian cultural counsellor at the Embassy of Iran, Hamid Mohammadi arrived in Canada in 2011 and left when the Iranian embassy staff were expelled. Hamid Mohammadi was shown on an Iran-based website, speaking in an interview about Iran's plan to win the hearts and minds of Iranians living in Canada[495] and telling Iranian-Canadians to "occupy high-level key positions" and "resist being melted into the dominant Canadian culture."[496]

The most glaring single example, however, might be the Shia Ithna Asheri Jamaat, otherwise known as the Thornhill Mosque or the Jaffari Mosque which is located at 9000 Bathurst Street in Toronto. It is reasonable to believe that the Imam and resident Alim of the mosque, Muhammad Rizvi, is a follower and outright supporter of the late Ayatollah Khomeini of Iran. On 2 June 2012, Imam Rizvi of the Jaffari Mosque travelled from Toronto to Ottawa to be the keynote speaker at Carleton University. This was in

---

http://www.thestar.com/news/gta/2010/04/14/is_iranian_government_tied_to_toronto_cultural_centre.html . Viewed 03 October 2017. **Rated B2.**

[490] Robin Wright, *Will Iran's 'Kennedys' Challenge Ahmadinejad?*, Time Magazine, Monday, Aug. 17, 2009. The article can be seen online at http://content.time.com/time/magazine/article/0,9171,1917720,00.html . Viewed 20 June 2017. **Rated B2.**

[491] Official land registry documents list Mahmood Khedmatgozar as president of the Mobin Foundation and Lida Madarshahian as director. See Michael Petrou, *Heroes' Welcome planned for expelled Iranian diplomats,* Macleans Magazine, 12 September 2012. The article is available online at http://www.macleans.ca/authors/michael-petrou/heroes-welcome-planned-for-expelled-iranian-diplomats/ . Viewed 20 June 2017. **Rated B2.**

[492] Stewart Bell, *Canadian bank accounts linked to Iranian government frozen as terror victims seek damages*, The National Post, 17 September 2013. The article and account information can be seen online at http://news.nationalpost.com/2013/09/17/canadian-bank-accounts-linked-to-iranian-government-frozen-as-terror-victims-seek-damages/ . Viewed 20 June 2017. **Rated B2.**

[493] C-CAT is the Canadian Coalition Against Terror. It is comprised of Canadian terror victims, counterterrorism professionals, lawyers and other individuals dedicated to building bridges between the private and public sectors in the battle against terrorism and to assisting terror victims in rebuilding their lives. For more on C-CAT see Annex H.

[494] Adrian Humphreys, *Iran's Canadian assets frozen over $13M U.S. terrorism payout*, The National Post, 01 November 2012. The article can be seen online at http://news.nationalpost.com/2012/11/01/irans-canadian-assets-frozen-over-13m-u-s-terrorism-payout/ . Viewed 20 June 2017. **Rated B2.**

[495] Iran Infiltrates Canada, Calls to Attack America, Jewish Info News, 12 July 2012. The article can be seen online at http://jewishinfonews.wordpress.com/tag/iranian-cultural-association-of-carleton-university/ . Viewed 20 June 2017. **Rated B3.**

[496] Kathryn Blaze Carlson, *Iranian embassy in Ottawa 'clearly' seeking to interfere in Canada's domestic affairs: expert,* The National Post, 12 July 2012. The article can be seen online at http://news.nationalpost.com/2012/07/12/iranian-embassy-in-ottawa-clearly-seeking-to-interfere-in-canadas-domestic-affairs-expert/ . Viewed 20 June 2017. **Rated B2.**

support of the Cultural Centre of the Islamic Republic of Iran (Ottawa) and the Iranian Cultural Association of Carleton University. The conference he attended was held to celebrate the anniversary of the death of Ayatollah Khomeini and was titled The Contemporary Awakening and Imam Khomeini's Thoughts.

At the conference, Imam Rizvi told the audience that Khomeini had:

> "proved that Islam is not just a religion of prayers and personal laws that only deals with matters of divorce and inheritance, rather it is a complete code of life that can govern all aspects of society — spiritual, material, as well as personal, social, economic and political aspects."[497]

This quotation can be reasonably interpreted as a cause for concern as Khomeneists believe that their interpretation of Sharia law takes precedence over all other forms of law and regulation – including the Canadian Constitution, the Charter of Rights and the Criminal Code of Canada.

Imam Rizvi has written extensively on marriages and morals within Islam while he has been in Canada.[498] Among some of his views are:

- "Girls can be considered sexually mature at the age of nine lunar years."
- "A girl/woman can only enter into her first marriage with the permission of her father and/or grandfather."
- "Girls/women can be entered into temporary (muta) marriages, apparently from the age of nine and upwards."

Imam Rizvi also raises the question "If a person cannot marry soon after becoming sexually and mentally mature, then how should he or she handle the sexual urge?" There are two acceptable practices in Islam according to Imam Rizvi. These are abstinence and temporary marriages.

The Jaffari Mosque formerly ran three schools in Toronto, one of which, the East End Madrassa, was closed after a 2012 hate propaganda investigation carried out by the York Regional Police.[499] No charges were laid, although the police noted that the complainant "has raised a legitimate concern and has prompted change." The school was removed from its rented premises by the Toronto District School Board. The two individuals responsible for the hate propaganda material - the principal, Ms. Masuma Jessa, and the mosque's Imam, Muhammad Rizvi - attempted to distance themselves from it, but the investigation made it clear they were aware of the Iranian produced material being used.

The East End Madrassa was located at David and Mary Thomson Collegiate and was run as part of the Jaffari Mosque organization. The school was founded in 1973 and had over 400 students at the time of

---

[497] Michael Petrou, *Carleton hosts event honouring Ayatollah Khomeini*, 6 June 2012, Maclean's Magazine. The article can be seen online at http://www.macleans.ca/education/uniandcollege/carleton-hosts-event-honouring-ayatollah-khomeini/ . Viewed 20 June 2017. **Rated B2.**

[498] See the book *Marriages and Morals in Islam* which is available online at: http://www.al-islam.org/marriageand-morals-islam-sayyid-muhammad-rizvi . The preface for this book states that it was written by S. M. Rizvi at Richmond, B.C. and dated Jamadi II 1410/January 1990. Viewed 20 June 2017. **Not Rated**.

[499] See the York Regional Police investigation report at: http://www.friendsofsimonwiesenthalcenter.com/downloads/news_110812.pdf . Viewed 20 June 2017. **Rated A1.**

the investigation. Throughout its early years, there appears to have been no major complaints or issues within the larger Thornhill/Vaughan community.

In 2012, the school was accused of inappropriate teachings advocated through Iranian-provided material, and the York Regional Police investigated it for hate propaganda issues. The school and the Madrassa are connected by common staff, common emails, and common physical addresses. Moreover, the mosque itself said that it was their school.

The school principal [falsely] stated that the teaching material did not come from Iran:

> "The EEM [East End Madrassah] has been renting space from the TDSB [Toronto District School Board] for 38 years (since 1974), and as the TDSB itself has noted, it has been an entirely positive relationship and we have never had any issues previously. We have more than 400 students from 265 families enrolled in our classes, with the age range from 5 to 17 years of age. **The curriculum is now under a comprehensive review and I can also confirm that the material at issue did NOT come from Iran.**"

The statements that the material did not come from Iran were shown to be false by the police investigation. The materials came from both Iran (Al Balagh Foundation) and from the Mostazafan Foundation of New York, which is identified as an arm of the Iranian government.[500] Most significantly, the school knew the material was in the curriculum, as they had a homework checking sheet that was sent home for parents to confirm the students were reading the material.

The Imam said the material was on the website without his knowledge or that of the principal. This would later also be shown to be false. As described in the press:

> "The chief Imam of the Islamic Shia Ithna Asheri Jamaat of Toronto, the EEM school's parent organization, said late Tuesday that the offensive content came from information taken from two websites without the permission of the "scholars" designing the school's lesson plans."
>
> "Police held Principal Masuma Jessa and Imam Syed Mohammed Rizvi responsible. As leaders in their respective roles the two must accept responsibility for failing to appropriately screen the learning material. Although not held criminally responsible, the complaint has raised a legitimate concern and has prompted change."
>
> "But police traced the most contentious passages to books published by the Al Balagh Foundation in Iran and the Mostazafan Foundation of New York, an alleged front for the Iranian regime."[501]

The curriculum also stated that girls were instead to stick to "hobbies" which prepare them to become wives and mothers.[502]

---

[500] See the East End Madrassah, Hate Propaganda Investigation, Occurrence Number 2012-126786.

[501] See, among others, http://www.torontosun.com/2012/05/08/islamic-school-apologizes-but-jewish-groupsays-they-need-to-do-more . Viewed 20 June 2017. **Rated B2.**

[502] Stewart Bell, *Police investigating Islamic school over curriculum comparing Jews to Nazis*, Stewart Bell | May 7, 2012 | Last Updated: May 9 3:23 AM ET. The article can be seen online at http://news.nationalpost.com/2012/05/07/toronto-islamic-school-removes-partsof-curriculum-casting-jews-as-treacherous-akin-to-nazis/ . Viewed 20 June 2017. **Rated B2.**

Hizb ut-Tahrir

Hizb ut-Tahrir was formed in Jerusalem (al-Quds) in 1952[503] as a spinoff of the Muslim Brotherhood. Hizb ut-Tahrir advocates their end goal is the Islamization of Canada as part of a global caliphate.[504] The UK based Quilliam Foundation notes that many Islamist groups, such as Hizb ut-Tahrir, continue to advocate separatist, confrontational ideas that, followed to their logical conclusion, lead to violence.

The City of Mississauga's Living Arts Centre hosted the 2015 annual conference of Hizb ut-Tahrir. This group calls upon Muslims not to vote, advocates the execution of anyone who leaves Islam and supports a global caliphate. The group says that jihad is a duty that should be commenced even if the enemy does not attack. The organizer, who calls all Canadian soldiers war criminals, has told Canadian Muslims it is Haram (forbidden) to vote in elections because Muslims can only vote for leaders who support Sharia Law.[505]

It is rational to believe that Hizb ut-Tahrir represents what might be Canada's smallest yet quickly growing Islamist group. It is small, but advocates an Islamic caliphate which would dominate all other religions and political systems. It tells its followers they must be loyal to the Ummah and Caliphate and not to their host country.

Mazin Abdul-Adhim, the perceived leading Imam of Hizb ut-Tahrir in Canada, was one of the organizers of the Mississauga conference. Based in London and the owner of Bismillah Meats, he advocates that it is time to move from Dawah (outreach, preaching) toward the stage of action which calls for the overthrow of corrupt regimes. Democracy, he notes, is not permissible because man is the legislator.[506] On 5 October 2016, Mazin Abdul-Adhim commented[507] on an Al Jazeera "Up Front" current affairs video (Twitter: @AJUpFront) posted on Facebook[508] 24 September 2016, as follows:

> "...The issue is very simple:
>
> 1- Sovereignty: **In a democracy, man is the sovereign legislator, so laws are legislated based exclusively on the will of the people. In Islam, on the other hand, Allah (swt) is the Sovereign Legislator, so laws are legislated based exclusively on the texts of the Quran and Sunnah; the**

---

503 For this and more on Hizb ut-Tahrir see their own website at http://english.hizbuttahrir.org/index.php/about/about-us . Viewed 20 June 2017. **Not rated.**

504 For more background on the aims of Hizb ut-Tahrir, see http://jonathanhalevi.blogspot.ca/2013/08/the-endgoal-is-islamization-of-canadian.html . Viewed 20 June 2017. **Rated B2.**

505 Thomas Quiggin, *Hizb ut-Tahrir in Canada: Providing the Mood Music to Which the Suicide Bombers Dance,* The Mackenzie Institute, 18 April 2016. The article can be seen online at http://mackenzieinstitute.com/hizb-ut-tahrir-in-canada-providing-the-mood-music-to-which-the-suicide-bombers-dance/ . Viewed 11 April 2017. **Rated A2.**

506 Thomas Quiggin, *Hizb ut-Tahrir in Canada: Providing the Mood Music to Which the Suicide Bombers Dance,* The Mackenzie Institute, 18 April 2016. The article can be seen online at http://mackenzieinstitute.com/hizb-ut-tahrir-in-canada-providing-the-mood-music-to-which-the-suicide-bombers-dance/ . Viewed 11 April 2017. **Rated A2.**

507 Mazin Abdul-Adhim, "*Yes, Islam is compatible with democracy - Mehdi Hasan's Reality Check,"* Al Jazeera, 5 October 2016. The article can be seen at http://www.aljazeera.com/upfront , Viewed 22 May 2017. **Rated C3.**

508 See the Facebook posting "*Yes, Islam is compatible with democracy - Mehdi Hasan's Reality Check*", 24 September 2016. The posting is available at https://www.facebook.com/AJUpFront/videos/1573689882939676/ . Viewed 22 May 2017. **Rated C3.**

people have no right or capability to make Halal into Haram, or Haram into Halal, no matter how many people vote in favor of it. (Emphasis added).

2- Authority: In a democracy, man has the right to elect his ruler. In Islam, man has the right to elect his ruler.

So, people tend to confuse these two things. Yes, people can elect their ruler in both Islam and democracy, but no, people cannot legislate their own laws in Islam, whereas they can in a democracy.

Therefore, Islam and democracy are contradictory and absolutely incompatible, because Islam forbids mankind from legislating laws in the place of the Creator, even if the overwhelming majority of the people vote in favor of it. (Emphasis added).

Allah (swt) says:

"If you were to obey the majority opinion of the people of the earth, they will lead you far astray from the path of Allah; they only follow guesses and they are only lying."

And:

"The right to legislate belongs exclusively to Allah." (Emphasis added).

We should stop chasing this old, outdated, failed Greek system that has led to the suffering of the majority of the world under its oppression today, and we should submit ourselves to the guidance of our Creator that has no flaws or gaps or loopholes, and leads to justice and balance. The Khilafah system is the system of government designed by Allah (swt), and no amount misuse of it by bloodthirsty militias will change that fact. **We should call for it, and work toward re-establishing it - and its return is a promise from Allah (swt) and His Messenger (saw).**" (Emphasis added).

Implications

The ideology of the Islamist front groups is clearly against the Constitution of Canada, the Charter of Rights and Freedoms and the Criminal Code of Canada. Advocating wife beating, gay killings and "approved" sex with nine-year-old girls does not seem to be part of "Canadian values."

However, it is a fact that Islamist front groups have raised millions of dollars through charities to support terrorism overseas. It can be assessed that they continue to infiltrate Canadian organizations and institutions to advance the Islamist ideology. Yet money from government continues to flow to these groups and a variety of individuals in government, the media, human rights groups and academia continue to support them.

Left unchecked, the Islamist ideology will continue to spread in Canada. It can be reasonably believed that Canada has had a series of warnings about this violence, yet they have been consistently ignored or explained away. In the future, Canada will look increasingly like France and Belgium, suffering from more attacks, segregation and the destruction of our social fabric and societal peace. Far from working towards "peace, order and good government" Canada is now sliding towards a situation whereby conflicts that used to occur between borders will now occur between neighbourhoods.

CHAPTER 14: THE MUSLIM STUDENT ASSOCIATION

Jonathan Cotler

Key Points

- Canada's most infamous terrorist, Ahmed Sayed Khadr, was radicalized while a member of the Muslim Student Association at the University of Ottawa, Ontario.[509]

- Calgary suicide bomber Salman Ashrafi was the President of the Muslim Student Association at the University of Lethbridge, Alberta.[510]

- Others such as Awso Peshdary; John Maguire; Khadar Khalib; Chiheb Esseghaier; Youssef Sakhir; Samir Halilovic; Zakria Habibi, and Ferid Imam all had ties to Muslim Student Association chapters across Canada.

- The list of individuals who have been members of the Muslim Student Association, and then gone on to be suicide bombers, jihadist fighters, propagandists, or to have leadership role in the Muslim Brotherhood is extensive. (See biographies below).

What is the Muslim Student Association? Where did it come from? Who founded it? Is it just a coincidence that so many extremists have come from its alumni? Or is something going on?

The Muslim Students Association (MSA) of the United States and Canada was established in January 1963 by members of the Muslim Brotherhood (MB) at the University of Illinois, Urbana-Champaign campus.[511] Its creation was the result of Saudi Arabia-backed efforts to create a network of international Islamic organizations in order to spread its Wahhabist ideology. It was essentially "an arm of the Saudi-funded, Muslim Brotherhood-controlled Muslim World League."[512] Since its inception, the MSA has emerged as the leading and most influential Islamic student organization in North America. Today, there are nearly six hundred MSA chapters in the United States and Canada.[513] This report will investigate the key principles the MSA is founded upon to gain a greater understanding of its activities. This requires establishing its clear nexus to the MB and its adherent organizations. The MSA will be further scrutinized with respect to its rampant anti-US, anti-Semitic and anti-Israel rhetoric both on and off campus. Within that framework, a greater perspective of its radical Islamist ideology, and the methods it is transmitted, can be gained. This report will also analyze the way the MSA provides material support to terrorism travel. Through the introduction of specific case studies, it will be evident that current and former members of

---

[509] Shephard, Michelle. *Guantanamo's Child: The Untold Story of Omar Khadr*. New York: John Wiley & Sons, 2008.

[510] http://www.torontosun.com/2015/02/06/extremist-links-to-muslim-students-association-not-new-group-has-been-monitored-for-years and http://calgary.ctvnews.ca/friends-shocked-calgary-man-became-suicide-bomber-1.1854253

[511] "Muslim Student Association: The Investigative Project on Terrorism Dossier," (2008, January 1). *The Investigative Project on Terrorism.* Retrieved from https://www.investigativeproject.org/documents/misc/31.pdf

[512] Mauro, R. (2013, February 3) "Islamist Organization Profile: Muslim Students Association (MSA)," *The Clarion Project.* Retrieved from http://www.clarionproject.org/analysis/muslim-students-association

[513] "Current size of MSA National." *MSA National Website.* Retrieved from http://www.msa-national.org/media/support.

the MSA account for a significant share of individuals who have left home to join in terror related activities abroad.

The Muslim Brotherhood Connection

The Muslim Brotherhood (MB) was founded in 1928 by Hassan al-Banna. It is an Egyptian based organization that is both staunchly conservative and highly secretive.[514] It is dedicated to true Islamic governance based on Sharia law. The motto of the MB is, "God is our objective, the Quran is our constitution, the prophet is our leader, jihad is our way, and death for the sake of God is the highest of our aspirations."[515] Further emphasizing the mindset of its leader, al-Banna, in addressing MB members, said, "We must prepare ourselves, our wives, our sons, our daughters, and those who follow in our path for a lengthy, uncompromising jihad, in which we seek [to gain] the status of martyrs."[516]

It can be reasonably assessed that the MSA promotes al-Banna's MB ideology openly. In a speech in Missouri in the 1980's Zaid Naman, a US Muslim Brotherhood official, made the relationship between the MSA and the MB clear. He stated that, "as for recruitment in the ranks of the Movement [the MB], its main condition was that a brother must be active in the general activism in the MSA."[517] Furthermore, Naman went on to say, "the most important resolution the Group [MB] might have taken was who was going to be a member of the MSA's executive committee."[518]

One of the core MB principles to be transmitted to, and adopted by the MSA, is the notion of 'Civilization Jihad.'(See Annex D) In a 1991 memorandum, Mohamed Akram, a MB operative, explained this process, that members of the MB "must understand that their work in America is a kind of grand jihad in eliminating and destroying the Western civilization from within and sabotaging its miserable house by their hands and the hands of the believers so that it is eliminated and God's religion is made victorious over all other religions."[519] The MSA was specifically named in the 1991 memorandum as one of the MB's "likeminded organizations of our friends" that shared the common goal of creating a Muslim nation in the West.[520]

It can be seen that to achieve their goals of spreading radical Wahhabi Islam, the MB and the MSA pay specific attention to the concept of dawah (a core issue for al-Banna). It can be defined as the calling for the practice or policy of conveying the message of Islam to non-Muslims. Taken within the mission of the MB and its adherent organizations, dawah can be better understood as a means of proselytizing Islam. In 1995, for example, at a Muslim Arab Youth Association (MAYA) conference in Toledo, Ohio, the world's

---

514 Noreen S. Ahmed-Ullah, Sam Roe and Laurie Cohen, (2004, September 19), A Rare Look at Secretive Brotherhood in America, *Chicago Tribune*. Retrieved from http://my.chicagotribune.com/#section/-1/article/p2p-14311665/

515 "Muslim Student Association: The Investigative Project on Terrorism Dossier," (2008, January 1). *The Investigative Project on Terrorism.* Retrieved from https://www.investigativeproject.org/documents/misc/31.pdf

516 MEMRI (2015), "Muslim Brotherhood Turn To Terrorism Against Al-Sisi Regime: Threats Of Attacks Against Foreign Diplomats, Workers In Egypt On Turkey-Based MB TV, Calls For Jihad And For Assassination Of Al-Sisi, Regime Heads," *The Middle East Media Research Institute,* issue 5792. Retrieved from http://www.memri.org/report/en/0/0/0/0/0/0/8446.htm

517 Ibid, 3.

518 Mauro, R. (2013, February 3) "Islamist Organization Profile: Muslim Students Association (MSA)," *The Clarion Project.* Retrieved from http://www.clarionproject.org/analysis/muslim-students-association

519 The Muslim Students Association and the Jihad Network. (2008). *Terrorism Awareness Project.* Retrieved from http://media0.terrorismawareness.org/files/MSA%20and%20Jihad%20Network%20v5b.pdf

520 Ibid, 4.

most influential Sunni scholar and unofficial spiritual leader of the MB and a life-long adherent, Yusuf al-Qaradawi, explained the importance of dawah, converting people to Islam, as a means of spreading the global Islamic movement. He said, "conquest through dawah, that is what we hope for. We will conquer Europe, we will conquer America! Not through the sword but through dawah."[521] Qaradawi himself is currently wanted by Interpol on charges of agreement, incitement and assistance to commit intentional murder, helping prisoners escape, arson and vandalism.[522]

The MSA's dawah campaign is of course largely composed of benign and righteous religious work protected by Free Speech. However, its true Islamist nature is frequently promoted by MSA members and guests. At the 2005 MSA West Conference, president of the University of California Los Angeles (UCLA) MSA, Ahmed Shama, discussed the ultimate goal of establishing Islamic governance through dawah. In his speech, he said "the only justification – the only justification – that Muslims have to live in this country is dawah. I say it again. It might be controversial... the only obligation that we have living in this country is dawah... and if we are not doing something to invite people to Islam, Muslims and non-Muslims, then we are missing the point of what [the] Islamic Movement is about."[523] This rhetoric is not isolated to small radical cells within the North American MSA network. The MSA National website posted a document entitled, "Dawa: Time to Come Out of Our Boxes," which advised its members to strategically adapt their dawah to the particular cultural sensibilities of North Americans. It suggested for example, that, "instead of using 'Holy War' to translate the word Jihad, use a more comprehensive and proper term like 'struggle' or 'striving'... Try to use language that is more appealing to North Americans."[524]

In Canada, a disturbing matter came to light upon the announcement of the investigation into Hussein Hamdani. Hamdani is a lawyer who, in 2005, was appointed to the Cross Cultural Roundtable that "provides advice and perspective to the Minister of Public Safety and the Minister of Justice, concerning matters of national security." He held this position for ten years despite the fact that his affiliation with Muslim Brotherhood entities dates back to 1995, at least, when he was the Muslim Students Association's treasurer at McMaster University where he studied political science from 1991-1995. He continued to work with the MSA at the University of Toronto while he was doing his Masters in International relations from 1995-1996. In 1998 and in 1999, the University of Western Ontario's student newspaper identified Hamdani as MSA Western's president. He was then studying Law (1997-2000).[525] In 1996, Hamdani published the text "The Islamicization of Campus Politics and the Politicization of the MSA." In it he discusses how Muslim student leaders in North America ought to take control of their respective student unions, and by extension the union's finances. He claims that in doing so, Muslim students would be ideally positioned to redirect funds towards their own Muslim associations on campus. Furthermore, Hamdani encourages Muslim student activists to try to control their student union's key committees,

---

521 Yusuf Qaradawi, Speech, MAYA Conference, Toledo, OH, 1995.

522 Wanted: Yusuf Qaradawi. Retrieved from http://www.interpol.int/notice/search/wanted/2014-58772

523 Ahmed Shama, Speech "Global Islamic Movements," Striving for Revival: Student Activism for Global Reformation. 7th Annual MSA West Conference. University of Southern California. January 14-17, 2005.

524 "Dawa: Tome to Come Out of Our Boxes!" MSA National Website. Retrieved from https://www.investigativeproject.org/documents/misc/31.pdf

525 Hussein Hamdani advocated "the Islamicization of campus politics" before being appointed public safety advisor by the government of Canada. (2015, April 30). Retrieved from http://pointdebasculecanada.ca/hussein-hamdani-advocated-the-islamization-of-campus-politics-before-being-appointed-public-safety-advisor-by-the-government-of-canada/

those "where the real politics lies." An excerpt from the text says, "It should be the long-term goal of every MSA to Islamicize the politics of their respective university."[526]

Between 2005 and 2009, two charities Hamdani worked with, the Halton Islamic Association and the Hamdani Foundation, gave more than $25,000 to IRFAN-Canada, a charity that transferred some $15 million to Hamas, a designated terrorist organization.[527] IRFAN-Canada also lost its official charity status in 2011 after a Canada Revenue Agency (CRA) audit exposed the organization as an "integral part" in Hamas' global financing infrastructure.[528] This is particularly worrying as it is a clear example that the goals and extremist rhetoric of the MB that is transmitted through the MSA does not only manifest itself among the student body. These messages of Islamist ideology are carried by its adherents to the highest levels of society and government. On May 1, 2015, Hamdani was suspended from his position on the cross-cultural roundtable on national security by the former Minister of Public Safety Steven Blaney. While Hamdani holds that his dismissal was politically motivated due to his opposition to Bill C-51 and his support of Justin Trudeau and the Liberal party, former Minister Blaney alleges "This individual's membership on the Cross-Cultural Roundtable on National Security has been suspended immediately pending a review of the facts. While questions surrounding this individual's links to radical ideology have circulated for some time, it was hoped that he could be a positive influence to promote Canadian values. It is now becoming clear this may not have been the case."[529]

Anti-Western, Anti-Israel, Anti-Semitic Rhetoric

It can also be reasonably believed that another aspect of the MSA's ideology is the promotion of anti-Western, anti-Semitic and anti-Israel rhetoric. Despite presenting themselves as an apolitical, religious and cultural organization, the MSA engages in radical lobbying, accusing America of being an imperialist power and Israel an oppressive, apartheid nation, if they will acknowledge its status as a state at all. Alex Alexiev of The Center of Security Policy stated, "The majority of Muslim Student Associations at US colleges are dominated by Islamist and anti-American agendas, as are most of the numerous Islamic centers and schools financed by the Saudis."[530] On October 22, 2000 at the Israeli Consulate in Los Angeles, MSA-UCLA members Arif Shaikh and Ahmed Shama (who was then president of the chapter), led a demonstration protesting 'Israeli aggression against Palestinians.' At the rally, chants of 'death to Israel,' and 'death to Jews,' were repeated amongst the crowd. Shama stated "Our solution is simple; our solution is the establishment of justice by Islamic means. This is the only solution to this Israeli apartheid."[531] At a San Francisco State University rally on April 9, 2002, Imam Amir Abdul Malik Ali, in discussing the Israel-Palestinian conflict, was cheered by the student crowd when he exclaimed, "stop calling them suicide bombers. When a person commits suicide, they are depressed... these brother, and sisters, before they go out on their martyr missions are doing videotapes and they are saying 'yah! I'm doing this! I'm doing

---

[526] Ibid.

[527] Hamas loving Canadian Islamist baffled by suspension. (2015, May 20). *The Counter Jihad Report.* Retrieved from http://counterjihadreport.com/tag/muslim-students-association/

[528] Canadian Homeland Security Advisor Suspended for Islamist Associations. (2015, May 1). *IPT NEWS.* Retrieved from http://www.investigativeproject.org/4840/canadian-homeland-security-adviser-suspended-for

[529] Carter, A. (2015, May 1). Hussein Hamdani says federal election politics behind his suspension. *CBC News.* Retrieved from http://www.cbc.ca/news/canada/hamilton/news/hussein-hamdani-says-federal-election-politics-behind-his-suspension-1.3056931

[530] Muslim Students Association of the U.S. and Canada (MSA). Retrieved from http://www.discoverthenetworks.org/groupProfile.asp?grpid=6175

[531] The Muslim Students Association and the Jihad Network. (2008). *Terrorism Awareness Project.* Retrieved from http://media0.terrorismawareness.org/files/MSA%20and%20Jihad%20Network%20v5b.pdf

this! And their mothers are right next to them saying, 'go ahead and go!'"[532] These are but a token few examples of the pervasive and ongoing Islamist, xenophobic and anti-Semitic messages that the MSA transmits.

Furthermore, the MSA and many of its campus affiliates have organized or participated in 'Israeli Apartheid Week' (IAW). Beginning in Toronto in 2005, and since becoming an annual event worldwide, the organization claims "the aim of IAW is to educate people about the nature of Israel as an apartheid system and to build Boycott, Divestment and Sanctions (BDS) campaigns as part of a growing global BDS movement."[533] It has at this point become a foregone conclusion that these annual events will descend into anti-Semitic diatribes, largely maintaining international support as legitimate freedom of expression. For example, a text that appeared at the top of the IAW campaign's website this year accuses Israel of "'fresh war crimes and crimes against humanity' and an 'incremental genocide' of Palestinians. It describes the Jewish state as 'the world's dangerous pariah.'"[534] Examples of IAW themes include accusations against Israel of 'pinkwashing,' a term used to accuse Israel of leveraging its tolerant and progressive record on LGBT issues as a means of whitewashing its policies towards Palestinians.[535]

Additionally, at the Yale 2011 IAW, Mazin Qumsiyeh, a Palestinian former Professor who had recently moved back to the West Bank "described Israel as the 'worst colonial venture in history' and defended the right of Palestinians to resist 'by any means,' including violent resistance."[536] He went on to accuse Israel of having an "apartheid system" worse than it was in South Africa and expressed support for boycott campaigns against Israel and companies that do business with Israel.[537]

At the University of Manitoba in 2009, the MSA put up posters that depicted Israeli fighter planes targeting baby strollers. Others featured a caricature of a hooked-nosed Hasidic Jew with a Star of David, pointing a bazooka at the nose of an Arab carrying a slingshot. Another showed an Israeli helicopter with a swastika on top, dropping a bomb on a baby bottle.[538] These annual conferences not only propagate the most vitriolic falsehoods, often not distinguishing between anti-Zionism and anti-Semitism, but IAW events allow for no discourse or debate on the facts. Rather than use university forums for open dialogue and the free expression of facts and opinions, the IAW events continue to nurture and spread hateful messages, and prevent any real progress from being made.

Mechanisms for Radical Ideological Dissemination

With an understanding of the true nature of the MSA and its radical ideology, it is important to enumerate the various mechanisms it uses to publicize its messages to college campuses and beyond. As was previously noted, the MSA regularly holds conferences, or engages guest lecturers with radical Islamist themes. Some of the MSA's past guest speakers have included: Abu Ali (Abdul-Alim) Musa, the Imam of

---

532 Amir Abdel Malik Ali, Speech. (2002, April 9). Anti-Israel Rally, San Francisco State University.
533 About Israeli Apartheid Week (2015). Retrieved from http://apartheidweek.org/about/
534 Bigman, P.M. (2015, February 23). Israeli Aprtheid Week. Anti-Semitism 101. The Louis D. Brandeis Centre for Human Rights Under Law. Retrieved from http://brandeiscenter.com/blog/israeli-apartheid-week-anti-semitism-101/
535 Israeli Apartheid Week: A year by year report. (2012). *Anti-Defamation League.* Retrieved from http://www.adl.org/assets/pdf/israel-international/Israeli-Apartheid-Week-Year-by-Year-Report.pdf
536 Ibid, 5.
537 Ibid.
538 Offman, C. (2009, March 2). Campuses awash in tension over Israel Apartheid Week. *National Post.* Retrieved from http://www.nationalpost.com/news/story.html?id=1343206

the Masjid al-Islam in Washington D.C. Musa is known for justifying the use of suicide bombers, saying in a July 2002 rally in D.C.:

> "When they go out and strike at the heart of Zionism, they are not suicide bombers they are heroes, isn't that right? That's a part of our deen, that's a part of our religion, let's not become weak bones and apologetic, and run around trying to appease this government and that government."[539]

Another notable figure engaged by the MSA as a guest speaker is Mohammed al-Hanooti. In November 2001, he was designated by FBI special agent Dale Watson, Assistant Director of the FBI Counterterrorism Division, as a significant and active supporter of Hamas. The report went on to say that al-Hanooti purportedly held fund-raising activities for Hamas, and supporting visitors to the US from Israel and Jordon to speak on behalf of Hamas.[540]

Lastly, another guest on the MSA roster was Omar Ahmed, who founded the Council on American-Islamic Relations (CAIR) in 1994. He was also an official of the Islamic Association for Palestine (IAP).[541] The IAP was mentioned in a memorandum opinion in the case of Holy Land Foundation v. Ashcroft, in which the Holy Land Foundation (HLF) unsuccessfully sued then-Attorney General John Ashcroft, challenging its designation as a Specially Designated Terrorist Entity. US District Judge Gladys Kessler found that "at the same time Hamas was funding HLF, it was also funding a network of organizations connected to HLF. There is evidence that at least one of these organizations, Islamic Association for Palestine (IAP), has acted in support of Hamas."[542] While again, this is hardly an exhaustive list of the radical Islamist guest list the MSA has hosted over the years, it is a compelling indicator of the kind of message being transmitted to students across the continent.

The MSA equally lends it support to a multitude of Islamic organizations, many of which have been identified as having terrorist ties. One such example is the Global Relief Foundation (GRF), based in Chicago Illinois, which grew into one of the largest Islamic charities in the US. The GRF described itself as a non-profit, non-governmental organization established to provide humanitarian assistance and charitable relief to Muslims, especially in conflict zones.[543] Aside from their charitable work however, the US government has also alleged that GRF funded jihadism.[544] By the end of the 1990's, GRF was reporting more than five million dollars in annual contributions, with tax filings indicating that ninety percent of the money donated between 1994 and 2000 was sent abroad.[545] An FBI memorandum notes that "some materials distributed by GRF glorify 'martyrdom through jihad' and state that donations will be used to

---

[539] Abdul Alim Musa, Rally, Freedom Plaza, Washington DC, July 2002.
[540] "Muslim Student Association: The Investigative Project on Terrorism Dossier," (2008, January 1). *The Investigative Project on Terrorism.* Retrieved from https://www.investigativeproject.org/documents/misc/31.pdf
[541] Awad, N. (2000, March). Muslim-Americans in Mainstream America. *The Link.*
[542] *Holy Land Foundation for Relief and Development v. John Ashcroft,* 02-442. "Memorandum Opinion," 21 (DC, August 8, 2002).
[543] John Roth, Douglas Greenberg and Serena Wille. Monograph on Terrorism Financing. *National Commission on Terrorist Attacks upon the United States.* Retrieved from http://www.9-11commission.gov/staff_statements/911_TerrFin_Monograph.pdf
[544] Ibid, 88.
[545] Ibid, 89.

buy ammunition, equip 'the raiders' and support the mujahedin."[546] The MSA provided a link to GRF until March 2003.[547]

Another notable of MSA affiliated charities linked to terrorism, is the case of the Holy Land Foundation for Relief and Development (HLF). As discussed above, HLF's assets were frozen by the FBI and Treasury Department in December 2001 based on charges that it raised money for Hamas. The 2007 trial led to the conviction of HLF's founders on charges of supporting a terrorist organization.[548] The MSA provided a link to HLF until March 2003.[549] In anticipation of the 2007 verdict in the HLF case, Farhad Noorzay, the president of MSA West, released a message requesting people:

> "make du'a and supplicate to Allah, the Almighty, asking Him to confirm the innocence of these men, that justice prevail, and that they be returned safely to their families."[550]

The MSA also releases several publications on various campuses, which maintain its radical position and respect of jihadist activity. UCLA's MSA newspaper al-Talib, for example, distributes approximately twenty thousand copies per issue to campuses, mosques and community centers.[551] UC-Irvine's MSA newspaper Alkalima circulates to roughly fifteen thousand people,[552] with some of the publications available online. In a July 1999 Issue of al-Talib, an editorial by MSA staff called "The Spirit of Jihad" included a portion stating, "When we hear someone refer to the great Mujahid Osama bin Laden as a 'terrorist,' we should defend our brother and refer to him as a freedom fighter."[553] The edition featured a photo of Bin Laden on the cover. In their June 2004 issue, Alkalima published a piece praising Hamas, Islamic Jihad, and Hezbollah. In it, it was written "Arab countries have come to realize that the only group able to liberate land from the Zionists was Hizb' Allah. Sheikh Ahmad Yassin, who only had control of his tongue, stuck to his correct legitimate ideology and was assassinated as a hero of the Palestinian people and Muslims worldwide."[554] Lastly, in a special report entitled "Zionism: The Forgotten Apartheid," both al-Talib and Alkalima staff joined to release a heavily anti-Semitic piece. The report stated:

> "As the Zionists continue to colonize, torture and ethnically-cleanse in the name of the 'peace process' and the Americans continue to fund them, the respective staffs of Al-Talib and Alkalima

---

[546] Fed Claim Muslim Charity Had Contact with Bin Laden Secretary. (2002, March 28). *Associated Press.* Retrieved from http://www.nwitimes.com/uncategorized/feds-claim-muslim-charity-had-contact-with-bin-laden-secretary/article_28314bb2-c861-529e-93cb-233f4d5d06f4.html

[547] Islamic Organizations (2003, March). *Muslim Student Association National Website.* Retrieved from Web Archive, http://web.archive.org/web/20030301041614/http://www.msa-national.org/resources/islamorg.html

[548] Herf, J. (2015, April 15). The Black Book of the American Left: Volume IV: Islamo Fascism and the War Against the Jews. *Front Page Mag.* Retrieved from http://www.frontpagemag.com/fpm/255024/black-book-american-left-volume-iv-islamo-fascism-jeffrey-herf?utm_source=feedburner&utm_medium=feed&utm_campaign=Feed%3A+FrontpageMag+%28FrontPage+Magazine+»+FrontPage%29

[549] Islamic Organizations (2003, March). *Muslim Student Association National Website.* Retrieved from Web Archive, http://web.archive.org/web/20030301041614/http://www.msa-national.org/resources/islamorg.html

[550] Noorzay, F. (2007, October 19). "URGENT: A Sincere Request from MSA West,"

[551] "Advertise," Al-Talib Website. Retrieved from http://www.al-talib.com/

[552] "FAQ," Alkalima Website. Retrieved from http://www.alkalima.com/?page=FAQ

[553] "Jihad in America; maintaining an Islamic identity in an un-Islamic environment," *al-Talib*, MSA University of California-Los Angeles, July 1999, editorial page.

[554] Abdulrahman Hachache. (2004, June 14). The Assassination of Sheikh Yassin and Dr. Rantissi: Why the assassinations will have serious consequences for 'Israel' and the Islamic Resistance Movement. *Alkalima.*

feel it to be their basic duty to expose Zionism, its evil and its effects. Zionist controlled world media has been purposefully distorting and misconstruing world events too long." [555]

The MSA and Foreign Travel

Unfortunately, the successful promotion and indoctrination of radical Islamist ideology by the MSA in the ways previously discussed, sometimes results in individuals undertaking jihadist missions from and within North America. The final section of this report will look at the way the MSA contributes to the radicalization of young people, providing material support to terrorism travel. In 2007, a New York Police Department report noted that the MSA acts as an "incubator" for Islamic radicalism. The report went on to say that:

> "Among social networks of the local university population, there appears to be a growing trend of Salafi-based radicalization that has permeated some Muslim Students Associations (MSAs). Extremists have used these university-based organizations as forums for the development and recruitment of likeminded individuals." [556]

One of the most notable Canadian examples of terrorism travel influenced by the MSA is the case of Ahmed Said Khadr. While he was an engineering student at the University of Ottawa, he joined the MSA, agreeing with their notions of Sharia law, and he became a vocal advocate for Islamic rule in his native Egypt.[557] After his graduation, Khadr moved to Pakistan to run the office of Human Concern International, another Muslim Brotherhood affiliated organization.[558] Through his work with multiple charitable NGO's serving Afghan refugees, Khadr was tied to multiple militant and Mujahedeen leaders in Afghanistan, including Osama bin Laden and Aymen al-Zawahiri. He was accused of being a senior associate and financier of al-Qaeda.[559] Khadr was killed on October 2, 2003, along with al-Qaeda and Taliban members, in a shootout by Pakistani security forces near the Afghanistan border. An al-Qaeda website profiling "120 Martyrs of Afghanistan" described him as a leader of Bin Laden's organization and praised him for "tossing his little child [Omar] in the furnace of the battle."[560]

Most recently, a report by the QMI Agency compiled a report of eleven individuals topping Canada's lists of Jihadi extremists, who all share ties to the MSA. While extended profiles of all the individuals on the list are discussed in the biographical data of MSA-linked terrorists section below, several of the cases bear mentioning here. Awso Peshdary, Khadar Khalib and John "Yahya" Maguire, all students and members of the [Ottawa campus] Algonquin College MSA, got connected and engaged in terrorist activities together. Khalib was apparently radicalized by Peshdary, and travelled to Syria in 2014 with Peshdary and Maguire's assistance. He was charged in abstentia in February 2015, as he is currently believed to be in Syria fighting

---

[555] "Zionism: The Forgotten Apartheid," *Alkalima*, MSA University of California-Irvine Publication.

[556] Mitchell D. Silber and Arvin Bhatt (2007) "Radicalization in the West: The Homegrown Threat," *New York Police Department*.

[557] Shephard, M. (2008) *Guantanamo's Child: The Untold Story of Omar Khadr*. New York: John Wiley & Sons.

[558] Point de Bascule. (2013, January 9). Ahmed Said Khadr's radicalization at the University of Ottawa. Retrieved from http://pointdebasculecanada.ca/ahmed-said-khadrs-radicalization-at-the-university-of-ottawa/

[559] Friscolanti, M. (2006, August 4). The House of Khadr. *Macleans.*

[560] Point de Bascule. (2013, January 9). Ahmed Said Khadr's radicalization at the University of Ottawa. Retrieved from http://pointdebasculecanada.ca/ahmed-said-khadrs-radicalization-at-the-university-of-ottawa/

with the Islamic State (IS).[561] Peshdary himself is accused of helping bankroll prospective homegrown jihadis seeking to join IS. He was described by CSIS as being a recruiter and talent spotter for a convicted terrorist when he was first arrested in 2010.[562] Maguire joined IS in 2012, travelling to Syria on a one-way ticket, and posted a propaganda video in 2014. He was charged in abstentia with participating in a terrorist group in Syria, Iraq, and Turkey, and conspiring with a terrorist network in Ottawa. He was reportedly killed in battle, but no official agency has confirmed his death.[563] What is most alarming is how these individuals allegedly did not show signs of extremist views prior to their time in the MSA. According to Awso Peshdary's father, Awso was not raised in a religious, much less radical, home.[564] Similarly, colleagues of Khalib at Algonquin College expressed their shock at the discovery of his radicalization, expressing that there were no prior signs of his extremist views.[565] Friends of Maguire similarly stated that he had a normal upbringing and, "had a pet horse. He played guitar in a punk band called the Shackles, which held concerts in church basements. He also played hockey."[566] What this shows is that young people who are raised far from repressive regimes and Islamist ideology, may still find their way to it. The MSA has developed and refined an effective method of identifying and recruiting the type of individuals susceptible to radicalization, and it is operating almost unimpeded.

Implications

The MSA has had over fifty years to expand across campuses in North America, and in that time, they have solidified their role in influencing both academic and political circles. They have remained true to their original purpose as an arm of the global Muslim Brotherhood Movement, and have been successful in implementing its policies and agendas. The MSA cultivates individuals, some who go on to hold important positions in mainstream society, to carry the radical ideology espoused by the organization with them, beyond the campus. This has created the situation we are confronted with today. The rate of extremist rhetoric from university MSA's is increasing, namely with the IAW and BDS movements gaining global momentum, while it has equally cultivated a vast network of likeminded organizations and people to accommodate its radical ideology through a stealth jihad.

Biographies of Canadian MSA Alumni

Awso Peshdary: Ottawa born accused terrorist Awso Peshdary was arrested in February 2015 as part of operation 'Project Servant' by the RCMP Integrated National Security Enforcement Team (INSET). He was

---

[561] Duffy, A. (2015, February 4). Former Algonquin Student Khadar Khalib charged with terror offences. *The Ottawa Citizen.* Retrieved from http://ottawacitizen.com/news/local-news/former-algonquin-student-charged-with-terror-offences

[562] Helmer, A. (2015, February 10). Terror Suspect Awso Peshdary worked closely with Ottawa Youth. *Ottawa Sun.* Retrieved from http://www.ottawasun.com/2015/02/10/terror-suspect-awso-peshdary-worked-closely-with-ottawa-youth

[563] Daly, B. (2015, February 6). Extremist links to Muslim Students Association not new; group has been monitored for years. *QMI Agency*. Retrieved from http://www.torontosun.com/2015/02/06/extremist-links-to-muslim-students-association-not-new-group-has-been-monitoed-for-years

[564] Hempstead, D (2015, February 3). Terror assused Awso Peshdary's dad believed he is innocent. *Ottawa Sun.* Retrieved from http://www.ottawasun.com/2015/02/03/terror-accused-awso-peshdarys-dad-believes-son-is-innocent

[565] Robbins, K (2015, February 3). Terror accused Khadar Khalib recognized from Muslim Students Association. *Ottawa Sun.* Retrieved from http://www.ottawasun.com/2015/02/03/terror-accused-khadar-khalib-recognized-from-muslim-students-association

[566] Who is John Maguire? Maguire urged Muslims in Canada to carry out lone-wolf attacks in video released Dec. 7. (2014, December 8). Retrieved from http://www.cbc.ca/news/world/who-is-john-maguire-1.2864159

charged with participation in the activity of a terrorist group (Sec. 83.18).[567] He is accused of helping bankroll prospective homegrown jihadis seeking to join the Islamic State (IS), and was connected to Canadian jihadi John Maguire. He was described by CSIS as being a recruiter and talent spotter for a convicted terrorist when he was first arrested in 2010. Peshdary was active within the Algonquin College Muslim Students Association (MSA), and conditions of his arrest prevent him from communicating with several members of the organization, including MSA executives Abdalrahman Naddaf and Mohammed Tulul. Peshdary was most recently employed at the Pinecrest-Queensway Community Health Centre as a youth services worker. Peshdary was hired to serve youth aged 13-17, an age range particularly vulnerable to radicalization.[568]

Khadar Khalib (aka AbdulBaqi Hanif): Grew up in Ottawa and later moved with his family to Calgary. Khalib was a member of the Algonquin College MSA. It is believed he was radicalized by Awso Peshdary. According to the RCMP, Khalib travelled to Syria in late March 2014 with the alleged assistance of Peshdary and former University of Ottawa business student John Maguire, who was already in Syria at the time. Khalib is now believed to be in Syria fighting with the Islamic State, therefore he was charged by the RCMP in abstentia in February 2015. Weeks before Khalib left for Syria, both he and Peshdary took part in Islam Awareness Week on Algonquin College's Woodroffe Avenue campus, which was sponsored by the MSA.[569]

John "Yahya" Maguire: Grew up in Kemptville, ON. He received a scholarship to study in Los Angeles in 2010 and returned to Canada enrolling at the University of Ottawa in 2011, at which point friends claimed he had already begun making extremist claims, and became involved with the university's MSA. He joined IS in 2012, travelling to Syria on a one-way ticket, and posted a propaganda video in 2014.[570] He was charged in abstentia with participating in a terrorist group in Syria, Iraq and Turkey, and conspiring with a terrorist network in Ottawa. He was reportedly killed in battle, but no official agency has confirmed his death.[571] He has made multiple comments online supporting the ideology of IS and extolling the virtues of Jihad. He wrote on twitter for example that "in this situation the son is to go for jihad regardless of what his parents say." To please God "one should sacrifice what he has in the West and make hijrah [migration] to a land of jihad."[572]

Ahmed Said Khadr: Born in Egypt, Khadr moved with his family to Montreal in 1975, and then to Toronto several months later. He enrolled at the University of Ottawa, studying engineering. While there he joined the MSA, agreeing with their notions of Sharia law, and became a vocal advocate for Islamic rule in

---

[567] RCMP Arrests One Individual and Charges Two Others with Terrorism Offences as part of Project SERVANT. (2015, February 3). Retrieved from http://www.rcmp-grc.gc.ca/on/news-nouvelles/2015/15-02-03-ottawa-eng.htm

[568] Helmer, A. (2015, February 10). Terror Suspect Awso Peshdary worked closely with Ottawa Youth. *Ottawa Sun.* Retrieved from http://www.ottawasun.com/2015/02/10/terror-suspect-awso-peshdary-worked-closely-with-ottawa-youth

[569] Duffy, A. (2015, February 4). Former Algonquin Student Khadar Khalib charged with terror offences. *The Ottawa Citizen.* Retrieved from http://ottawacitizen.com/news/local-news/former-algonquin-student-charged-with-terror-offences

[570] Who is John Maguire? Maguire urged Muslims in Canada to carry out lone-wolf attacks in video released Dec. 7. (2014, December 8). Retrieved from http://www.cbc.ca/news/world/who-is-john-maguire-1.2864159

[571] Daly, B. (2015, February 6). Extremist links to Muslim Students Association not new; group has been monitored for years. *QMI Agency*. Retrieved from http://www.torontosun.com/2015/02/06/extremist-links-to-muslim-students-association-not-new-group-has-been-monitoed-for-years

[572] Bell, S. (2014, August 25). Extremist named John Maguire: Ottawa student likely joined ISIS after converting to Islam and moving to Syria. *National Post.* Retrieved from http://news.nationalpost.com/news/canada/extremist-named-john-maguire-ottawa-student-likely-joined-isis-after-converting-to-islam-and-moving-to-syria

his native Egypt.[573] After his graduation, Khadr went to Pakistan to run the office of Human Concern International, another Muslim Brotherhood affiliated organization.[574] Through his work with multiple charitable NGO's serving Afghan refugees, Khadr was tied to multiple militant and Mujahedeen leaders in Afghanistan, including Osama bin Laden and Aymen al-Zawahiri. He was accused of being a senior associate and financier of al-Qaeda.[575] Khadr was killed on October 2, 2003, along with al-Qaeda and Taliban members, in a shootout by Pakistani security forces near the Afghanistan border. An al-Qaeda website profiling "120 Martyrs of Afghanistan" described him as a leader of Bin Laden's organization and praised him for "tossing his little child [Omar] in the furnace of the battle."[576]

Qutbi al-Mahdi: Involved with the Islamic movement in Sudan from a young age. While studying for his PhD in Islamic Studies at McGill University, Qutbi was active with MSA and then ISNA, where he served as President from 1984-1986. Immediately after receiving his PhD in 1989, he served as Director General of the Muslim World League in NY for two years. Returning to Sudan, Qutbi became involved with the newly formed Islamic government. He has served in many posts since the early 1990's: Ambassador to Tehran, Director General of Political Affairs in the ministry of Foreign Relations, Minister of Hajj, Minister of Social Planning, and Political Advisor to the President.[577] He also served as the head of external intelligence in Sudan in the 1990s under President Omar al-Bashir, who faces an International Criminal Court arrest warrant for war crimes and crimes against humanity in the Darfur crisis.[578]

Salman Ashrafi: Originally from Pakistan but raised in Calgary, Ashrafi was enrolled at the University of Lethbridge, where he completed a bachelor degree in management. During his university years, Ashrafi started to practice Islam in a more serious manner and became heavily involved with Islamic activism in the campus, serving as president of the MSA. Following graduation, he worked at Calgary's Talisman `energy for one year before quitting in 2012, and flying to the Persian Gulf.[579] He blew himself up in November 2013 in a double suicide bombing at an Iraqi military base, reportedly killing 46 people on behalf of ISIS, using the nom de guerre Abu Abdullah al-Khorasani.[580]

Chiheb Esseghaier: A Tunisian national and scientist, who was a doctoral student with a research arm at the Université du Québec at the time of his arrest. Esseghaier admitted to "La Presse" in an interview to only becoming immersed in religion after arriving at the University of Sherbrooke, when he read books and web sites about Islam and joined the local chapter of the MSA, and began attending a local Mosque. He was charged with plotting an attack on a VIA rail train in the Niagara region, and did not deny the charges, stressing that there is "no shortage of reasons" to launch a terrorist attack on North America. He

---

[573] Shephard, M. (2008) *Guantanamo's Child: The Untold Story of Omar Khadr*. New York: John Wiley & Sons.
[574] Point de Bascule. (2013, January 9). Ahmed Said Khadr's radicalization at the University of Ottawa. Retrieved from http://pointdebasculecanada.ca/ahmed-said-khadrs-radicalization-at-the-university-of-ottawa/
[575] Friscolanti, M. (2006, August 4). The House of Khadr. *Macleans*.
[576] Point de Bascule. (2013, January 9). Ahmed Said Khadr's radicalization at the University of Ottawa. Retrieved from http://pointdebasculecanada.ca/ahmed-said-khadrs-radicalization-at-the-university-of-ottawa/
[577] Muslim Alliance in North America. (2008) Grassroots Interview with Qutbi al-Mahdi. Retrieved from https://www.mana-net.org/pages.php?ID=activism&ID2=&NUM=13
[578] Daly, B. (2015, February 6). Extremist links to Muslim Students Association not new; group has been monitored for years. *QMI Agency.* Retrieved from http://www.torontosun.com/2015/02/06/extremist-links-to-muslim-students-association-not-new-group-has-been-monitoed-for-years
[579] Bell, S. (2014, June 12). It's a mystery how middle-class Calgary man turned suicide bomber was recruited into ISIS terror group: family. *National Post.* Retrieved from http://news.nationalpost.com/news/canada/its-a-mystery-how-middle-class-calgary-man-turned-suicide-bomber-was-recruited-into-isis-terror-group-family
[580] Suicide bomber killed in Iraq part of wider jihadi base in Calgary. (2014, June 4). *CBC News.* Retrieved from http://www.cbc.ca/news/canada/suicide-bomber-killed-in-iraq-part-of-wider-jihadi-base-in-calgary-1.2663890

is currently on trial in Toronto for the failed 2013 VIA Rail bomb plot, the first known al-Qaida plot against Canada. He refused to be judged under the Criminal Code of Canada, deeming it a human-created law that was subordinate to the divine law of the Koran.[581]

Youssef Sakhir, Samir Halilovic and Zakria Habibi: All three are from Sherbrooke QC, and became friends through a local Muslim association in the Eastern Townships. They were Facebook friends with the University of Sherbrooke MSA. They vanished from Quebec last year at around the same time and are being sought by RCMP and CSIS. They are believed to be travelling overseas, possibly joining forces with local Islamist forces in Syria or elsewhere in the Middle East.[582]

Ferid Imam: University of Manitoba student who served as president of the local chapter of the MSA.[583] He is wanted by the RCMP on terrorism related charges following a four-year investigation. He was completing a degree in biochemistry when he disappeared. He travelled to Pakistan in March 2007 to participate as an insurgent in the war in Afghanistan. He became involved as a weapons instructor at a terrorist training camp aligned with Al Qaeda. According to RCMP interviews, Imam was positively identified as an Al Qaeda weapons instructor using the alias "Yousef." An RCMP witness interview showed that Imam's goal was to fight and kill NATO soldiers in Afghanistan.[584] He was charged in abstentia with instructing to carry out terrorism activities and conspiracy to participate in the activities of a terrorist group. He is also accused of training others for terrorist activities. According to an indictment that was unsealed in federal court in Brooklyn, N.Y., Imam has also been charged in the foiled al-Qaeda plot against New York City subways. The court documents allege Imam, who also went by the name Yousef, was part of a conspiracy to attack the subways with suicide bombers in September 2009. Canada's Anti-Terrorism Act, passed shortly after the Sept. 11, 2001, attacks, allows police to charge people suspected of committing terrorist offences outside Canada's borders. The case against Imam is the first time RCMP have charged someone with acts taking place entirely overseas, according to the Globe and Mail. [585]

Dr. Jamal Badawi: Egyptian born Canadian, and possibly the most influential member of the North American Muslim Brotherhood. He is a former professor who taught at the Sobey School of Business and Saint Mary's University in Halifax, Nova Scotia, where he taught in the Departments of Religious Studies and Management. He is a well-known author, activist, preacher and speaker on Islam. He has been serving as a volunteer imam of the local Muslim community in the Halifax Regional Municipality since 1970. He cites Hassan al-Banna and the Muslim Brotherhood as his source for inspiration.[586] He has been identified

---

[581] Hopper, T. (2013, September 26). VIA terror suspect Chiheb Esseghaier calls 9-11 attacks a 'tap on the cheek.' *National Post.* Retrieved from http://news.nationalpost.com/news/canada/via-terror-suspect-chiheb-esseghaier-calls-9-11-attacks-a-tap-on-the-cheek

[582] Daly, B. (2015, February 6). Extremist links to Muslim Students Association not new; group has been monitored for years. *QMI Agency.* Retrieved from http://www.torontosun.com/2015/02/06/extremist-links-to-muslim-students-association-not-new-group-has-been-monitoed-for-years

[583] The growing list of Muslim Student Association (MSA) terrorists – updated, (2015, April 25). Retrieved from https://creepingsharia.wordpress.com/2015/04/25/the-growing-list-of-muslim-student-association-msa-terrorists/

[584] Wanted by the RCMP: Ferid Ahmad Imam. (2011, March 29). Retrieved from http://www.rcmp-grc.gc.ca/en/wanted/ferid-ahmed-imam

[585] Freeze, C. (2012, May 6). Fugitive Canadian alleged to have trained al-Qaeda recruits. *The Globe and Mail.* Retrieved from http://www.theglobeandmail.com/news/world/fugitive-canadian-alleged-to-have-trained-al-qaeda-recruits/article4107071/

[586] *On Mount Nur with Dr. Jamal Badawi*. (2004. April). *Emel,* Issue 4. Retrieved from http://www.emel.com/article?id=5&a_id=1516

by the MB of North America has being on its board of directors (Shura Council).[587] He is active in the North American ISNA and sat on their board in 2005, was on the board of CAIR-CAN for every year they have had a published list of members (2000-2012), and was on the board of MAC from at least 2002-2006. He is a member of the Islamic Juridical (Fiqh) Council of North America, The European Council of Fatwa and Research and the International Union of Muslim Scholars. Badawi has made repeated comments over the years holding Islam as superior to democracy and defending jihad, including suicide bombings, as a form of martyrdom.[588] During a February 2009 speech on "Understanding Jihad and Martyrdom," at the Chebucto Mosque in Halifax, Nova Scotia, Badawi explained that Gaza-based terrorists were fighting a jihad and that those who were killed were martyrs.[589] In July 2007 Dr. Badawi was a featured speaker at a conference in Qatar honoring Muslim Brotherhood spiritual leader Yousef Qaradawi, where Badawi shared the speaker's podium with Khaled Mashal, the head of Hamas and a designated terrorist by both the U.S. and Canada. Badawi's remarks were posted on Qaradawi's website (now since removed). Badawi also sits on the board of directors of Qaradawi's International Association of Muslim Scholars (IAMS), which just a few months after its founding in 2004 issued a fatwa authorizing the killing of American troops in Iraq. The Iraqi resistance even published the news of the IAMS fatwa on their own English website.[590]

Dr. Mohammed Bekkari: Dr. Mohamed Bekkari was born in Morocco in 1947 and resides in Ottawa, Ontario. He is a registered child clinical and school psychologist employed by Timiskaming Child and Family Services. Dr. Bekkari has served for more than thirty years on various ISNA committees, as ISNA Vice President-Canada, on MSA boards, and as the current President of ISNA Canada.[591]

He was President when an ISNA charitable organization lost its charitable status (for cause) as a resulting of using the charity's money to fund a terrorist organization. A Canada Revenue Agency audit found that ISNA distributed funds to an agency linked to a terrorist organization in Pakistan.[592] Dr. Bekkari is also involved in a lawsuit with a former ISNA member (Mohammad Ashraf) over allegations of the mismanagement of funds. The problems were noted in the Toronto Star article "Muslim charity squandered money for poor."[593] He also sits on the board of the Canadian Islamic Trust Foundation, a subsidiary of the ISNA that is part of the broader global Muslim Brotherhood network.[594]

---

[587] *ANALYSIS: Holy Land Document May Resolve Mystery of Jamal Badawi Affiliation*. (2007, August 28). Retrieved from http://www.globalmbwatch.com/2007/08/28/analysis-holy-land-document-resolve-mystery-jamal-badawi-affiliation/

[588] *RECOMMENDED READING: "Jamal Badawi: Enduring Link to ISNA's Radical Past*." (2012, May 15). *The Global Muslim Brotherhood Daily Watch.* Retrieved from http://www.globalmbwatch.com/2012/05/15/recommended-reading-jamal-badawi-enduring-link-to-isnas-radical-past/

[589] Jamal Badawi: Enduring Link to ISNA's Radical Past. (2012, May 8). *The Investigative Project on Terrorism.* Retrieved from http://www.investigativeproject.org/3569/jamal-badawi-enduring-link-to-isna-radical-past

[590] Poole, P. (2012, March 16). *Homeland Insecurity: Why is Jamal Badawi still allowed inside the United States? PJ Media.* Retrieved from http://pjmedia.com/tatler/2012/05/16/homeland-insecurity-why-is-jamal-badawi-still-allowed-inside-the-united-states/

[591] Dr. Mohamed Bekkari Bio. (2013). *ISNA.* Retrieved from http://www.isna.net/mohamed-bekkari.html

[592] Jeffords, S. (2013, September 20). Islamic group's charitable status revoked over alleged link to terror organization. *Toronto Sun.* Retrieved from http://www.torontosun.com/2013/09/20/islamic-groups-charitable-status-revoked-over-alleged-link-to-terror-organization

[593] Jesse Mclean, *Muslim charity squandered money for poor.* 20 January 2011, The Toronto Star. This article is available online at: http://www.thestar.com/news/gta/2011/01/20/muslim_charity_squandered_money_for_poor.html . Viewed 24 July 2017. **Rated B2**.

[594] The Canadian Islamic Trust Foundation. (2008). Retrieved from http://www.jamimosque.com/about_cit.php

Dr. Rida Beshir: According to his own website, Dr. Mohamed Rida Beshir has over 35 years of experience in da'wah work [the concept of the proselytizing of Islam forwarded by the Muslim Brotherhood] in North America, and is a regular speaker at ISNA, ICNA, MSA, MAC, and MAS conventions. He received the Ottawa Muslim Association and Ottawa Muslim Community Circle appreciation awards in 1993 and 1999 for his volunteer Islamic work in the National Capital region. Currently he is advising the Muslim Association of Canada (MAC) and the Muslim American Society (MAS) departments on Tarbiyah matters. He is also a member of the advisory board of SIFCA "Shura of Islamic Family Counselors of America."[595] He was listed in a 1992 directory of the Muslim Brotherhood in North America as being as being on its board of directors (Shura Council) as well as being the "Masul" (Leader) of the Educational Committee for the same organization.[596]

Dr. El-Tantawy Attia: Dr. El-Tantawy Attia is very active within the Muslim community and organizations affiliated with the Muslim Brotherhood. He sits on the board of directors of Islamic Relief Canada, and has previously served as President of the Muslim Investment Group and the Canadian Islamic Trust Foundation. He also serves as the Executive Director of Toronto Masjid. Recently Dr. Attia was awarded the Queen Elizabeth II Diamond Jubilee Medal by the Governor General of Canada for his lifetime of achievements and services to Canada.[597] Dr. Attia is also a leading figure in the Muslim Association of Canada. In 2011, he told the press that: "Here [the Toronto Masjid] we follow the teachings of the Muslim Brotherhood." Dr. Attia's son in law was in jail in Egypt. Khaled al-Qazzaz was the Foreign Secretary for the Muslim Brotherhood's government of Egypt when Dr. Morsi was President. His daughter, Sarah, was a leading figure in the Muslim Student Association and left Canada to go to Egypt with Mr. Qazzaz.[598]

Sarah Attia: Sarah Attia is the daughter of Dr. El-Tantawy Attia. She is the former Vice President of the Muslim Students Association and was a speaker at May 18-19, 2002, 28th Annual Islamic Society of North America (ISNA) Canada Convention in Toronto. She is a graduate of the Faculty of Engineering, University of Toronto, with a master's degree in chemical engineering.[599] Sarah Attia is the wife of Khaled Aa-Qazzaz.

Khaled al-Qazzaz: Khaled al-Qazzaz was born on July 3, 1979 in Cairo, Egypt. He moved to Toronto in 2000 to do a Masters in Mechanical Engineering at the University of Toronto, where he met his wife, Sarah Attia. He served as the UTSG MSA President in 2002-2003.[600] In 2005, al-Qazzaz returned to Egypt. In 2011, and according to his own Twitter account, al-Qazzaz was working in Egypt as "Secretary on Foreign Relations, Office of the President Politics: Freedom & Justice Party." This refers to Dr. Morsi, the Muslim Brotherhood president of Egypt in 2012 and 2013. The Freedom and Justice Party is the political wing of the Muslim Brotherhood in Egypt. He was taken in a wave of arrests alongside several other top Muslim Brotherhood aides after a military coup toppled the government on July 3, 2013. After spending 18 months in prison, he was released by Egyptian authorities in January 2015.[601]

---

[595] Posts by Mohamed Rida Beshir. (2015). Retrieved from http://familydawn.com/author/mrbeshir/

[596] 1992 phone directory retrieved from http://www.investigativeproject.org/documents/case_docs/1083.pdf

[597] Board of Directors. (2015) Retrieved from http://islamicreliefcanada.org/about/bod/

[598] *Here are the facts about Islamic Relief.* (2014, August 22). *Jewish Defense League.* Retrieved from http://www.jdl-canada.com/tag/cair-canada/

[599] Attia, S. (2011, February 11). I Took My Kids to Tahrir Square. *Bangor Daily News.* Retrieved from https://bangordailynews.com/2011/02/11/opinion/i-took-my-kids-to-tahrir-square/

[600] Free Khaled al-Qazzaz. Retrieved from http://www.freekhaledalqazzaz.com/personal-life/

[601] Carville, Olivia. (2015, January 11). Canadian resident Khaled Al-Qazzaz freed after 558 days. *Toronto Star.* Retrieved from

Khadija Haffajee: Khadija Haffajee is originally from South Africa, and according to her biography on the Women's Islamic Initiative on Spirituality and Equality website, is an educator and community activist in Ottawa, Canada. Ms. Haffajee is also a member of the Board of Directors for the Council on American-Islamic Relations - Canada (CAIR- CAN). For more than 30 years Ms. Haffajee has held leadership positions in local, national and international Muslim associations. In 1997 she was the first female elected to the Majlis ash Shura of the Islamic Society of North America and continued there until 2008. [602] She is on the board of the newly formed National Council of Canadian Muslims (NCCM), the new name for CAIR-CAN. She is one of the few to have been there every year along with Dr. Jamal Badawi.[603] Ms. Haffajee has also held various positions with the ISNA, and joined its board of directors in 1997. She won additional terms in 2001 and 2004. During that time, she was on the editorial advisory board of ISNA's Islamic Horizons magazine. A 1999 issue released under her supervision put Muslim Brotherhood founder Hassan al-Banna on the cover with the heading, "A Martyr of Our Times."[604]

Hisham al-Talib: One of the most significant founders of the MSA of the United States and Canada, which was formed in January 1963.[605] He is a founding member and the current vice president of finance of the Herndon, VA based International Institute of Islamic Thought (IIIT), an organization the FBI believes was part of a terrorist financing network. He was a founding member and Director of the SAAR Foundation from 1983-1995. A U.S. Government investigation found that the SAAR Foundation is part of a network, known as the Safa Group, of up to 100 non-profit and for-profit organizations, inter-related through corporate officers and holding companies, which facilitate terrorist funding.[606] In November 1992, IIIT wrote a letter to Sami al-Arian supporting the funding of WISE, a Tampa, Florida think-tank that housed four members of the Palestinian Islamic Jihad's (PIJ) governing board, including al- Arian. The PIJ is a U.S.-designated foreign terrorist organization. The IIIT letter named the IIIT officials who supported WISE, including al-Talib.[607]

Maiwand Yar: Born in Pakistan in 1983, Yar is a former student of Mechanical Engineering at the University of Manitoba, and was the local MSA chapter's treasurer.[608] According to the RCMP, in 2007, it is believed that Yar departed Canada with accomplice Ferid Ahmed Imam for Pakistan. According to witnesses, Yar advised that he and Imam were going to ally themselves with the Taliban and attend a terrorist training camp in order to receive instruction on firearms, explosives and guerilla warfare. Their specific objective for joining the Taliban was to fight and kill NATO soldiers in Afghanistan. In a letter sent in 2009, Yar stated that he had in fact spent time in both the Taliban and Al Qaida.[609] Yar is being sought on charges of conspiracy to participate in the activities of a terrorist group and participation in the

---

http://www.thestar.com/news/gta/2015/01/11/canadian_resident_freed_in_cairo_after_18_months_says_family.html

[602] Khadija Haffajee Bio. Retrieved from http://www.wisemuslimwomen.org/muslimwomen/bio/khadija_haffajee/

[603] NCCM board of directors. Retrieved from http://www.nccm.ca/about/our-board/

[604] Mauro, R. (2014, April 17). CAIR-Canada Directors Praise Muslim Brotherhood. *The Clarion Project.* Retrieved from http://www.clarionproject.org/analysis/cair-canada-directors-praise-muslim-brotherhood

[605] The truth about the Muslim Students Association. (2014, April 10). Retrieved from http://counterjihadreport.com/2014/04/10/the-truth-about-the-muslim-students-association/

[606] Hisham al-Talib. Retrieved from http://www.investigativeproject.org/documents/misc/720.pdf

[607] Ibid.

[608] MSA University of Manitoba (UM_MSA). (2014, August 19). Retrieved from http://pointdebasculecanada.ca/10022329/

[609] Wanted by the RCMP. (2011, March 29). Retrieved from http://www.rcmp-grc.gc.ca/en/wanted/maiwand-yar

activities of a terrorist group.[610]

Muhannad al-Farekh: Born in Texas, al-Farekh grew up in the United Arab Emirates and was educated in Jordan.[611] In Canada he lived with his grandmother in Winnipeg. He is a former business student at the University of Manitoba, who served as the office manager of that chapter's MSA from 2005-2006. On April 2, 2015, an arrest warrant for Muhannad al-Farekh was unsealed after an RCMP investigation. The allegations against al-Farekh date back to 2007.[612] It was then that he disappeared to Pakistan along with University of Manitoba colleagues Farid Imam and Maiwand Yar. Though both Imam and Yar were charged in 2011 with terrorism offences following an RCMP national security investigation called Project Darken, al-Farekh was only indicted in April 2015. The criminal complaint accused him of travelling "to Pakistan to join al-Qaida" and helping a terrorist group targeting American citizens and military personnel.[613]

Abdalrahman Naddaf and Mohammad Tulul: President and event coordinator at Algonquin college MSA respectively (as of 2014). Both were part of a group of Muslim students who claimed they were not being given fair use of their school's spirituality centre.[614] Naddaf and Tulul are both on a court-ordered no contact list for Awso Peshdary, among others with college ties such as Thair Hafez, Samr Farhat, Mohammad Ali Farhat, Ayyub Arab, and Ibrahim Soukary.[615]

Omar Kalair: President and CEO of United Muslims (UM) Financial, Kalair is wanted by the RCMP with respect to a Sharia banking fraud investigation. Videos of previous RIS (Reviving the Islamic Spirit) conventions available on YouTube show that UM Financial sponsored the Toronto Islamist convention in 2005 and 2006. A profile of Omar Kalair posted on a Wilfrid Laurier University alumni's website indicates that, during his years as an Economics student, "Kalair founded the Muslim Students' Association [MSA] and remained its President for four years."[616] Furthermore, the alumni website goes on to say that Kalair founded UM in 2004, initially with eight regional branches to service Canada's over one-million Muslims. It is now Canada's premier Islamic financial institution, profiled in over 200 print, TV and radio interviews. Partnering with other institutions UM has launched many Islamic financial products including: Home financing, UM Investment, Islamic ETF, Sukuks (Islamic bonds), and an interest-free MasterCard. Kalair has

---

[610] Terror charges laid against former Winnipeggers. (2011, March 15). *CBC News.* Retrieved from http://www.cbc.ca/news/canada/manitoba/terror-charges-laid-against-former-winnipeggers-1.1015496

[611] McArthur, G et al. (2010, October 1). Global manhunt for Canadian students. *The Globe and Mail.* Retrieved from http://www.theglobeandmail.com/news/national/global-manhunt-for-canadian-students/article4327862/?page=1

[612] Muhanad Al Farekh – Another former MSA-Manitoba leader charged with supporting terrorism. (2015, April 3). Retrieved from http://pointdebasculecanada.ca/muhanad-al-farekh-former-msa-manitoba-leader-charged-supporting-terrorism/

[613] Bell, S. (2015, April 2). Muhanad Mahmoud Al Farekh, former University of Manitoba student, charged with supporting terrorism. *National Post.* Retrieved from http://news.nationalpost.com/news/canada/muhanad-mahmoud-al-farekh-former-university-of-manitoba-student-charged-with-supporting-terrorism

[614] Desrosiers, S. (2014, March 25). Muslim students, Algonquin College, clash over spirituality centre. *Ottawa Sun.* Retrieved from http://www.ottawasun.com/2014/03/25/muslim-students-algonquin-college-clash-over-spirituality-centre .

[615] Helmer, A. (2015, February 14). Alleged jihadists in Ottawa share common link. *Ottawa Sun.* Retrieved from http://www.ottawasun.com/2015/02/14/alleged-jihadists-share-common-link

[616] Omar Kalair, founder of UM Financial – Past sponsor of the Islamist RIS convention wanted by the RCMP for sharia banking fraud. (2014, March 7). Retrieved from http://pointdebasculecanada.ca/omar-kalair-um-financial-ris-rcmp-sharia-banking-fraud/

become the face of the Islamic finance industry in Canada, being invited by governments and royalty, presenting papers at international conferences, and was selected to accompany Prime Minister Jean Chrétien's business trade delegation to Saudi Arabia, among other missions. Kalair's honours include: Entrepreneur of the Year Award by the Islamic Canadian Chamber of Commerce, top 20 Pioneer Muslim Business Leadership Award at the Canadian Parliament and World Finance's Islamic Finance Business Leader Award – North America.[617]

Hussein Hamdani: Hussein Hamdani was an advisor to the Canadian government on public safety matters since 2005. He was appointed that year to the Roundtable that "provides advice and perspective to the Minister of Public Safety and the Minister of Justice, concerning matters of national security." His affiliation with Muslim Brotherhood entities dates back to 1995, at least, when he was the Muslim Students Association's treasurer at McMaster University where he studied political science from 1991-1995. He continued to work with the MSA at the University of Toronto while he was doing his Masters in International relations from 1995-1996. In 1998 and in 1999, the University of Western Ontario's student newspaper identified Hamdani as MSA Western's president. He was then studying Law (1997-2000).[618] In 1996, Hamdani published the text "The Islamicization of Campus Politics and the politicization of the MSA." In it he discusses how Muslim student leaders in North America ought to take control of their respective student unions, and by extension the union's finances. He claims that in doing so, Muslim students would be ideally positioned to redirect funds towards their own Muslim associations on campus. Furthermore, Hamdani encourages Muslim student activists to try to control their student union's key committees, those "where the real politics lies." An excerpt from the text says, "It should be the long-term goal of every MSA to Islamicize the politics of their respective university."[619] In addition to his roles at the MSA, Hamdani has held roles in several other Islamic organizations. He was board chair at the Settlement and Integration Services Organization (SISO shut down after its CEO and its finance director were convicted of defrauding the federal government for millions of dollars). He's been listed as: a Senior Advisor of Muslim Youth of North America Organization (MYNA), Vice-Chair of North American Spiritual Revival (NASR), and was founding member of the Ihya Foundation (Ihya launched the Muslim Brotherhood-linked RIS Conventions in 2003), among others.[620] On May 1, 2015, Hamdani was suspended from his position on the cross-cultural roundtable on national security by Minister of Public Safety Steven Blaney. While Hamdani holds that his dismissal was politically motivated due to his opposition to Bill C-51 and his support of Justin Trudeau and the Liberal party, Minister Blaney alleges "This individual's membership on the Cross-Cultural Roundtable on National Security has been suspended immediately pending a review of the facts. While questions surrounding this individual's links to radical ideology have circulated for some time, it was hoped that he could be a positive influence to promote Canadian values. It is now becoming clear this may not have been the case."[621]

---

[617] Omar Kalair profile. Retrieved from https://www.laurieralumni.ca/alumni/OmarKalair

[618] Hussein Hamdani advocated "the Islamization of campus politics" before being appointed public safety advisor by the government of Canada. (2015, April 30). Retrieved from http://pointdebasculecanada.ca/hussein-hamdani-advocated-the-islamization-of-campus-politics-before-being-appointed-public-safety-advisor-by-the-government-of-canada/

[619] Ibid.

[620] Hussein Hamdani profile, (2013, September 20). Retrieved from http://pointdebasculecanada.ca/hamdani-hussein/

[621] Carter, A. (2015, May 1). Hussein Hamdani says federal election politics behind his suspension. *CBC News.* Retrieved from http://www.cbc.ca/news/canada/hamilton/news/hussein-hamdani-says-federal-election-politics-behind-his-suspension-1.3056931

CHAPTER 15: CHARITABLE STATUS REVOKED FOR CONNECTIONS TO EXTREMISM

Thomas Quiggin

Key Points

- The Jihad Fund of the former Libyan dictator Muammar Gaddafi[622,623,624,625] operated openly in Canada for years as a taxpayer supported charity. During that time, this government approved "charity" helped fund a coup in a Caribbean country and built a mosque in Toronto.

- Hamas received millions of Canadian taxpayer dollars in a nationwide registered charity scheme aimed at deliberate terrorist fund raising, calculated to mislead the Government of Canada. IRFAN ran it.

- One of the south Asia's largest terrorist groups received funding from Canada, again from a government approved charity, while the charities host organization was defrauding its own supporters. The ISNA, which ran this fraud, has been involved in three charity revocations related to the funding of terrorism.

As of 2017, it can be assessed that the Government of Canada continues to fund Islamist operations both directly through government handouts and indirectly by allowing them to operate taxpayer supported charities. While terrorism and extremism funding continue to flow into and out of Canada, not all the news has been bad. Between 2011 and 2014 the Government of Canada did take several steps to shutter charities that were involved in Islamist terrorist funding activities

It is a fact that some of these charities had Muslim Brotherhood connections. Three of them were revoked for cause which the CRA states occurs only in the "most severe cases of non-compliance, or cases where there is continuous non-compliance."[626] Another was revoked for failing to conduct any substantive charitable activity during the three years under audit while providing a private benefit to a Director. All the money provided to this particular "charity" came from Colonel Gaddafi in Libya and his Jihad Fund.

The CRA directly identifies that funding terrorism is a major factor in all these cases and that in one case, a charity was claiming to be raising funds for victims of disasters in Asia, yet was using the money to fund terrorism in the Middle East. In other words, it is reasonable to say that individuals in Canada who may

---

[622] Eoin O'Carroll, "*Gaddafi? Kadafi? Qaddafi? What's the correct spelling?*" *Christian Science Monitor*, 22 February 2011. The article can be seen online at http://www.csmonitor.com/World/2011/0222/Gaddafi-Kadafi-Qaddafi-What-s-the-correct-spelling Viewed 21 May 2017. **Rated B2.**

[623] BBC News, *Libya country profile*, www.bbc.com, 01 March 2017, The article can be seen online at http://www.bbc.com/news/world-africa-13754897. Viewed 21 May 2017. **Rated A2.**

[624] *The World Factbook 2013-14*, Central Intelligence Agency, 2013. The article can be viewed online at https://www.cia.gov/library/publications/the-world-factbook/index.html . Viewed 21 May 2017. **Rated B2.**

[625] Wikipedia contributors, "Muammar Gaddafi," Wikipedia, The Free Encyclopedia. https://en.wikipedia.org/w/index.php?title=Muammar_Gaddafi&oldid=777967303 Viewed 21 May 2017. **Rated C2.**

[626] For an explanation of CRA terms in these types of cases see the glossary of the CRA at http://www.cra-arc.gc.ca/chrts-gvng/chrts/glssry-eng.html#revokedcause . Viewed 24 July 2017. **Rated A1.**

have thought they were funding a charity to help those suffering from a natural disaster were in fact having their money used to fund terrorism. Additionally, all Canadians are subsidizing this activity due to the tax breaks that accrue to charitable donations.

These noteworthy charities, location, and their charitable status revocation dates are:

- International Relief Fund for the Afflicted and Needy (IRFAN-Canada), Mississauga ON; charitable status revoked 9 April 2011;

- Islamic Society of North America (ISNA) Development Foundation (ISNA-DF), Mississauga ON; charitable status revoked 21 April 2013;

- World Islamic Call Society (WICS), London ON; charitable status revoked 26 March 2011, and

- World Assembly of Muslim Youth (WAMY), Mississauga ON; charitable status revoked 11 February 2012.

- Islamic Society of North America: Canadian Islamic Trust Foundation Islamic Services of Canada, Mississauga ON; revocation reported July 2017.

- Islamic Society of North America: Islamic Services of Canada, Mississauga, ON; revocation reported July 2017.

Additionally, the Government of Canada declared IRFAN-Canada itself to be a terrorist entity in 2014, when it continued to operate following its charitable status revocation in 2011.

International Relief Fund for the Afflicted and Needy Canada (IRFAN Canada) Mississauga ON: CRA Charitable Status Revoked 9 April 2011

In 2011, the CRA revoked (for cause) the charitable status of IRFAN-Canada due a series of failures and for the funding of the terrorist group Hamas. The short form of the statement as it appears on the CRA website reads:

> "On the basis of our audit, we have concluded that IRFAN-Canada has: ceased to comply with the requirements of the Act for its continued registration; failed to comply with or contravened sections 230 to 231.5 of the Act; issued a receipt for a gift or donation otherwise than in accordance with the Act and the Regulations or that contains false information; and failed to file an information return as required under the Act-[o]ur analysis of the audit information has led the CRA to believe that IRFAN-Canada provides support to Hamas, a listed terrorist organization. Our findings indicate that IRFAN-Canada provided over $14.6 million in resources to operating partners that were run by officials of Hamas, openly supported and provided funding to Hamas, or have been listed by various jurisdictions because of their support for Hamas or other terrorist entities."

In addition to failing to comply and funding a terrorist group, the CRA also noted that IRFAN was raising money by appeals made to the public under misleading circumstances. Specifically, CRA notes that IRFAN requested pledges for money for the 2004 Tsunami disaster, the South-East Asia Earthquake Disaster of 2006, the Indonesian Earthquake of 2006, the Bangladesh Cyclone of 2007, the Burma Cyclone of 2007, the Pakistan Earthquake of 2008 and the Indonesian Earthquake of 2008. The CRA audit discovered that the money raised through these campaigns was not sent to assist those in need. Rather, the money was then co-mingled with the general monies of IRFAN and then used to fund other activities such as funding terrorism. (Section 2.5 Public Breech Test/Deceptive Funding).[627]

The CRA audit and investigation also reveals that IRFAN was an integral part of the international fund-raising efforts to support Hamas. They add that there is a strong possibility that IRFAN was created to circumvent the CRA's refusal to grant charitable status previously to charitable status to the Povrel Jerusalem Fund for Human Services (JFHS). The CRA believes that there are "strong indicators" that the JFHS acted in Canada on behalf of the American based Holy Land Foundation.[628] The Holy Land Foundation has been the subject of an extensive criminal investigation in the USA which resulted in convictions for funding terrorism.[629]

The CRA also stated that "clear evidence" existed that at their earliest inception, the HLF and JFHS were in close communication, their identities overlapped, and they were part of the North American network established by the Muslim Brotherhoods Palestine Committees to support Hamas.[630] Furthermore, the CRA notes that JFHS and IRFAN had a past pattern (1992-2002) of funding organizations that have been recognized as having links to Hamas and that despite its 2004 undertaking, IRFAN continued to do so.[631]

The founding members of the board of directors of IRFAN were Nadeem Siddiqi, Mohamed Farhad Khadim, Reyad Hobba, Mohammad Ammak and others.[632]

From this factual government reporting, it can be assessed that some of these individuals were in a position of authority and influence when the IRFAN was being conceived, set up and as it began operations as well as being a voting member until 2004. During this time, IRFAN was involved in a series of deceptive practices, including false claims of fund raising for disasters and funding terrorism.

---

[627] For more information on the deceptive fund-raising efforts of IRFAN see Section 2.5 *Public Breech Test/Deceptive Funding,* (page 22/27) of the CRA report/letter dated 14 December 2010 (file number 3001490). The subject line of the letter was RE: Audit of Registered Charity: International Relief Fund for the Afflicted and Needy (Canada). The PDF can be seen online at http://www.globalphilanthropy.ca/images/uploads/02_20101214_IRFAN_AFL_FINAL.pdf . Viewed 24 July 2017. **Rated A1**.

[628] Page 3/27 of the CRA report/letter dated 14 December 2010 (file number 3001490). *RE: Audit of Registered Charity: International Relief Fund for the Afflicted and Needy (Canada).* The PDF can be seen online at http://www.globalphilanthropy.ca/images/uploads/02_20101214_IRFAN_AFL_FINAL.pdf . Viewed 24 July 2017. **Rated A1**.

[629] See the United States Department of Justice 2009 statement *Federal Judge Hands Downs Sentences in Holy Land Foundation Case, Holy Land Foundation and Leaders Convicted on Providing Material Support to Hamas Terrorist Organization*. It is available online at: http://www.justice.gov/opa/pr/2009/May/09-nsd-519.html

[630] See page 15/27 of the CRA report/letter dated 14 December 2010 (file number 3001490). *RE: Audit of Registered Charity: International Relief Fund for the Afflicted and Needy (Canada).* The PDF can be seen online at http://www.globalphilanthropy.ca/images/uploads/02_20101214_IRFAN_AFL_FINAL.pdf . Viewed 24 July 2017. **Rated A1**.

[631] See page 15/27 of the CRA report/letter dated 14 December 2010 (file number 3001490). *RE: Audit of Registered Charity: International Relief Fund for the Afflicted and Needy (Canada).* The PDF can be seen online at http://www.globalphilanthropy.ca/images/uploads/02_20101214_IRFAN_AFL_FINAL.pdf . Viewed 24 July 2017. **Rated A1**.

[632] As listed on the T3010 form of IRFAN as submitted to the CRA for the year 2000. Available on the CRA website.

As made clear by the Hamas charter itself, Hamas is part of the Muslim Brotherhood.[633] The CRA audit of IRFAN and the Holy Land Foundation trial in the USA make it clear that IRFAN, the JFHS and others are part of the various Palestine Committees set up by the Muslim Brotherhood in North America.

Both the Canadian based Jerusalem Fund for Human Services and IRFAN were also identified as unindicted co-conspirators in the terrorism funding trial of the Holy Land Relief Foundation (formerly Occupied Land Fund). This major trial in the USA resulted in multiple criminal convictions.[634] The terrorism funding money in question was sent to Hamas, which claims to the Muslim Brotherhood in Palestine.

Islamic Society of North America (ISNA): Development Fund (ISNA-DF) Mississauga ON

CRA Charitable Status Revoked: 21 September 2013

In 2013, the CRA revoked (for cause) the charitable status of the ISNA Development Foundation for funding terrorism.[635] Specifically, the CRA had concerns that the charity's money "may have been used to support the political efforts of Jamaat-e-Islami and/or its armed wing, Hizbul Mujahideen."[636]

The ISNA is located at 2200 South Sheridan Way in Mississauga Ontario. The same address houses/housed a number of other charities and organizations run by the ISNA, including, but not limited to the Islamic Schools Association of Canada (ISAC), The Canadian Islamic Trust Foundation, The Canadian Muslim Relief Committee of ISNA Canada, the Indian Muslim Relief Committee of ISNA Canada, the Canadian Muslim Council, the Islamic Book Service, ISNA-IDB Education Trust, the Muslim Youth of North America and the Islamic Centre of Canada. The ISNA itself has direct links to the Muslim Brotherhood and was one of its first North American organizations set up in Canada and the USA.

The short version of the CRA revocation statement reads as follows:

> "On the basis of our audit, we have concluded that the Organization has: ceased to comply with the requirements of the Act for its continued registration; failed to comply with or contravened any of sections 230 to 231.5 of the Act; issued a receipt for a gift or donation otherwise than in accordance with the Act and its Regulations; and failed to file an information return as required under the Act. Our analysis of the information obtained during the course of the audit has led the CRA to believe that the Organization had entered into a funding arrangement with the Kashmiri Canadian Council/Kashmiri Relief Fund of Canada (KCC/KRFC), non-qualified donees under the Act, with the ultimate goal of sending the raised funds to a Pakistan-based non-governmental organization named the Relief Organization for Kashmiri Muslims (ROKM) without maintaining direction and control. Under the arrangement, KCC/KRFC raised funds for relief work in Kashmir,

---

[633] Section Two of the charter begins with the line: *The Islamic Resistance Movement is a branch of the Muslim Brotherhood chapter in Palestine.* The entire charter of HAMAS can be seen at http://avalon.law.yale.edu/20th_century/hamas.asp . Viewed 24 July 2017. **Rated A1.**

[634] See page 3/27 of the CRA report/letter dated 14 December 2010 (file number 3001490). *RE: Audit of Registered Charity: International Relief Fund for the Afflicted and Needy (Canada).* A copy of this report is available online at file:///C:/Users/User/Pictures/IRFAN%20CRA%20admin%20letter.pdf . Viewed on 27 February 2017. **Rated A1.**

[635] For a short description of the reasons for revoking the charitable status of the ISNA Development Foundation, see the CRA's website at: http://www.cra-arc.gc.ca/ebci/haip/srch/revcausesumm-eng.action?bn=863919262RR0001. Viewed 24 July 2017. **Rated A1**.

[636] This statement can be seen at http://www.cra-arc.gc.ca/ebci/haip/srch/revcausesumm-eng.action?bn=863919262RR0001. Viewed 24 July 2017. **Rated A1**.

and the Organization supplied official donation receipts to the donors and disbursed over $281,696 to ROKM, either directly, or via KCC/KRFC. Our research indicates that ROKM is the charitable arm of Jamaat-e-Islami, a political organization that actively contests the legitimacy of India's governance over the state of Jammu and Kashmir, including reportedly through the activities of its armed wing Hizbul Mujahideen is listed as a terrorist entity by the Council of the European Union and is declared a banned terrorist organization by the Government of India, Ministry of Home Affairs, under the Unlawful Activities (Prevention) Act of 1967. Given the commonalities in directorship between ROKM and Jamaat-e-Islami, concerns exist that the Organization's resources may have been used to support the political efforts of Jamaat-e-Islami and/or its armed wing, Hizbul Mujahideen."

Dr. Mohamed Bekkari was on the board of directors of the ISNA Development foundation for at least the last five years before it lost its status for funding terrorism (2008-2012) including being the Vice Chair and President. He also sits on the boards of many other organizations that sit under the ISNA umbrella as well. Dr. Bekkari was also involved in a lawsuit involving the ISNA, himself and a former staff member Mohammad Ashraf. The outcome of the lawsuit was unclear, but some background information has been covered in the Toronto Star. The articles noted that a Muslim charity squandered money for poor[637] as well as Federal audit raises concern that Canadian charity funded terror.[638]

Khalid Tarabain was also on the board of directors of the ISNA Development Foundation for three of the last five years before the charity lost its status for funding terrorism.

The ISNA and its Previous Connections to Terrorism Funding

It can be assessed that the ISNA has repeatedly been tied to the promotion of terrorist groups or the funding of terrorism. The most well documented of these was the above noted Canada Revenue Agency statement of September 2013 which revoked the charitable status of the ISNA Development Foundation.[639]

However, the ISNA has a previous history with the Jamaat-e-Islami such as when they invited the head of Jamaat-e-Islami to be a speaker at the 34th annual ISNA Convention. Zazi Hussain Hamad (also reported as Qazi Hussain Hamad) was the head of Jamaat-e-Islami in Pakistan at the time. The group has been banned as a terrorist group in numerous countries. He would have been a speaker on Saturday 23 May

---

637 For more on the audit and the problems at ISNA, see Jesse Mclean, *Muslim charity squandered money for poor.* 20 January 2011, The Toronto Star. This article is available online at: http://www.thestar.com/news/gta/2011/01/20/muslim_charity_squandered_money_for_poor.html . Viewed 24 July 2017. **Rated B2**.

638 Jesse McLean, *Star Investigation: Federal audit raises concern that Canadian charity funded terror*, The Toronto Star, 25 July 2017. The article is available on line at http://www.thestar.com/news/canada/2013/07/25/star_investigation_federal_audit_raises_concern_that_canadian_charity_funded_terror.html Viewed 24 July 2017. **Rated B2**.

639 A PDF version of the 36-page letter on the audit of the ISNA Development Foundation by CRA is available online at: http://www.thestar.com/content/dam/thestar/static_images/IDF-complete-audit-letter.pdf . Viewed 24 July 2017. **Rated A1**.

2008 from 1:45 to 2:45 PM and on Sunday 24 May 2008 from 1:45 to 2:45 PM. Following that, he was to have been a moderator on a panel from 7:15 PM to 8:45 PM.[640]

The conference was called "Our Youth, Our Future: Path to Paradise." The conference was endorsed by CAIR CAN, the ICNA, the Muslim Association of Canada (MAC) and the event was sponsored by Human Concern International (HCI). Among many others, Khalid Tarabain was on the board of directors of HCI at the time. Dr. Bekkari was the Vice Chair of the ISNA Development Foundation, the charity that would have its status revoked in 2013 for concerns about funding terrorism: Jamaat-e-Islami and/or its armed wing, Hizbul Mujahideen.

Mr. Ahmad did not make it to the convention as the Canadian government pulled his visa shortly before the conference after a complaint from the NGO Canadian Coalition for Democracies (CCD).[641]

Islamic Society of North America (ISNA): Canadian Islamic Trust Foundation and Islamic Services of Canada, Mississauga ON

In July of 2017, it was reported that two other charities run by ISNA also suffered charity revocations by the CRA. The Canadian Islamic Trust Foundation and Islamic Services of Canada[642] both had their status revoked for not complying with the requirements set out by the charities act. According to Global News, "the findings that led to the latest two revocations was that ISNA Islamic Services tax receipts had been issued for collections by a Toronto mosque for the "charitable arm" of a Pakistani group whose armed wing was fighting Indian forces."[643]

World Islamic Call Society (WICS) London ON: CRA Charitable Status Revoked: 26 March 2011

In 2011, the World Islamic Call Society lost its charitable status for failing to meet the definition of being a charity and for providing private benefits to its director. The case is interesting as WICS-Canada was a chapter of the World Islamic Call Society that was set up by the former President of Libya and funded through his "jihad fund." The short statement from CRA concerning this revocation reads:

> "On the basis of the Canada Revenue Agency audit, we have concluded that the World Islamic Call Society (Society) has ceased to comply with the requirements of the Act for its continued registration as it has failed to meet the definition of a charitable organization under the Act by failing to conduct any substantive charitable activity during the three years under audit. It has also provided a private benefit to a Director."

---

640 The poster for this convention can be seen online at http://bp2.blogger.com/_2B8hNLTjAH0/SDXUV4hwHbI/AAAAAAAAAAk/wGSRiST7y54/s1600-h/isna_brother_qazi_hussain_ahmad.jpg . Viewed 24 July 2017. **Rated C3.**

641 Guest Column, *CCD urges immediate action on eligibility of Qazi Hussain Ahmad to enter Canada*, Canada Free Press, 22 May 2008. The article can be seen online at http://canadafreepress.com/print_friendly/ccd-urges-immediate-action-on-eligibility-of-qazi-hussain-ahmad-to-enter-ca . Viewed 24 July 2017. **Rated C3.**

642 For more on this, see *Summary of reasons for revocation — ISNA, ISLAMIC SERVICES OF CANADA.* This CRA statement can be seen online at http://www.cra-arc.gc.ca/ebci/haip/srch/revcausesumm-eng.action?bn=884802356RR0001 . Viewed 24 July 2017. **Rated A1.**

643 Stewart Bell and Sean Craig, *Government revokes group's charity status, audit cites possible funding of Pakistani militants,* Global News, 19 July 2017. The article can be seen online at http://globalnews.ca/news/3606224/government-revokes-groups-charity-status-audit-cites-pakistani-militants/ . Viewed 24 July 2017. **Rated B2.**

In its longer audit report, CRA also noted: [644]

> "The Society acts at the direction of, and receives all of its funding from, the Libyan-based World Islamic Call Society (WICS-Libya), an organization founded by Muammar al-Qadaffi (Gadhafi) in 1972 whose objects and activities are not confined to the advancement of religion as that term is understood under Canadian law."
>
> "According to various sources, WICS-Libya is operated under the control of the Government of Libya and funded by allocations made by Muammar al-Qadaffi. (Gadhafi) from "the Jihad Fund". (FN3) An affidavit and the Plea Agreement filed in the successful U.S. conviction of Abdurahman Muhammad Alamoudi in 2004 on charges of wilfully attempting to violate U.S. economic sanctions against Libya imposed because of Libya's involvement in terrorist bombings and the downing of Pan Am Flight 103 over Lockerbie, Scotland, attest to the use of the WICS-Libya's network to move funds on behalf of the Libyan government in violation of the sanctions against Libya."

The head of the charity was Assem Fadel.[645] Assem Fadel was president of the organization from its inception until it lost its charitable status.[646] One of the recipients of the WICS money was a jihadist political party that tried to overthrow the government of Trinidad and Tobago (Jamaat al-Muslimeen). Assem Fadel was the holder of the bank account that transferred the monies in question. The CRA also noted that for many years much of the money from the charity was used for administrative expenses including rent of an office in a building owned by Mr. Fadel himself as well as paying for his cell phone etc.[647]

Mr. Fadel is also the President and former treasurer of the Islamic Centre of Southwest Ontario (ICSO), which was first registered as a charity in 1995.[648] The ICSO is also the co-funder of the new chair of Islamic

---

[644] Mark Blumberg, *CRA letters on revocation of World Islamic Call Society - various CRA concerns noted*, Canadian Charity Law, 03 June 2011. The article can be seen online at http://www.canadiancharitylaw.ca/index.php/blog/comments/cra_letters_on_revocation_of_world_islamic_call_society_-_various_cra_conce . Viewed 24 July 2017. **Rated B2**.

[645] CRA Charity number 894381573RR0001.

[646] CRA letter concerning revocation of the charitable status of the WICS, dated 04 October 2010. The letter can be seen online at http://www.globalphilanthropy.ca/images/uploads/World_Islamic_Call_Society.pdf . Viewed 24 July 2017. **Rated B2**.

[647] CRA letter concerning revocation of the charitable status of the WICS, dated 04 October 2010. The letter can be seen online at http://www.globalphilanthropy.ca/images/uploads/World_Islamic_Call_Society.pdf . Viewed 24 July 2017. **Rated B2**.

[648] CRA charities website. For one example of Mr. Fadel as treasurer, see http://www.cra-arc.gc.ca/ebci/haip/srch/t3010form22officers-eng.action?b=897762696RR0001&fpe=2011-12-31&n=THE+ISLAMIC+CENTRE+OF+SOUTHWEST+ONTARIO&r=http%3A%2F%2Fwww.cra-arc.gc.ca%3A80%2Febci%2Fhaip%2Fsrch%2Ft3010form22-eng.action%3Fb%3D897762696RR0001%26amp%3Bfpe%3D2011-12-31%26amp%3Bn%3DTHE%2BISLAMIC%2BCENTRE%2BOF%2BSOUTHWEST%2BONTARIO%26amp%3Br%3Dhttp%253A%252F%252Fwww.cra-arc.gc.ca%253A80%252Febci%252Fhaip%252Fsrch%252Fbasicsearchresult-eng.action%253Fk%253DIslamic%252BCentre%252Bof%252BSouthwest%252BOntario%252B%2526amp%253Bs%253Dregistered%2526amp%253Bp%253D1%2526amp%253Bb%253Dtrue Viewed 24 July 2017. **Rated A1**.

Studies at Huron College (University of Western Ontario). The other funder of this chair is the Muslim Association of Canada, whose President played a role in the announcement of the project.[649]

World Assembly of Muslim Youth (WAMY) Mississauga ON: CRA Charitable Status Revoked: 11 February 2012

The CRA short statement on the revocation of charitable status read:

> "On the basis of our audit and of our review of the Organization's Registered Charity Information Returns for the years from 2005 to 2009, we have concluded that the Organization: failed to comply with or contravened subsection 230(2) of the Act; ceased to comply with the requirements of the Act for its continued registration; and failed to file an information return as required under the Act. Our analysis of the Organization's operations has led the CRA to believe that the Organization, which has been inactive since at least 2005, was established to support the goals and operations of its parent organization located in Saudi Arabia. Our analysis particularly noted that the Organization shared a common director, contact information, and a bank account with the Benevolence International Fund in Canada (BIF-Canada), and provided $50,246 to the Benevolence International Foundation in the United States (BIF-USA) in 2001. On November 21, 2002, BIF-Canada and BIF-USA were added to the Consolidated List of the United Nations Security Council's Al-Qaida and Taliban and Sanctions Committee."

WAMY was founded in part by a member of the Muslim Brotherhood, according to the biography of Kamal Helbawy, who has been identified as one of the longest serving adherents of the Muslim Brotherhood. His biography is posted on IkhwanWeb, the official English language website of the Muslim Brotherhood in an article titled: A brother and a scholar:[650]

> "For 58 years, Kamal Helbawy has been a member of the Muslim Brotherhood, making him one of the oldest members of the Islamic movement. He joined the MB when he was 12 - in 1951 - and since then the Brotherhood, Islam and political Islam have been the centre of his life.
>
> Helbawy has established several organisations, associations and research centres with a focus on Islam as a religion and as a political ideology. **In the early 1970s, he took part in founding the World Assembly of Muslim Youth (WAMY) in Saudi Arabia and served as its executive director until 1982.** (Emphasis added).
>
> Dr Helbawy was then in charge of Muslim Brotherhood activities in Afghanistan from the late 1980s until 1994. He then moved to the United Kingdom and has been based there ever since. Upon his arrival in London, he established the Muslim Council of Britain (MCB) and the Muslim Association of Britain (MAB), which have helped establish him as one of the leaders of the Islamic community in the UK."

---

[649] The MAC announcement of the new chair in Islamic Studies can be seen online at http://www.macnet.ca/English/PressRelease/C_NAT-NewsRoom-PressRelease2011Oct14_Content.pdf . Viewed 24 July 2017. **Rated B2**.

[650] See the official site of the Muslin Brotherhood for the article *A Brother and a Scholar* dated 21 January 2010. The article can be seen online at http://www.ikhwanweb.com/article.php?id=22724 . Viewed 27 April 2017. **Rated B2**.

As noted by the CRA as well, WAMY is an organization based in Saudi Arabia which has funded several projects outside of Saudi Arabia itself. One of those organizations was CAIR (USA) whose leadership has had a long-standing relationship with WAMY and the Organization of the Islamic Conference. CAIR founder Nihad Awad has meet with the Secretary General of WAMY in Saudi Arabia and WAMY and CAIR have had joint projects.[651]

CAIR USA has also made it clear that they have derived funding from Saudi Arabia in the past, at least according to their own executive director:[652]

> "Elaborating on the CAIR campaign to dispel misunderstandings of Islam and Muslims, Nihad Awad, CAIR executive director, said that his group proposes to spend $10 million annually for five years in a media campaign. He said that CAIR would also recruit volunteers and produce educational material as part of its initiative. "We are planning to meet Prince Alwaleed ibn Talal[653] for his financial support to our project. He has been generous in the past," he added."

The Use of Monies Raised by the Various "Palestine Committees"

It is reasonable to believe that a variety of adherent Muslim Brotherhood organizations have raised money for the Palestinian cause, both legally and illegally in Canada and the USA (and elsewhere). The loss of the chartable status for IRFAN-Canada highlights how a Muslim Brotherhood led organization has transferred millions of dollars of "charity" money overseas to Hamas. Much the same can be said for the Islamic Association for Palestine and for the Holy Land Foundation (among others). This is not a new problem.

In a special non-periodical bulletin (Issue 1- dated 01 October 1992)[654] the Muslim Brotherhood sends the following information to its various Masuls (leaders). It is worth noting that the bulletin itself says it should not be photocopied (underlined) but that the ideas should be spread among the Ikhwan. In the section titled "Inside News" the bulletin, the examples of how Hamas is operating with the money are given, including the claimed killing of a Canadian and the wounding of two others by Muhammad Arif Bisharat (a.k.a. Abu Suhayb):

> "The pioneering role played by the Hamas Movement among the Palestinian people sectors inside and outside and on all the horizons is known to you. This is a [blessing and] a favor from God.
>
> The Movement has become the first organization in the field as your brothers bear the burdens of the Intifadah and are in the front row of the distinguished operations against the enemy and its collaborators. The Movement has now a weight that is taken into consideration abroad and it

---

[651] According to a Dec. 23, 1999 Arab News article, WAMY announced at a Riyadh press conference that it "was extending both moral and financial support to CAIR in its effort to construct a $3.5 million headquarters in Washington, D.C." For more on this see the IPT article on CAIR's funding at https://www.investigativeproject.org/documents/misc/110.pdf . Viewed 24 July 2017. **Rated B3**.

[652] *Javid Hassan, Media Campaign in US to Dispel Islamophobia,* Arab News, 21 June 2006. The article can be seen online at http://www.arabnews.com/node/286568 . Viewed 24 July 2017. **Rated C3**.

[653] Prince Talal is the grandson of Saudi King Abdulaziz.

[654] For a copy of this document as it was presented in an American court, see http://coop.txnd.uscourts.gov/judges/hlf2/09-25-08/Elbarasse%20Search%2035.pdf Viewed 21 May 2017. **Rated A2**.

is the one leading the powers that are opposed to the peaceful settlement, and it amasses all the capabilities for that purpose.

Due to the brothers' conviction of the necessity of keeping you abreast of the different developments inside the Movement, and also the news of your brothers inside and outside, and in order for you to be aware and informed of the Movement's policies and plans, something which helps you to perform your duties, and in order to gather efforts, program them and coordinate between them ... , due to all of this, it was decided to issue a private, non-periodical bulletin dealing with all of the aforementioned. (The Movement's positions and news, news of the inside, directions.)

The first issue of "The Trust" is between your hands and we ask God to help us and you to fulfill the proper duty towards the trust. We find it necessary to make some remarks which should be observed precisely:

1- The bulletin is specifically for the brothers, the Masuls of (Palestine Committee in every country only), and it is a trust in their necks.

2- The brothers are to study the bulletin in the periodical meeting of the committee and it is **not to be photocopied,** meaning that the original copy should remain the only one. (Emphasis added).

3- The brothers should work on spreading the contents of the bulletin and the ideas contained in it among the Ikhwans and the collective Islamists. (Emphasis added).

News of the Inside

The Jerusalem Operation:

Two units of Izz al-Din d-Qassam attacked a group of soldiers. One of the Mujahedeen fired his M16 machine gun at one of the soldiers, killing him immediately. This operation caused a massive reaction among the Jews as [it] took place in Jerusalem. The news agencies broadcasted the news. We received a report from the inside about the brother who carried out the Jerusalem operation.

Name: Muhammad Arif Bisharat (Abu Suhayb).

Town: Tammun - Jenin

Age: Approximately 20 years.

Status: Single

He carried out a previous heroic operation as on June 13, 91, brother Bisharat stabbed three Canadian settlers, killing one of them and inflicting medium wounds on the two other ones and this took place at al-Aghwar region. The army identified him and started to chase him, Fatah Movement tried to claim responsibility for this operation and did not succeed. The brother carried out several operations after that and was wounded during one of them and managed to flee before the army found him. Finally, he carried out the operation of the attack on the soldier in Jerusalem." (Emphasis added).

Implications and Outlook

It is reasonable to believe, based on Canadian government reports, that Canadian registered "charities" have raised, quite literally, millions of dollars for overseas terrorist groups such as Hamas and Hizbul Mujahideen. Money from some of the world's worst dictators such as Muammar Gaddafi has built mosques in Canada and been recycled for Islamist causes in the USA and the Caribbean. In addition to the funding of terrorism, some of these same organizations have received funding from countries such as Qatar and Saudi Arabia.

Canada may need to examine the patterns involved in fund raising for terrorism. One effective plan would be that any organization that has a charity revoked for cause should be banned for life from running any future charities. CRA clearly needs greater resources to both check into new applications for charities as well as pursuing audits against those who have suspicious transactions or histories.

In 2017, it is reasonable to assess that Canada's reputation as a civil society that promises peace, order and good government is at risk as terrorism financing is increasingly on the radar of many countries. In the event of future terrorist attacks, the Government of Canada may find itself both financially and politically responsible for such deaths.

CHAPTER 16: THE KILLING OF APOSTATES AND NON-BELIEVERS

Thomas Quiggin

Key Points

- This chapter was to have addressed the issues of how apostates and non-believers are often killed, especially by adherents of the Islamist interpretation of Islam.

- The hoped-for author, who was born into the Muslim faith and then left it, did not write the chapter. The reason given was fear of retaliation by Islamist against the family of the author.

This empty chapter symbolizes a key problem associated with the discussion of Islamist ideology. Speaking out against Islamists can get your family threatened or killed.

Implications

It is reasonable to believe that even in Canada, fear of retribution by Islamists is silencing free speech and open discussion.

CHAPTER 17: REPORTING OF ISLAMISTS AND EXTREMISM BY THE CANADIAN PRESS

Thomas Quiggin

Key Points

- An effective, free, and open press is the cornerstone of a democracy, as it provides the citizens with the information necessary for the freedom of thought, speech, expression, and association.

- Threats to freedom of the press exist in the Western democracies.

- Our courts and the legislative bodies have, to a degree, worked to ensure this freedom remains intact.

- Self-censorship and political correctness may be the greatest threats to a free press in Canada, not government surveillance or the courts. This self-censorship, abetted by politically-correct managers and reporters who call themselves social justice activists[655], has already weakened the debate in Canada about the role of the Islamists.

CBC, ISIS Supporters and Maisonneuve College in Montreal

On 19 February 2016, the Canadian Broadcasting Corporation (CBC) published an article on certain events occurring at Maisonneuve College in Montreal. The story carried the rather innocuous title of *Collège de Maisonneuve teachers' union wants action over alleged library threats.*[656] According to the story, the teacher's union wanted the college management to intervene due to threats made to staff in the college's library. The story also quotes Line Légaré, the college's spokesperson, who stated that teachers have intervened and asked students to lower their voices. She added "It's quite loud, more than we would like for a library." In addition, it is noted that an act of violence occurred in a parking lot at the library and the Montreal Police were called as a result. At the end of the story, the college spokesperson notes that the college has two committees dedicated to re-arranging the library fifth floor space in question and considering claims by the teachers.

---

[655] Catherine Porter of the Toronto Star is described on the Toronto Star's own website as a "social justice columnist." This description is online at http://www.thestar.com/authors.porter_catherine.html . She is also described as a "social justice activist/columnist" by the Toronto Star's own public editor. This article can be seen at http://www.thestar.com/opinion/2015/07/17/catherine-porter-ezra-levant-and-journalism-standards.html . Catherine Porter came to public attention in July of 2015 when she and the Toronto Star were both forced to apologize to Ezra Levant of "The Rebel" TV for her deliberately misleading report of a climate change protest and her confrontation with Mr. Levant. Viewed 24 July 2017. Ms. Porter has since left the Toronto Star. **Rated B3.**

[656] *Collège de Maisonneuve teachers' union wants action over alleged library threats*, CBC News, Posted: Feb 19, 2016 1:55 PM ET. The article is available online at http://www.cbc.ca/news/canada/montreal/college-maisonneuve-library-teachers-sanctions-1.3455443 . Viewed 24 July 2017. **Rated E5.**

On the same day, La Presse, a Montreal based French language newspaper ran a story on the same event. This story ran with the title *Tensions et intimidation au collège de Maisonneuve* (Tensions and intimidation at Maisonneuve College).[657]

Unlike the CBC story, however, La Presse noted that the student at the heart of the actions had tried to leave Canada to become jihadist fighter for ISIS. Additionally, the story notes that five other Maisonneuve students had left to be fighters in Syria and Iraq in January 2015 while a further four Maisonneuve students had tried to leave Canada in May of 2015 (including the one at the centre of the problems). Another two students from Maisonneuve College were in jail at the time of the article awaiting trial on a bombing plot. In the La Presse version of the story, it is also noted that the students at the centre of the troubles had also taken down the licence plate numbers of the staff's cars and took pictures of them as well. At the end of the story, it is noted that a common space called "The Source" existed and that it was available to all students. However, non-Muslim students quit using the space for activities such as yoga as they were afraid of using it. The college spokesperson confirmed the space had been closed for security reasons, quoting concerns about crowds and fire escapes. According to the author of the story, their sources told them that radical students wanted to use the space alone, so they could not be heard by other students.

In short, the reader of the CBC story is left with the view that students at Maisonneuve College have been rude and noisy. Additionally, this misbehavior has risen the level of a distraction and the teachers feel action must be taken.

By contrast, those who read the article by La Presse are left with the impression that the college has an Islamist problem, with multiple students having left Canada to fight for ISIS or at least have tried to leave. Other students are in jail, having been arrested for a bombing plot which was also related to Islamist ideology. Students at the college, apparently sympathetic to ISIS, have tried to take over parts of the college and have threatened the staff in doing so.

In both stories, the spokesperson for the college denies there is any extremism problem, saying in the CBC story that it was mostly a "noise problem."

The CBC story has been linguistically and political cleansed of any words, phrases or name that might suggest an Islamist problem. How can this be?

Does a Pattern Exist?

One misleading and ineffective story by the CBC does not prove a pattern of behaviour. This story is worrying, however, as it is just one of many such stories in Canada where the press has published misleading, incorrect or highly biased pieces of journalism.

False Information: The Toronto Star, Haroon Siddiqui and the Muslim Brotherhood

---

[657] *Tensions et intimidation au collège de Maisonneuve,* Gabrielle Duchaine, La Presse, 19 February 2016. The article can be seen online at http://www.lapresse.ca/actualites/education/201602/18/01-4952337-tensions-et-intimidation-au-college-de-maisonneuve.php . Viewed 24 July 2017. **Rated B2.**

Consider the Toronto Star article of 7 March 2015 entitled Conservative senators hold kangaroo court on security: Siddiqui.[658] The author of this is Haroon Siddiqui, who is identified as the Star's editorial page editor emeritus. In other words, a writer of some status, according to the Toronto Star.

In the article, Mr. Siddiqui raises the issue of whether the Muslim Brotherhood exists or has infrastructure in North America. Mr. Siddiqui asks the question to Dr. Jamal Badawi who has been noted in public testimony as being a key player in Muslim Brotherhood organizations. He quotes Dr. Badawi by saying:

> "Muslim Brotherhood is not a registered entity in Canada or the USA, nor does it have any branch in North America."

Asking Dr. Badawi if the Muslim Brotherhood exists in North America is like asking the head of a mafia family if corruption and racketeering exist in civic government. However, the proverbial "reasonable individual" would read the article and come away with the opinion that the Muslim Brotherhood does not have any infrastructure, branches or members in Canada and the USA.

Is this true and why would we take the word of Dr. Badawi on such an issue? Dr. Badawi has been identified by the Muslim Brotherhood itself as a leading figure in the organization and one to be emulated.[659] He is part of their North American Muslim Brotherhood Shura Council and his name appears as such on its board of directors along with his phone numbers in Halifax , Nova Scotia.[660] He has also been a member of the board of directors of multiple organizations[661] that themselves claim to be followers of Hassan al-Banna and the Muslim Brotherhood.[662] This includes the Muslim Association of Canada. He is also an unindicted co-conspirator in the Holy Land Relief terrorism funding trials.[663] Dr.

[658] The article can be seen online at http://www.thestar.com/opinion/commentary/2015/03/07/conservative-senators-hold-kangaroo-court-on-security-siddiqui.html . Viewed 25 July 2017. **Rated E5.**

[659] In 1991, the Muslim Brotherhood issued *An Explanatory Memorandum on the General Strategic Goal for the Group In North America 5/22/1991*. In this document, which took 10 years to produce, Dr. Badawi is lauded for his leading role in outreach (Dawa) for the Muslim Brotherhood. See Section 20 of this document which can be seen online at http://www.investigativeproject.org/documents/misc/20.pdf . Viewed 25 July 2017. **Rated A2.**

[660] A copy of the court document used in the Holy Land Relief terrorism funding trials reveals the name and phone numbers of Dr. Badawi and places him on the Muslim Brotherhood Shura Council or Board of Directors for North America. The document can be seen online at http://www.investigativeproject.org/documents/case_docs/1083.pdf . Viewed 25 July 2017. **Rated A2.**

[661] Dr. Badawi has been on the board of directors of CAIR-CAN (now NCCM) for every year they had had a published list (2000-2012) as well as having been on the board of directors of the Muslim Association of Canada from at least 2002 to 2006. Both of these organizations were identified as Muslim Brotherhood front groups on a variety of occasions including Senate Testimony by Lorenzo Vidino. See the Ottawa Citizen report by Ian MacLeod *Beware the Muslim Brotherhood, expert warns* at http://ottawacitizen.com/news/politics/beware-of-the-muslim-brotherhood-expert-warns. Viewed 25 July 2017. **Rated A2.** The full Senate Testimony can be seen at http://www.parl.gc.ca/content/sen/committee/412/SECD/52124-E.HTM . Viewed 25 July 2017. **Rated A2.**

[662] In its website, the Muslim Association of Canada claims to be followers of Hassan al-Banna, the founder of the Muslim Brotherhood as well as the Muslim Brotherhood itself. The link for this statement is http://www.macnet.ca/english/pages/about%20mac.aspx. Viewed 25 July 2017. **Rated A2.**

[663] The Holy Land Relief trails were a series of criminal proceedings concerning terrorism fund raising in the United States. Dr. Badawi was listed as an unindicted co-conspirator is these proceedings. A copy of the relevant court document can be seen at https://www.investigativeproject.org/documents/case_docs/423.pdf . Viewed 25 July 2017. **Rated A2.**

Badawi has also described Hassan al-Banna, the founder of the Muslim Brotherhood, as being the most influential person in his life.[664]

Of broader interest, Dr. Badawi was on the founding board of directors (1993) of the Muslim American Society[665] which has since been designated as a terrorist entity and Muslim Brotherhood front organization by the United Arab Emirates (2014).[666]

Separate from this, but related, Dr. Badawi also maintains a website on the proper procedures for wife beating which details the level of progressive steps to be taken in the beating procedure.[667]

Given that Dr. Badawi is a leading figure in the Muslim Brotherhood and that all of the above information is a matter of public record, several questions arise:

- Did Haroon Siddiqui know that Dr. Badawi was a leadership figure in the Muslim Brotherhood when he asked the question?

- Did Haroon Siddiqui try to verify if Dr. Badawi was a valid source? Is Dr. Badawi a long time personal contact of Siddiqui?

- Does the Toronto Star make any effort to fact check articles of the columnists who write for them even allowing that these are columns and not reporting?

- Given that the fundamental facts in the article appear flawed, what level of credibility should we apply to the overall column and the newspaper?

The public editor of the Toronto Star, Kathy English, was sent an extensive email on this situation on 04 May 2017. The email included background information concerning the Muslim Brotherhood. No response, beyond the automated one, was received.

The Toronto Star, The Toronto Sun and Girls Forced to the Back of the Room

On Monday, 4 July 2011, the Toronto Sun ran an article concerning protests at the Valley Park Middle School. The protests were against Friday Muslim prayers run at the public school and noted that girls were forced to sit at the back of room while boys sat at the front. In the story, the Toronto District School Board said that prayer sessions had been taking place for three years.[668]

---

664 EMEL Magazine, On Mount Nur with Dr. Jamal Badawi, Issue 4 Mar / Apr 2004. The magazine article can be seen online at http://www.emel.com/article?id=5&a_id=1516 . Viewed 25 July 2017. **Rated C3.**

665 Three of the founding directors of the Muslim American Society had direct connections to the Muslim Brotherhood in North America. They were Jamal Badawi, Ahmad Elkadi and Omar Soubani.

666 A list of the designated terrorist entities can be seen at http://www.wam.ae/en/news/emirates-international/1395272478814.html . Viewed 25 July 2017. **Rated A2.**

667 For more on wife beating and the proper procedures for it, see *Is wife beating allowed in Islam?* By Dr. Jamal Badawi. The article is available online at: http://www.themodernreligion.com/women/w_abuse_badawi.htm . Viewed 25 July 2017. **Rated C3.**

668 *Hindus protest Muslim prayers at public school*, By QMI Agency. First posted: Monday, July 04, 2011 04:32 PM EDT. The article can be seen online at http://www.torontosun.com/2011/07/04/hindus-protest-muslim-prayers-at-public-school . Viewed 25 July 2017. **Rated B2.**

This Toronto Sun story appears to have been a response to a blogger posting made the week before (29 June 2011) at the website Blazing Cat Fur.[669] The blog posting stated:

> "Islamic ritual prayers are done in my 13-year-old daughter's middle school every Friday. Every Friday my daughter's school cafeteria changes into a mosque as dozens of Muslim boys and their imams (Islamic preachers) lead Islamic ritual prayers and no one else can even walk through the cafeteria. Some imams (Islamic preachers) come from the outside of the school and lead Muslim students in the Islamic prayer and this happens at the school cafeteria after lunch on Fridays. All other non-Muslims are in classes in the afternoon when they are using the cafeteria as a mosque. There is a mosque nearby but the Muslim kids pray in the school. School administration take part preparing the cafeteria and making it into mosque every Friday and no one but Muslims can use the cafeteria during the Islamic prayers on Friday.[670]

Following the Toronto Sun article of 04 July 2011, the story then broke across multiple news agencies. As the story emerged, it became clear that girls were forced to sit behind the boys during prayer sessions while "unclean"[671] girls were forced to the back of the room or had to sit outside.

It is reasonable to believe that forcing girls to the back of the room in a taxpayer funded public school is a violation of the Charter of Rights and Freedoms. The issue of Friday Muslim prayers is also questionable, given the Christian Lord's Prayer has been forced out of public schools.

The prayers had been ongoing for approximately three years. The minutes of the Valley Park Middle School Council Meeting of 24 November 2008 record that:

> Prayer Service, the school is providing a venue for the Muslim students to have prayers at school on Fridays. An Imam from the neighbouring mosque comes to our school and conducts the prayers. Prior to this, students signed out early on Friday afternoons to go to mosque. By staying at school, valuable instructional time is saved for our students.

Without any sense of irony, the meeting Valley Park Middle School meeting also said a Girls Unlimited program would be happening at the school. The program would help girls improve their "confidence and self-esteem." No explanation was given on how forcing girls to sit at the back of the room while a male Iman and the boys ran the prayer service would help the girls with their self-esteem.

The administrator of the mosque that provides the Imam was Abdul Huq Ingar.[672] He was one of those who sent out a mass email on behalf of Kathleen Wynne, then running for the leadership of the Liberal Party of Canada. The email and a follow-on letter specifically claims that Ms. Wynne had, as an MLA, supported the "Muslim prayer issue at the Valley Park Middle School."[673] By way of context, it should be

---

[669] Blazing Cat Fur. www.blazingcatfur.ca .

[670] http://www.blazingcatfur.ca/2011/06/29/islamic-ritual-prayer-conducted-at-toronto-district-school-board-middle-school/ . Viewed 25 July 2017. **Rated B3**.

[671] In the language of Islamists, girls and women who are menstruating are described as "unclean" which serves as another example of the misogyny which is at work in their circles.

[672] He has also been identified as President of the Islamic Society of Toronto. See the article online at http://www.cbc.ca/news/canada/toronto/muslims-killed-in-yukon-crash-were-on-faith-mission-1.615634 . Viewed 25 July 2017. **Rated B3**

[673] Tarek Fatah, *Kathleen Wynne's Muslim support: Will Valley Park Middle School, with its Friday prayers, become a model for all Ontario public schools*?, Toronto Sun. First posted: Tuesday, January 29, 2013 08:06 PM EST. The

noted that the Valley Park Middle School is in the home riding of Ms. Wynne. When students leave Valley Park Middle School in Grade 8, they automatically transfer to Marc Garneau Collegiate Institute, which has its own Friday prayer program.

The Toronto Star eventually ran an article on 08 July 2011, complete with photos of the prayer session.[674] The article is of interest, as it shows a photo of the prayer session in process, even though the story had not broken until after the school term was over for the year. The photo appears to have been taken in January of 2015.

Stated differently, the Toronto Star had the story on school prayer and chose to not run it. The photo used in their July story is evidence of that. What is not clear is whether or not Graham Parley, the (former) City Editor,[675] decided to kill the story on his own or if he did so after a call from the Office of the Premier of Ontario in early 2011. The Toronto Star was sitting on a major "coup" of a story, but did not run it for either political reasons or for reasons of political correctness.

At any rate, the story went on to be a major news event for 2011. Its effect was limited however, as Valley Park Middle School, Teston Valley School, Stephen Lewis High School, Agincourt Collegiate and multiple others in Toronto and Ottawa have similar programs. Although the situation clearly violates the rights of girls and women in Canada, no level of government appears to be willing to address this issue.

The Toronto Star, Noor Javed and Islamist Groups in the GTA

Another Toronto Star story of interest was that written by Noor Javed and Ben Spurr on 7 June 2015 entitled What it's like to be Muslim in the GTA. The article says that they have interviewed Muslims in the Greater Toronto Area.

The article does not explain the methodology behind choosing the interviewees, but a closer look at them is revealing. It does say that the individuals interviewed are "inherently Torontonian" folks who "hate the traffic and worry about the Blue Jays bullpen."

It is possible to believe, however, that the reality is quite different. Far from being any sort of cross section of GTA Muslims, this is a group of individuals who are political activists who have been involved in promoting Sharia and advocating for an Islamist government. They come from groups known for radicalization and extremism which are almost exclusively front groups for the Muslim Brotherhood. **Therefore, when the articles' authors prompt them to discuss how they are misunderstood and discriminated against, the answers should be taken with a grain of salt.**

Among the most interesting case examples are:

---

article can be seen online at www.torontosun.com/2013/01/29/kathleen-**wynnes**-muslim-support . Viewed 25 July 2017. **Rated B3.**

[674] Kristin Rushowy and Louise Brown, Education Reporters, *Board runs afoul of Education Act with prayer services*, The Toronto Star, 08 July 2011. The article can be seen online at http://www.thestar.com/life/parent/2011/07/08/board_runs_afoul_of_education_act_with_prayer_services.html Viewed 25 July 2017. **Rated B3.**

[675] Mr. Parley has since left the Toronto Star.

Alaa Elsayed is an Islamic Society of North America (Canada) Imam and he is the Director of Religious Affairs - ICC Mosque.[676] The ISNA Canada's parent organization (ISNA) was as an unindicted co-conspirator in a terrorism funding trial and one of several "entities who are and/or were members of the US Muslim Brotherhood." Following an appeal, the ISNA and CAIR USA had their names removed from the list of co-conspirators, but the judge ruled that "the government has produced ample evidence to establish the associations of CAIR, ISNA, NAIT, with the Islamic Association for Palestine, and with (terrorist group) Hamas."[677] ISNA Canada lost the federal charitable status for one if its charities (Development Fund) when it was found to be using charitable money for funding terrorism.[678] ISNA also made the news in Toronto when it was found to have fraudulently spent some $600,000 in charity money that had been intended for the poor.[679]

Although this story was printed on 7 June 2015, it did not note that in May of 2015, the ISNA school made the news when it objected to two girls on an opposing boys' soccer team which they were playing. The ISNA objected to the girls playing for "religious reasons" and the two girls were forced to sit out the second half of the game, contrary to league rules and the Charter of Rights and Freedoms of Canada.[680]

Selma Djukic is described as a business owner in the article. She is also a former board member of CAIR-CAN which has now been renamed to the National Council of Canadian Muslims. The name change occurred after its parent organization, CAIR USA was named as an unindicted co-conspirator in an American terror-financing criminal trial. CAIR USA has also been named as a terrorist entity and a Muslim Brotherhood front group by the United Arab Emirates.[681] The current head of CAIR-CAN/NCCM is Ihsaan Gardee.

Despite statements made in TV interviews with CBC by Ihsaan Gardee[682] and his further misleading testimony to the Parliament of Canada,[683] CAIR-CAN is a subsidiary of CAIR USA. According to CAIR-CAN's

---

676 A list of staff appointments of the ISNA in Mississauga can be seen on their website. This is available online at http://webcache.googleusercontent.com/search?q=cache:W4US8jxoiKUJ:www.isna.ca/1/about-us/staff+&cd=1&hl=en&ct=clnk&gl=ca . Viewed 25 July 2017. **Rated B2.**

677 The decision of the court on this issue is available online at http://www.scribd.com/doc/43380629/2009-order-on-Holy-Land-Foundation-unindicted-coconspirator-list . Viewed 25 July 2017. **Rated A2.**

678 The Canada Revenue Association ruling on this matter can be seen online at http://www.marketwired.com/press-release/canada-revenue-agency-revokes-registration-isna-development-foundation-as-charity-1833203.htm . Viewed 25 July 2017. **Rated A2.**

679 For more on the misspent charity money, see the story online at http://www.thestar.com/news/gta/2011/01/20/muslim_charity_squandered_money_for_poor.html . Viewed 25 July 2017. **Rated B2.**

680 *Muslim school which objected to girls on boys soccer team told to abide by rules,* Diana Mehta, The Canadian Press, Published Friday, May 29, 2015 5:25PM EDT. The article can be seen online at http://Bww.ctvnews.ca/canada/muslim-school-which-objected-to-girls-on-boys-soccer-team-told-to-abide-by-rules-1.2397987 . Viewed 25 July 2017. **Rated B2.**

681 A list of the designated terrorist entities can be seen at http://www.wam.ae/en/news/emirates-international/1395272478814.html . Viewed 25 July 2017. **Rated A2.**

682 *Muslim group demands apology from Harper, chief spokesman*, Posted: Jan 28, 2014 12:24 PM ET Last Updated: Jan 28, 2014 6:18 PM ET. See: http://www.cbc.ca/news/muslim-group-demands-apology-from-harper-chief-spokesman-1.2514099 . Viewed 25 July 2017. **Rated B2.**

683 For more on his testimony to the Parliament of Canada, see http://www.cbc.ca/news/politics/bill-c-51-hearings-diane-ablonczy-s-questions-to-muslim-group-mccarthyesque-1.2993531 . Viewed 25 July 2017. **Rated B2.**

website,[684] CAIR-CAN has a parent organization which is identified as CAIR USA based in Washington DC. In this extract from a 2003 publication titled "A Journalist's Guide to Islam" on a website belonging to CAIR-CAN the following statement makes this statement:

> "CAIR (Council on American-Islamic Relations) This Washington-based organization is CAIR-CAN's parent organization. It has an email newsletter for the news media, providing news releases and background materials about important Islamic events. It is worth receiving. Tel: 202-488-8787 Fax: 202-488-0833 Email: webmaster@cair-net.org, Web site: www.caircan.org (A Journalist's Guide to Islam (version 2003) Conceived by the Council on American Islamic Relations Canada." Published by Islamic Social Services Association Canada. [23]

Katherine Bullock is described in the newspaper article as an "academic". It does not mention her position with the ISNA. She is a Muslim convert who has been active in promoting political Islam in the GTA. She campaigned to introduce Sharia arbitration tribunals in Ontario.[685] As a spokesperson[686] for the ISNA she had denied that they had received millions of dollars of Saudi money to fund the ISNA centre at its high school. This turned out to be false as the ISNA had indeed received funding from the Islamic Development Bank (five million dollars in grants plus annual payments). The ISNA's own website stated that the funding had in fact occurred.[687] The Saudi government has regularly funded Muslim Brotherhood front groups such as the ISNA, so the funding of the ISNA high school was consistent with this pattern.

As noted in Chapter 13, this is the same individual Katherine Bullock who, as a Lecturer in the Department of Political Science, University of Toronto at Mississauga[688], stated in a speech that:

> "from an Islamic point of view this absolutely **nothing radical about wanting Caliphate or wanting Sharia**. These are completely normal traditional points of view." [689] (Emphasis added).

---

[684] The website referred to here is www.caircan.ca. The site was caircan.ca was registered originally with a creation date of 2001/05/16 according to the WHOIS website using information from the Canadian Internet Registration Authority, (http://www.cira.ca/). When checked the site showed as active with an expiry date of 2018/05/16 and a last update of 2013/06/25. The DMOZ Title for the site is: CAIR-CAN – Council on American - Islamic Relations Canada.

[685] Marina Jiménez and Omar El Akkad, *Values at heart of Islamic tensions*, Globe and Mail, Published Tuesday, 08 November 2005, 12:00 AM EST. The article can be seen online at http://www.theglobeandmail.com/news/national/values-at-heart-of-islamic-tensions/article989709/?page=all . Viewed 15 April 2017. **Rated B2.**

[686] Marina Jiménez and Omar El Akkad, *Values at heart of Islamic tensions*, Globe and Mail, Published Tuesday, 08 November 2005, 12:00 AM EST. The article can be seen online at http://www.theglobeandmail.com/news/national/values-at-heart-of-islamic-tensions/article989709/?page=all . Viewed 15 April 2017. **Rated B2.**

[687] Marina Jiménez and Omar El Akkad, *Values at heart of Islamic tensions*, Globe and Mail, Published Tuesday, 08 November 2005, 12:00 AM EST. http://www.theglobeandmail.com/news/national/values-at-heart-of-islamic-tensions/article989709/?page=all . Viewed 15 April 2017. **Rated B2.**

[688] Katherine Bullock, "Katherine Bullock," *University of Toronto Mississauga*, https://www.utm.utoronto.ca/political-science/katherine-bullock Viewed 22 May 2017. **Rated B1.**

[689] For the speech see *ISIS, Violence and the Politics of Deradicalization.* This is available online at http://digitalcommons.osgoode.yorku.ca/video_lectures/12/ . Viewed 15 April 2017. **Rated A1.**

Rebia Khedr has spoken at ISNA events[690] as well as those organized by Islamic Relief Canada. Islamic Relief Canada has been identified as a Muslim Brotherhood front group[691] and its parent organization in the United Kingdom has had its bank accounts shut[692] due to terrorism funding issues.[693] The parent organization of Islamic Relief Canada is Islamic Relief UK, which was also listed as a terrorist entity by the United Arab Emirates.[694] The UAE list focuses heavily on the Muslim Brotherhood and groups that the UAE identifies as front groups or proxy groups.

In 2014, Islamic Relief's (UK) donation page was removed from Charities Aid Foundation website. The CAF would not comment directly as to why it ceased to have an affiliation with Islamic Relief, but it did release a statement which said:

> "It would be wrong for us to discuss our processes, but like any financial intermediary, we have robust systems in place to ensure we comply with our UK and international obligations to protect against fraud, money laundering, bribery and corruption and terrorism financing while working with charitable organisations to support their work in conflict zones and elsewhere."[695]

Boonaa Mohammed and **Yusuf Zine** have both performed at the annual Mississauga MuslimFest, which bans female singers. MuslimFest also states that "All submitted artwork must be compliant to the boundaries set by Shariah."[696] In 2009, the Globe and Mail ran an article concerning Zuriani (Ani) Zonneveld, a "Grammy-award-winning singer from Los Angeles who would have liked to have been part of the festival." She was denied, however, as she was female.[697] MuslimFest is organized, in part, by

---

[690] Ms. Khedr's name can be seen on the 34th annual ISNA conventions speakers list in the Way Back Machine web archive at http://web.archive.org/web/20080626074943/http://www.isnacanada.com/Convention/Toronto/34/isna_program_glance.html . Viewed 25 July 2017. **Rated B3.**

[691] See the Ottawa Citizen report by Ian MacLeod *Beware the Muslim Brotherhood, expert warns* at http://ottawacitizen.com/news/politics/beware-of-the-muslim-brotherhood-expert-warns. Viewed 25 July 2017. **Rated A2.** The full Senate Testimony can be seen at http://www.parl.gc.ca/content/sen/committee/412/SECD/52124-E.HTM . Viewed 25 July 2017. **Rated A2.**

[692] This material can be seen on the web archive at https://web.archive.org/web/20121124044239/http://www.civilsociety.co.uk/finance/news/content/13757/banking_sector_nerves_blocking_international_relief_says_islamic_relief_finance_director . Viewed 25 July 2017. **Rated B3.**

[693] For more on this see https://moneyjihad.wordpress.com/2012/11/09/ubs-closes-islamic-relief-account-over-terror-risk/ . Viewed 25 July 2017. **Rated B3.** See also the very last line in the article at: http://www.civilsociety.co.uk/finance/news/content/17903/hsbc_to_close_bank_account_of_muslim_charity_working_in_gaza Viewed 25 July 2017. **Rated B3.**

[694] The official list is online at http://www.thenational.ae/uae/government/list-of-groups-designated-terrorist-organisations-by-the-uae . Viewed 11 April 2017. **Rated A1.**

[695] *Islamic Relief's donation page is removed from CAF website*, Civil Society News, 03 September, 2014. The article is available online at http://www.civilsociety.co.uk/fundraising/news/content/18091/islamic_reliefs_donation_page_is_removed_from_caf_website . Viewed 20 June 2017. **Rated B3**.

[696] Tarek Fatah, *Chasing a Mirage: The Tragic Illusion of an Islamic State*, John Wiley and Sons Canada, 2008. The specific references can be seen on pages 300 and 301 of the PFD version online which can be seen at http://tarekfatah.com/wp-content/uploads/2013/09/Chasing-a-Mirage-The-book-copy1.pdf . Viewed 25 July 2017. **Rated B2.**

[697] Marina Jimenez, *Women artists, performers criticize Muslim festival restrictions*, Globe and Mail, Published Saturday, Aug. 13, 2005 12:00AM EDT. The article is available online at

SoundVision, the company that hired Ms. Javed for a three-day news media training event in July 2012, although this is not noted in the article. The advertising poster notes that a complimentary lunch was to be provided for the 7 July session by IRFAN, the events sponsor. As noted elsewhere, IRFAN lost its federal charity status for funding a terrorist group (HAMAS) and was later declared a terrorist entity itself.[698]

SoundVision is identified as being the media wing of the ICNA (Islamic Circle of North American).[699] The ICNA in Canada is noteworthy for its online syllabus that legalizes "slave-girls"[700] has a section on wife beating,[701] says that pregnant adulteresses should be stoned to death after giving birth,[702] and also says Allah will "give us victory over the disbelieving people."[703]

The ICNA is the organization that employs Zunera Ishaq, the individual who challenged the Government of Canada over her "right" to wear the face covering niqab at a citizenship swearing in ceremony.[704] The ICNA notes that "Islam is totally incompatible with Western democracy."[705]

Dalia Hashim served on the executive of the University of Toronto's Muslim Student Association. The Muslim Students Association (MSA) of the United States and Canada was established in January 1963 by members of the Muslim Brotherhood at the University of Illinois, Urbana-Champaign campus.[706] Its creation was the result of Saudi Arabia-backed efforts to create a network of international Islamic organizations to spread its Wahhabist ideology. It was essentially "an arm of the Saudi-funded, Muslim Brotherhood-controlled Muslim World League."[707] The Muslim Student Association of Canada has had a

---

http://www.theglobeandmail.com/news/national/women-artists-performers-criticize-muslim-festival-restrictions/article18243631/. Viewed 25 July 2017. **Rated B2.**

698 See Chapter 15 for more on IRFAN and its connections to terrorism.

699 *The North American Muslim Resource Guide: Muslim Community Life in the United States and Canada*, Mohamed Nimer, Routledge 2002, Page 69.

700 *ICNA Canada's online syllabus legalizes "slave-girls"*, Posted by: Jonathan D. Halevi, February 15, 2016. The article is available online at http://en.cijnews.com/?p=26432 . Viewed 25 July 2017. **Rated B2.**

701 *ICNA Canada's online syllabus on wife beating*, Posted by: Jonathan D. Halevi, February 18, 2016. The article can be seen online at http://en.cijnews.com/?p=26599 . Viewed 25 July 2017. **Rated B2.**

702 *ICNA Canada's online syllabus: pregnant adulteress to be stoned after giving birth*, Posted by: Jonathan D. Halevi, February 19, 2016. The article can be seen online at http://en.cijnews.com/?p=26659 . Viewed 25 July 2017. **Rated B2.**

703 *ICNA Canada syllabus: "Give us victory over the disbelieving people"* Posted by: Jonathan D. Halevi, January 12, 2016. The article can be seen online at http://en.cijnews.com/?p=19137 . Viewed 25 July 2017. **Rated B2.**

704 Debra Black Immigration Reporter, *Fight to wear niqab a matter of principle for Zunera Ishaq*, The Toronto Star, Published on Thu Oct 08 2015. The article can be seen online at http://www.thestar.com/news/canada/2015/10/08/fight-to-wear-niqab-a-matter-of-principle-for-zunera-ishaq.html. Viewed 25 July 2017. **Rated B3.**

705 *ICNA Canada refutes Trudeau: "Islam is totally incompatible with Western democracy"* Posted by: Jonathan D. Halevi. February 25, 2016. The article can be seen online at http://en.cijnews.com/?p=27451 . Viewed 25 July 2017. **Rated B2.**

706 *"Muslim Student Association: The Investigative Project on Terrorism Dossier,"* (2008, January 1). *The Investigative Project on Terrorism.* Retrieved from https://www.investigativeproject.org/documents/misc/31.pdf . Viewed 25 July 2017. **Rated B2.**

707 Mauro, R. (2013, February 3) "Islamist Organization Profile: Muslim Students Association (MSA)," *The Clarion Project.* Retrieved from http://www.clarionproject.org/analysis/muslim-students-association . Viewed 25 July 2017. **Rated B2.**

rather dubious list of alumni who have gone on to be suicide bombers, jihadists fighters and ISIS propagandists.[708]

Jeewan Chanicka is identified as an elementary school principal who has "been taken off a plane for no reason and had security officers laugh at me about it, and I had no recourse." The article does not mention that he has been a speaker for the ISNA[709], which as noted above is a Muslim Brotherhood front group which had lost status for one if it charities caught funding terrorism. His presentation was on Saturday, 18 May 2002 2:15 – 3:45 pm and was listed as the Muslim Student Association Workshop Session #3. As noted earlier, the Muslim Student Association was originally founded by the Muslim Brotherhood and the MSA in Canada has produced a rather long list of alumni who have gone off to be suicide bombers, jihadist fighters, ISIS propagandists and leadership figures in Muslim Brotherhood led organizations overseas.[710]

The article also does not mention he has been a speaker at the "Reviving the Islamic Spirit' conference which has hosted a veritable who's-who of the Muslim Brotherhood (and other) speakers.[711] Of note, the "Reviving the Islamic Spirit" conference was frequently funded the IRFAN Canada, the International Relief Fund for the Afflicted and Needy. IRFAN lost its charitable status in 2011 for funding the terrorist groups Hamas[712] and was listed as a terrorist entity in 2014. Also of interest is that Hamas itself is a Muslim Brotherhood organization, as stated by the Hamas Charter in Article 2.[713]

Farrah Marfatia is identified as an Islamic school principal. Not in this article, but elsewhere in her own words she as stated that "her experience at ISNA in her elementary years she feels solidified in her Islamic identity."[714] Given the history of the ISNA as a Muslim Brotherhood front group that lost the charitable status (Development Fund) for funding terrorism, this is not encouraging.

Noor Javed and the Hajj

---

[708] *Is the Muslim Student Association of Canada/USA a Recruiting Point for Extremism?* Chapter 14 of this book.

[709] Mr. Chanika was a speaker at the 28th Annual ISNA convention in 2002. That conference had other speakers such as Tariq Ramadan, a close relative of the founder of the Muslim Brotherhood and Dr. Jamal Badawi who is listed by the Muslim Brotherhood itself as one of their Shura Council members and a leading educator in their organization. The 28th Annual Convention was held on Saturday & Sunday, Rabi' Awwal 5 & 6, 1423 / May 18 & 19, 2002 at the Toronto Congress centre.

[710] *Is the Muslim Student Association of Canada/USA a Recruiting Point for Extremism*? Chapter 14 of this book.

[711] Among many others, see http://www.globalmbwatch.com/2014/01/11/2013-reviving-islamic-spirit-conference-featured-usual-cast-global-muslim-brotherhood-leaders/ . Viewed 25 July 2017. **Rated C3.** See also http://www.torontosun.com/2011/12/23/controversial-islamic-conference-set-for-toronto-this-weekend . . Viewed 25 July 2017. **Rated B2**. See also http://www.globalmbwatch.com/2009/12/29/8th-annual-reviving-the-islamic-spirit-convention-features-muslim-brotherhood-leaders/ . Viewed 25 July 2017. **Rated C3**.

[712] For details on this, see the CRA summary at http://www.cra-arc.gc.ca/ebci/haip/srch/revcausesumm-eng.action?r=http%3A%2F%2Fwww.cra-arc.gc.ca%3A80%2Febci%2Fhaip%2Fsrch%2Fbasicsearchresult-eng.action%3Fk%3D%26amp%3Bs%3DrevokedForCause%26amp%3Bb%3Dtrue%26amp%3Bp%3D2&bn=885408849RR0001 . Viewed 25 July 2017. **Rated A1**.

[713] Section Two of the HAMAS charter begins with the line: *The Islamic Resistance Movement is a branch of the Muslim Brotherhood chapter in Palestine.* The entire charter of HAMAS can be seen at http://avalon.law.yale.edu/20th_century/hamas.asp . Viewed 25 July 2017. **Rated A1**.

[714] Helal Musleh, *Leaving a Legacy Behind: Farrah Marfatia,* by Helal Musleh, The Link Canada, August 18, 2015. The article can be seen online at http://thelinkcanada.ca/leaving-legacy-interview-farrah-marfatia/ Viewed 25 July 2017. **Rated C3**.

In 2007, Noor Javed, as a staff reporter of the Toronto Star, wrote a three-part series entitled Joining Muslim pilgrims on the Hajj. The first part in the series was published on Monday, December 17, 2007.[715] At the time of the publishing, neither Noor Javed nor the Toronto Star disclosed that Ms. Javed had her expenses paid for by the Minister of Culture of the Government of Saudi Arabia. This failure to disclose such information would appear to be a serious lapse in journalist standards. However, seven years later, the Toronto Star did update the article:

> **"Note - June 25, 2015:** Noor Javed's pilgrimage to Mecca and Medina was partially funded by the government of Saudi Arabia and arranged through the Ministry of Culture."

The Ministry of Culture in Saudi Arabia originally called the Ministry of Information was established in 1962. In 2003, responsibility for culture was added to the Ministry's portfolio, hence the name change. The Ministry of Culture now controls the state-run press as well as the education system.[716]

Noor Javed and Media Training

Ms. Javed has been actively involved in providing media response training for a number of organizations outside of the Toronto Star. Among these have been IRFAN, the ISNA and the Muslim Association of Canada (MAC).

IRFAN sponsored the training session of 6-8 July 2012. By that point in time, IRFAN's charitable status for funding terrorism had been revoked for more than a year (9 April 2011 revocation date). The Toronto Star itself had run an article on the revocation. Its seems questionable that a Toronto Star reporter should be giving media training to an organization that had been identified publicly as a funder of terrorism. Naheed Mustafa of the CBC was also an instructor on this same course.

Ms. Javed was also an instructor for a media relations workshop that was run at McMaster University on 15 March 2009. The event was run in collaboration with the Muslim Association of Canada. The MAC, on its own website, states that:

> "MAC's roots are deeply enshrined in the message of Prophet Mohammad. Its modern roots can be traced to the vigorous intellectual revivalist effort that took hold in Muslim societies starting in the early twentieth century. This revival aimed at reconciling faith with the challenges of modernity and providing a clear articulation of balance and moderation in understanding Islam. In the Arab world, this revival culminated in the writings of the late Imam Hassan al-Banna and the movement of the Society of Muslim Brothers (commonly known as the Muslim Brotherhood). Al-Banna's core messages of constructive engagement in society, focus on personal and communal empowerment, and organizational development had a deep impact on much of the Muslim world." [717]

---

[715] See the article online at http://www.thestar.com/life/2007/12/17/joining_muslim_pilgrims_on_the_hajj.html . Viewed 25 July 2017. **Rated B2.**

[716] For more on the Ministry of Culture, see their own website at http://www.saudinf.com/main/c6e.htm . Viewed 25 July 2017. **Not rated.**

[717] This statement from the MAC website can be seen at http://www.macnet.ca/english/pages/about%20mac.aspx. Viewed 25 July 2017. **Rated B2.**

The other two speakers of the event were Naheed Mustafa of the CBC and one individual from the MAC and another from the MAS. Though it was NOT/NOT known at the time of the event, the MAS would be listed as a terrorist entity by the United Arab Emirates.[718]

On another occasion in March of 2015, the ISNA identified that Noor Javed had "spoken at length" in January of 2015 on how to communicate with the media. This was more than two years after the ISNA had lost the charitable status for its Development Fund after having been caught funding terrorism.

The public editor of the Toronto Star was sent an email (2017-05-04 6:59 AM) with a set of questions referring to this issue.[719] No substantive response was received beyond an automated response.

CBC, the Toronto Star and Al Jazeera

A documentary on the life of Omar Khadr entitled Omar Khadr: Out of the Shadows was initially broadcast in late May 2015. A longer version of the production premiered to four screenings at the 2015 Toronto International Film Festival.[720]

In a variety of press stories and postings, it is stated that the film was a cooperative project with a Toronto Star reporter, the CBC and White Pine Pictures.[721] This can be seen on the CBC website[722] as well as the Toronto Star.[723]

What was not broadly reported in Canada, however, was that Al Jazeera English, Al Jazeera Arabic and Al Jazeera American were all collaborators in the production. This is overlooked or omitted in many Canadian references. The Al Jazeera version claims that the film was a collaboration "between Al Jazeera, White Pine Pictures, and the Canadian Broadcasting Corporation."[724] White Pine pictures does note the

---

[718] A list of the designate terrorist entities can be seen at http://www.wam.ae/en/news/emirates-international/1395272478814.html . Viewed 25 July 2017. **Rated A1.**

[719] In the mail, an extensive amount of supporting material was sent. The questions asked were: *Does the Toronto Star stand behind the work of Noor Javed, one of its reporters? Does the Toronto Star still believe that a reporter who worked as a PR consultant for fund-raising organizations that had lost their charitable status for funding terrorism is an appropriate employee? Will the Toronto Star retract the article What it's like to be Muslim in the GTA or will it at least add a clarification to the article explaining who was interviewed?*

[720] For more information on this see http://www.cbc.ca/firsthand/episodes/omar-khadr-out-of-the-shadows . Viewed 25 July 2017. **Rated B2**. and See also http://freeomar.ca/ . Viewed 25 July 2017. **Not rated.**

[721] See, among others, the CBC website that states the documentary was "Directed by Patrick Reed and co-directed by Toronto Star journalist Michelle Shephard, Omar Khadr: Out of the Shadows is a White Pine Pictures production in association with the CBC." This can be seen at http://www.cbc.ca/firsthand/episodes/omar-khadr-out-of-the-shadows . There is no mention here of the three different arms of Al Jazeera that were involved.

[722] *Omar Khadr: Out of the Shadows*, Thursday, December 3, 2015. The article can be seen at http://www.cbc.ca/firsthand/episodes/omar-khadr-out-of-the-shadows . Viewed 25 July 2017. **Rated C3**. See also http://www.cbc.ca/news/canada/omar-khadr-tells-his-guantanamo-story-in-new-documentary-1.3089953 . Viewed 25 July 2017. **Rated C4**.

[723] The Toronto Star has a short promotional video of the production on their website at http://www.thestar.com/news/2015/05/27/omar-khadr-out-of-the-shadows.html . At 1:08 of 1:13, the film is shown as White Pine Production with CBC and Radio Canada. Viewed 25 July 2017. **Rated C3.**

[724] *Guantanamo's Child - Omar Khadr, Unprecedented access and an exclusive interview with Omar Khadr during his first days of freedom*. 07 Jun 2015 20:07 GMT. The Al Jazeera article is available online at http://www.aljazeera.com/programmes/witness/2015/06/guantanamo-child-omar-khadr-150531111517474.html . Viewed 25 July 2017. **Rated C4.**

role of Al Jazeera Arabic, Al Jazeera English and Al Jazeera America in the fine print on its sales site for the documentary.[725]

This is a serious issue, as the Al Jazeera news service is largely seen as the mouthpiece of the Government of Qatar and takes a pro-Muslim Brotherhood line on editorial issues. Al Jazeera's overt support for the Muslim Brotherhood[726] and other extremist groups has resulted in internal problems for Al Jazeera when reporters quit the organization, reporting that they did not want to work for the Muslim Brotherhood.[727]

Al Jazeera also has a history of glorifying Osama bin Landen. As the New York Times Magazine noted in November of 2001, "A huge, glamorous poster of bin Laden's silhouette hangs in the background of the main studio set at Al Jazeera's headquarters in Doha, the capital city of Qatar."[728]

Omar Khadr's father, the (in)famous Ahmed Sayed Khadr, was originally radicalized into the Muslim Student Association while at the University of Ottawa. Given that the Muslim Student Association was created by the Muslim Brotherhood, as noted in the book *Guantanamo's Child*[729], this is a serious omission.

Given the ties between the CBC and Al Jazeera[730] and the history of ownership,[731] this is a particularly worrisome issue. It raises interesting questions.

- How much influence did Al Jazeera have in the making of the film?
- How much money did they provide?
- If Al Jazeera played only a minor role, then why sometimes omit that they were involved?
- And most importantly, why would CBC even be involved with al Jazeera after it was known that Al Jazeera is a front operation that supports the Muslim Brotherhood, as identified by the journalists who quit Al Jazeera rather than work for a listed terrorist group?

---

[725] The fine print reads: Produced by White Pine Pictures in association with CBC, Radio-Canada, Al Jazeera English, Al Jazeera Arabic, Al Jazeera America and with the participation of Shaw Media Hot Docs Fund and the Canada Media Fund. The statement can be seen at http://www.whitepinepictures.com/guantanamos-child/?v=3e8d115eb4b3 . Viewed 31 August 2017. **Not rated.**

[726] Nicholas Noe and Walid Raad, *Al-Jazeera Gets Rap as Qatar Mouthpiece*, Bloomberg News, 10 April 2012. The article can be seen online at https://www.bloomberg.com/view/articles/2012-04-09/al-jazeera-gets-rap-as-qatar-mouthpiece . Viewed 31 March 2017. **Rated C2.**

[727] Bob Dreyfuss, *Al Jazeera's Muslim Brotherhood Problem, Staff quits en masse over Qatar-imposed favoritism for the Brothers*, The Nation, 10 July 2013. The article can be seen online at https://www.thenation.com/article/al-jazeeras-muslim-brotherhood-problem/ . Viewed 31 March 2017. **Rated B2.**

[728] Fouad Ajami, *What the Muslim World Is Watching*, 18 November 2001, The New York Times Magazine. The article is available online at http://www.nytimes.com/2001/11/18/magazine/what-the-muslim-world-is-watching.html?smid=tw-share . Viewed 12 September 2017. **Rated C2.**

[729] Michelle Sheppard, *Guantanamo's Child: The Untold Story of Omar Khadr*, John Wiley & Sons Canada, Apr 8, 2008. **Not rated.**

[730] Tony Burman, formerly of CBC, also worked for the government funded media organization of Qatar, Al Jazeera, in both Doha as managing director for their English Network and in the Washington DC office as chief strategic advisor for the Americas.

[731] Al Jazeera America (closed April 2016) was created when it took over Current TV, which had major shareholders in Al Gore, Joel Hyatt, and Ronald Burkle. Before it was Current TV, the channel had been called News World International whose majority holder was the CBC.

It would be difficult for the CBC or the Toronto Star to say they were unaware of the relationship between the Muslim Brotherhood, Al Jazeera and Qatar. Canadian journalist Mohamed Fahmy was arrested in Egypt in December of 2013. The entire basis of his arrest and subsequent trials rotated around the question of Al Jazeera and its relationship to the Muslim Brotherhood. Both the CBC[732] and the Toronto Star[733] reported on this.

The CBC and its Editorial Policies

The Islamist mass murder of journalists in France which came to be known as the "Charlie Hebdo killings" placed many members of the media in a difficult situation. On the one hand, obvious pressure existed to support the journalists at the heavily satirical Charlie Hebdo publication who had been murdered by Islamists. Free speech, a fundamental principle of both journalism and democracy, was at stake. Many would rise to the occasion, as did the public in France. However, many others failed to react and would not reprint the Charlie Hebdo cartoons.

It is a reasonable opinion to hold that Canada's national broadcaster, the CBC, was one of those who failed.

> "This is not a ban, and it isn't censorship," said David Studer, CBC's director of Journalistic Standards and Practices which was sent in an email to CBC's news staff. "We are being consistent with our historic journalistic practices around this story, not because of fear, but out of respect for the beliefs and sensibilities of the mass of Muslim believers about images of the Prophet. Similarly, we wouldn't publish cartoons likely to dismay or outrage mainstream followers of other religions."[734]

Tony Burman, was formerly the editor in chief of CBC news. He is quoted as saying:

> "Tony Burman of the CBC explained that "most media in Canada dealt with the story in the same way." The CBC felt that it could "easily describe the drawings in simple and clear English without actually showing them. That was indeed, without embarrassment, as an act of respect not only for Islam but for all religions." Burman also felt there was no reason to offend part of its audience for "absolutely no public value."[735]

Putting some of this in context, Tony Burman, formerly of CBC, also worked for the government funded media organization of Qatar, Al Jazeera, in both Doha as managing director for their English Network[736] and in the Washington DC office as chief strategic advisor for Al Jazeera in the Americas. Qatar is a known

---

[732] See, among others, *Egyptian-Canadian Journalist Mohamed Fahmy Sentenced To 7 Years In Prison,* CBC News, 23 June 2014. The article is available online at http://www.cbc.ca/strombo/news/mohamed-fahmy-sentenced-to-7-years . Viewed 07 October 2017. **Rated B3**.

[733] See, among others, Olivia Ward, *Canadian journalist Mohamed Fahmy says his 'patience is at an end,'* Toronto Star, 24 October 2017. Viewed 07 October 2017. **Rated B3**.

[734] *Prophet Muhammad cartoon in Quebec papers after Charlie Hebdo shooting,* Jan 08, 2015 8:35 AM ET, http://www.cbc.ca/news/canada/montreal/prophet-muhammad-cartoon-in-quebec-papers-after-charlie-hebdo-shooting-1.2893662 . Viewed 25 July 2017. **Rated B2**.

[735] *Freedom of the Press and Self-Censorship in the Media*. By Graham Darling, University of Alberta LL.B. student.

[736] *Tony Burman appointed as Managing Director at Al Jazeera English*, Qatarliving.com, 14/05/2008. The article is available online at http://web.archive.org/web/20120207122411/http://www.qatarliving.com/news/107195/tony-burman-appointed-as-managing-director-at-al-jazeera-english#ixzz42cMO6j1b . Viewed 25 July 2017. **Rated C3**.

funder of a variety of terrorism groups[737] and it is providing shelter for the Muslim Brotherhood's chief theoretician Yusuf Qaradawi (wanted in 2014 on an INTERPOL Red Notice).[738] Al Jazeera itself is noted for its editorial support for the Muslim Brotherhood which has been listed as a terrorist group by Egypt, Saudi Arabia, Bahrain and the United Arab Emirates. The government of the UK, following an extensive study of the Muslim Brotherhood stated:

> "Parts of the Muslim Brotherhood have a highly ambiguous relationship with violent extremism. Both as an ideology and as a network it has been a rite of passage for some individuals and groups who have gone on to engage in violence and terrorism." [739]

The UK government also believes that "that membership of, association with, or influence by the Muslim Brotherhood should be considered as a possible indicator of extremism." Individuals closely associated with the Muslim Brotherhood in the UK have supported suicide bombing and Hamas is a Muslim Brotherhood organization.[740]

The policy is also hypocritical. The CBC has published articles which are hugely offensive to Christians, for example, and shows no sign of backing down. The photo of a plastic crucifix submerged in urine, (Immersion Piss Christ) was published by the CBC and remains there, even though it is gratuitously offensive to Christians. The article, complete with photos of the exhibit, remain on the CBC website six years after it was originally published in 2011.[741]

What is most worrying, however, is that the CBC choses to decide what is offensive and unprintable based on views advanced by extremist groups. The issue of images of the Prophet Mohammed is largely a fake crisis generated as another means of shutting down any criticism of Islamist views. Images of the Prophet appear regularly throughout history. The idea of killing someone for this is new and advocated only be the most extreme of groups. It can be reasonably assessed that rather than using the Constitution of Canada, the Charter of Rights or the Criminal Code of Canada, individuals such as Tony Burman and David

---

[737] A variety of articles have discussed the role of Qatar in funding extremist and terrorism groups. Among them are Qatar and *Terror Finance*. Part I: Negligence, by David Andrew Weinberg of FDD. This article is available online at http://www.defenddemocracy.org/content/uploads/publications/Qatar_Part_I.pdf . Viewed 25 July 2017. **Rated B2**. Another view of Qatar's financing of extremism and terrorism is *Qatar and ISIS Funding: The U.S. Approach* by Lori Plotkin Boghardt of the Washington Institute. This article can be seen online at http://www.washingtoninstitute.org/policy-analysis/view/qatar-and-isis-funding-the-u.s.-approach. Viewed 25 July 2017. **Rated B3**.

[738] For more on the Interpol Red Notice see *FEATURED: INTERPOL Issues "Red Notice" For Youssef Qaradawi; Notice Considered By Many Countries As Provisional Arrest Warrant*, dated 05 December 2014. The article can be seen online at https://www.globalmbwatch.com/2014/12/05/featured-interpol-issues-red-notice-youssef-qaradawi-notice-considered-countries-provisional-arrest-warrant/ . Viewed 24 July 2017. **Rated B2**.

[739] *Muslim Brotherhood review: statement by the Prime Minister*, 17 December 2015. The statement can be seen online at https://www.gov.uk/government/speeches/muslim-brotherhood-review-statement-by-the-prime-minister . Viewed 24 July 2017. **Rated A1.**

[740] For more on the position of the UK government on the Muslim Brotherhood, see the Statement by Prime Minister David Cameron on the findings of the internal review to improve the government's understanding of the Muslim Brotherhood. It is available online at: https://www.gov.uk/government/speeches/muslim-brotherhood-review-statement-by-the-prime-minister . Viewed 24 July 2017. **Rated A1.** The full report can be seen at: https://www.gov.uk/government/publications/muslim-brotherhood-review-main-findings . Viewed 24 July 2017. **Rated A1.**

[741] The article and photo can be seen on the CBC website at http://www.cbc.ca/news/entertainment/french-museum-reopens-after-crucifix-art-attacked-1.1075952 . Viewed 23 August 2017. **Not rated**.

Studer appeared to have fallen to the fear and ideology of extremism. As the national broadcaster which is heavily taxpayer subsidized, it is reasonable to believe that a higher standard might be expected.

The Globe and Mail – Sheema Khan

The Globe and Mail regularly publishes columns by Sheema Khan with the byline "Special to The Globe and Mail." She is also the founder of CAIR CAN/NCCM, which has been openly identified as a Muslim Brotherhood front group in Canadian Senate testimony by Dr. Lorenzo Vidino (and many others).

CAIR CAN/NCCM parent organization (CAIR USA) was founded in the USA as a front group for HAMAS. CAIR USA has been openly identified as an unindicted co-conspirator in terrorism funding trials as well as being a Muslim Brotherhood/HAMAS front group. HAMAS itself states in Article 2 of its charter that it is Muslim Brotherhood. CAIR Can/NCCM's parent organization (CAIR USA) has also been listed as a terrorist entity by the United Arab Emirates.

It is a reasonable question to ask: Does the Globe and Mail think it is appropriate to have a columnist who also founded a front group for a listed terrorist entity? This same entity has also been involved in terrorism funding trials in the USA. Should the Globe and Mail identify this background when presenting articles by Sheema Khan?

This question was sent to the Public Editor of the Globe and Mail on 04 May 2017 (publiceditor@globeandmail.com). Included in the email was a list of primary and secondary sources detailing and supporting the question at hand.[742] The email also included a seven-page document consisting of 2795 words and 35 footnotes, with each footnote individually rated for source reliability and information credibility.

As of 05 September 2017, the Globe and Mail had not responded to this question.

Conclusion – The Voldemort Effect

The Voldemort Effect is the state of being fearful of naming someone or something out of fear of being attacked or killed. The phrase takes a cue from the line associated with "Lord Voldemort" in the Harry Potter series: "He who must not be named". The phrase, with respect to Islamists, was coined by British activist Maajid Nawaz in context of Islamism: individuals are fearful or reluctant to call out the ideology of Islamism as the underlying cause of Jihadist terrorism.[743]

---

[742] The information provided was: 1. For a transcript of the testimony of Dr. Vidino before the Standing Senate Committee on National Security and Defence, see: https://sencanada.ca/en/Content/Sen/committee/412/secd/52124-e . 2. For more on the Senate Testimony of Dr. Vidino see: Ian MacLeod, Beware of the Muslim Brotherhood, expert warns., Ottawa Citizen, 16 May 2015. The article is available online at: http://ottawacitizen.com/news/politics/beware-of-the-muslim-brotherhood-expert-warns . 3. UAE global listing of terrorist entities including CAIR USA. http://www.thenational.ae/uae/government/list-of-groups-designated-terrorist-organisations-by-the-uae . 4. Court document showing relationship between CAIR USA, NAIT, HAMAS, ISNA and the Muslim Brotherhood etc etc https://www.investigativeproject.org/documents/case_docs/1425.pdf . 5. Further court document showing relationship between CAIR USA, ISNA, HAMAS etc etc https://www.investigativeproject.org/documents/case_docs/1424.pdf .

[743] The Urban Dictionary. See definition at http://www.urbandictionary.com/define.php?term=Voldemort+Effect . Viewed 24 July 2017. **Rated B2.**

It is reasonable to believe that the effects of Islamists on Canada are self-evident. The terrorist attacks in Ottawa, St Jean sur Richelieu, Toronto, Edmonton and the failed suicide bomber attack in London Ontario are the most visible. The decision of young Canadians to become suicide bombers, jihadist martyrs, ISIS fighters and ISIS propagandists cannot be denied. Canadian registered charities have funded terrorist activities overseas and allow "jihad fund" money to enter Canada to spread the message of extremism.

It can be reasonably argued that the most visible effects of Islamists in Canada are the all-out assault on the rights of women. It is now acceptable in Canada to openly advocate wife beating as a form of education for women and worse still, it can be said that women enjoy being beaten as a "sign of love and concern" for them. This is done without any reaction from the Government of Canada or the main stream press.

Much of what is called the "main stream media" in Canada will not address the issues created by Islamists, nor will they investigate or report on the extremist groups that operate in Canada which are foreign based. The Toronto Star story with references to the Muslim Brotherhood by Haroon Siddiqui demonstrates the degree of denial (deliberate or otherwise) that is being displayed.

The degree to which this level of denial is policy or self-censorship is difficult to assess. Clearly, the CBC has attempted to pass off some of its denial as deliberate policy, claiming that they do not want to offend religious groups. The uneven way in which the policy is applied, however, suggests that it is the fear of Islamists that drives the coverage, but not that of any other religious group. Adding to this is the CBC's indirect and direct connections to Al Jazeera. Why the CBC chose to deny its collaboration with Al Jazeera in the Khadr documentary raises uncomfortable questions, given the links of the Khadr family and Al Jazeera to Muslim Brotherhood?

It is reasonable to believe that self-censorship and political correctness, may be at the heart of the problem. The Toronto Star 's policy on the Islamic State naming convention[744] and the CBC reporting on Maisonneuve College show the degree to which voluntary linguistic cleansing is affecting reporting.

It is also reasonable, however, to express some sympathy to journalists, authors and newspaper owners. Multiple journalists have been killed by Islamist forces and others, such as Salman Rushdie, have had fatwas levelled against them which are deadly serious. Michel Houellebecq, author of a satirical fictional futurist novel about the role of Islamists in France had disappeared from public view since 2015 due to death threats. Such death threats and lawsuits by Islamist groups are a fact of life, including Canada.

It is also reasonable to believe that journalists, however, are often part of the problem itself. Lars Hedegaard is a Danish historian, journalist and author and a former member of the Danish Socialist Workers Party. He is also an outspoken critic of the Islamist movement in Europe and has received death threats. On 5 February 2013, an unknown person attempted to assassinate him in his own house. Following that, he was relocated in an operation assisted by the police. However, his moving day activities were observed by another journalist and a photographer from the newspaper Ekstra Bladet. The two newspaper employees followed the moving van with the intent of being able to publicly report his new address, thus greatly increasing the likelihood of his assassination. The police intervened twice, pulling the two Ekstra Bladet and delaying them so they could not follow the moving van. Most shocking, the journalist involved, Bo Poulsen, published an article the next day which sarcastically attacked the police

---

[744] Olivia Ward Foreign Affairs Reporter, *The Star now says 'Daesh' instead of 'the Islamic State' or ISIS*, Published on Thu Mar 03 2016. The article is available online at h2tp://www.thestar.com/news/world/2016/03/03/the-star-now-says-daesh-instead-of-the-islamic-state-or-isis.html. Viewed 24 July 2017. **Rated B3.**

for detaining him from his work.[745] The journalist in question, Bo Poulsen, did not agree with the views of Lars Hedegaard and therefore seemed to think exposing him to assassination was a credible activity to be carried out while an employee of a newspaper.

Only half-jokingly, comedian and actor John Cleese, famous for his role in the Monty Python TV series and films, was asked if he would repeat his comedic and satirical attacks of his younger years. He would, he said, except for Muslims. When asked why not, he said "They'll kill you."[746]

---

[745] *Lars Hedegaard flytter: Islamkritikeren, der blev forsøgt likvideret i februar, flytter fra sin lejlighed på Frederiksberg,* 03 March 2013. The article can be seen online at http://ekstrabladet.dk/112/article3989674.ece . An English language commentary on the article can be seen at http://www.frontpagemag.com/fpm/180655/media-try-report-lars-hedegaards-new-address-bruce-bawer . Viewed 24 July 2017. **Rated B3.**

[746] *John Cleese says you can't make jokes about Muslims - because 'they'll kill you',* By Annabel Grossman for MailOnline, Published: 14:16 GMT, 27 November 2014. The article can be seen online at http://www.dailymail.co.uk/news/article-2851888/John-Cleese-blasts-political-correctness-protecting-select-groups-ridicule.html#ixzz42usroMWE . Viewed 24 July 2017. **Rated B2.**

CHAPTER 18: INTELLIGENCE, LAW ENFORCEMENT, AND THE MULLAH SYNDROME

Thomas Quiggin

Key Points

- Increasing indicators suggest that the role of policing may be changing over time, driven by political correctness, rather than societal needs.
- Instead of enforcing the law and supporting community values, police are increasingly expected and/or willing to enforce political orthodoxy. The same can be said for the intelligence services.
- Political correctness outweighs law enforcement in many police forces.

Mullah Syndrome

The term Mullah Syndrome, coined by Danish politician Naser Khader,[747] refers to the tendency of government officials, especially policy makers, police and intelligence agencies, to engage with predominantly Islamist groups. They do this while ignoring the much larger population of secular and reformist Muslims. This attitude has played into the hands of Western Islamist groups.[748]

It is reasonable to suggest that Mullah Syndrome may be at its worst at the local level, but the problem runs from city police forces right up to federal agencies. Newspapers suffer from the same issue, frequently using quotes and information from extremist front groups who pass themselves off as human rights groups or "grass roots activists."[749]

Mullah Syndrome, it can be said, is damaging on many different levels. One of the primary side effects is that many Muslims are frightened about dealing with the police and intelligence services. They believe that those organizations have been infiltrated by Islamist supporters. Another level of damage occurs when the police and intelligence agencies have their views shaped by individuals who advocate for the Islamist ideology.

These engagements with the representatives of Islamist groups may be a simple failure to do a background check. It may also be that the organization involved did a background check, but was simply not able to understand who they were dealing with at the time. Others have been told by extremist group members that their group "condemns terrorism" and is therefore "moderate." The officials then naively believe these are the "good guys."

---

[747] Hudson Institute Senior Fellow (non-resident) Naser Khader serves as a member of the Conservative Party in the Danish Parliament, Folketinget, having previously served from 2001 until 2011. Khader's main research areas include freedom of speech and the fight for democracy and democratic values in multicultural societies. For more on him see the Hudson Institute at http://www.hudson.org/experts/660-naser-khader . Viewed 25 July 2017. **Not rated.**

[748] Dr. Lorenzo Vidino, *The New Muslim Brotherhood in the West*, Columbia University Press, New York, 2010. Chapter Four.

[749] See Chapter 17 in this book for examples of how the press report on Islamist extremism in Canada.

As noted elsewhere, the police and intelligence agencies are often under pressure from "above" in order to get the right photos and press briefings to placate their politically correct bosses. Many politicians, captured by their own ambition or being believers in political correctness are far more worried about community outreach than they are in enforcing the law or stopping extremist ideologies. The grooming and rape of 1,400 girls aged eleven to fourteen in Rotherham, UK, is evidence of that. In Rotherham, the police, social workers and city council did not respond to reports of mass rapes being carried out by Kashmiri Muslims in their town. They were more afraid of being called racists than they were interested in protecting 11-year-old girls from rape and sex trafficking.[750]

The York Regional Police and the NCCM

On 29 March 2014, Mark Topping of the York Regional Police (Toronto area) accepted an award from the National Council of Canadian Muslims (formerly Council for American Islamic Relations Canada) for "community service and professionalism." The photo of his accepting the award appeared in multiple settings, including a Toronto Star article[751] as well as NCCM's own "Good News Alert" internet posting.[752] This was not an 'one off' event as the Chief of the York Regional Police, Eric Jolliffe, also met with the NCCM/CAIR CAN Chief, on 28 March 2014.[753]

It is reasonable to believe that the problem with such a meeting is that the NCCM/CAIR CAN is part of CAIR USA (Council of American Islamic Relations USA). After this meeting, CAIR USA was also declared to be a terrorist group by the United Arab Emirates, [754] but it had been well known that CAIR USA was an unindicted co-conspirator in terrorism funding trials in the USA. It was also known that CAIR-USA had been repeated linked directly to Hamas in that it was funding that terrorist organization. Mr. Gardee, of the NCCM. has attempted to suggest to the press and to Parliament that his organization has no links to CAIR USA, but this is doubtful, based on the statements of his own organization, CAIR USA and that of others such as the US State Department.[755]

By allowing such (public) meetings to take place or awards accepted, the York Regional Police are sending a message to Muslims (and others) that they have been co-opted or infiltrated by front groups for Islamists. The perception is that any information given to them may fall into the hands of the groups who have done the infiltrating.

---

[750] The Jay Report on mass rape in Rotherham can be seen online at file:///C:/Users/User/Downloads/Independent_inquiry_CSE_in_Rotherham%20(10).pdf . Viewed 25 July 2017. **Rated A2.**

[751] Peter Edwards, *National Muslim group condemns latest Islamic State threat*, The Toronto Star, 08 December 2014. The article is available on line at http://www.thestar.com/news/canada/2014/12/08/national_muslim_group_condemns_latest_islamic_state_threat.html . Viewed 25 July 2017. **Rated B3.**

[752] For a copy of the NCCM article, see http://myemail.constantcontact.com/Good-News-Alert--NCCM-Holds-Successful-2014-Gala-.html?soid=1114179096563&aid=beJmtSZHf1Q . Viewed 25 July 2017. **Rated B3.**

[753] Others from the York Regional Police who attended the brief were Superintendent Tony Cusimano, Sgt. Brett Kemp from the Hate Crime Unit and Det. Cst. Mark Topping. For more on this meeting see http://www.nccm.ca/wp-content/uploads/2014/07/NCCM-Events-Roundup-January-to-July-2014.pdf . Viewed 25 July 2017. **Rated B2.**

[754] For a list of the organizations designated as terrorist entities, front groups or proxy groups, see http://warontherocks.com/2016/03/the-islamic-state-in-europe-terrorists-without-borders-counterterrorists-with-all-borders/ . Viewed 25 July 2017. **Rated B3.**

[755] For more on how the NCCM/CAIR CAN is connected to CAIR USA, see the examples in Chapter 13.

It is clear that police forces need to deal with many groups and individuals in the line of duty. This sometimes means dealing with unsavoury elements to gain insight or evidence. It is a common practice based on the principle of supporting the "larger good." However, it is reasonable to believe that being seen in public accepting awards from groups such as the NCCM/CAIR CAN is a questionable practice. Again, it is reasonable to assess that such actions either demonstrates a lack of judgment on the part of the police force in question, or it demonstrates submissiveness on the part of the police. Either can be assessed as frightening.

The York Regional Police were sent an email on 04 May 2017 (2017-05-04 7:11 AM) asking questions about this situation.[756] A polite and timely email was returned (2017-05-12 5:48 PM) but none of the questions were answered.

The Toronto Police Service

One of the chaplains to Toronto Police is Musleh Khan, who was officially appointed on Wednesday, October 26, 2016. It is reasonable to question why this appointment was made.

Born in Madinah, Saudi Arabia and raised Toronto, Musleh Khan graduated from the Islamic University of Madinah (Medina) where he completed a BA in Islamic Law from the faculty of Da'wah and Usool al-deen. He lectures in the Muslim community on Islamic Law, Islamic identity and marital relationships among other things. The University of Medina is well known for its severe, Wahhabist interpretation of Islam. As the New York Times noted:

> The University of Medina recruits students from around the world, trains them in the bigotry of Salafism and sends them to Muslim communities in places like the Balkans, Africa, Indonesia, Bangladesh and Egypt, where these Saudi-trained hard-liners work to eradicate the local, harmonious forms of Islam.[757]

Chaplain Khan has been noted for his teachings in Canada. Women, he believes must obey their husbands, and makes themselves sexually available on demand. They also "must seek permission from their husbands whenever they want to leave the house because the man is the "main decision-maker of the home."[758]

Islamist apologists, including Khan himself, made the usual statements that his views had been taken out of context and that those unfamiliar with his meaning could misinterpret them.[759] According to Khan, the

---

[756] The questions asked were (1.) Is it appropriate for the YRP to accept "community awards" from an organization that has been publicly identified as a front group for terrorist listed organizations? For instance, the following photo shows Detective Constable Mark Topping (left) accepting an award for community service and professionalism on behalf of the York Regional Police from NCCM Executive Director Ihsaan Gardee. (2.) Does the YRP feel that such exposure has a chilling effect on other Muslims in the community? Specifically those Muslims who feel they wish to communicate information to the police but are aware that the YRP has been comprised in its dealings with an extremist front group such as the CAIR CAN/NCCM? (3.) Is the YRP aware that Durham Regional in Canada and the FBI in the USA no longer deal with these organization due to their links to extremism?

[757] Ed Husain, *Saudis Must Stop Exporting Extremism; ISIS Atrocities Started with Saudi Support for Salafi Hate,* the New York Times, 22 August 2014. Viewed 25 July 2017. **Rated C3**.

[758] Farzana Hassan, *Muslim Toronto Police chaplain's views troubling,* The Toronto Sun, 03 November 2016. Viewed 25 July 2017. **Rated B3**.

[759] Shanifa Nasser, *Toronto police chaplain under fire for women's 'obedience' comments to stay with force for now, Musleh Khan met recently with Toronto police Chief Mark Saunders,* 04 November 2017. This article can be seen

Arabic translation for obedience really denotes "loyalty and devotion." By contrast, a search on a variety of Arab-English dictionaries turns up the terms compliance, obedience, submission, surrender and yielding.

It is a reasonable question to ask. Why does the Toronto Police Service have an Imam from the University of Medina who teaches that women are inferior and must be house bound unless they seek permission from their husbands? How does the Toronto Police Board allow such a person to be an Imam when their domestic violence policy states that "Women who have been victimized by violence are a Toronto Police Service Priority."[760] Of interest, the policy includes the line "DOMESTIC VIOLENCE includes acts used to **maintain power and control over a person by creating fear and isolation**. Abuse can take many forms, including physical, sexual, emotional, psychological and financial."[761] (Emphasis added).

The Royal Canadian Mounted Police and the Muslim Student Association

In November of 2014, Superintendent Best of the Royal Canadian Mounted Police met with the Muslim Student Association of the University of Windsor. Superintendent Best is publicly identified as having a national security role for the RCMP in the province of Ontario[762] and was aware of the nature of the organization.[763]

The Muslim Student Association (MSA) was originally founded by the Muslim Brotherhood as their first 'above ground' organization in North America.[764] Its creation was the result of Saudi Arabia-backed efforts to create a network of international Islamic organizations to spread its Wahhabist ideology. It was, at that time, essentially an arm of the Saudi-funded, Muslim Brotherhood-controlled, Muslim World League."[765]

It is reasonable to believe that there are a number of Canadian MSA alumni who have gone onto become suicide bombers, al Qaeda funders and senior members of listed terrorist organizations.[766] It includes, among others, Ahmed Sayed Khadr, a martyr of al Qaeda, suicide bomber Salman Ashrafi, and John Maguire, a propagandist of ISIS.

---

online at http://www.cbc.ca/news/canada/toronto/toronto-police-chaplain-under-fire-for-women-s-obedience-comments-to-stay-with-force-for-now-1.3837565 . Viewed 25 July 2017. **Rated B3.**

760 The Toronto Police Service policy on domestic violence is available on their website at http://www.torontopolice.on.ca/community/domesticviolence/ . Viewed 23 August 2017. **Not rated.**

761 This statement can be seen at http://www.torontopolice.on.ca/community/domesticviolence/20090422-domestic_violence_pamphlet.pdf . Viewed 23 August 2017. **Not rated.**

762 *Violent radicalization at a high in Canada, though still an extreme minority*, Craig Pearson, Windsor Star, Published on: November 26, 2014. The article can be seen online at http://windsorstar.com/news/violent-radicalization-at-a-high-in-canada-though-still-an-extreme-minority . Viewed 25 July 2017. **Rated C3.**

763 Superintendent Best was sent an expansive email and 200-page report on the MSA and the Muslim Brotherhood in advance of his meeting. The email as sent to him on 2014-11-30 at 11:53 AM. Additionally, his own unit of the RCMP was investigating IRFAN, another Muslim Brotherhood front group which had lost its charity status for funding terrorism (HAMAS). Neither he nor his staff responded to the email.

764 *Muslim Student Association: The Investigative Project on Terrorism Dossier*, (2008, January 1). The Investigative Project on Terrorism. The article can be seen online at https://www.investigativeproject.org/documents/misc/31.pdf . Viewed 25 July 2017. **Rated B2.**

765 Islamist Organization Profile: Muslim Students Association (MSA), Mauro, R. (2013, February 3), *The Clarion Project. The article is available online at* http://www.clarionproject.org/analysis/muslim-students-association . Viewed 25 July 2017. **Rated B2.**

766 For a partial listing of MSA alumni with terrorist connections, see Chapter 14 of this book.

It is reasonable to believe that by sending a senior authority to such an event and allowing himself to be photographed, the Superintendent is signalling to the larger (non-radicalized) Muslim community that he engages with Islamist groups. Law enforcement and intelligence agencies feel they have to engage Muslims who have credentials. It becomes hard to tell if this is part of the failed strategy of engaging such groups, formerly known as Preventing Violent Extremism, or they literally just do not know what is going on in the Canadian context of Islamist radicalization.

The Canadian Security and Intelligence Service and Sheema Khan

On 11 April 2006, Sheema Khan did a presentation at the headquarters of the Canadian Security and Intelligence Service (CSIS). The title of the presentation was, ironically enough, Partners in Security. Sheema Khan is noteworthy as she was the founder of CAIR Montreal, CAIR Ottawa and CAIR CAN which has recently changed its name to the NCCM.

According to Sheema Khan, the stated purpose of the Montreal chapter of CAIR USA, was to promote awareness of CAIR USA in Montreal. Ms. Khan states that she was director of this chapter until 1998 and that CAIR USA had control over the character and quality of the activities of the Canadian chapter.[767] CAIR CAN itself was founded in 2000.

CAIR USA, as noted already, was as an unindicted co-conspirator in the Holy Land Relief terrorism funding case, until their name was removed from the list. At that point, however, the judge ruled, that "the government has produced ample evidence to establish the associations of CAIR, ISNA, NAIT, with the Islamic Association for Palestine, and with (terrorist group) Hamas."[768] Since then, CAIR USA has been listed as a terrorist entity by the United Arab Emirates. As such, the Canadian chapter, set up by its founder to advance the cause of CAIR USA, is a front group for the Muslim Brotherhood and closely tied to Hamas, itself a part of the Muslim Brotherhood.

It is a reasonable question to ask how CSIS could believe it would advance their cause to have public connections to the front group for two different terrorist entities at the time (Muslim Brotherhood and Hamas).

Conclusions

Following the section on Sheema Khan above, it is noteworthy that at a conference in Ottawa in late 2015, a very senior Canadian intelligence official stated that "there are many different Muslim Brotherhoods, and not all of them are bad." It is reasonable to assess that CAIR CAN/NCCM's investment in infiltrating CSIS is working well.

The statement by the intelligence official is, of course, absurd. All Muslim Brotherhood front groups and proxies are Islamist and supremacist in nature as their aim is to create a global, Islamist caliphate which they believe has the right to dominate all others. By definition, the Muslim Brotherhood and other such groups are an affront to the Constitution of Canada and the Charter of Rights and Freedoms. It should be noted that the Muslim Brotherhood did, from the mid-1970s to the early 1990s, try to move away from

---

[767] For more on Sheema Khan and how CAIR CAN was created, see Chapter 13.

[768] The decision of the court on this issue is available online at http://www.scribd.com/doc/43380629/2009-order-on-Holy-Land-Foundation-unindicted-coconspirator-list . Viewed 25 July 2017. **Rated A1.**

the worst of its violence. This has now ended, and the Muslim Brotherhood has made repeated claims to its own audience that it supports violence.[769]

It is reasonable to believe that the difference between the various Muslim Brotherhood front groups is that some are overtly violent, such as Hamas, while others make dubious claims of non-violence. Others front groups are fundraisers for terrorist groups. In Canada, this includes IRFAN which was fundraising for Hamas[770] and the Islamic Society of North America (ISNA) which was fundraising for the Kashmiri Canadian Council/Kashmiri Relief Fund of Canada. The ISNA funds, it was stated, were eventually headed for Jamaat-e-Islami and/or its armed wing, Hizbul Mujahideen.[771] The Jamaat-e-Islami is often called the 'Muslim Brotherhood in South Asia.'

Implications

So why do police and intelligence agencies co-operate with front groups for the Muslim Brotherhood, Hizb ut-Tahrir and the Khomeneists (among others)?

The reasons, it can be said, appear to fall into three main areas. These are:

- Direct examples of Mullah Syndrome. Agencies want to be seen to be cooperating and do "community engagement" in order to achieve "community balance." The need or desire for good photo ops and selfies outweighs any assessment of whether this is truly a practical idea.

- Violent extremism. Another less likely, but possible issue, is that of the failed idea of preventing violent extremism versus the idea of confronting it. Several agencies, especially in the United Kingdom, decided to knowingly engage with Islamist groups in the (false) hope that this would be a fire break or bulwark against the overtly violent groups. As learned by experience, however, the "line between extremism and terrorism is not always precise. It correctly concludes from this that preventing people becoming terrorists will require a challenge to extremist ideas where they are used to legitimize terrorism and are shared."[772]

- A third option. As always, a third option is possible, however unlikely given the amount of time that has past since 9-11. Some police forces, especially smaller ones, may simply have no idea

[769] For more on this see MEMRI Project. For this quotation and other information see *Muslim Brotherhood Turn to Terrorism Against Al-Sisi Regime: Threats of Attacks Against Foreign Diplomats, Workers in Egypt On Turkey-Based MB TV, Calls For Jihad And For Assassination Of Al-Sisi, Regime Head*, 20 February 2015. The articles can be seen online at http://www.memri.org/report/en/0/0/0/0/0/0/8446.htm . Viewed 19 June 2017. **Rated B2.**

[770] The Government of Canada statement on the revocation of the charitable status of IRFAN and its listing as a terrorist entity can be seen at https://www.publicsafety.gc.ca/cnt/ntnl-scrt/cntr-trrrsm/lstd-ntts/crrnt-lstd-ntts-en.aspx#2052 . Viewed 25 July 2017. **Rated A1**.

[771] The CRA statement on the charity revocation for the ISNA Development Fund can be seen at http://www.marketwired.com/press-release/canada-revenue-agency-revokes-registration-isna-development-foundation-as-charity-1833203.htm . Viewed 25 July 2017. **Rated A1**.

[772] For more on the failures of the prevent extremism policy, see the Quilliam Foundation's report *Quilliam response to UK's government's new 'Prevent' policy.* It can be seen online at https://www.quilliaminternational.com/quilliams-response-to-uk-governments-new-prevent-policy/ . Viewed 25 July 2017. **Rated B2**. For more on this see also Quilliam Launches White Paper on the role of Prevent in Countering Online Extremism, 02 December 2014. The report can be seen online at http://www.quilliamfoundation.org/press/quilliam-launches-white-paper-on-the-role-of-prevent-in-countering-extremism/ . Viewed 25 July 2017. **Rated B2.**

with whom they are communicating. Lacking the background and with the lack of guidance from national level agencies, they may believe they are doing the right thing. As bureaucratic insiders are aware the age-old excuse is sometimes valid: Never assume malice when stupidity could adequately explain the situation.

CHAPTER 19: THE MONTREAL KIDNAPPING

Thomas Quiggin

Key Points

- The investigation of an attempted kidnapping by Chiheb Battikh raises more questions than it answers with respect to his involvement with an Islamist group.
- The judge in the proceedings where Mr. Battikh was sentenced after changing his plea to guilty raised questions about the likelihood of an accomplice.
- Police forces at the local level do not appear to be getting support and intelligence from national level agencies on Islamist groups in Canada.

It is a court proven fact that in December 2012, Chiheb Battikh attempted the kidnapping of the three-year-old grandson of a Montreal area billionaire.[773] His intent was to extort a ransom. The kidnapping attempt was derailed during its execution phase due to the swift reactions of local citizens and a nearby police patrol car responding to the 911 call.

The kidnapping, arrest and subsequent investigation resulted in a sudden change of plea from "not guilty" to "guilty" by the defense lawyers. Consequently, no trial occurred. There was, however, a significant investigation carried out by Andrew McIntosh[774], formerly of the Journal de Montreal. The result of the press investigation was a five-page story published on 20 June 2014. The headline for the story was:

> "Mystérieux enlèvement d'enfant manqué, Le coupable avait-il un complice? Était-il lié aux Frères musulmans?" [Mysterious child abduction failed; did the culprit have an accomplice? Was it linked to the Muslim Brotherhood?]

The same story appeared in the English language press on 8 Augusts 2014 with the headline:

> "Questions linger in failed kidnapping of billionaire's grandson"

Many questions remain unanswered, despite the arrest and conviction of Mr. Battikh. The most important questions may be these:

- Was the kidnapping an attempt to raise money for a Muslim Brotherhood front organization project in Canada?

---

[773] The names of the victim, his father and grandfather are the subject of a publication ban imposed by the courts in Quebec. The intent of the publication ban was to protect the three-year-old minor. The ban also protects how Chiheb Battikh came to target this family specifically.

[774] The five-page original story by Andrew McIntosh can be seen in French at: http://www.journaldemontreal.com/2014/06/20/mysterieux-enlevement-denfant-manque . A shorter version of the story in English can be seen at: http://www.ottawasun.com/2014/08/08/questions-linger-in-failed-kidnapping-of-billionaires-grandson . Both viewed 24 July 2017. **Both rated A1**.

- Has the practice of kidnapping the children of the rich for funding extremist operations arrived in Canada?

When news first broke about the kidnapping, an overseas French language paper, the Tunis Tribune[775], also picked up and republished the kidnap for ransom story. The headline read:

> "Canada: Un Tuniso-canadien, proche d'Ennahdha accusé d'enlèvement d'enfant" [776] [Canada: A Tunisian Canadian, close to Ennahdha accused of kidnapping a child]

The Ennahda Movement was formerly known as the Movement of Islamic Tendency which itself was the successor to Islamic Action. The party is closely associated to beliefs of Sayyid Qutb and Abul Ala Maududi, two of the most (in)famous theoreticians of the Muslim Brotherhood and Jamaat-e-Islami. While claiming to be moderate, the party's general secretary in Hamadi Jebali, called the Tunisian revolution "a divine moment in a new state, and in, hopefully, a 6th caliphate," and that "the liberation of Tunisia will, God willing, bring about the liberation of Jerusalem."[777] Shortly after that, leaders of the Hamas party visited Tunisia.

Mr. Battikh was born in Tunisia in approximately 1962, but had lived in Canada for 25 years at the time of the kidnapping. His most recent address was in Montreal Quebec, but he has also lived in Mississauga Ontario.

The Muslim Association of Canada

The Muslim Association of Canada has been identified by Dr. Lorenzo Vidino (and many others) as a Muslim Brotherhood front organization in Canada.[778] During his testimony to the Canadian Senate[779] in May of 2015, Dr. Vidino was reported as warning that the Muslim Brotherhood movement has planted its revivalist interpretation of Islam, political ideology, and activism among some Muslims here and sees itself as a minder and broker between them and the rest of society. He also added that in addition to the Muslim Association of Canada, the National Council of Canadian Muslims (NCCM), is another front group along with the International Relief Fund for the Afflicted and Needy (IRFAN). The list also included Islamic Relief Canada. IRFAN lost its charitable status for funding terrorism in 2011 and was declared to be a

---

[775] The main web page of the newspaper is available online at http://news.tunistribune.com/ .

[776] See more at: http://news.tunistribune.com/?q=node/6#sthash.ThVG0Wo2.dpuf . The paper is published in Paris, France. Viewed 28 April 2017. **Rated C3**.

[777] Mischa Benoit-Lavelle, *Hamas Representative Addresses Tunisian Political Rally*, Tunis Alive, 15 November 2011. The article can be seen online at http://www.tunisia-live.net/2011/11/15/hamas-representative-addresses-tunisian-political-rally/. Viewed 24 July 2017. **Rated C3**.

[778] Ian MacLeod, The Ottawa Citizen, *Beware of the Muslim Brotherhood, expert warns*. Published on 16 2015. The article is available online at http://ottawacitizen.com/news/politics/beware-of-the-muslim-brotherhood-expert-warns . Viewed 17 April 2017. **Rated A2**. The article is based on the Senate of Canada testimony of Dr. Lorenzo Vidino. For a full transcript of his testimony on the Muslim Brotherhood in Canada see: http://www.parl.gc.ca/content/sen/committee/412/SECD/52124-E.HTM . Viewed 17 April 2017. **Rated A2.**

[779] Ian MacLeod, The Ottawa Citizen, *Beware of the Muslim Brotherhood, expert warns*. Published on: May 16, 2015. The article is available online at: http://ottawacitizen.com/news/politics/beware-of-the-muslim-brotherhood-expert-warns . Viewed 17 April 2017. **Rated A2**. The article is based on the Senate of Canada testimony of Dr. Lorenzo Vidino. For a full transcript of his testimony on the Muslim Brotherhood in Canada see: https://sencanada.ca/en/Content/Sen/committee/412/secd/52124-e . Viewed 17 April 2017. **Rated A2**.

terrorist entity in 2014.[780] Islamic Relief Canada's parent organization, Islamic Relief Worldwide was listed as a terrorist entity by the United Arab Emirates.

Mr. Battikh has been involved with the Muslim Association of Canada (MAC) for more than 14 years and has filled several leadership roles. He has been quoted in the press on numerous occasions in an MAC role. He was on the Board of Directors as far back as the year 2000[781], on the executive committee and he has also been the Head of the MAC Education Department and played a role in the MAC's "Springs of Knowledge" program as well. His name was also quoted as being a representative of the MAC responsible for the purchase of a building when the MAC announced[782] that they would purchase a new property for an Islamic Centre at 615 rue Belmont, Montreal QC, H3B 2L8. His name was also listed as a contact for an MAC West Island sports camp for children with the office contact number of 514-983-5566.

The $4.7 million deal for the premises at 615 rue Belmont was the subject of a court action due to the breakdown of the financing in the deal. The MAC eventually went to court to try and force the transfer, but it appears they did not have the money and unsolved discussions about an environmental cleanup remained. In the six-page court document, Mr. Battikh's name appears as acting on behalf of the MAC in paragraphs 22, 24, 25 and26.[783] The status of the purchase was unclear at the time of his arrest and the failure to come up with the appropriate financing appears to have been at the heart of the problems.

Of note, the project eventually went ahead, and the location is now known as the Institute of Islamic Civilization.

The Muslim Association of Canada and the Muslim Brotherhood

It is reasonable to believe that the Muslim Association of Canada has a strong and long-standing link to the Muslim Brotherhood and its founder, Hassan al-Banna. Specifically, the MAC believes:

> "MAC's roots are deeply enshrined in the message of Prophet Mohammad. Its modern roots can be traced to the vigorous intellectual revivalist effort that took hold in Muslim societies starting in the early twentieth century. This revival aimed at reconciling faith with the challenges of modernity and providing a clear articulation of balance and moderation in understanding Islam. In the Arab world, this revival culminated in the writings of the late Imam Hassan al-Banna and the movement of the Society of Muslim Brothers (commonly known as the Muslim Brotherhood). Al-Banna's core messages of constructive engagement in society, focus on personal and

---

[780] For more on the status of IRFAN, see the Government of Canada document at https://www.canada.ca/en/revenue-agency/services/charities-giving/charities/whats-new/revoked-canadian-charity-listed-under-criminal-code-terrorist-entity.html . Viewed 24 July 2017. **Rated A1**.

[781] See the CRA charities website for further information on the MAC and its board members.

[782] Assalalamou alaikom, L'association musulmane du Canada est heureuse de vous annoncer l'acquisition d'un nouveau centre islamique dans le centre ville de Montréal. Il s'agit d'un édifice de cinq étages sise à l'adresse suivant: 615 Rue Belmont, Montréal, QC H3B 2L8. The announcement can be seen at http://studylibfr.com/doc/3797588/mohamed-hamrani-annonce-l-acquisition-du-615-belmont-%C3%A0 . Viewed 24 July 2017. **Rated C3**.

[783] The court document can be seen online at http://pointdebasculecanada.ca/wp-content/uploads/2012/07/0%20org%20mac%20belmont%20motion.pdf . Viewed 24 July 2017. **Rated B2**.

communal empowerment, and organizational development had a deep impact on much of the Muslim world." [784]

"It is now 75 years since Al-Banna initiated that blessed effort. The efforts of the Muslim Association of Canada are separate from the writings and organization of Al-Banna by time and space. The assertion that much of our philosophy and vision derive from the efforts of Al-Banna should not be taken to mean that we adopt in wholesale fashion all of the ideas developed and put forward by Al-Banna or the Muslim Brotherhood. However, **we believe that the efforts of Al-Banna and subsequent generations of the Muslim Brotherhood remain the truest reflection of Islamic practice in the modern era.**" [785] (Emphasis added).

The Kidnapping Attempt and Arrest

The actual kidnapping attempt failed during execution. It appears Chiheb Battikh had carried out basic surveillance and was aware that the three-year-old child victim was regularly picked up by the mother from a place of care and walked home. On the day of the kidnapping, however, it was the father who picked up the child and was walking home in the snow with the child in a sled behind him. As they were walking through F.X. Garneau Park in Outremont, the father noticed someone walking behind him.

The father was then tasered three times in the neck by Mr. Battikh, but fended off the worst of the attack as he had turned just as the attack commenced. His awareness and ability to raise his hand against the Taser prevented him from being completely immobilized.

The father fell to the snow and was bleeding from his ear as a result. However, he could stand up again after a few seconds and gave chase. A woman nearby observed the events and called 911 while a passing citizen on a bicycle entered the fray as well. Fortunately, the Service de Police de la Ville de Montréal (SPVM, City of Montreal Police Service) had a patrol car nearby.

Mr. Battikh grabbed the child from the sled as the father lay on the ground. He began to run away from the scene. Strangely, he ran in the direction opposite from where his car was later found. This raised one of the first questions about the whole kidnapping attempt. If he was operating alone, why run away from his car and not towards it? Was there another car waiting for him?

Once Mr. Battikh's escape was frustrated by the passing citizen and the father of the child, he threatened the father and said that he would kill him the next time he saw him. Shortly after that, the SPVM arrived and Mr. Battikh was removed from the park in handcuffs.

The Investigation

The SPVM did ask questions about the possibility of links to terrorism. Specifically, they inquired as to whether he had links to al Qaeda (which he probably does not).

It is fair to say that the three-year-old grandson of a billionaire was kidnapped by an individual whom even the foreign press noted had links to an extremist group, but no one in Canada noticed it. It appears,

---

[784] For the views of the Muslim Association of Canada and their relationship to Hassan al-Banna and the Muslim Brotherhood, see http://www.macnet.ca/English/Pages/About%20MAC.aspx . Viewed 24 July 2017. **Rated B2.**
[785] A screenshot of this document can be seen at http://pointdebasculecanada.ca/wp-content/uploads/2012/07/MAC-Maududi-Endorsement.jpg . Viewed 24 July 2017. **Rated B2.**

however, that CSIS and the RCMP became interested in the investigation only after court proceedings had begun. Most likely, they were tipped to the issue by the investigation by the press and not their own networks of information. The outcome of any CISIS or RCMP later involvement has not been made public.

The investigation left many questions unanswered. Even the judge in the proceedings where Mr. Battikh was sentenced after changing his plea to guilty raised questions about the likelihood of an accomplice. The judge also questioned the amount of money that was going to be demanded for ransom.

The Son of Chiheb Battikh

Shortly after his father was arrested, Moez Battikh (rapper stage name Moez Melon)[786] posted on his Facebook a message: "God is the only authority." The message and similar material were taken down shortly after the media contacted him. His name also came up when the police asked Chiheb Battikh about the one walkie talkie that was found in his car. He claimed it belonged to his son, there was only one and it did not work anyway. In the light of the overall investigation, this statement seems doubtful and it raises the issue of whether Moez Battikh was involved in the events.[787] Who owns one walkie talkie?

The Twitter account of Moez Battikh is also interesting. On 16 June 2013 (after the failed kidnapping attempt) Moez Tweets a Happy Father's Day to his father, and then rather bizarrely notes that his father is a role model for him.

In other Tweets, Moez quotes the founder of the Muslim Brotherhood (Hassan al-Banna) on 12 February 2012 and says, "And do not despair, for despair is not from the character of a Muslim."

Moez stated in a Tweet on 7 September 2011 that he gave one of his CDs to Tariq Ramadan who was visiting Montreal and part of a Muslim Association of Canada conference. Mr. Ramadan is the grandson of the founder of the Muslim Brotherhood Hassan al-Banna.

Moez also sends out a Tweet in support of Islamic Relief USA. Islamic Relief Worldwide was originally founded in the United Kingdom and has a series of international satellite organizations in countries such as those in Canada and the USA. The parent organization has been identified on repeated occasions as a Muslim Brotherhood front and it has had its bank accounts closed by major international banks for undisclosed reasons related to "risk" and "terrorism concerns."[788]

---

[786] The family name Battikh can be translated as melon or watermelon in English.

[787] More on Moez Battikh can be seen in the five-page original story by Andrew McIntosh. The French version is at French at: http://www.journaldemontreal.com/2014/06/20/mysterieux-enlevement-denfant-manque . A shorter version of the story in English can be seen at: http://www.ottawasun.com/2014/08/08/questions-linger-in-failed-kidnapping-of-billionaires-grandson . Both viewed 24 July 2017. **Both rated A1**.

[788] For more on why UBS closed the accounts of Islamic Relief see https://web.archive.org/web/20121124044239/http://www.civilsociety.co.uk/finance/news/content/13757/banking_sector_nerves_blocking_international_relief_says_islamic_relief_finance_director . Viewed 24 July 2017. **Rated B2**. See also *HSBC to close bank account of Muslim charity working in Gaza*, 25 July 2014. The article can be seen online at https://www.civilsociety.co.uk/news/hsbc-to-close-bank-account-of-muslim-charity-working-in-gaza.html . Viewed 24 July 2017. **Rated B2**. See also *UBS closes Islamic Relief account over terror risk*, 09 November 2012. The article is available online at https://moneyjihad.wordpress.com/2012/11/09/ubs-closes-islamic-relief-account-over-terror-risk/ Viewed 24 July 2017. **Rated C3.** See also the very last line in the article *HSBC to close bank account of Muslim charity working in Gaza*, dated 25 July 2014. The article is available online at

As noted above, the founding organization (Islamic Relief Worldwide) and the local UK operation (Islamic Relief UK) have been listed as terrorist entities by the United Arab Emirates.[789]

In 2014, Islamic Relief's donation page was removed from UK Charities Aid Foundation website. The CAF would not comment directly as to why it ceased to have an affiliation with Islamic Relief, but it did release a statement which said:

> "It would be wrong for us to discuss our processes, but like any financial intermediary, we have robust systems in place to ensure we comply with our UK and international obligations to protect against fraud, money laundering, bribery and corruption and terrorism financing while working with charitable organizations to support their work in conflict zones and elsewhere."[790]

The Financial Post of Canada removed Islamic Relief Canada from its "25 Charities of the Year" list stating that it was "pulled from this year's list since its international arm has been banned elsewhere (though not in Canada) for allegedly funneling funds to the terrorist organization Hamas."[791] Hamas, in its own charter, claims it was founded as an arm of the Muslim Brotherhood.[792]

The Unanswered Questions[793]

Because of this event, many questions remain unanswered, especially the potential question of whether the kidnapping was carried out to profit Mr. Battikh himself to cover for his own alleged financial troubles, or if it was to fund the MAC project. They are perhaps best captured by the press article of Andrew McIntosh as noted below:

- **Dubious Motive?** Battikh told police he'd lost most of $250,000 that a brother and several friends entrusted to him to invest in currency markets. He refused to identify them to police. Police never checked out that story. QMI Agency did. Battikh never had $250,000. His known losses were $115,000, sources said.

- **Wrong Way Battikh:** After he grabbed the child from the dazed father he had tasered, Battikh ran not toward his parked car at one end of the park, but rather in the opposite direction to a busy boulevard at the opposite end of the small park. To the police, this suggested the presence of an

---

http://www.civilsociety.co.uk/finance/news/content/17903/hsbc_to_close_bank_account_of_muslim_charity_working_in_gaza . Viewed 24 July 2017. **Rated B3.**

789 This was after Moez Battikh had sent them Tweeted in support of them.

790 Tania, Mason, *Islamic Relief's donation page is removed from CAF,* Civil Society, 03 September 2014. The article can be seen online at http://www.civilsociety.co.uk/fundraising/news/content/18091/islamic_reliefs_donation_page_is_removed_from_caf_website . Viewed 24 July 2017. **Rated B3.**

791 Claire Brownell, *Financial Post's Charities of the Year: Why these 25 are worth your donations (and which ones we're cautious about),* The Financial Post, 12 December 2014. The article can be seen online at http://business.financialpost.com/news/financial-post-charities-of-the-year-2014 . Viewed 24 July 2017. **Rated B2.**

792 *The Covenant of the Islamic Resistance Movement* (HAMAS) 18 August 1988. The entire covenant can be seen online at http://avalon.law.yale.edu/20th_century/hamas.asp . Viewed 24 July 2017. **Rated A1.**

793 This list of questions was taken from the story by Andrew McIntosh. It can be seen online at: http://www.ottawasun.com/2014/08/08/questions-linger-in-failed-kidnapping-of-billionaires-grandson . Viewed 24 July 2017. **Rated A1.**

accomplice. "Was another car waiting for Mr. Battikh? This bothered me a bit," one officer testified.

- **A Lone Walkie Talkie in His Car:** A single walkie-talkie was found in Battikh's car. Battikh said it belonged to his son Moez Battikh and didn't work. Police never seized the device and never checked to see if it was working after the kidnapping.

- **Mysterious 600 Number:** Battikh received several calls from a 600 number just prior to the kidnapping. A 600 number indicates a satellite phone or pre-paid cell often used by criminals. Police said they were unable to trace the calls.

- **Mysterious Pack of Smokes:** A fresh pack of cigarettes was found in the snow beside Battikh's car after his arrest. Battikh is not a smoker, one friend said. A butt was also found, and a bottle of half-drunk water was never DNA tested, police admitted.

- **A Visa for Saudi Arabia:** Battikh received a text message following his arrest saying his request was approved for a visa to Saudi Arabia a few weeks later. Police never investigated this. Battikh's lawyer has no idea why he was going here, but at the time Saudi Arabia was a favourite meeting place for Muslim Brotherhood members. The group is now outlawed there.

- **Two USB Flash Drives:** Montreal police seized two of the data storage tools at Battikh's home but never even opened them to review their contents.

- **Battikh's Home Under Police Surveillance:** Battikh's home in suburban Laval was put under surveillance after his arrest but before he was named publicly as the kidnapping suspect. Police identified his wife and daughter visiting a mosque after midnight for unknown reasons. The family reported Battikh missing at 2:30 a.m. though he'd been under arrest since 4 p.m. the day before.

- **Ties to Muslim Association of Canada and Muslim Brotherhood Never Verified:** Battikh denied he was a member of an al-Qaida sleeper cell, but police never probed his links to the Muslim Association of Canada, a group with reported ties to the banned Muslim Brotherhood. Battikh was a consultant for the Muslim Association. His job was to identify and negotiate the purchase of a six-story office building in downtown Montreal for $4.7 million. Battikh was also charge of fundraising for the project, to house the Canadian Institute of Islamic Civilization.

- **Disturbing Remarks by Battikh's Son:** Two days after his father was arrested for the attempted child kidnapping for ransom, Moez Battikh posted on his Facebook a message: "God is the only authority." Muslim Brotherhood members consider themselves above local laws and national constitutions. When we contacted Moez Battikh about the remarks, and another posting of a symbol favoured by Muslim Brotherhood members, both were erased.

CHAPTER 20: THE QUEBEC CITY MOSQUE SHOOTING AND THE CYCLE OF VIOLENCE IN CANADA

Thomas Quiggin

Key Points

- Violence begets violence.
- The cycle of Islamist inspired violence was completed in Canada on 29 January 2017 when a mosque in Quebec City was attacked and six people died in a blaze of gunfire. Alexandre Bissonnette, the alleged assailant, has been charged with six counts of first degree murder.
- Was the Quebec City mosque shooting aimed at "Muslims" or the "Muslim Brotherhood."
- We either learn to understand the cycle of violence and struggle against it – or we learn to continue living with it.

The Cycle of Islamist Violence in Canada

It is reasonable to assess that Canada has suffered from a series of Islamist attacks. These attacks have included:

- The October 2014 murder of Canadian Forces Warrant Officer Vincent;[794]
- The October 2014 attack on the National War Memorial and the Parliament of Canada, including the killing of Canadian Forces Corporal Nathan Cirillo[795] and the wounding of House of Commons Protective Service guard, Samearn Son;[796]
- The May 2016 attack on the Canadian Forces Recruiting Centre in Toronto, and
- The August 2016 failed suicide bombing attack of Arron Driver in Ontario which is alleged to have targeted a major transportation facility.[797] Arron Driver was the only causality.

---

[794] Sonja Puzic, *Patrice Vincent, the soldier who put 'country before himself'*, CTVNews.ca, October 21, 2015. The article can be seen online at http://www.ctvnews.ca/canada/patrice-vincent-the-soldier-who-put-country-before-himself-1.2620897 . Viewed 22 March 2017. **Rated A1.**

[795] Lama Nicolas, *Cpl. Nathan Cirillo honoured on 1-year anniversary of his death,* Global News, October 20, 2015. The article can be seen online at http://globalnews.ca/news/2289126/cpl-nathan-cirillo-honoured-on-1-year-anniversary-of-his-death/ . Viewed March 22, 2017. **Rated A1**.

[796] Ottawa Citizen, *Samearn Son, the man who took a bullet in the leg, and his fellow Commons' security guards were honoured today*, December 11, 2014. The article can be seen online at http://ottawacitizen.com/storyline/samearn-son-the-man-who-took-a-bullet-in-the-leg-and-his-fellow-house-of-commons-security-guards-were-honoured-today . Viewed 22 March 2017. **Rated A1.**

[797] David Schum, *Toronto transit authorities 'made aware' of RCMP terror threat investigation,* . The article can be seen online at http://globalnews.ca/news/2876860/toronto-transit-authorities-made-aware-of-rcmp-terror-threat-investigation/ . Viewed March 22, 2017. **Rated B2.**

- The September 2017 Edmonton attack against one police officer and four pedestrians.

Other Islamist inspired violence in Canada has made the news. The Toronto 18 were building a major bomb. Ottawa resident Momin Khawaja was a key player in a London UK plot. Canada's first Islamist suicide bomber was Salman Ashrafi of Calgary, who had previously been president of his Muslim Student Association. Canadians from London, Ontario played leading roles in an attack on an Algerian gas plant in which some forty workers died. ISIS video propagandist John Maguire was also a member of the Muslim Student Association at the University of Ottawa. Ahmed Said Khadr, also from the University of Ottawa Muslim Student Association was listed by Al Qaeda as one of its top martyrs. Ten students attempting to leave Montreal to join ISIS, but were stopped in one operation alone.[798] Hundreds of others may have left Canada to join ISIS. The list goes on.

The Quebec City Mosque Attack

The investigation and trial in the Quebec City shooting at the Centre culturel islamique de Québec will be complex. The fallout may be significant as it focuses attention on intelligence, law enforcement, the Government of Canada and the Muslim Brotherhood. How much of this is public knowledge is not clear, as the main stream media in Canada has seemingly avoided any discussion on why this mosque was the scene of a murderous attack.

Background on the Mosque

The mosque in the Quebec City shooting was originally formed by Muslim Student Association according to its own history.[799] The Muslim Student Association was founded by adherents (see Chapter 13) of the Muslim Brotherhood. The mosque donated money on a yearly basis (2001 to 2010) to the International Relief Fund for the Afflicted and Needy (IRFAN).[800] IRFAN, according to the Canada Revenue Agency, was set up to skirt Canadian law (Chapter 15) and send millions of dollars to Hamas. The parent organization of Hamas is the Muslim Brotherhood according to Article Two of the Hamas charter. IRFAN has now listed as a terrorist entity by the Government of Canada.[801]

A regular attendee of the mosque is Abdallah Assafiri, according to his own statement to the press. He was listed as the "directeur de la formation et de l'animation religieuse au Centre culturel islamique de Québec." [802] Mr. Assafiri is also major leadership figure in the Muslim Brotherhood, according to the Muslim Brotherhood itself. He was listed as the "Masul" or the leader for Eastern Canada.[803] He told the

---

[798] 10 Montreal young people arrested on suspicion of wanting to join jihad, 19 May 2015, CBC News. The article can be seen online at http://www.cbc.ca/news/canada/montreal/10-montreal-young-people-arrested-on-suspicion-of-wanting-to-join-jihad-1.3079873 . Viewed 19 October 2017. **Rated B3.**

[799] For more on the history of the mosque, see the Laval University website at https://croir.ulaval.ca/fiches/c/centre-culturel-islamique-de-quebec-ccig/ . Viewed 19 April 2017. **Rated B2.**

[800] *Le CCIQ, le Hamas et le projet de nouvelle mosquée dans le quartier Saint-Sauveur de Québec*, Point de Bascule, 5 March 2012. The article can be seen online at http://pointdebasculecanada.ca/le-cciq-le-hamas-et-le-projet-de-nouvelle-mosquee-dans-le-quartier-st-sauveur-de-quebec/ . Viewed 19 April 2017. **Rated B2.**

[801] For more on the terrorism listing for IRFAN see the Government of Canada website at http://www.cra-arc.gc.ca/chrts-gvng/chrts/whtsnw/trrrst-ntty-eng.html . Viewed 19 April 2017. **Rated A1.**

[802] For more on the position of Mr. Assafiri with the mosque see the website at http://kissislam.free.fr/index.php?idM=50. Viewed 19 April 2017. **Rated B2.**

[803] For more on his position with the Muslim Brotherhood in North America, see the Holy Land Foundation court trial document at http://counterterrorismblog.org/site-resources/images/1992_Phone_Directory.pdf . Viewed 19 April 2017. **Rated A1.**

press he normally would have been there on Sunday night, but he did not attend when the shooting occurred because his son borrowed his car (c'est parce que son fils avait emprunté sa voiture).[804]

In July 2016, the Journal de Quebec and TVA ran an article which showed a pamphlet delivered in the neighbourhood of the mosque claiming that the Centre Culturel Islamique de Québec (CCIQ) was a Muslim Brotherhood organization.[805] It is also fair to say that the mosque also has a series of other connections to the Muslim Brotherhood, most of which were publicly available to anyone with an Internet search engine.

Will the shooting at the Quebec City mosque of 29 January 2017 result in a terrorism charge? Three incidents around one mosque (see below), including the shooting attack of 29 January 2017, suggests a pattern of activity by an individual or group that has grievances with the Muslim Brotherhood. If the two previous incidents plus the shooting are connected by the police investigation through a single individual or group, then this is close to the legal definition of terrorism. As such, it would seem logical that the alleged perpetrator should be charged with terrorism. Terrorism is, however, a political crime and the decision to charge an individual with terrorism in Canada has political and many other factors.

Factors for the Terrorism Charge

It is reasonable to believe that a variety of factors suggest a charge of terrorism should result from the murder of six individuals at the mosque. The shooting incident was the final one of three seemingly connected incidents involving the mosque. In June of 2016 a pig's head was placed at the door of the mosque. Three weeks later a pamphlet was distributed around the neighborhood which claimed that the mosque was run by the Muslim Brotherhood. The pamphlet also said that the headquarters of the Muslim Brotherhood in Quebec was none other than the CCIQ. At the end of the pamphlet, the anonymous author suggested viewing the website http://fmquebecinfo.blogspot.ca/. This blog posting was dated 08 July 2016 and it has much of the same text that was in the pamphlet distributed around the mosque.

Six months later, the shooting occurred.

As such, it is reasonable to suggest that given the "pig's head" incident of 20 June 2016,[806] the pamphlet distributed around the mosque in July 2016, and the website are connected. The question must be raised if this was a planned and targeted shooting aimed at "Muslims" or if the target was the "Muslim Brotherhood."

---

[804] Tommy Chouinard, Martin Croteau, Audrey Ruel-Manseau, Denis Lessard, *SIX MUSULMANS TUÉS DANS UN ATTENTAT TERRORISTE*, La Presse, (no date given). The article can be seen online at http://plus.lapresse.ca/screens/cfa07dc0-e3be-4e00-86c6-5be77c328335%7CXm8tAMC-0T4Z.html . Viewed 19 April 2017. **Rated B2**.

[805] Pierre-Paul Biron, *Lettre islamophobe distribuée à Sainte-Foy*, TVA Nouvelles, 8 July 2016. The article can be seen online at http://www.tvanouvelles.ca/2016/07/08/lettre-islamophobe-distribuee-a-sainte-foy . Viewed 19 April 2017. **Rated B2**.

[806] Jason Magder, *Pig head left on door of Quebec City mosque during Ramadan*, Montreal Gazette, 20 June 2016. The article can be seen online at http://montrealgazette.com/news/local-news/pig-head-left-on-door-of-quebec-city-mosque-during-ramadan . Viewed 19 April 2017. **Rated A2**.

Following the shooting attack, another attack occurred. On or about the 6th of August 2017, a car belonging to Mohamed Labidi, the President of the CCIQ mosque was burnt. The Quebec City Police (SPVQ) have confirmed that the fire was deliberately set, and a criminal investigation is underway.[807]

A regular attendee of the mosque, according to himself, is Abdullah Assafiri. He has been identified as a "Masul" or leadership figure for the Muslim Brotherhood.[808] If his name appears in the investigation before the shooting, this would strongly support the concept of a terrorism charge.

Abdallah Assafiri, the senior member of the mosque noted above, was also identified (but not charged and not listed as a co-conspirator) in a US terrorism funding case involving the Holy Land Relief Foundation – another organization with multiple links to Hamas and its parent organization, the Muslim Brotherhood. He has also testified (2011) to the Quebec Provincial Legislature on behalf of the CCIQ.[809]

The mosque has also given money to IRFAN, an organization in Canada which was determined to be a terrorist entity by the Government of Canada itself after it was caught funding Hamas[810] which itself is a Muslim Brotherhood front group.

If (stressing "if") it can be shown that these incidents are connected through a common individual, group or campaign, then the attack is close to what constitutes terrorism today in Canada.[811]

Factors Against the Terrorism Charge

Charging and convicting an individual with terrorism in Canada is a high bar to clear. In addition to proving the crime occurred, the Crown Prosecutor must address the issue of motive and intent. Terrorism by its nature is a political crime, the intent of which is to have an outcome which affects the political sphere around the targeted group. Simply showing that the accused in the case killed the individuals does not rise to terrorism. If the Crown cannot connect the three events or if the Crown cannot show through other means that the shooter had a political motive against the targeted group, the charge would likely fail in court.

Working against the charge of terrorism is the (informal) prosecutorial belief that you should charge the individual in a case with the crime which is easiest to prove. In the case of the mosque shooting, it is reasonable to assess that proving a murder charge appears to be a relatively straightforward case. Why

---

[807] Sophie Side, *The Vehicle of The President of the Islamic Cultural Center of Quebec Fire,* 30 August 2017, The Sherbrooke Times. The article can be seen online at https://sherbrooktimes.com/the-vehicle-of-the-president-of-the-islamic-cultural-center-of-quebec-fire/2479 . Viewed 31 August 2017. **Not rated.**

[808] See, among others, court documents from the Holy Land Relief terrorism funding trial. Mr. Assafiri's role as a senior figure in the Muslim Brotherhood appears in https://www.investigativeproject.org/documents/case_docs/1083.pdf . Viewed 24 August 2017. **Rated A1.**

[809] The full transcript of this appearance can be seen online at file:///C:/Users/User/Downloads/ci_v41_121.pdf . Viewed 23 August 2017. **Not rated.**

[810] For more on the terrorist designation of IRFAN, see the Government of Canada statement *Revoked Canadian charity listed under the Criminal Code as terrorist entity.* This statement can be seen at https://www.canada.ca/en/revenue-agency/services/charities-giving/charities/whats-new/revoked-canadian-charity-listed-under-criminal-code-terrorist-entity.html . Viewed 19 October 2017. **Rated A1.**

[811] Criminal Code of Canada 83.01. This section of the criminal code can be seen online at http://laws-lois.justice.gc.ca/eng/acts/C-46/page-12.html#h-26 . Viewed 19 April 2017. **Rated A1.**

complicate matters for yourself if you are the prosecutor? Take the most straightforward charge and proceed.

The workload and the case complexity for the prosecutor may also be complicated if a terrorism charge is placed. The mosque itself has multiple perceived ties to the Muslim Brotherhood, which itself is listed as a terrorist group in many countries.

It is reasonable to believe that the name of Mr. Assafiri appearing in that case would be a complication for the prosecution which they may not wish to explain. Ironically, Mr. Assafiri's role may be both a help and a hindrance for the prosecution depending on the direction followed by the investigation.

Other complications may also occur, given that Mr. Assafiri was a public servant in Quebec for several years on worked on IT related projects for them. Ironically, Mr. Assafiri is/was the holder of the domain name **"gouv.qc.ca"** who previously had the office phone number of 1 (418) 644-4667 and the government email address of admin@gouv.qc.ca.[812]

Also working against the terrorism charge is the rather large list of inconsistencies that came out of the initial news reports and police statement. There was one, two or three shooters according to early reports. They did, or did not, yell out a political message at the start of the shooting. The case may not have been helped by the Prime Minister sending a letter to Fox News complaining about the reporting.[813] Misleading or wrong information is a common occurrence, especially in a crisis, and dealing with it at trial, is part and parcel of what the prosecution had to deal with.

The Outcome

The decision to lay a terrorism charge (or not) will be a difficult one for the prosecution. National attention would be focused on a trial and every shred of evidence (and inconsistencies) will be seized upon by the defence. Evidence of motive may be the toughest barrier in reaching for this charge.

The Muslim Student Association founded the Quebec City mosque. It was attended by a senior leadership figure of the Muslim Brotherhood who also had a leadership role inside the mosque while representing the mosque to the public. The leadership of the mosque gave money for years to IRFAN/HAMAS. The mosque had been the target of a letter campaign in its own neighbourhood that singled it out as a Muslim Brotherhood organization. A website singled out the mosque as a Muslim Brotherhood institution. It is then reasonable to ask the following questions:

- It is coincidence that the mosque was singled out for violence?
- Did the belief systems of this mosque and its leadership serve the reason for the attack?
- Did its activities and leadership serve as an attractor to the fatal violence?

---

812 For more on this see the domain name information at http://gouv.qc.ca.hypestat.com/ . Viewed 19 April 2017. **Rated A1.**

813 David Akin, *Trudeau's PMO takes on Fox News over 'false and misleading' tweet about Quebec mosque shooting,* National Post, 31 January 2017. The article can be seen online at http://news.nationalpost.com/news/canada/canadian-politics/trudeaus-pmo-takes-on-fox-news-over-a-fox-tweet-about-the-mosque-shooting . Viewed 19 April 2017. **Rated A2**.

Whatever the case, Canada has now been the scene of murderous reactionary violence that involves the presence of Islamist ideology. The cycle of violence has begun and if other countries are an example, the problem will get worse before it improves.

Implications

Intelligence: In the near term, it is reasonable to believe that it should be seen as an intelligence failure on the part of the Government of Canada. The various agencies have done little significant work on the Muslim Brotherhood in Canada (and their various front groups.) There is no indication that federal level agencies gave any warning or information to the local police after the posters accusing the mosque of supporting the Muslim Brotherhood came out. As such, little is understood about this international group that has a structured presence in 81 countries.

Law Enforcement: Local, provincial, and federal law enforcement agencies depend on intelligence agencies for understanding larger and more complex problems like extremism, terrorism, and organized crime. If the intelligence agencies are not doing their jobs, this make investigations and prevention more difficult for police. This problem was seen earlier in a kidnapping case when Chiheb Battikh of the Muslim Association of Canada attempted to kidnap a child[814] for ransom.[815]

Government of Canada: Much of the Federal Government's policies on Islamism and immigration seem based on platitudes or fluffy thinking. This case, it could be reasonably argued, should force the Government of Canada to examine how an individual shooter came to shoot up a mosque founded by an Islamist group which was attended by a high-profile Islamist figure.

---

[814] Andrew McIntosh, *Mystérieux enlèvement d'enfant manqué, Le coupable avait-il un complice? Était-il lié aux Frères musulmans?* QMI Agency, 20 June 2014. The article can be seen online at http://www.journaldemontreal.com/2014/06/20/mysterieux-enlevement-denfant-manque . Viewed 19 April 2017. **Rated A1**.

[815] Andrew McIntosh, *Questions linger in failed kidnapping of billionaire's grandson*, QMI Agency, 8 August 2014. The article can be seen online at http://www.ottawasun.com/2014/08/08/questions-linger-in-failed-kidnapping-of-billionaires-grandson . Viewed 19 April 2017. **Rated A1**.

CHAPTER 21: IT'S NOT A DEFECT! IT'S A FEATURE! ANTI-SEMITIC AND ANTI-CHRISTIAN MESSAGES IN CANADIAN MOSQUES

Thomas Quiggin

Key Points

- Calls for violence in Canadian mosques are being normalized by Imams who come from organization as such the International Union for Muslims Scholars (IUMS) or are educated at the University of Medina and similar institutions.
- Repeated claims from mosques that such events are mistakes, or the result of poor translations are simply cover ups for the Islamist message.
- Key among the issues is the normalization of the subjugation of women.

Canadians were surprised to hear in February 2017 that mosques in Toronto and Montreal were calling for the killing of Jews, polytheists and anyone who had "displaced the sons of Muslims." Such events are not new, of course, as a variety of mosques in Canada have been caught making similar calls for action.

It is reasonable to believe that the calls were clear and direct. The supplications from the Dundas Street Mosque in Toronto stated:

> "[O Allah!] Give us victory over the disbelieving people...,O Allah! Give victory to Islam and raise the standing of the Muslims. And humiliate the polytheism and polytheists. O Allah! Give victory (help) to your slaves who believe in the oneness of Allah, O the Lord of the Worlds! O Allah! Give them victory over the criminal people. O Allah! **Destroy anyone who killed Muslims**. O Allah! Destroy anyone who displaced the sons of the Muslims. O Allah! Count their number; slay them one by one and spare not one of them. O Allah! **Purify Al-Aqsa Mosque from the filth of the Jews**! O Allah! Purify Al-Aqsa Mosque from the filth of the Jews!" [816](Emphasis added).

The Montreal mosque (Al Andalous Islamic Centre) had a similar message with calls for the Jews to be killed "one by one." The Jews were also described as "people who slayed the prophets, shed their blood and cursed the Lord."[817]

When attending the Montreal Al Sunnah Mosque on Friday, 21 July 2006, undercover reporter Mohamed Sifaoui listened to the sermon of "Sheikh" Omar Soufyane, who was a bayat[818] swearing member of al Qaeda.[819] The sermon discussed the Middle East crisis and Mr. Soufyane called for God to kill all the

---

[816] *Supplications at Masjid Toronto Mosque: "Slay them one by one and spare not one of them,"* CiJ News. 18 February 2017. The article can be seen online at http://en.cijnews.com/?p=205803 . Viewed 20 April 2017. **Rated A2**.

[817] Stewart Bell, *Montreal mosque facing calls for investigation after imam preaches on anti-Semitic conspiracy theories*, National Post, 28 February 2017. The article can be seen online at http://www.nationalpost.com/m/wp/tag/blog.html?b=news.nationalpost.com/news/world/montreal-mosque-facing-calls-for-investigation-as-video-shows-imam-preaching-anti-semitic-conspiracy-theories&pubdate=2017-04-04&t=israel . Viewed 20 April 2017. **Rated B2**.

[818] A bayat is an oath of allegiance.

[819] *U.S. lists Montreal mosque as al-Qaeda 'recruiting' place; Detainee who lived in Montreal disputes U.S. claims of links to millennium bomb plot, 9/11*, CBC News Posted: Apr 25, 2011 9:17 PM ET. The article can be seen online at

enemies of Islam to the last. On Friday, August 11, 2006 Mr. Sifaoui again attended the Al Sunnah Mosque. This time the Imam (a replacement) told they youth that they should mobilize prepare to fight a Holy War. Referring to the youth, he told them that they were the "ammunition of our community."[820]

Apologists for the most recent (2017) events have tried to explain the situation by saying that the supplications were the result of "clumsy and unacceptable phrasing" by a substitute imam.[821] The Imam stated that he had been "misspeaking" and that he regretted his statements.[822] It is hard to imagine how a call to kill all the Jews or to "Purify Al-Aqsa Mosque from the filth of the Jews" it a matter of clumsy phrasing.

Some Basic Realities

Both mosques in the 2017 events have a direct affiliation to the Muslim Association of Canada (MAC). From this, several observations can be made.

- The MAC website states that the "Muslim Brotherhood remains the truest reflection of Islamic practice in the modern era." (Chapter 13).
- The Dundas Street Mosque Executive Director El-Tantawi Attia[823] stated that "Here we follow the teachings of the Muslim Brotherhood."[824]
- The current Imam of the Dundas Street Mosque is Dr. Wael Shehab. He holds a PhD in Islamic Studies from Al-Azhar University and was the Head of the Shari`ah and Fatwa sections at the English website, OnIslam.net.[825] This now defunct website was set up and run by Yusuf Qaradawi, according to the Muslim Brotherhood's own website.[826]

---

http://www.cbc.ca/news/world/u-s-lists-montreal-mosque-as-al-qaeda-recruiting-place-1.1124571 . Viewed 20 April 2017. **Rated B2**.

[820] *À l'intérieur des mosques*, Publié le vendredi 8 septembre 2006. The article is available online at http://ici.radio-canada.ca/nouvelles/national/2006/09/08/004-zl_islam_mosquees.shtml . Viewed 20 April 2017. **Rated B2.**

[821] Stewart Bell, *Montreal mosque facing calls for investigation after imam preaches on anti-Semitic conspiracy theories*, National Post, 28 February 2017. The article can be seen online at http://www.nationalpost.com/m/wp/tag/blog.html?b=news.nationalpost.com/news/world/montreal-mosque-facing-calls-for-investigation-as-video-shows-imam-preaching-anti-semitic-conspiracy-theories&pubdate=2017-04-04&t=israel . Viewed 20 April 2017. **Rated B2.**

[822] Ron Csillag, *Ryerson Probing TA Who Made Anti-Semitic Statements At Mosque,* CJN, 28 February 2017. The article can be seen online at http://www.cjnews.com/uncategorized/ryerson-probing-ta-made-anti-semitic-statements-mosque . Viewed 20 April 2017. **Rated B2.**

[823] The MAC describes Dr. Attia (as of 20112) as: *Dr. El-Tantawy Attia, Executive Director of MAC's Masjid Toronto.* See http://www.macnet.ca/English/Pages/Home.aspx . Viewed 20 April 2017. **Rated A2.**

[824] Jessica Hume, *Cancelled debate highlights tension among Canadian Muslims*, National Post, 7 February 2011. The article can be seen online at http://life.nationalpost.com/2011/02/07/cancelled-debate-highlights-tension-among-canadian-muslims/ . Viewed 20 April 2017. **Rated B2.**

[825] *Masjid Toronto welcomes new Imam and resident scholar*, posted by iqradotca, 20 April 2015. The article is available online at http://iqra.ca/2015/masjid-toronto-welcomes-new-imam-and-resident-scholar/ . Viewed 20 April 2017. **Rated B2.**

[826] *Sheikh Qaradawi's First Interview with Onislam.net*, Ikhwan Web, 21 November 2010. The article can be seen online at http://www.ikhwanweb.com/article.php?id=27233 . Viewed 20 April 2017. **Rated A2.**

- Yusuf Qaradawi is regarded as the chief inspirational cleric of the Muslim Brotherhood and he holds a prominent intellectual role in their teachings. Qaradawi stated himself that he grew up in the Muslim Brotherhood traditions.[827] For this role, Qaradawi was wanted on an INTERPOL Red Notice.[90]

- The International Union of Muslim Scholars (IUMS) was founded in 2004 with Yusuf Qaradawi as its chairman.

- Qaradawi stated that: Allah Imposed Hitler On the Jews to Punish Them – 'Allah Willing, the Next Time Will Be at the Hand of the Believers.'[828]

- Among many other contentious views, Qaradawi also believes that some women enjoy being beaten. On an al Jazeera TV program, he stated "There is a woman who cannot agree to being beaten, and sees this as humiliation, while some women enjoy the beating and for them, only beating to cause them sorrow is suitable..."[829]

- Consistent with the general views of the Muslim Brotherhood, the new Imam at the Dundas Street Mosque believes that homosexuality is a sin, Muslims should avoid gays as homosexuality is evil, transgender people should return to their original gender and seek counselling. Additionally, Dr. Shehab believes Muslims should read the book by Qaradawi titled *Fiqh of Jihad* and follow its teachings. This book has concepts such as Muslims do not fight to achieve material or worldly goals. On the contrary, the objective of fighting is only to make the Word of Allah (Exalted and Glorified be He) the uppermost. In other words, fighting is allowed to make Islam the dominant if not the only religion in the world. It can be reasonably believed that this is a statement in support of offensive jihad.

It can be assessed that the messages from these mosques were not the result of misspeaking or clumsy phasing. The messages from these mosques on killing those who oppose Islam are entirely consistent with the message of the Islamist ideology as expressed by a variety of individuals such as Yusuf Qaradawi of the Muslim Brotherhood. The same can be said for the role of women. The head of the IUMS openly states that some women enjoy being beaten. This is, of course, the same position taken by the book handed out by the York University Muslim Student Association. (See Chapter 9 for more on this)

Implications

As is often said in the world of software: It's not a defect! It's a feature!

It is reasonable to believe that these messages, along with those concerning wife beating (Chapter 10) and those that state that Islam(ist) beliefs are not compatible with democracy (Chapter 13) suggest a

---

[827] In an introduction to one of his books, Dr. Qaradawi states: *However, in most examples I will be citing the Muslim Brotherhood, because that is the movement where I grew up; I experienced all its hardships and good times, and shared in many of the events it witnessed over almost a half-century.* See: http://www.islambasics.com/view.php?bkID=48&chapter=1 . Viewed 20 April 2017. **Rated A2.**

[828] *Sheikh Yousuf Qaradawi: Allah Imposed Hitler On the Jews to Punish Them – 'Allah Willing, the Next Time Will Be at the Hand of the Believers'*, MEMRI, 04 February 2009. Viewed 20 April 2017. **Rated A2.**

[829] Steven Stalinsky and Y. Yehoshua, "*Muslim Clerics on the Religious Rulings Regarding Wife-Beating,*" MEMRI, Special Report #27, March 22, 2004 http://memri.org/bin/articles.cgi?Page=archives&Area=sr&ID=SR2704 . Viewed 20 April 2017. **Rated A2.**

pattern. It can be reasonably assessed that these statements are not occurring in isolation, but rather they are part of the overall Islamist message of the Muslim Brotherhood and other Islamist groups such as the Iranian Khomeneists.

CHAPTER 22: WILL HASSAN AL-BANNA AND THE MUSLIM BROTHERHOOD DESTROY ISLAM?

Thomas Quiggin

Key Points

- Hassan Ahmed Abdel Rahman Muhammed al-Banna (1906-1949) founded the Muslim Brotherhood in Egypt in 1928.

- This organization now has adherents in over 80 countries.

Throughout history, many individuals have dreamed of re-establishing an Islamic caliphate. Today, this includes those who have plans for re-establishing the highwater marks of the various Islamic Empires.

What was different about Hassan al-Banna, however, was his insistence on mixing the religious and the political which has led to a collectivist and totalitarian view of Islam. In short, he advocated what we now call the concept of "Islamism."

It is possible that future historians may record him as the individual who destroyed Islam.

Hassan al-Banna was born in 14 October 1906, in Mahmoudiyah, a small town in the Nile Delta northwest of Cairo, Egypt. He was exposed to the al-Hassafiyya Sufi order in his youth, but would later become a Sunni. He was trained as a school teacher and worked in that role in Ismailia, which was also the headquarters of the Suez Canal. Distressed at what he saw as an encroaching way of life from colonialism, he began to form ideas about how Islam needed to resist foreign influences. While working as a school teacher, he was also preaching as an Imam in a local mosque, much the same as his father had done.

At the age of 22, the young Egyptian is believed, according to popular legend, to have approached a Sufi "Sheik" (respected religious and community leader). His purpose was to ask for permission and/or advice about forming the association which would become known as the Muslim Brotherhood. What happened next is unclear and it has become the stuff of much discussion and disagreement. One version of the meeting suggests that the Sheik gave his approval. Another version suggests that the Sheikh did not approve of the idea, but told Hassan al-Banna that he was young and would go ahead and try his plan whether he received approval or not.

A third, and more nuanced version of events, suggests that the Sheikh gave his conditional approval to al-Banna, but after al-Banna left the meeting the Sheik told the rest of the gathering that the ideas were dangerous. The reality of what happened has been lost to history.

The Basis for Destruction

At the basis of al-Banna's ideology lies a dangerous concept. Hassan al-Banna believed there would be only one form of faith (Islam) and that it could only be practiced one way: the supremacist Muslim Brotherhood interpretation. From this comes his statement that it is the nature of Islam to dominate all others.

Needless to say, this idea of domination leads to constant conflicts with modernity and with the current law in any number of countries.

But perhaps the most damning (pun intended) feature of Hassan al-Banna was his insistence on the complete politicization of the faith. To al-Banna and those he has inspired, Islam must be both the only religion and the only political system for everyone. In his mind, the Muslim Brotherhood version of reality would have the Muslim Brotherhood version of Islam as the religious, political, social, cultural and financial system for everyone. There are no exceptions. As a result, the Muslim Brotherhood has produced the slogan "Islam is the solution."

To round this out, al-Banna and his adherents have justified the assassination of leadership figures who do not follow their beliefs. A leader must not only be Muslim, he must also follow their version of the faith or he can be assassinated in the name of (their) Islam. This applies not only to leaders such as prime ministers and presidents, but also to lower level leaders in society such as mayors, judges and Imams. As such, the Muslim Brotherhood can be described as "Takfirist." They believe they have the right to call another Muslim an apostate which then justifies them being killed.

The followers and adherents of Hassan al-Banna and the Muslim Brotherhood will find themselves in perpetual conflict. This conflict is not just with most other Muslims, but it will be – quite literally – with every other faith, belief, political and social structure in the world.

Spreading the Word

The Muslim Brotherhood's belief structure has been the well spring of inspiration for a variety of organizations such as al-Qaeda, ISIS, Jamaat-e-Islami, and, to a certain degree, the Khomeneists. Many of them have taken on and then extrapolated the ideas of Hassan al-Banna which then lead to perpetual confrontation and conflict.

How this virulent infection in the body of Islam plays itself out if not clear. The body politic of Islam may eventually clear itself of this virus. Alternatively, if the virus is proven capable of taking control of the body, it may lead to a situation where the ideas of Hassan al-Banna takes root in most of the Arab/Muslim world. If this happens, the virus, by putting the Muslim Brotherhood's version of Islam into conflict with all other Muslims and the rest of the world, may ultimately weaken the body and lead to the destruction of Islam as a coherent faith.

Implications

The current struggle for the soul and future of Islam may produce a modernist and humanist Islam. At this point in time, however, it is hard to see how modernist voices can become ascendant when they are regularly silenced in both the West and in the world of Islam. If the modernist voices can be heard in the West where freedom of speech and thought are at least still concepts. Ironically, the future of Islam may lie the West.

CHAPTER 23: SUBMISSION OR FREE WILL?

Thomas Quiggin

Key Points

- "Islam does not attribute [the principle of free] will to people with respect to the laws of Allah and his ordained punishments.... freedom is dependent on the Sharia." [830] Sheik Houssein Muhammad Amer, the Imam of Centre Aljisr, Laval, Quebec.

- Western values, founded in the Reformation, the Renaissance and the Enlightenment are based on free will, agency, and the rights of the individual. These are expressed in the ideals of free speech, freedom of thought, belief, conscience, opinion and association.

In many of the 49 Muslim majority countries,[831] a struggle is ongoing for the soul of Islam between the Islamists and reformers. The struggle is often violent as can be seen in Pakistan, Bangladesh, Afghanistan, Iran, Iraq, Saudi Arabia, Lebanon, Syria/ISIS, Bahrain and others. Countries with a significant Muslim minority population are also having struggles involving Islamist minorities. This includes the Philippines, Thailand, Nigeria and Mali. It is worth noting that 47 of the 49 Muslim majority countries are in the lesser developed world. The other two are in Europe: Kosovo and Albania. Both European countries are synonymous with poverty and instability.

The Differences between Islamists and the West

It is reasonable to assess that the following serve points to highlight the basic points of contention between the Islamists and the values of the West:

- Free will vs submission.

- Democracy vs theocracy.

- Free speech vs blasphemy.

- Freedom of religious belief vs the killing of apostates.

- Honour killing vs the rights of the child.

- The rights of the individual vs submission to the will of the Islamists.

- The rights of women vs absolute domination by men.

Most Islamists believe that no discussion about the validity of their ideology is allowed, and that they have, quite literally, a right to absolute domination over all others. This has been stated by individuals

---

[830] *Trudeau: We strive to show that "Islam is not incompatible" with Western values*, CIJ News, 03 February 2016. The article can be seen online at http://en.cijnews.com/?p=25349 . Viewed 27 April 2017. **Rated A2.**

[831] For more on this issue see the Pew Research Report *Muslim Majority Countries.* It is available online at http://www.pewforum.org/2011/01/27/future-of-the-global-muslim-population-muslim-majority/. Viewed 29 May 2017. **Rated B2**.

such as Hassan al-Banna and Abul A'la Maududi. This was seen in the massacre of the staff of Charlie Hebdo in Paris, the various attacks against Kurt Westergaard (Danish Cartoons) and the fatwa against Salma Rushdie. In Egypt, the 1992 killing of Dr. Farag Foda was justified in a court room by Dr. Muhammad al-Ghazali, a leading Islamist theoretician. After the Egyptian murder of Dr. Foda, al-Ghazali argued that the killing was legitimate. As he put it:

> "They killed one person who should be killed because he was an apostate, they did it on behalf of the nation and the state, and there is no penalty for those who carried out the law of God himself, rather than the state. The apostate cannot stay in the community and act as a germ that emits toxins so that people leave Islam. The ruling says that you must kill him, though it does not have to be the duty of an individual person."

Of general interest, the Ottawa Library and many others in Canada and the USA have copies of al-Ghazali's books where he says that Muslim living in a non-Muslim majority country should be in state of war with their government.[832]

It is a valid opinion that, as with many of their Islamist beliefs, this kind of violence (Charlie Hebdo etc.) is required as they cannot defend their belief systems in a rational manner or in open public debate. There is consistency, however, in how they act. A wife who does not obey her Islamist husband can be beaten – it is an education for her and some wives will enjoy it. Children who do not submit to the will of their Islamist parents can be killed in the process of honour killing or forced suicides. Women who dress "improperly" in public can be harassed and raped. Other Muslims who disagree with the Islamists can be killed as they are apostates. Such is the logic of domination.

The Islamist Logic Trap for Politicians – Tolerate Our Takeover or We Will Kill You

It is reasonable to believe that Islamists are using the traditional media and social media to set a logic trap for politicians. In Western countries, Islamists first make the claim that they are the victims of oppression and racism (Islamophobia). They ignore the reality of what is happening in their communities (youth going off to ISIS etc., terrorist attacks etc.) and they use this false narrative of Islamophobia to indirectly threaten politicians.

The logic trap for the (generally) weak willed and ill-informed politicians is this: They either allow the Islamist to continue to infiltrate the system gradually, or if they respond and try and stop it, the politicians are faced with the threat of violence. In most cases, the politicians chose to submit once again. Either way, the spread of the Islamist ideology continues unabated.

It can be assessed that most politicians today collapse immediately in the face of special interest groups, especially if threatened with being called racist, homophobic or Islamophobic. Combined with the threat of violence, few, if any, politicians are willing to tackle the issue of the spread of political Islam, even in the face of a series of attacks and the tearing of society's social fabric (France, Belgium, UK). Political correctness, virtue signalling, and selfies outweigh all other prerogatives.

Political Correctness and Competitive Virtue Signalling

---

[832] Saied Shoaaib, *What is a Killer Imam Doing in Public Libraries in Canada?,* The Gatestone Institute, 21 February 2017. The article can be seen online at https://www.gatestoneinstitute.org/9974/ottawa-public-library-islam . Viewed 27 April 2017. **Rated A1**.

It is reasonable to say that most Western politicians today, especially progressives, will watch mass rape and terrorist murders occur, rather than state that the integration, diversity and multiculturalism problems are real. In fact, a UK Labour female Member of Parliament supports the idea that victims of mass rape by Kashmiri/Muslims rape gangs should keep their mouths shut "for the good of diversity."[833] The comment was in response to the 1400 girls aged 11 to 14 who were victims of rape in the UK city of Rotherham.

In 2014, the Government of the United Kingdom released the "Jay Report" also known as the Rotherham Report which was accepted by the Parliament.[834] The report found that between 1997 and 2013, a minimum of 1,400 primarily white girls between the ages of 11 and 14 were raped, beaten, drugged and used as prostitutes by a complex network of traffickers around Rotherham. The perpetrators were mainly Kashmiri Pakistani Muslims. Those charged with protecting children, such as social services and the police were found to have repeatedly covered up allegations, destroyed evidence and threatened anyone who reported the problem. By example, Rotherham police arrested a father and charged him with assault after he tried to liberate his daughter from a pimp, who was not charged. The report even details how one professional employee who attempted to address the mass rapes was sidelined, threatened with dismissal and sent on a two-day ethnicity and diversity course.[835]

A variety of other civic officials, town councillors and the local Member of Parliament had been aware for years of the abuse, but had remained silent or punished those who spoke out. Three of the previous inquiries from 2002, 2003 and 2009 had found similar issues, but those reports were "effectively suppressed."[836] One researcher who reported the rapes faced hostility from the city council and her records and information were stolen and destroyed by an unknown person who also likely worked for the council.[837]

What was the cause of this silence? The UK Home Secretary at described it as "institutionalized political correctness." The Member of Parliament for Rotherham, Denis McShane, is worth quoting, He said, that he was a "Guardian reading lefty" added that:

---

[833] Joseph Curtis, *Labour MP and key Corbyn ally shares Twitter message telling Rotherham sex abuse victims to 'shut their mouths for the good of diversity' - just days after attacking a fellow party member for speaking out over the issue,* 22 August 2017, The Daily Mail. The article can be seen online at http://www.dailymail.co.uk/news/article-4813870/MP-shares-Twitter-post-telling-abuse-victims-shut-up.html . Viewed 23 August 2017. **Rated B3**.

[834] The official UK report on the Rotherham mass rapes as accepted by the Parliament can be seen at: http://www.parliament.uk/business/committees/committees-a-z/commons-select/communities-and-local-government-committee/inquiries/parliament-2010/jay-report-rotherham/. Viewed 26 April 2017. **Rated A1.**

[835] For more information on the abuse of researchers in this area of inquiry see the following article online at http://www.huffingtonpost.co.uk/2014/09/02/rotherham-abuse-researcher-diversity-course_n_5750560.html . Viewed 26 April 2017. **Rated B2.**

[836] *Rotherham child abuse scandal: 1,400 children exploited, report finds*, BBC News, 6 August 2014. The article can be seen online at http://www.bbc.com/news/uk-england-south-yorkshire-28939089 . Viewed 26 April 2017. **Rated A1.**

[837] Alison Holt, *Rotherham abuse: Researcher 'faced council hostility,'* BBC Panorama, 01 September 2014. The article can be seen online at http://www.bbc.com/news/uk-england-south-yorkshire-29012571 . Viewed 26 April 2017. **Rated B2.**

"I think there was a culture of not wanting to rock the multicultural community boat, if I may put it like that."[838]

Mr. McShane also said he was aware of the problem of cousin marriage and the oppression of women within parts of the Muslim community in Britain. He added, however that:

"Perhaps yes, as a true Guardian reader, and liberal leftie, I suppose I didn't want to raise that too hard."

The Canadian Situation

In Canada, the Canadian Council of Imams is headed by Dr. Mohammad Iqbal Al-Nadvi who is also the president (Emir) of the Islamic Circle of North America. His organization (ICNA) openly advocates in the stoning of gays, sexual slavery for women, honour killings and the victory of Islam over the Jews and the non-believers. His organization has also stated the "Islam is incompatible with democracy."

Yet, the Canadian press constantly refers to the Canadian Council of Imams when talking about Islamophobia. Is this political correctness gone mad, the willing submission of the press to Islamists or simply a case of the press being too uninformed to understand with whom they are speaking? The events of Rotherham are not encouraging when thinking about this issue.

It Has "Something to Do with Islam"

After almost every Islamist inspired terrorist event, the apologists issue statements saying that "It has nothing to do with Islam" and "Islam is the religion of peace." It can be reasonable believed that these statements are little more than extreme expressions of political correctness or acts of submission and appeasement.

"There is little room for doubt that Europe is in the midst of something akin to a jihadist guerrilla war" says Nawaz Maajid of the Quilliam Foundation of the UK. As a former member of Hizb ut-Tahrir he has some first-hand insights into the methods and direction of the Islamists. He further adds:

"Extremism certainly has something to do with Islam. We must accept that the world is in the midst of a generational struggle to distinguish the faith from Islamism, a political ideology that seeks to impose itself on society and its violent arm of jihadism. The task ahead of us is to name this ideology, isolate it and then discredit it while supporting those who seek to reform Islam today." [839]

It cannot be denied that there are problems as the global struggle for the soul of Islam continues. Even the United Nations served to highlight the issue of violence in their Arab Development Report of November 2016. The Economist reported on this document and stated:

---

[838] Gordon Rayner, *Denis MacShane: I was too much of a 'liberal leftie' and should have done more to investigate child abuse,* The Telegraph, 27 Aug 2014. The article can be seen online at: http://www.telegraph.co.uk/news/uknews/crime/11059643/Denis-MacShane-I-was-too-much-of-a-liberal-leftie-and-should-have-done-more-to-investigate-child-abuse.html . Viewed 26 April 2017. **Rated B2.**

[839] For more on the Quilliam Foundation and the views of Nawaz Maajid see the Quilliam website at https://www.quilliaminternational.com/we-need-to-pull-up-islamism-by-its-roots/ . Viewed 24 April 2017. **Rated A1.**

"Horrifyingly, although home to only 5% of the world's population, in 2014 the Arab world **accounted for 45% of the world's terrorism**, 68% of its battle-related deaths, 47% of its internally displaced and 58% of its refugees. War not only kills and maims, but destroys vital infrastructure accelerating the disintegration." [840] (Emphasis added).

All the Arab states are Muslim majority. Clearly, the issues in these states are driven by more that just the Islamist's uprising. History, demographics, colonialism and despotism play a major role as well. But the level of conflict and terrorism in the Arab/Muslim world is truly disturbing.

The 2015 Global Terrorism Index has a rating scale that list countries based on the prevailing trends of peace and terror. The top five countries listed as Iraq, Afghanistan, Nigeria[841], Pakistan, and Syria. All of them have majority Muslim populations. These five countries alone represented 78 percent of global terrorism-related deaths.[842]

The top 15 countries from this list include Iraq, Afghanistan, Nigeria, Pakistan, Syria, India, Yemen, Somalia, Libya, Thailand, Philippines, Ukraine, Egypt, Central African Republic, and the South Sudan. Most of these countries have a Muslim majority population as well. The exceptions are countries such as Thailand, but much of its terrorism problem comes from an Islamist insurgency on its southern border with Malaysia. The same goes for the Philippines, where terrorism is largely confined to Islamist groups such as the Moro Islamic Liberation Front, the Abu Sayyaf Group and now ISIS. India has a substantial Muslim minority population of Muslims (120 million). The terrorist attacks in India are a confusing mix of communists, Islamists and separatists. Communists probably account for the largest number of deaths with the Islamists at number two. The Central African Republic has a majority Christian population, but the terrorism attacks are between Muslim and Christian groups. The only one of the top 15 counties where the terrorist attacks do not involve Islamists is Ukraine, where the violence is driven by primarily by Ukrainian and Russian nationalists.

In short, it is reasonable to assess that the Islamist violence has "something to do with Islam."

Western Values and Canadian Values

Canadian values are expressed through the Constitution and the Canadian Charter of Rights and Freedoms. The Constitution and the Charter are both founded in traditional Western values that emerged from the Reformation, the Enlightenment, the Renaissance, and the Industrial revolution.

Western society, like most of the world, has a long history of internal and external conflict. However, Western societies have also created the first democracies, ridded themselves of systemic slavery and granted rights to minorities. The West has also granted women status as legal persons, a relatively new

---

[840] *Another Arab awakening is looming, warns a UN report*, The Economist, 29 November 2016. The article can be seen online at http://www.economist.com/news/middle-east-and-africa/21710934-arabs-make-up-just-5-worlds-population-they-account-about-half . Viewed 24 April 2017. **Rated A2**.

[841] The exact division in the population of Nigeria by religion are not clear. A variety of estimate suggest that the population of Nigeria may be roughly evenly divided between Muslims and Christians. Other estimates suggest a growing population of "others" and/or those who express no religious affiliation.

[842] For more on this see the Global Terrorism Index discussion at http://www.worldatlas.com/articles/the-global-terrorism-index-countries-most-affected-by-terrorist-attacks.html . Viewed 24 April 2017. **Rated A2**.

concept in many societies. In Canada, this only occurred in October of 1929.[843] Women do not have any such legal status in countries where Islamists have a strong influence (Saudi Arabia, Pakistan etc.).

Western societies in the Modern Era (i.e. since 1500) have also broadly implemented the idea of separation of church and state, albeit a process rather than an immediate change. Academics (and others) were also able to exploit the idea of freedom of thought and speech, which was at least in part responsible for the explosion of ideas and creativity in Europe since 1500.

By contrast, the Islamists would see all this overturned. Women would have no rights beyond those granted to them by Islamist ideology, interpreted by men. Women can be beaten into subjugation and subdued. Religion and the state would become one again, as witnessed by what is happening in Turkey now and what was tried in Egypt between 2012 and 2013. Freedom of speech would be denied, and the dissenters killed. Freedom of thought is denied. Freedom of expression is to be met with death if it offends the Islamists. Slavery of both women and defeated minorities is to be allowed.

The Future

It can be reasonable stated that conflict is the logical consequence of the Islamist ideology. The importation of Islamist and globalist people and values means that conflict between nations will now move towards violence between neighbours.

The importation of the Islamist values in Canada began in 1958 when Ismail al-Faruqi moved to Montreal. He was a previously a governor/mayor in the Palestinian Governate (British Mandate – district of Galilee) and left the area after the founding of Israel. He would move to the USA after ten years in Canada and would become well known for his books and his co-founding of the International Institute of Islamic Thought (IIIT) in 1980/81. His major intellectual contribution was the concept of the Islamization of Knowledge. The IIIT bears the motto: Towards Islamization of Knowledge and Reform of Islamic Thought.[844] Al-Faruqi remains a revered figure in Islamist circles. He was murdered in his own home by a convert to Islam.

Following his ground-breaking work, many other Islamists arrived in Canada and began to create the series of deep networks we now have. Not coincidently, confrontation follows them whether it is the attack on the War Memorial and Parliament Hill or the angry confrontations at the Peel Regional Board of Education.

It is not just Canada, of course, where this ideology is spreading.

France, it appears, has already committed an act of submission and has lost the will to fight the Islamist internal violence issue. Following the Charlie Hebdo attacks, much was made of the right to freedom of speech and the defence required for it. After the Bataclan attacks, President Hollande of France declared that France was at war with ISIS, yet he made no real determinations on the troubles with extremist Islam inside of France.

---

[843] The question put to the Privy Council of England was "Does the word 'Persons' in section 24 of the British North America Act 1867, include female persons?" The Privy Council of England was still serving as Canada's "Supreme Court" at that time. Their answer was "women were indeed persons" and the "exclusion of women from all public offices is a relic of days more barbarous than ours."

[844] For this and more on the International Institute of Islamic Thought, see http://iiit.org/ . Viewed 29 September 2017. **Not rated**.

However, Patrick Calvar, France's director general of intelligence, says he fears a civil war in France if more Islamist terrorist attack occur. He also believes that "The confrontation is inevitable," and that there are an estimated 15,000 Salafists among France's seven million Muslims, "whose radical-fundamentalist creed dominates many of the predominantly Muslim housing projects at the edges of cities such as Paris, Nice or Lyon. Their preachers call for a civil war, with all Muslims tasked to wipe out the miscreants down the street".[845]

In Belgium, the socialist Mayor of Brussels stated publicly that all the mosques in Brussels were in the hands of the Safafists. ("ici, toutes les mosquées sont aux mains de salafistes".)[846] He asked that the mosques be put under the control of local authorities who could monitor the mosques. His statements, shocking as they were, gathered little interest in the main stream media outside of Belgium.

Also in Belgium, it was reported by the Het Laatste Nieuws that radicalization problems are occurring at the kindergarten level as well.[847] A internal school report, titled Indoctrination in Toddlers, stated that Muslim children were seen making hand gestures of throat slitting, calling other children infidels and unbelievers and were said to treat other children like pigs. This activity also included death threats. School officials responded by saying the number of children was small and that young children do not always understand the meaning of the gestures they are making.[848]

In the UK, besides several recent terrorist attacks, intelligence services there now say they have 23,000 persons on the radar for Islamist related threats as well as having some 500 investigations in 3,000 individuals.[849] It is not clear what has caused the number to have jumped from approximately 3,000 only a few years ago to that number now.

Also in the United Kingdom, female genital mutilation continues apace. According to the Health and Social Care Information Centre (HSCIC), 5,700 new cases of female genital mutilation (FGM) recorded in England

---

[845] John Vinocur, *Averting France's War of All Against All*, The Wall Street Journal, 18 July 2016. The article can be seen online at https://www.wsj.com/articles/averting-frances-war-of-all-against-all-1468870986 . Viewed 24 April 2017. **Rated A2.**

[846] *L'influence du salafisme dans les mosquées - La question est celle de la manière dont on aide les croyants à s'organiser - Y. Mayeur*, RBTF, 22 March 2017. The article can be seen online at Viewed 24 April 2017. **Rated B2.** https://www.rtbf.be/info/belgique/detail_l-influence-du-salafisme-dans-les-mosquees-la-question-est-celle-de-la-maniere-dont-on-aide-les-croyants-a-s-organiser-y-mayeur?id=9561685 .

[847] *Radicalisering bij kleuters: "Ze noemen klasgenootjes varkens en bedreigen hen met vinger over de keel,"* Sven Spoormakers, 21 August 2017. The article can be seen online at http://www.hln.be/hln/nl/1265/Onderwijs/article/detail/3237324/2017/08/21/Radicalisering-bij-kleuters-Ze-noemen-klasgenootjes-varkens-en-bedreigen-hen-met-vinger-over-de-keel.dhtml . Viewed 21 August 2017. **Not rated.**

[848] Many other online press agencies have reported on this story. Among others, see http://www.7sur7.be/7s7/fr/1502/Belgique/article/detail/3237585/2017/08/21/Des-signes-de-radicalisation-chez-des-enfants-de-maternelle.dhtml , http://www.7sur7.be/7s7/fr/1731/Islam/article/detail/3237840/2017/08/21/Enfants-radicalises-a-Renaix-Une-tempete-dans-un-verre-d-eau-selon-le-directeur-de-l-ecole.dhtml , and http://www.ouest-france.fr/societe/un-rapport-belge-pointe-des-signes-de-radicalisation-des-la-maternelle-5199948 . Viewed 21 August 2017. **Not rated.**

[849] *23,000 people have been 'subjects of interest' as scale of terror threat emerges after Manchester attack*, The Telegraph, 27 May 2017. The article is available online at http://www.telegraph.co.uk/news/2017/05/27/23000-people-have-subjects-interest-scale-terror-threat-emerges/ . Viewed 24 August 2017. **Rated B3.**

in 2015/2016.[850] The City of Birmingham reported 120 new cases of FGM in just three months in 2016.[851] These reporting numbers are thought to be the "tip of the iceberg."[852]

The New York Times, however, suggests that the term "Female Genital Mutilation" should not be used as it is "culturally loaded."[853] This echoes the Prime Minister Trudeau and his suggestion that we need to have terms that use "responsible neutrality" when discussing such barbaric practices. In Canada, a growing body of evidence suggests that FGM is a problem and girls are often shipped out of country for the procedures.[854] Others in Canada, however, have come forward and said that FGM is practiced on Canadian girls within Canadian borders. Those making the claims they were the victims were members of a Muslim sect. The same report also states that girls have been taken from Canada and had FGM performed on them elsewhere. In Ontario, 308 operations have been carried out to reverse some of the worst aspects of FGM.[855] There are no signs of any legal action having been taken. Despite the evidence, the media and government remain largely silent on the issue, even as arrests of doctors for carrying out FGM occur just across the border in Detroit.[856]

While the UK is taking steps to prevent FGM and the USA is laying criminal charges against doctors in Detroit for carrying out FGM operations, the Government of Canada is moving in the opposite direction. The new citizenship guide (2017) has removed any reference to honour killings and FGM

Violence in Canada

The Islamist violence and its reaction has already begun in Canada. The country has produced a string of Islamist suicide bombers, jihadist fighters and an ISIS propagandist. Four terrorist attacks have occurred and a suicide bombing in a transportation hub was narrowly adverted due to quick action and insights that originated from the American FBI. The cycle of violence has also turned, as a Muslim Brotherhood associated mosque in Quebec City was attacked in early 2017. (Chapter 20).

---

[850] Haroon Siddiqui, *England had 5,700 recorded cases of FGM in 2015-16, figures show,* The Guardian, 21 July 2016. The article can be seen online at https://www.theguardian.com/society/2016/jul/21/england-fgm-cases-recorded-2015-2016 . Viewed 26 April 2017. **Rated A2.**

[851] Anuji Varma, *Female genital mutilation: Birmingham has highest number of UK cases,* The Birmingham Mail, 09 September 2017. The article can be viewed online at http://www.birminghammail.co.uk/news/midlands-news/female-genital-mutilation-birmingham-highest-11858839 . Viewed 26 April 2017. **Rated B2.**

[852] Mark Tran, *Female genital mutilation increase in England 'only tip of iceberg,'* The Guardian, 30 April 2015. The article can be seen online at https://www.theguardian.com/society/2015/apr/30/female-genital-mutilation-england-fgm-girls . Viewed 26 April 2017. **Rated B2.**

[853] Mythili Sampathkumar, *New York Times refuses to use term 'female genital mutilation' for being 'culturally loaded,'* The Independent, 26 April 2017. The article can be seen online at http://www.independent.co.uk/news/world/americas/new-york-times-female-genital-mutilation-culturally-loaded-response-a7702221.html . Viewed 26 April 2017. **Rated A2**.

[854] For more on the issue of FGM in Canada, the Ontario Human Rights Commission report at http://www.ohrc.on.ca/es/node/2754. Viewed 26 April 2017. **Rated A1.**

[855] Michele Henry and Jayme Poisson, *Women in small Muslim sect say they have had FGM in Canada*, The Toronto Star, 21 August 2017. The article is available online at https://www.thestar.com/news/fgm/2017/08/21/women-in-small-muslim-sect-said-they-had-fgm-in-canada.html . Viewed 24 August 2017. **Rated B3**.

[856] For more on the arrest of Detroit doctors on charges of FGM, see the US Justice Department reports online at https://www.justice.gov/opa/pr/detroit-doctor-and-wife-arrested-and-charged-conspiring-perform-female-genital-mutilation and at https://www.justice.gov/opa/pr/detroit-emergency-room-doctor-arrested-and-charged-performing-female-genital-mutilation . Viewed 26 April 2017. **Rated A1**.

Other confrontations are occurring. Citizens have been protesting the Dundas Street mosque in Toronto due to its Islamists calls for the killing of Jews. Confrontations have occurred at the Peel Regional District School Board as Islamists insist on prayers being allowed in schools despite a general prohibition on religion interfering in public schools. Assaults are alleged to have occurred at these meetings. The rate at which the violence and confrontations are occurring is increasing as a variety of Islamist front groups and individuals begin to impose their will by claiming oppression and Islamophobia.

The current government of Prime Minister Justin Trudeau appears to be fully committed to supporting a wide variety of Islamist front groups and causes. Additionally, the Prime Minister now tells us that Canada must move "beyond tolerance towards acceptance and friendship" with our "fellow citizens." It is not clear why Canadians have to be accepting of those who create suicide bombers, advocate wife beating, promote genocide, advocate temporary marriage with nine-year-old girls and tell the youth of Canada that they need to become "Lovers of Death."[857]

The views of Prime Minister Trudeau do not exist in isolation, however. In Sweden, a government backed charity has a campaign that tells Swedes they must be the ones to change to integrate with foreign cultures and languages. The "New Country" film put out by the charity Individual Relief (IM), also says that "It's time to realise the new Swedes will claim their space" and "Sweden will never be like it was."[858] Most shocking, perhaps, is that this government sponsored body also denounces the assimilation of migrants. They also believe that "Integration does not mean that one party should adapt to the other, or that everyone should think, do and feel the same. Integration is about meetings, and real meetings are built on reciprocity."

Sweden, it seems, is being told that it must learn to adapt to child marriages, the systemic subjugation of women, the advocacy of genocide and offensive jihad.

The message of submission and acceptance also comes from then French Presidential candidate Emmanuel Macron who stated that terrorism is "part of our daily lives for the years to come".[859]

Europe, of course, has a land bridge to Asia, the Middle East and Africa. The flows of economically and ideologically motived migrants will continue, especially as welfare payments remain generous and governments have no will to resist or physically control their borders. The number of migrants on the move in Africa who are looking to move to Europe and North America is not clear. NGOs sometimes suggest the number is around 60 million while security agencies have suggested this number could be 100 million. Whatever the reality, this is just Africa. Other countries such as Pakistan and Afghanistan also have millions of people who lead miserable lives.

---

[857] For more on the issues of Islamist education for Muslim Youth in Canada see the report *The Lovers of Death"? Islamist Extremism in Our Mosques, Schools and Libraries.*

[858] The film can be seen at https://www.youtube.com/watch?v=X3-_KZExlJ0 or also on the charity's website at https://manniskohjalp.se/integration/det-nya-landet . For more background on the film see the report at http://www.friatider.se/det-finns-ingen-vag-tillbaka-nu-ska-svenskarna-integreras-i-mangkulturen . Viewed 24 April 2017. **Rated B2**. See also https://www.thenewamerican.com/world-news/europe/item/24472-swedes-and-germans-told-to-integrate-into-their-new-country . Viewed 24 April 2017. **Rated B2.**

[859] Kim Willsher, *Fears Paris shooting will affect presidential election as first round looms*, The Guardian, 21 April 2017. The story can be seen online at https://www.theguardian.com/world/2017/apr/21/fears-that-paris-shooting-will-affect-presidental-election-as-first-round-looms . Viewed 24 April 2017. **Rated A2.**

In Canada, the flow of illegal economic migrants also appears to be increasing. Prime Minister Trudeau has signalled to the world (literally) that Canada will not enforce its border controls and that anyone is welcome to just cross the border and declare refugee status, regardless of their country of origin, status or criminal record. One sampling of recently arrived illegal border crossers suggests that approximately 50% of them already have criminal records.[860] His statement that "To those fleeing persecution, terror & war, Canadians will welcome you, regardless of your faith," is obviously flaunting 150 years of Canadian immigration policy and little is being done to stop this new flow of illegal migration.

Prime Minister Trudeau has told us that Canada is now a post-national state and our previously accepted value system based on our European history and ancestry is now over. With no "core values" we must instead accept a "pan-cultural heritage" with all that he perceives this means.

Implications

Unless this slide into accepting the values of the dark past and the ideology of the Islamists is corrected, the Government of Canada will continue one path: **Submission**.

Submission on the part of the government will lead to resistance on the part of the population.

[860] *Nearly half of illegal border crossers have criminal records, CBSA union says*, CBC News Manitoba, 13 April 2017. The article and video can be seen online at http://www.cbc.ca/player/play/920868419922 . Viewed 26 April 2017. **Rated B2.**

CHAPTER 24: A WARNING TO AMERICA

Thomas Quiggin

Key Points

- The Canadian government's practice of conciliation to Islamist causes and increasing international cooperation with countries such as Iran will have direct negative implications for both Canada and America.

- Islamists (primarily Sunni/Ikhwani) and Iranian Khomeneists (Shia) are increasingly seeing Canada as a soft target for infiltration and Entryism.

The current Canadian government is accommodating Islamist enablers at a time when the violence emanating from these ideologies is increasing. As the spread of the Islamist ideology and violence accelerates, the respective positions of the Canadian and American governments are evolving.

The previous Administration of President Obama (2009 to 2017) allowed Muslim Brotherhood leadership figures into the White House and other corridors of influence such as the State Department. Under the influence of Valerie Jarrett, the Obama Administration was also accommodating to the demands of the Iranian regime. At roughly the same time, from 2006 to 2015, Prime Minister Harper of Canada took a relatively hard-line stance against the Islamists resident in Canada and went so far as to remove the Iranian Ambassador and his staff from Canada in 2012. Several charities in Canada with Islamist connections had their charitable status revoked for funding terrorism (See Chapter 15 on IRFAN and the ISNA Development Fund etc.).

Now the roles have reversed. The Administration of President Trump is taking a harder line against the Islamists and the Iranians. By contrast, Prime Minister Trudeau has shown himself to be repeatedly submissive to the Islamist cause. While difficult to categorize, Western leaders appear to be split into to "globalists" who favour immigration without integration and "sovereigntists" who favour national priorities over globalist agendas. Trudeau regularly appears in the globalist anti-border camp, while Trump is moving in a nationalist, pro-border direction.

Prime Minister Trudeau has defended Islamists from when he was a Member of Parliament (2008) and carrying over into his time as Prime Minister (2015 to the present). His position on re-opening Iran's Embassy appears fluid, but Canadian sanctions against Iran have been lifted and Iranian parliamentarians have been visiting Canada, including personal home visits to Canadian Members of Parliament.

With respect to terrorist fighters returning from ISIS, Prime Minister Trudeau feels that Canada needs to "ensure that resources are in place to facilitate disengagement from violent ideologies."[861] Canada, as of the time of the statement from the Prime Minister, did not have a deradicalization program. Nor has

[861] Tonda McCharles, *Conservatives slam Trudeau as soft on terror as push for security changes begins*, 20 November 2017, The Toronto Star. The article can be seen online at https://www.thestar.com/news/canada/2017/11/20/conservatives-slam-trudeau-as-soft-on-terror-as-push-for-security-changes-begins.html . Viewed 22 November 2017. **Rated B3**.

anyone been nominated to be charge of government's *Centre for Community Engagement and Prevention of Violence*, despite the government having been in power for two years.

The position of Prime Minister Trudeau on China and Cuba, both communist dictatorships, is worrying to many observers as well. Trudeau's open and unprompted admiration for China's "basic dictatorship" and his stated affection for Fidel Castro are both worrying. (See Chapter 12) Either Trudeau is hopelessly naive and uninformed about the world around him, or he has true affection for absolutist systems. The position of his brother and advisor Sacha on Iran does little to dispel this.

History

Canada and USA have a strong history in security cooperation. The North American Air Defence Command (NORAD) is jointly staffed and commanded by both countries. Canadian and American troops landed together on the beaches of Normandy on D-Day in World War II. The 2nd Battalion, Princess Patricia's Canadian Light Infantry (2 VP) played a pivotal role (along with an Australian battalion) in defeating an entire Chinese division which had attacked US and UN forces. For their efforts, 2 VP was awarded a United States Presidential Unit Citation.

During the war in the former Yugoslavia, Canada was only able to open and operate the Sarajevo airport by knowing that "Uncle Sam" was providing intelligence and some top cover. General Colin Powell, the Chairman of the US Joint Chiefs of Staff, personally intervened into the CANUS intelligence process to make sure Canada received intelligence support. Cooperation is, of course a two-way street, with Canadians having a better look at the reality on the ground, and making intelligence assessments that national technical means just cannot do.

During 9/11, Canadian airports found themselves hosts to a variety of mostly American aircraft suddenly ground. Gander Newfound land with a population of just over 10,000 people suddenly found it had 6,600 new guests.

Cross-Border Terrorism

Not all Canadian/American interaction on security has been positive. In 2000, Islamist bomber Ahmed Ressam (AKA Benni Antoine Norris) left Canada and crossed into the US with a bomb in his car. His intent was to bomb the Los Angeles Airport (LAX). It was only the quick thinking and observational skills of American border agent Diana Dean that saved the day.

Attempted terrorist attacks have also originated in the USA and moved north. Jamaat al Fuqra was in the process of carrying out a plot to kill some 5,000 people in an attack on Toronto. Based outside of Syracuse, New York, the followers of Pakistani cleric Sheik Gilani were tripped up by Canadian police and border agents who questioned their behaviour and possessions. The result was a multi-jurisdictional investigation that derailed a major terrorism plot.

The 1997 cross-border case of Gazi Ibrahim Abu Mezer, and his attempt to bomb the Atlantic Avenue subway in Brooklyn, New York, is another example. His efforts served to underline how a person from a third country could exploit the Canada/USA border in a terrorism plot. Despite have been rejected three times from entering the USA, he was able to do so on a Canadian issued student visa.

In 2013, Chiheb Esseghaier was involved in a cross-border plot and was convicted of terrorism charges in Canada. Esseghaier, a Muslim Student Association member (Chapter 14), was leading a plot to attack a

Via Rail passenger train as it crossed a bridge into the USA. Both Canadians and Americans would have been the victims.

Senator Hillary Clinton and Senator John McCain both claimed that some of the 9/11 bombers crossed over into the USA from Canada. This was false, but it caused tensions on both sides as the US sought greater border security following the 2001 terrorist attack. That they can make such claims years after they have been debunked shows how security issues on the Canada/USA border can be politicized.

The Terrorism Nightmare Scenario for Canada – and America

Pundits frequently discuss terrorist "nightmare" scenarios such as a terrorist group with a dirty bomb or biological weapon. Rapidly advancing technology and communications suggest such scenarios are a possibility.

But what do the nightmare scenarios look like for Canada and the USA?

For the USA, a nightmare scenario could be a biological or chemical attack against a major urban centre such as New York City or Los Angeles. It could also be a combined gun or explosives attack against a major sporting or entertainment event.

For Canada, a different set of nightmare scenarios exist. An attack such as that envisaged by the "Toronto 18" would be devastating (6,000+ pounds of ammonium nitrate). A suicide bomb such as that attempted by Islamist convert Aaron Driver in 2016 could have been ruinous to public confidence in public transportation.

However, the real nightmare scenario for Canada may be something different. If a major terrorist attack in America were to be carried out by individuals who entered the USA from Canada, the results could be catastrophic. That was the 2000 Ressam scenario. This point was just driven home when it was revealed that 19-year-old Canadian Abdulrahman El Bahnasawy from Mississauga was convicted (2016) of a terrorist plot in New York City. The planned attacks included detonating bombs in Times Square and the New York City subway system, and shooting civilians at specific concert venues.[862]

In the face of casualties or significant infrastructural damage, the American government would be (rightfully) angry at the attack and may chose to close the Canadian border. This would continue until such time the Canadian government was able to assure American authorities that the security situation in Canada was under control. The American position might be more drastic, given the recent views of the Canadian government that convicted terrorists should be allowed to keep Canadian citizenship. Prime Minster Trudeau's ongoing positive interactions with Islamists organizations in Canada and around the world would come under scrutiny as would his views that returning ISIS fighters should not face arrest.

This point was just driven home again when President Trump stated he wanted to see immigration changes made following a terrorist attack in Edmonton Alberta on 30 September 2017. In this case, the terrorist attacker had been ordered deported from the USA, but had left the USA and was granted refugee

---

[862] For more on this terrorism plot see the United States Department of Justice Statement *Acting Manhattan U.S. Attorney Announces The Court's Unsealing Of Charges Against Three Men Arrested For Participating In International Plot To Carry Out Terrorist Attacks In New York City For Isis In The Summer Of 2016*. This statement is available online at https://www.justice.gov/usao-sdny/pr/acting-manhattan-us-attorney-announces-court-s-unsealing-charges-against-three-men. Viewed 11 October 2017. **Rated A1**.

status in Canada, notwithstanding his problems in the USA.[863] To further make the point, it turns out the alleged attacked had illegally crossed the Mexican/US border as well as the Canadian/US border. Cross border terrorism remains an issue.

The economic and social results for Canada could be devastating, given Canada's dependence on trade with the USA. The Office of the United States Trade Representative stated that US/Canada trade (import/export) was valued as some $662.7 billion in 2015. For Canada, this represents more than 70% of its export trade.

Prime Minister Justin Trudeau

By allowing both the Sunni Islamist and Iranian/Khomeneist forces to build in Canada, Prime Minister Trudeau is taking a risk with the lives and welfare of both Canadians and Americans. This is occurring at a time when the capabilities of groups and countries looking to harm the USA and Canada are increasing. Allowing these forces to build up their strength in Canada is dangerous to US interests directly. All of this while Iran and the USA remain in a state of potential conflict over a variety of issues involving the spread of the Khomesiests political influence, nuclear weapons, oil pricing and Iran's "competition" with Saudi Arabia for influence in the Gulf Region and around the world.

Implications

The backdrop to this is worrying. Islamists, on a global basis, appear to be increasingly violent and growing in both strength and audacity. Islamist violence is spreading in Indonesia, Pakistan, Afghanistan, Nigeria, Kenya, Somalia, Russia, France, the UK, Germany, Belgium, Turkey, ISIS, Syria, and Iraq. (to mention just the highlights). Canada and the USA have both suffered from Islamist inspired or directed attacks in recent years.

Unfortunately for all concerned, the problem is growing. Canada is doing little address the issues while accommodating those who form the basis of the problem. Canada will not be able to plead ignorance or inability while facing accusations of complicity from future American victims. The price of Canada's submission to the Islamists may indeed be high.

---

[863] Adrian Morrow, *Trump administration cites Edmonton attack in call for immigration changes,* 09 October 2017, the Globe and Mail. The article can be seen online at https://beta.theglobeandmail.com/news/world/us-politics/trump-administration-cites-edmonton-attack-in-call-for-immigration-changes/article36524833/?ref=http://www.theglobeandmail.com&. Viewed 11 October 2017. **Rated B2.**

CHAPTER 25: WHAT IS TO BE DONE?

Thomas Quiggin

Key Points

- This book has examined a few of the key issues concerning the role of Islamist ideology in Canada.
- It has not taken a deep dive into all the front organizations, rather it has only exposed a few of the leading ones or the most egregious examples.
- This book does, however, lay out enough of the threat to begin a discussion on what must be done in Canada.

Globally, it can be assessed that there are increasing problems with Islamists, including the country with the world's largest Muslim population – Indonesia. Hizb ut-Tahrir, also active in many countries including Canada, is one of the driving forces of Islamist ideology there.[864] The growing list of countries with Islamist and Sharia problem is extensive. Among others, it includes Muslim majority countries such as Pakistan, Turkey, Qatar, Malaysia, Bangladesh, Lebanon, Syria, Jordan, Egypt, Saudi Arabia, Morocco, Algeria, and Tunisia. Non-Muslim majority countries have dangerous Islamist problems as well. Leading this list is India, followed by other countries such the Philippines, China, Spain, Italy, Russia, Australia, Singapore, and the USA.

In other countries with an Islamist problem, the rate of Islamist terrorism attacks and Islamist related incidents is increasing. In France, the government has repeatedly extended a state of emergency while keeping some 7500 to 10,000 troops on the street for public order. French police have demonstrated against the government, claiming they are exhausted and overwhelmed.[865] Women in France report that they are unable to enter certain cafes and shops in Paris – because they are female.[866] The United Kingdom's internal security service officially states that there are 23,000 jihadists of concern[867], while the EU head of counter terrorism, Gilles de Kerchove suggests the real number could be as high as 35,000.

---

[864] Jewel Topsfiled and Karuni Rompies, *Indonesia bans Islamic organisation Hizbut-Tahrir to protect Pancasila*, 19 July 2017, The Sydney Morning Herald. This article can be seen online at http://www.smh.com.au/world/indonesia-bans-islamic-organisation-hizbut-tahrir-to-protect-pluralism-20170719-gxeaae.html . Viewed 13 October 2017. **Rated B2.**

[865] Henry Smith, *'Exhausted' French police plead with unions to postpone fresh protests so they can recover*, 21 June 2016, The Telegraph. This article can be seen online at http://www.telegraph.co.uk/news/2016/06/21/exhausted-french-police-plead-with-unions-to-postpone--fresh-pro/ . Viewed 13 October 2017. **Rated B2.**

[866] David Chazan, *'This isn't Paris. It's only men here' - Inside the French Muslim no-go zones where women aren't welcome,* 18 December 2016, The Telegraph. The article is available online at http://www.telegraph.co.uk/news/2016/12/17/french-bar-tells-women-isnt-paris-men/ . Viewed 13 October 2017. **Rated B2.**

[867] See, among others, *Britain is 'home to 35,000 Islamist fanatics', more than any other country in Europe, top official warns*, 31 August 2017, The Telegraph. The article is available online at http://www.telegraph.co.uk/news/2017/08/31/britain-home-35000-islamist-fanatics-country-europe-top-official/. Viewed 21 September 2017. Rated **B2**.

Other official numbers in Europe place Belgium at 18,000, France 15,000[868], Germany 10,000[869] and Switzerland 500.[870]

Canada is not immune from such issues, as demonstrated by the series of four Islamist attacks from 2014 to 2017 and one failed suicide bombing. Young Canadians are also dying overseas, having been recruited by Islamist groups such as ISIS and al Qaeda in the Islamic Maghreb. We also have a variety of Imams calling for the beating of women in Canada and the murder of Jews and apostates as part of their support for the installation of Sharia in Canada. (Chapter 21)

What is to be done?

How Canada reacts to this civilizational challenge posed by the Islamists is unclear. Limited efforts have been undertaken, such as withdrawing charitable status from Islamist organizations like IRFAN. At the same time, however, Islamist Imams continue to openly advance their ideology by calling for the killing of apostates and the organized subjugation of women. Clearly, Canada lacks any strategy for identifying and attacking the issues. What could be done? The following is a short initial list of recommendations.

Recommendations

1. PRECISE LANGUAGE: The Government of Canada, the press and others need to adopt and use precise language to debate the issues. The problem is not Muslims nor is it Islam. The problem is the Islamists – those who would impose any given interpretation of Islamic religious law (called Sharia) over society. Terrorism is a tactic used by those who employ violence to force political change. Terrorism is not “the problem” nor is terrorism an existential threat to Canadian society. The existential threat is a civilizational one and that is driven by the Islamist who believe it is the right of politicized Islam to dominate all others. At the tactical level, terrorism must be fought. The real problem is at the strategic level and again, that problem is the Islamists, their demands for Sharia and their multiple front groups.

2. INVESTIGATIVE ACTION: An investigation should be carried out into the role of the Muslim Brotherhood in Canada, including its call for Sharia Law, history, front groups, ideology, financing, foreign connections, number of front groups listed as terrorist entities, overseas connections, the

---

868 For more on the figures for France, Spain and Belgium see the article by Noor Nanji, *'50,000 militant Islamists in Europe', warns top security chief*. This article is available online at https://www.thenational.ae/world/europe/50-000-militant-islamists-in-europe-warns-top-security-chief-1.624849 . Viewed 21 September 2017. **Not rated.**

869 *Germany must brace for more attacks by radicalized Muslims: officials,* 04 July 2017, Reuters News Service. The article can be seen online at https://www.reuters.com/article/us-germany-security/germany-must-brace-for-more-attacks-by-radicalized-muslims-officials-idUSKBN19P1MY . Viewed 21 September 2017. **Rated A2.** For more on this see also Allan Hall, *WE'VE LOST CONTROL' Germany cannot cope with ISIS terror cells because the country's Muslim population has grown so rapidly, top intelligence official admits*, 09 January 2017, The Sun. This article can be seen online at https://www.thesun.co.uk/news/2573862/germany-cannot-cope-isis-terror-cells-muslim-population-grown-intelligence-official-admits/ . Viewed 21 September 2017. **Rated C3.** There may be as many as 400 potentially violent Islamist individuals being tracked in just Berlin by itself. For more on this see *Mehr als 400 gewaltbereite Salafisten leben in Berlin*. The article can be seen online at http://www.berliner-zeitung.de/28387288 . Viewed 21 September 2017. **Not rated.**

870 The Swiss authorities are believed to be monitoring some 500 Islamists. For more on this see *Swiss monitor 500 people for online jihadist propaganda*, 14 March 2017, Swissinfo.ch. Viewed 21 September 2017. **Rated B3.**

role of Halal Certification and financing, and the role of Muslim Brotherhood members in Canada as they play leading roles in foreign governments. The starting point of such an investigation could begin with IRFAN, a terrorist listed organization whose founding members and actions were widely spread across Canada. The investigation could also be based on the UK model, which established the links of the Muslim Brotherhood in the UK to a variety of Islamist issues. Various reports on the Muslim Brotherhood have also been done in Belgium[871], Austria[872] and Sweden.[873]

3. LISTING OF FOREIGN ENTITIES: The Government of Canada should list the Muslim Brotherhood in Egypt, Qatar, Turkey, and Libya as terrorist entities. Additionally, a review should be undertaken to determine if the increasingly powerful and influential IRGC (Iranian Revolutionary Guards Council) should be listed as a terrorist entity in a similar manner to what has been done in the USA. Canada already lists the Quds Forces of the IRGC as a terrorist entity.

4. CHARITY REVIEW: A major review of charities in Canada should be undertaken. Those which have already organizational links to Islamist ideology, support for Sharia and terrorist funding should be considered first, along with others which have donated money repeatedly to terrorist organizations.

5. CHARITY LAW: Changes should be made so that board members and executive committee members of organizations that have lost charitable status for funding terrorism should be barred from serving on other charitable boards.

6. CHAPLAINS: The police, military and prison services should be examined for the hiring process of their chaplains. Muslim chaplains who belong to organizations that advocate for Sharia Law, against democracy, or in favour of violent behaviour such as beating women or killing apostates, should not be allowed to fill such positions.

7. HUMAN RIGHTS: The Canadian Human Rights Commission needs to examine its outreach partners, particularly with respect to education programs. If its outreach partners advocate in favour of Sharia Law or violent behaviour such as wife beating and the killing of apostates, they are not acceptable partners. If an outreach partner has a parent organization that is listed as a terrorist group, this could be considered as an indicator that further examination is required.

---

[871] Pieter Van Berkel, *Blootgelegd: De Moslimbroederschap in België,* 14 October 2017, Sceptr News. The article can be seen online at https://sceptr.net/2017/10/moslimbroederschap-belgie-kaart-gebracht/ . Viewed 14 Octover 2017. **Not rated**.

[872] Dr. Lorenzo Vidino, *The Muslim Brotherhood in Austria*, Program on Extremism at George Washington University and the University of Vienna, August 2017. The article can be seen online at https://extremism.gwu.edu/sites/extremism.gwu.edu/files/MB%20in%20Austria-%20Print.pdf . Viewed 03 October 2017. **Rated B2**.

[873] Lee Roden, *Debate rages in Sweden over Muslim Brotherhood report,* 03 March 2017, The Local SE. This news report can be seen online at https://www.thelocal.se/20170303/debate-rages-in-sweden-over-muslim-brotherhood-report . Viewed 14 October 2017. **Rated B3**. The report in its original Swedish can be seen at https://www.msb.se/Upload/Kunskapsbank/Studier/Muslimska_Brodraskapet_i_Sverige_DNR_2107-1287.pdf . An English language version of the report can be seen at https://clarionproject.org/wp-content/uploads/2017/06/Muslim-Brotherhood-Sweden-Magnus-Norrell.pdf .

8. HALAL CERTIFICATION: Canada needs to determine the flow and usage of money raised by Halal Certification. This is critical with respect to the growth of Islamist ideology as this form of funding is being set up to ensure a stable future for the Islamist supporters. Leading Islamist leadership figures such as Yusuf Qaradawi have advocated Halal Certification as a means of funding the Muslim Brotherhood. Given the role played by the ISNA and their repeated role in funding terrorism, this is a critical question.

9. THE CHARTER OF RIGHTS AND FREEDOMS: Canada needs to discuss if the Charter of Rights and Freedoms stands for anything and if it guides life in Canada. Clearly at this point, the Charter has lost significance as a guiding document. A variety of charities and organizations openly call for the beating of women, sex with underage children, and the killing of those who leave a religion. The M-103 Islamophobia motion is an extension of Islamist inspired blasphemy laws as it demands protection for Islamist views. It is ironic that Islamist want special protection when it is gays, Jews and women who suffer the most from hate crimes.

10. "FORCED SUICIDES:" A national level investigation into forced suicides (family induced honour killings), Female Genital Mutilation, child marriage, muta marriages and off-the-book marriages at mosques needs to be conducted. Canada could look at the UK, USA, and France where these issues are already being investigated.

11. EDUCATION: Provincial education authorities need to examine what is being taught in schools. Initial official investigations have already shown that questionable material has and is being used. Schools have been shut in the middle of such investigations. The provincial authorities may wish to look to OFSTED (Office for Standards in Education, Children's Services and Skills) in the United Kingdom. OFSTED has already had a series of disturbing school investigations and school closures based on the application and teaching of Islamist ideology.

12. UNIVERSITES: The Muslim Student Association of Canada and the USA needs to be examined more critically by the press, the government, and the universities. Besides a rather high rate of ex-MSA individuals who have gone off to be jihadist fighters, it has regularly called for the abuse of women. Some MSA's have constitutions which focus on Salafism and Sharia law. The MSA "starters guide" written by individuals such as "Lady Al Qaeda" (Aafia Siddiqui) and calls for the politicization of university campuses.

13. IMAMS: The Government of Canada needs a position on Imams in mosques. Countries such the UK and France have already examining such issues. Should an Imam be allowed to head a major mosque if he belongs to an organization which calls for sharia law or is listed as a terrorist group in other countries? Should advocating Sharia concepts which are in direct violation of Canadian law such as wife beating, and child molestation be grounds for removal from such positions? Is it acceptable for Imams to call for the killing of ex-Muslims/apostates?

14. THE MEDIA: Journalists and the media need to reassess their position on Islamism. The Canadian Association of Journalists exists, but it is not clear what, if any, influence it has on ethical issues. For instance, many journalists from Al Jazeera in Qatar (and the Middle East) quit the organization when it became clear that Al Jazeera had become little more than a mouthpiece for the Muslim Brotherhood (2013). Yet CBC and the Toronto Star both appeared to have taken money and

cooperated with Al Jazeera in media productions (2014-2015). Do journalists in the Middle East have higher standards of ethical behaviour and are they willing to take higher risks?

15. INTERFAITH DIALOG: Interfaith groups need to examine their partners. Merely asking if their partners denounce terrorism is not sufficient. Instead, interfaith groups need to make an in-depth examination of their partners to see if they support the imposition of Sharia Law. If the outreach partner or its parent organization has been listed as a terrorist group, this is an indicator of potential problems. If a partner group has an official position that wife beating is permissible, sexual slavery for women is OK and temporary marriages with girls as young as nine is allowed, this should be a warning.

16. ASSOCIATION OF CHIEFS OF POLICE: Community outreach is a critical police function. The Canadian Chiefs of Police Association needs a position on refusing to work with community groups that support sharia law, fund terrorism, or have a parent organization which is listed as a terrorist group.

17. CSIS: An overall review of Canadian Security Intelligence Service (CSIS), its mandate and competency are needed. Has it been infiltrated and have its policies been influenced by organizations which advocate sharia law? Do any of their partners have a parent group that funds terrorism or been listed as a terrorist entity? Can CSIS identify the major organizations in Canada that advocate Sharia and Islamist ideology and therefore hold anti-democratic positions?

18. PUBLIC TESTIMONY: Organizations that receive public money or testify to Parliament and Legislatures should be asked if they support the imposition of sharia law or if they have funded terrorist groups. Should they also be asked if they recognize the Constitution and the Charter as the supreme law of the land, or do they feel they are superior to it? It is not sufficient for them to say they reject terrorism. Government officials such as Minsters of the Crown should not be taking "community awards" from organizations which support Sharia Law, advocate violence, or have parent organizations which are listed as terrorist groups.

19. FOREIGN FUNDING: Should "religious" groups in Canada be allowed to receive foreign financing? The principle of reciprocity needs to be applied. For instance, Saudi Arabia and Qatar finance mosques and schools in Canada. Would a Canadian group be allowed to finance a church or religious school in either of those countries? If not, then the foreign funding should be disallowed.

20. IRAN: Canada needs to examine the increasing role of Khomeneism and its Islamist ideology in Canada. This includes Iranian agents of Khomeneism, including incoming money, Imams, and charities with Khomeneist connections. Do they advocate for the Khomeneist interpretation of Sharia Law?" Are their Canadian based charities sending money to Qom, Iran? This is a direct violation of charity law. Are Iranian agents of influence in Canada advocating that Iranian Canadians should infiltrate the government of Canada to advance Iranian/Khomeneist ideology?

21. NEIGHBOURS: Canada is a sovereign state, but its only land border is shared with the United States of America. Canadian policy thinking needs to be informed that a terrorist attack in the USA carried out by a Canadian, or a foreign national from Canada, could have massive implications for the Canadian economy. At least two close calls have already occurred. Ahmed Ressam was intent on blowing up the Los Angeles Airport (LAX) in 2000. An alert American border agent

stopped this attack. Abdulrahman El Bahnasawy of Mississauga Ontario was convicted in 2016 for his role in an ISIS inspired plot that the attackers were calling "the next 9/11." The FBI disrupted the plot.

ANNEX A: LEXICON

Ahmadi: A minority sect of Islam based on the beliefs of the founder of the movement Mirza Ghulam Ahmad. Other Muslim groupings often persecute them, including being declared apostates.

Apostate: An apostate is defined as one who rejects in word or deed the beliefs of one's former religion. In many parts of Islam, especially in the Islamist strain, being an apostate is punishable by death.

Bayat: A bayat is a pledge of obedience given to the Emir or leader of a group. Within Islamist circles, the term has come to mean a lifelong commitment which cannot be broken. Breaking the bayat can mean being identified as a kafir or non-believer afterwards.[874]

Cultural Relativism: This is a rather contested term. At one level, it simply means that that an individual's beliefs can only be understood in the context of where they were born and how they grew up (i.e. cultural). A more pernicious set of beliefs has grown out of this that says no one can say one culture can be considered superior to another as to do so is a form of racism etc. Consequently, many now believe that we simply must accept the cultural views of others as they enter our society and we cannot challenge them. The result is that wife beating, child marriages and pedophilia are now accepted or at least not being challenged due to a growing belief in 'cultural relativism.'

Daru Islam: To the Islamists, this term holds that to establish the dominance of the true religion (Islam), it is first necessary to establish an Islamic state, which, in turn, will then lead to the re-establishment of the Caliphate (Khilafah Islamiyah). It is obligatory for all Muslims to contribute both financially and physically to this end.[875]

Enlightenment: "The Enlightenment is the period in the history of Western thought and culture, stretching roughly from the mid-decades of the seventeenth century through the eighteenth century, characterized by dramatic revolutions in science, philosophy, society and politics; these revolutions swept away the medieval world-view and ushered in our modern Western world. Enlightenment thought culminates historically in the political upheaval of the French Revolution, in which the traditional hierarchical political and social orders (the French monarchy, the privileges of the French nobility, the political power and authority of the Catholic Church) were violently destroyed and replaced by a political and social order informed by the Enlightenment ideals of freedom and equality for all, founded, ostensibly, upon principles of human reason."[876]

Entryism (Political Entryism): This is the policy or practice of members of a particular group joining an existing political party with the intention of changing its principles and policies, instead of forming a new party.[877] Sourcewatch defines this practice and adds that Entryism is "a political tactic in which an organization or group enters a larger organization in an attempt to gain recruits, gain influence or to take control of the larger organisations' structure."[878] The term Entryism may have first been popularized by

---

874 For more on this term see http://www.terrorismanalysts.com/pt/index.php/pot/article/view/67/html .

875 For more on this term see http://www.terrorismanalysts.com/pt/index.php/pot/article/view/67/html .

876 For more on the Enlightenment see, among many others, the Stanford Encyclopedia of Philosophy entry on this subject which can be seen online at http://plato.stanford.edu/entries/enlightenment/ .

877 http://www.thefreedictionary.com/entryism

878 The Sourcewatch definition can be seen online at http://www.sourcewatch.org/index.php/Entryism .

the entry French Trotskyists into the party Section Française de l'International Ouvrière (SFIO). This effort which began 1934 was discussed by Trotsky in his work The French Turn.[879]

Extremism: In the context of this book, any set of beliefs that would seek to overthrow the Constitution of Canada, the Charter of Rights and Freedoms or the Criminal Code of Canada.

Hijrah (also Hirja): According to the Islamist view of Hijrah, volunteers should leave their homes, properties, jobs and families for the sake of Allah. They do not need permission from their families to do this. Islamists also advocate that they should disregard the needs of their parents, wives, and children for the sake of their struggle. They believe that the volunteers should migrate (Hijrah) from worldly inclinations to heavenly goals. They can achieve this heavenly goal through suicide bombings. Hirjah in the physical also means migration into a non-Muslim majority area for establishing Muslim control of that area. For many Islamists, the inflow of migrants into Europe is in fact of form of hirjah.[880]

Hizb ut-Tahrir: Founded in the Middle East in 1952 as a spinoff of the Muslim Brotherhood, the "Party of Liberation" has the main objective of creating a caliphate. As with most other Islamist groups, they are also Salafist, Takfirist, and Jihadist in orientation. They believe directly in the principle of offensive jihad once the caliphate is founded.

Humanist: A humanist is one who is a believer in the principles of humanism, those who believe or are concerned with the interests and welfare of humans.

Imam: A person who leads prayers in a mosque is known as an Imam. These individuals, almost always male, may be highly educated individuals with a deep knowledge of Islam or simply an individual who accepts the responsibility even if they have limited theological knowledge.

Ikhwan: The Muslim Brotherhood is also known as the Society of the Muslim Brothers or simply as the "Ikhwan" (i.e. The Brethren.) One who belongs to or follows the Muslim Brotherhood can be called an Ikhwani. This is not to be confused with a revolt in Arabia of the same name.

Islam: The religion founded by the Prophet Mohammed.

Islamist: An Islamist is one who would impose any given interpretation of politicized Islam over society by law. For Islamist groups such as ISIS, al Qaeda and the Muslim Brotherhood, this means a heavily politicized form of Islam which is Salafist, jihadist, and Takfirist. In short, it is a form of theocratic extremism with a distinctive relationship with violence.

Islamophobia: This is a highly-contested term. To some, it is simply the dislike of or prejudice against Islam or Muslims, especially as a political force. To others, it is a blunt tool of oppression used to silence anyone who is critical of extremist Islamist organization such as the Muslim Brotherhood, Hizb ut-Tahrir or similar groups.

Jihad: This is perhaps the most overworked and misused term in all discussion surrounding Islam and Islamists. To the Islamists such as al-Qaeda and the Muslim Brotherhood, jihad is war in both the defensive and offensive sense of the term. It is an obligatory act for all Muslims. This obligation is 'fardh

---

[879] See, among many other articles, *'Lessons from the Struggle for the Fourth International, The 'French Turn'* which is available online at http://www.bolshevik.org/1917/no9/no09frnt.html .

[880] For more on this term see http://www.terrorismanalysts.com/pt/index.php/pot/article/view/67/html .

ain'. Permission from parents or other relatives is not required if the jihadist is of an age of understanding. The aim of jihad is to achieve Muslim dominance over Daru Islam. Armed jihad is the highest form of jihad and should be undertaken against all enemies of Islam. This includes infidels, polytheists, as well as those who support them. When the term is used by more humanist scholars, the concept of jihad refers to 'striving for excellence'. There are multiple goals for this form of jihad. Among them are jihad for goodness (al khair), human development, prosperity, education, family, friendship, and nation-building. There is also jihad against the human condition as well. This includes jihad against evil (asy-syarr), one's inner self, and intrusions upon one's laziness, stupidity, hatred, and arrogance.[881]

Jamaat-e-Islami: Founded in 1941 in what was then British India, this group is an Islamic political organization with strong and often austere views. It was founded by Abul A'la Maududi and is often referred to as the Muslim Brotherhood in South Asia.

Khomeneist: One who follows the teachings of the Shia Ayatollah Khomeini (1902-1989). Khomeneist beliefs are the founding ideology of the Islamic Republic of Iran. In this system, the Supreme Leader of Iran is an Ayatollah who is referred to as "the Jurist." The President of Iran and its Parliament are subject to the rulings of the Jurist. Among other beliefs, the Iranian Constitution believes that the Jurist (currently Ayatollah Khamenei) is a placeholder who sits in this position until the return of the Mahdi or savior. Iran, therefore, is a theocratic regime.

Lawfare: This is the use or misuse of the law to silence critics or drive them into submission rather than using other means such as civil discourse or discussion. Islamist groups in North America regularly use well-funded lawfare cases to silence or frighten those who expose their extremist beliefs.

Mullah Syndrome: The tendency of government officials, especially policy makers, police, and intelligence agencies, to engage with predominantly Islamist/conservative Muslim groups at the expense of ignoring the larger population of secular and humanist Muslims. This syndrome has played into the hand of Islamist organizations.[882]

Muslim: One who self-identifies religious as a follower of Islam.

Muslim Brotherhood: An Islamic organization founded by Hassan al-Banna in Egypt in 1928. Its orientation is Islamist, Salafist, Takfirist, and Jihadist. It is often seen as the well spring of ideology for almost all other Islamist organizations.

Niqab: This is a veil worn by Muslim women in public which covers all the face except the eyes. For some, it is an article of clothing of choice for Muslim women. For others, it is the uniform of militant Islam.

Political Correctness: This is a belief system or philosophy that believes "the idea that people should be careful to not use language or behave in a way that could offend a particular group of people."[883] A culture

---

[881] For more in this term see http://www.terrorismanalysts.com/pt/index.php/pot/article/view/67/html .

[882] This term appears to have been coined Naser Khader who served as a member of the Conservative Party in the Danish Parliament. Outside of politics, Khader's main research areas include freedom of speech and the fight for democracy and democratic values in multicultural societies. For more on him see the Hudson Institute at http://www.hudson.org/experts/660-naser-khader . For more on Mullah Syndrome see Dr. Lorenzo Vidino, *The New Muslim Brotherhood in the West*, Columbia University Press, New York, 2010, Chapter Four.

[883] See the Meriam Webster dictionary definition at http://www.merriam-webster.com/dictionary/politically%20correct .

of extreme political correctness is now used in the media and universities as a means of shutting down any discussion on any topic to enforce the orthodoxy of beliefs as determined by those using political correctness as a weapon. It has now become the exact opposite of freedom of thought and freedom of speech which underlies democracy, secularism, and humanism.

Political Islam: It is the belief that Islam is a political ideology, as well as a faith. It is a modernist claim that political sovereignty belongs to God, that the Shari'ah should be used as state law, that Muslims form a political rather than a religious bloc around the world and that it is a religious duty for all Muslims to create a political entity that is governed as such. Islamism is a spectrum, with Islamists disagreeing over how they should bring their 'Islamic' state into existence. (Quillian Foundation Definition)

Reformation: "The Protestant Reformation (~ 1517-1648) was a major 16th century European movement aimed initially at reforming the beliefs and practices of the Roman Catholic Church. Its religious aspects were supplemented by ambitious political rulers who wanted to extend their power and control at the expense of the Church. The Reformation ended the unity imposed by medieval Christianity and, in the eyes of many historians, signaled the beginning of the modern era. A weakening of the old order was already under way in Northern Europe, as evidenced by the emergence of thriving new cities and a determined middle class. Popular belief holds that the Reformation started when Martin Luther, a German Augustinian monk, posted his 95 theses on a church door in the university town of Wittenberg.[884]

Renaissance: Literally "rebirth," the Renaissance Aga was a period in European civilization immediately following the Middle Ages. It is conventionally held to have been characterized by a surge of interest in Classical scholarship and values after a long period of cultural decline and stagnation.[885]

Salafi: A Salafist in one who believes that Islam should be constructed around an idealist and often fantasist interpretation of how Islam operated in the first three generations after the death of the Prophet. Their views are austere, misogynistic, and totalitarian while being strongly opposed to democracy, secularism, and humanism. Many, but not all, Salafis believe in the use of violence to support their views.

Shaheed or Istisyhad: Islamist theorists argue that an individual becomes a shaheed or 'martyr' by the act of suicide bombing. This istimate (suicide act) is part of their hijrah or migration to God. They believe that they will be rewarded in heaven for this action. Humanist scholars in Islam tend to believe that dying in the defence of Islam when an Islamic majority land is invaded constitutes martyrdom. However, they also believe that suicide is strongly forbidden in the Quran and Hadith. Allah has granted you a body. Only Allah can decide when the body will be taken back. There are no justifications for exceptions to this rule. Lives, be they human or others, are sacred, and must be honoured. Whoever commits suicide will be considered eternally committed to hellfire. Once in hell, the individual will spend the rest of eternity dying repeatedly in the same way they committed suicide. Therefore, suicide bombers will spend the rest of eternity having their arms, legs and head pulled off.[886]

Shia: The largest single minority within Islam are the Shia. This order or denomination believes that they trace their roots and legitimacy back to the Prophet's son-in-law and cousin Ali ibn Abi Talib. They are

---

[884] For more on the Reformation, see, among many others, the Theopedia entry at http://www.theopedia.com/protestant-reformation .

[885] For a brief description of the Renaissance, see http://www.britannica.com/event/Renaissance .

[886] For more on this term see http://www.terrorismanalysts.com/pt/index.php/pot/article/view/67/html .

frequently in conflict with the Sunnis and the main dividing concept is who was the legitimate successor to the Prophet.

Sufi: The more esoteric or mystic form of Sunni Islam is called Sufism. There are a variety of orders, each with a master or "sheik" who is presumably one of a series of scholars and teachers who can track his origins back to the time of the Prophet. Other Muslims often persecute Sufis as they are seen as heretics or non-believers.

Sunni: The largest order or denomination within Islam are the Sunnis. They believe that they trace their roots and legitimacy to the first Islamic Caliph Abu Bakr who was the father-in-law of the Prophet. The Sunni conflict with the Shia lies ion who they believe was the legitimate successor to the Prophet.

Submission: The word Islam is believed to originate from the Arabic word "al-Salaam." Depending on linguistics and political views, the word Islam can translate into either Peace or Submission. For the Islamists, the term means submission as they believe that (quite literally) everyone must submit themselves to the will of Allah in accordance with their politicized interpretation of Islam.

Takfir: According to Islamist theorists, Takfir is the action of accusing others of being infidels or non-believers. This is considered a very serious act. Groups such as ISIS, Al-Qaeda and the Muslim Brotherhood have regularly employed the term to discredit or disparage other Muslims who oppose them. By doing so, fellow Muslims are now turned into enemies. In more mainstream and humanist circles it is believed that the act of declaring someone Takfir should only be undertaken under the gravest of circumstances and then only by a very senior authority acting on the larger will of the affected population.[887]

Ummah (also Uma and Umah): The Ummah is the collective community of all Muslims. The rules for the Ummah are those of the "rightful way." Anyone who follows the "rightful way" is a member of the chosen community. According to Islamist theorists, anyone who does not believe or follow the rules is a non-believer. Every Muslim must follow the Ummah, but if the states in which they live are run by non-believers, Muslims do not have to follow the laws of those states.[888]

Wahhabism: This is a religious movement within the Sunni branch of Islam. It is the predominant form of the Sunni faith in Saudi Arabia. Extremely austere in its outlook, it was founded in the 18th Century by Muhammad ibn Abd al-Wahhab who lived from 1703 to 1792. The government of Saudi Arabia 'exports' Wahhabism through a variety of financial and operational means. It has significant influence in Qatar as well as part of Africa and Asia. In the West, an increasing number of mosques have Wahhabist Imams 'provided' to them by Saudi money or influence.

---

[887] For more on this term see http://www.terrorismanalysts.com/pt/index.php/pot/article/view/67/html .

[888] For more on this term see http://www.terrorismanalysts.com/pt/index.php/pot/article/view/67/html.

ANNEX B: SOURCE RELIABILITY AND INFORMATION CREDIBILITY RATING SYSTEM

A Revised and Updated Admiralty Rating System

Rick Gill

Key Points

- Since its initial development in the 1940s during World War Two, the original UK Admiralty rating system for source reliability and information credibility has remained unchanged in its original form until 2006.

- Little or no details have ever been provided on the use of the UK Admiralty rating system. Coupled with users' tendencies to correlate source reliability ratings with information credibility ratings, these factors have led to little or no use of this rating system in recent years.

- Revisions to this rating system which first began appearing in 2006 in U.S., NATO and other national military doctrinal and open-source publications have begun to make useful improvements to this (now) seven-decade old rating system.

- This revised and updated version of the original UK Admiralty rating system serves to identify ratings of sources and information will be used throughout this publication.

In the second edition of his book[889] published in 2015, Dr. Prunckun expanded upon his earlier work, addressing issues related to the potential for deception by the source, in addition to misinformation and disinformation. He did this by including additional ratings in both source and information categories to indicate:

- A source which is either "unintentionally misleading" or "deliberately deceptive", and

- Information which is either "misinformation" or "disinformation".

In his 2015 second edition of his book, Dr. Prunckun included new source ratings of F-G and information ratings of 6-7, pushing back the original "F" and "6" ratings of "Cannot be Judged" to "H" and "8", respectively. We believe that this change causes issues of backward compatibility with the original Admiralty rating system, for its many long-time military and other users, who easily remember the meaning of a rating of "F6" as "source reliability and information credibility cannot be judged".

Initial thoughts on adopting Dr. Prunckun's additions to the Admiralty rating system were to leave "F" and "6" where they were in the UK Admiralty rating system, and added his additional ratings for "Unintentionally Misleading" (F) and "Deliberately Deceptive" (G) for source reliability, and "Misinformation" (6) and "Deception" (7) below "F" and "6". These modifications would retitle his additional ratings to "Unintentionally Misleading" (G) and "Deliberately Deceptive" (H) for source reliability, and "Misinformation" (7) and "Deception" (8). This modification to Dr. Prunckun's revised UK

---

889 Hank Prunckun, *Scientific Methods of Inquiry for Intelligence Analysis.* Second Edition (Lanham, MD: Rowman & Littlefield, 2015.), 53-54. **Rated A1.**

Admiralty rating system would now keep his revisions backwardly compatible with the original UK Admiralty rating system.

Subsequent discussions with colleagues in the Defence Research and Development, and Security and Intelligence communities decided that Dr. Prunckun's ratings and descriptions of "Unintentionally Misleading" (F) and "Deliberately Deceptive" (G) for source reliability, and "Misinformation" (6) and "Deception" (7) were in fact regarded as subsets of the categories "Unreliable (E) and "Improbable" (5). Dr. Prunckun's descriptions for his additional ratings of "Unintentionally Misleading" and "Deliberately Deceptive" for source reliability, and "Misinformation" and "Deception" have now been included under "Unreliable" (E) and "Improbable" (5) in the revised UK Admiralty rating system used in this publication.

Background

The first known source reliability and information accuracy (credibility) rating system was developed by the UK Royal Navy's Admiralty staff during the Battle of the Atlantic in World War Two. The Admiralty staff needed a method by which they could systematically evaluate and rate mass volumes of reporting being received from a wide variety of sources. What quickly became known as the Admiralty Source Reliability and Information Accuracy rating system (shown below) was developed at that time, and subsequently adopted for use in subsequent years by British and other NATO military forces.

Evaluation of Source Reliability

Code: Description

- A: Reliable
- B: Usually Reliable
- C: Fairly Reliable
- D: Not Usually Reliable
- E: Unreliable
- F: Cannot be Judged

Evaluation of Information Accuracy

Code: Description

- 1: Confirmed
- 2: Probably True
- 3: Possibly True
- 4: Doubtfully True
- 5: Improbable
- 6: Cannot be Judged

A report or information received would be rated for source reliability and information accuracy by a combination of the letter-number codes shown above. For example:

> A report or information received from a source that is "**usually reliable**" and whose information provided at that point in time is believed to be "**probably true**" would be rated as "**B2**".

Since its initial development, the original Admiralty rating system shown above has been published in British, U.S., Canadian and other NATO nations' doctrinal publications "as-is" for nearly six decades. Other than one or two examples like that provided above, the Admiralty rating system in these various doctrinal publications were accompanied by little or no explanation on how to effectively select ratings using this system.

Research, Revisions, and Updates

U.S. Army research[890] conducted in 1975 on the use of the Admiralty rating system conducted found:

> "About one-fourth of the [37] subjects treated reliability and accuracy as independent dimensions; the majority treated reliability as highly correlated with accuracy, and their judgement of a report's truth was influenced more strongly by its accuracy rating. Numerical (probabilistic) interpretations of scale levels were consistent within individuals but varied widely between them. Development of a new scale is suggested."

This revised and updated Source Reliability and Information Credibility rating system provided below are an amalgam of the U.S. doctrinal publications discussed above, and rearranged additional elements of that published by Dr. Prunckun in 2015. This source reliability and information credibility rating system is backwardly compatible with both the original UK Admiralty rating system, and recent military doctrinal updates to the UK Admiralty rating system. Source reliability and information credibility ratings used in this and subsequent publications will be indicated in bold, to clearly delineate ratings from a document's content, citations, footnotes, or endnotes. Examples of this are "**rated B2**" (source is usually reliable; information is probably true), "**rated C4**" (source is fairly reliable; however, this information is doubtful), and "**rated F6**" (source reliability and information credibility cannot be judged). This revised source reliability and information credibility rating system tables will be included as an annex or appendix in all publications and other products.

Implications

These enhancements to the original UK Admiralty rating system and its use in this publication intend to provide readers with the best possible understanding of the authors' deliberations about sources being cited and information provided by those sources.

The Revised and Updated Admiralty Rating System

Source Reliability

Code: Description: Issues to be considered by Users when selecting a Rating

- **A: Completely Reliable:** No doubt of source's authenticity, trustworthiness, or competency; source has a history of complete reliability.
- **B: Usually Reliable:** Minor doubt about source's authenticity, trustworthiness, or competency; source has a history of valid information most of the time.
- **C: Fairly Reliable:** Doubt of source's authenticity, trustworthiness, or competency, but source has provided valid information in the past.
- **D: Not Usually Reliable:** Significant doubt about source's authenticity, trustworthiness, or competency, but source has provided valid information in the past.

---

[890] Michael G. Samet, Technical Paper 260 "Subjective Interpretation of Reliability and Accuracy Scales for Evaluating Military Intelligence", *U.S. Army Research Institute for the Behavioral and Social Sciences*, January 1975, accessed 23 May 2017. http://www.dtic.mil/dtic/tr/fulltext/u2/a003260.pdf **Rated B1.**

- **E: Unreliable:** Lacking authenticity, trustworthiness, and competency; the source has a history of invalid information. Alternately, the source is unintentionally misleading or deliberately deceptive, having been contradicted by other independent and reliable sources on the same subject.
- **F: Reliability Cannot Be Judged:** No basis exists for evaluating the reliability of the source.

In every instance, the ratings above are based on previous reporting from that source. If there has been no prior reporting, the source must initially be rated "F". **NOTE:** An "F" rating does not mean that the source cannot be trusted, but that there is no reporting history and therefore no basis for making any other determination.

Information Credibility

Code: Description: Issues to be considered by Users when selecting a Rating

- **1: Confirmed by Other Sources:** Confirmed by other independent sources; logical by itself; consistent with other information on the subject.
- **2: Probably True:** Not confirmed; logical by itself; consistent with other information on the subject.
- **3: Possibly True:** Not confirmed; reasonably logical by itself; agrees with some other information on the subject.
- **4: Doubtful:** Not confirmed; possible but not logical; no other information on the subject.
- **5: Improbable:** Not confirmed; not logical by itself; contradicted by other information on the subject. Alternately, the information is unintentionally false or deliberately false, having been contradicted by other independent and confirmed information on the same subject.
- **6: Truth Cannot Be Judged:** No basis exists for evaluating the validity of the information.

The highest degree of confidence in reported information (1) is given to that which has been confirmed by other sources. The table above provides the evaluated ratings for information credibility. The degree of confidence decreases if the information is not confirmed, and/or does not logically make sense. **The evaluated rating of "5" means that the information is evaluated as false; unintentionally false, or deliberately false.** **NOTE:** A rating of "6" does not necessarily mean false information, but is generally used to indicate that no determination can be made since the information is completely new.

ANNEX C: STRUCTURED ANALYTIC TECHNIQUES (SATS)

Rick Gill

Key Points[891]

- Structured analytic techniques are debiasing techniques; they assist the analyst in overcoming their cognitive biases.
- Structured analytic techniques do not replace intuitive judgement.
- The role of structured analytic techniques is to question intuitive judgements being made, by identifying a wider range of options for the analyst to consider.
- The structured analytic techniques detailed in this annex were used during the writing of this book.

Background

The first use of the term "structured analytic techniques" in the US Intelligence Community was noted in 2005. However, the origin of the concept goes back to the 1980s, when the eminent teacher of intelligence analysis at the CIA, Jack Davis, first began teaching and writing about what he called "alternative analysis".

In 1975, after 24 years at the CIA, Richards J. Heuer, Jr. moved from operations to the (then) new Analytic Methodology Division[892]. During the annual International Studies Association convention in 1977, Richards J. Heuer was introduced to the ground-breaking research in cognitive psychology by Daniel Kahneman and Amos Tversky. Heuer's review of Kahneman and Tversky's research on cognitive psychology was the beginning of his personal interest in this field of study. Heuer retired in 1979 after 28 years of service with the CIA, continuing his work on analytic and cognitive psychology issues as a CIA contractor.

Heuer's studies and writings over the next two decades included the development in the mid-1980s of an interagency course on deception analysis. He stated in his 2009 presentation The Evolution of Structured Analytic Techniques[893] that his Analysis of Competing Hypotheses methodology was the centerpiece of this course. Heuer's Psychology of Intelligence Analysis[894] was first published by the Center for the Study of Intelligence in 1999. Chapter 6, Keeping an Open Mind, Heuer speaks to various aspects of mindsets. On this subject, Heuer states:

> Beliefs, assumptions, concepts, and information retrieved from memory form a mind-set or mental model that guides perception and processing of new information.

---

[891] Richards J. Heuer, Jr., and Randolph H. Pherson. "Structured analytic techniques for intelligence analysis, Second Edition" *Thousand Oaks CA: CQ Press*, 2015, 6. **Rated A1.**

[892] Richards J. Heuer, Jr., "The Evolution of Structured Analytic Techniques" presentation, *National Academy of Science, National Research Council Committee on Behavioral and Social Science Research to Improve Intelligence Analysis for National Security*, Washington, DC, 8 December 2009. Accessed 5 June 2017. https://www.e-education.psu.edu/geog885/sites/www.e-education.psu.edu.geog885/files/file/Evolution_SAT_Heuer.pdf **Rated A1.**

[893] Heuer, "The Evolution of Structured Analytic Techniques", 2009. **Rated A1.**

[894] Richards J. Heuer Jr., "Psychology of Intelligence Analysis", *Center for the Study of Intelligence, Central Intelligence Agency*, 1999. Accessed 6 June 2017. https://www.cia.gov/library/center-for-the-study-of-intelligence/csi-publications/books-and-monographs/psychology-of-intelligence-analysis **Rated A1.**

> A mind-set is neither good nor bad. It is unavoidable. It is, in essence, a distillation of all that analysts think they know about a subject. It forms a lens through which they perceive the world, and once formed, it resists change.

Analysts must maintain an open mind, and constantly be aware of their personal beliefs and mindsets; how they are affecting their judgement, and assumptions they are making at any point in time. In chapter 6, Heuer discusses cognitive biases; his initial defining thoughts on this subject were:

> Cognitive biases are mental errors caused by our simplified information processing strategies. It is important to distinguish cognitive biases from other forms of bias, such as cultural bias, organizational bias, or bias that results from one's own self-interest. In other words, a cognitive bias does not result from any emotional or intellectual predisposition toward a certain judgment, but rather from subconscious mental procedures for processing information. A cognitive bias is a mental error that is consistent and predictable.

The ability to think creatively and critically, combined with the use of structured analytic technqiues, allow the analyst to systematically produce well-developed, rational and logical answers to analytic problems. It is for this reason that this annex on Structured Analytic Techniques has been included in this work.

In chapter 8, Heuer described his methodology Analysis of Competing Hypotheses (ACH). No doubt due to his earlier interest in the work of Kahneman and Tversky, chapters 8 through 13 addressed various aspects of cognitive biases, and how they relate to the analysis of intelligence. Heuer's Psychology of Intelligence Analysis is now also commercially available in hardcopy and Kindle formats through Amazon.[895]

The US government published A Tradecraft Primer: Structured Analytic Techniques for Improving Intelligence Analysis on 4 May 2009.[896] It is now also commercially available in hardcopy and Kindle formats through Amazon[897]. In 2010, Heuer collaborated with Randy Pherson to produce and publish the first edition of the widely acclaimed Structured Analytic Techniques for Intelligence Analysis.[898] This publication is one of the few commercially available references on the subject of structured analytic techniques.

Other methodologies and techniques that are today known as structured analytic techniques come from a variety of other areas. For example, the technique of brainstorming[899] originated in business advertising and marketing circles. The term "brainstorming" was popularized by Alex Faickney Osborn in the 1953 book Applied Imagination. The use of a "Devil's Advocate"[900] originated with the Roman Catholic Church beginning in the late sixteenth century, as part of the church's canonization process.

---

[895] Richards J. Heuer Jr., "Psychology of Intelligence Analysis", *Center for the Study of Intelligence, Central Intelligence Agency*, 1999. Accessed 6 June 2017. https://www.amazon.ca/Psychology-Intelligence-Analysis-Richard-Heuer/dp/1907521046 **Rated A1.**

[896] United States Government, *A Tradecraft Primer: Structured Analytic Techniques for Improving Intelligence Analysis*, (Washington: Center for the Study of Intelligence, March 2009), accessed 6 June 2017, https://www.cia.gov/library/publications/publications-rss-updates/tradecraft-primer-may-4-2009.html **Rated A1.**

[897] United States Government, *A Tradecraft Primer: Structured Analytic Techniques for Improving Intelligence Analysis, Amazon.com*, March 2009, accessed 6 June 2017, https://www.amazon.com/Tradecraft-Primer-Structured-Techniques-Intelligence/dp/1478361182 **Rated B1.**

[898] Richards J. Heuer, Jr., and Randolph H. Pherson. *Structured analytic techniques for intelligence analysis, Second Edition* (Thousand Oaks CA: CQ Press, 2015) **Rated A1.**

[899] Wikipedia contributors, "Brainstorming," Wikipedia, The Free Encyclopedia. Accessed 6 June 2017. https://en.wikipedia.org/w/index.php?title=Brainstorming&oldid=782442844 **Rated B1.**

[900] Wikipedia contributors, "Devil's advocate," Wikipedia, The Free Encyclopedia. Accessed

Analytic Problems

A favourite analogy which aptly describes often complex problems faced by analysts is described in this way:

- An analytic problem is like a thousand-piece puzzle box, with no picture of the completed puzzle on the cover of the box;
- Upon opening the puzzle box, it is discovered that there are far less then a thousand pieces in the box. The puzzle pieces represent evidence or answers to the problem which the analyst is attempting to solve. The apparent lack of many pieces of the puzzle is indicative of the reality that the analyst is highly unlikely to ever have all the answers to his or her analytic problem;
- Some of the pieces in the puzzle box also have no part of the overall picture on them. This represents a lack of understanding by the analyst of the meaning of these pieces of evidence;
- Many of the pieces in the puzzle box are obviously a different size and shape compared to most other puzzle pieces in the box. This represents extraneous information which has been collected, ("white noise") that has little or nothing to do with the analytic problem;
- Despite all the above, the goal of the analyst is to provide answers to the questions posed by the analytic problem, and typically within (often short) time constraints imposed by management, consumers, and decision makers.

As stated by Heuer and Pherson in the second edition of their influential reference publication Structured Analytic Techniques for Intelligence Analysis[901]:

> "No formula exists, of course, for always getting it right, but the use of structured analytic techniques can reduce the frequency and severity of errors. These technqiues can help analysts mitigate the proven cognitive limitations, sidestep some of the known analytic biases, and explicitly confront the problems associated with unquestioned mental models or mindsets. They help analysts think more rigorously about an analytic problem and ensure that preconceptions and assumptions are not taken for granted but are explicitly examined and, when possible, tested."

Starting an Analytic Project

At the beginning of an analytic project, analysts are always wise to consider brainstorming and assumptions checks to insure that important factors are not being missed or taken for granted. Similarly, outside-in-thinking can sometimes put an analytic project into a broader international context, in which factors outside the lead analyst's area of responsibility might impact on his or her analytic judgments. For instance, economic assumptions about the price of oil might be key to a regional political analyst's understanding the prospects for political stability in an oil-exporting country or a underdeveloped country entirely dependent on expensive energy imports. A High-Impact/Low-Probability assessment can also sensitize analysts early on to the significance of dramatic events that might affect their analytic lines.

Some techniques like Indicators or Analysis of Competing Hypotheses (ACH) can be useful throughout a project and revisited periodically as new information is absorbed and analyzed. ACH, in particular, is a

---

June 6, 2017. https://en.wikipedia.org/wiki/Devil%27s_advocate **Rated B1.**

[901] Heuer and Pherson. *Structured analytic techniques*, 7.

good tool to use throughout a project to prevent premature closure and to highlight evidence that is most "discriminating" in making an analytic argument.

Selected Structured Analytic Techniques

A selection of the structured analytic techniques used at various stages in the preparation of this book are described below. The vast majority of the information on the techniques detailed below has been drawn from:

- Heuer's Psychology of Intelligence Analysis, 1999;
- United States Government's A Tradecraft Primer: Structured Analytic Techniques for Improving Intelligence Analysis, 4 May 2009, and
- Heuer and Pherson's Structured Analytic Technqiues for Intelligence Analysis, second edition, 2015.

Brainstorming

An unconstrained group process designed to generate new ideas and concepts.[902]

When to Use

Brainstorming is a widely used technique for stimulating new thinking. Typically, analysts will conduct a brainstorming session beginning a new project to help generate a range of ideas and hypotheses about the subject at hand.

Brainstorming, almost by definition, involves a group of analysts meeting to discuss a common challenge. This modest investment of time at the beginning or critical points of a project can take advantage of the range of different perspectives to help structure a problem. This group process allows others to build on an initial idea suggested by a member of the brainstorming session.

Analysts can also brainstorm on their own to produce a range of ideas, without regard for others' egos, opinions, or objections. However, analysts will not have the benefit of others' perspectives in helping to develop their ideas. An individual may have difficulty breaking free of his or her own cognitive biases without the benefit of a diverse group. See Timeline for Using Structured Analytic Techniques graphic above.

Benefits

This technique can maximize creativity in the thinking process, forcing analysts to avoid their personal judgments about their individual ideas or approaches. More generally, brainstorming allows analysts to see a wider range of factors that might bear on the topic than they would otherwise consider. Analysts typically censor out ideas that seem farfetched, poorly sourced, or seemingly irrelevant to the question at hand. Brainstorming gives permission to think more radically or "outside the box." It can spark new ideas, ensure a comprehensive look at a problem or issues, raise unknowns, and prevent premature consensus around a single hypothesis.

Related Techniques

As seen above, structured brainstorming is also known as Divergent/Convergent Thinking. Other forms of brainstorming include Virtual Brainstorming, which is typically conducted online by participants in

---

[902] United States Government, *A Tradecraft Primer: Structured Analytic Techniques for Improving Intelligence Analysis*, (Washington: Center for the Study of Intelligence, March 2009), 27. **Rated A1.**

distributed locations. The Nominal Group Technique is also recommended, to ensure that all participants' insights and choices are given equal weight in group decisions.

Indicators

Periodically review a list of observable incidents or trends to track events, monitor targets, spot emerging trends, and warn of unforeseen change.

When to Use

An individual or a team can create an indicators or signposts list of observable events that one would expect to see if a postulated situation is developing; e.g., economic reform, military modernization, political instability, or democratization. Constructing the list might require only a few hours or as much as several days to identify the critical variables associated with the specific issue. The technique can be used whenever someone needs to track an event over time to monitor and evaluate changes. However, it can also be a very powerful aid in supporting other structured methods explained later in this primer. In those instances, an individual or team would be watching for mounting evidence to support a particular hypothesis, low-probability event, or scenario. See Timeline for Using Structured Analytic Techniques graphic above.

Benefits

By providing an objective baseline for tracking events or targets, indicators instill rigor into the analytic process and enhance the credibility of analytic judgments. An indicators list included in a finished product also allows the decisionmaker to track developments and builds a more concrete case for the analytic judgments. By laying out a list of critical variables, an individual or team also will be generating hypotheses regarding why they expect to see the presence of such factors. In so doing, analysts make the analytic line much more transparent and available for scrutiny by others.

Related Techniques

See What if? Analysis.

Key Assumptions Check

Analytic judgements are always based on a combination of evidence and assumptions, or preconceived ideas, which influence how the analyst interprets evidence. The Key Assumptions Check is structured process to clearly state and questions assumptions that guide the analyst's comprehension of evidence and reasoning about the problem at hand. The Key Assumptions Check is one of most commonly used structured analytic techniques, because the analyst typically need to make assumptions to fill gaps in his or her knowledge.

When to Use

A Key Assumptions Check is most useful at the beginning of an analytic project. An individual analyst or a team can spend an hour or two articulating and reviewing the key assumptions. Rechecking assumptions also can be valuable at any time prior to finalizing judgments, to ensure that the assessment does not rest on flawed premises. Identifying hidden assumptions can be one of the most difficult challenges some individual faces, as they are ideas held—often unconsciously—to be true and, therefore, are seldom examined and almost never challenged.

A key assumption is any hypothesis that analysts or a group have accepted to be true and which forms the basis of the assessment. For example, military analysis may focus exclusively on analyzing key technical and military variables (sometimes called factors) of a military force and "assume" that these forces will be operated in a physical environment (desert, open plains, arctic conditions, etc.). Postulating other conditions or assumptions, however, could dramatically impact the assessment. Historically, analysis of Soviet-Warsaw Pact operations against NATO had to "assume" a level of non-Soviet Warsaw Pact reliability (e.g., would these forces fight?). In this case, there was high uncertainty and depending on what level of reliability one assumed, the analyst could arrive at very different conclusions about a potential Soviet offensive operation. Or when economists assess the prospects for foreign economic reforms, they may consciously, or not, assume a degree of political stability in those countries or the region that may or may not exist in the future.

Likewise, political analysts reviewing a developing country's domestic stability might unconsciously assume stable oil prices, when this key determinant of economic performance and underlying social peace might fluctuate. All of these examples highlight the fact that analysts often rely on stated and unstated assumptions to conduct their analysis. The goal is not to undermine or abandon key assumptions; rather, it is to make them explicit and identify what information or developments would demand rethinking them. See Timeline for Using Structured Analytic Techniques above.

Benefits

Explicitly identifying working assumptions during an analytic project helps:

- Explain the logic of the analytic argument and expose faulty logic;
- Understand the key factors that shape an issue;
- Stimulate thinking about an issue;
- Uncover hidden relationships and links between key factors;
- Identify developments that would cause you to abandon an assumption, and
- Prepare analysts for changed circumstances that could surprise them.

Related Techniques

Heuer and Pherson suggest that some form of brainstorming is normally used in generating indicators by a group or team, to gain insight from different perspectives and specialities. "What If?" Analysis and High Impact / Low Probability Analysis depend on the development and use of indicators. Indicators are often entered as items of relevant information in Analysis of Competing Hypotheses (ACH) when generating and testing hypotheses. Heuer and Pherson have also developed the Indicators Validator tm as a tool used in testing the diagnosticity of indicators; see page 157 in their publication.

Chronologies and Timelines

A chronology is a list that place events or actions in the order in which they occurred. A timeline is a graphic depiction of those events put in context of the time of the events and the time between events.[903]

When to Use

Whenever it is important to understand the sequence and timing of events; to identify gaps in time or between events, and key events. See Timeline for Using Structured Analytic Techniques graphic above.

Benefits

[903] Richards J. Heuer, Jr., and Randolph H. Pherson. *Structured analytic techniques for intelligence analysis, Second Edition* (Thousand Oaks CA: CQ Press, 2015), 56. **Rated A1.**

Chronologies and timelines assist in pattern analysis and the relationship between events. These techniques assist the analyst in making connections between events and the bigger picture. Multiple-level timelines or "swim lanes" allow analysts to track concurrent activities or events that may influence one another. Chronologies and timelines can lead an analyst or analysts to hypothesize the existence of previously unknown events. A series of known events may only make sense if other previously unknown events have also occurred. Finally, chronologies and timelines can be very useful in organizing information in ways that can be easily understood in a briefing.

"What-If?" Analysis

Assumes that an event has occurred with potential (negative or positive) impact and explains how it might come about.

When to Use

"What If?" analysis is another contrarian technique for challenging a strong mind-set that an event will not happen or that a confidently made forecast may not be entirely justified. It is similar to a High-Impact/Low-Probability analysis, but it does not dwell on the consequences of the event as much as it accepts the significance and moves directly to explaining how it might come about. See Timeline for Using Structured Analytic Techniques graphic above.

Benefits

By shifting the focus from whether an event could occur to how it may happen, analysts allow themselves to suspend judgment about the likelihood of the event and focus more on what developments - even unlikely ones - might enable such an outcome. An individual analyst or a team might employ this technique and repeat the exercise whenever a critical analytic judgment is made.

Using this technique is particularly important when a judgment rests on limited information or unproven assumptions. Moreover, it can free analysts from arguing about the probability of an event to considering its consequences and developing some indicators or signposts for its possible emergence. It will help analysts address the impact of an event, the factors that could cause or alter it, and likely signposts that an event is imminent.

A "What If?" analysis can complement a difficult judgment reached and provide the policymaker a thoughtful caution to accepting the conventional wisdom without considering the costs and risks of being wrong. This can help decision-makers consider ways to hedge their bets, even if they accept the analytic judgment that an event remains unlikely.

Related Techniques

High-Impact / Low-Probability analysis.

Analysis of Competing Hypotheses (ACH)

Identification of alternative explanations (hypotheses) and evaluation of all evidence that will disconfirm rather than confirm hypotheses.

When to Use

Analysis of Competing Hypotheses (ACH) has proved to be a highly effective technique when there is a large amount of data to absorb and evaluate. While a single analyst can use ACH, it is most effective with a small team that can challenge each other's evaluation of the evidence. Developing a matrix of hypotheses and loading already collected information into the matrix can be accomplished in a day or less. If the data must be reassembled, the initial phases of the ACH process may require additional time. Sometimes a facilitator or someone familiar with the technique can lead new analysts through this process for the first time.

ACH is particularly appropriate for controversial issues when analysts want to develop a clear record that shows what theories they have considered and how they arrived at their judgments. Developing the ACH matrix allows other analysts (or even policymakers) to review their analysis and identify areas of agreement and disagreement. Evidence can also be examined more systematically, and analysts have found that this makes the technique ideal for considering the possibility of deception and denial. See Timeline for Using Structured Analytic Techniques graphic above.

Benefits

ACH helps analysts overcome three common mistakes that can lead to inaccurate forecasts:

- Analysts often are susceptible to being unduly influenced by a first impression, based on incomplete data, an existing analytic line, or a single explanation that seems to fit well enough.
- Analysts seldom generate a full set of explanations or hypotheses at the outset of a project.
- Analysts often rely on evidence to support their preferred hypothesis, but which also is consistent with other explanations.

Essentially, ACH helps analysts to avoid picking the first solution that seems satisfactory instead of going through all the possibilities to arrive at the very best solution.

Related Techniques

ACH is often used in conjunction with other techniques. For example, Structured Brainstorming, Nominal Group Technique, the Multiple Hypotheses Generator tm or Delphi Method may be used to identify hypotheses or relevant information to be included in the ACH analysis, or to evaluate the significance of relevant information. Deception Detection may identify an opponent's motive, opportunity, or means to conduct deception, or past deception practices. Information about these factors should be included in the list of ACH-relevant information. The Diagnostic Reasoning technique is incorporated within the ACH method. The final step in the ACH method identifies indicators for monitoring future developments.

ACH Matrix Example - Am Shinrikyo Terrorism in Tokyo: In March 1995, a largely unknown group attacked the Tokyo subways by using a highly lethal nerve agent known as sarin. ACH provides a mechanism to carefully examine all the evidence and possible explanations for understanding what type of group could have been responsible. In simplified form, the above matrix arrays each piece of evidence on the vertical axis and then evaluates each in terms of the item's consistency with four possible explanations for the terrorist attack in Tokyo (horizontal axis). Analysts rate a piece of evidence as consistent (C); inconsistent (I); or neutral (N). This process allows analysts to see that some evidence will be consistent with more than one hypothesis and be less valuable in disproving hypotheses.

Devil's Advocacy

Challenging a single, strongly held view or consensus by building the best possible case for an alternative explanation.

When to Use

Devil's Advocacy[904] is most effective when used to challenge an analytic consensus or a key assumption regarding a critically important intelligence question. On those issues that one cannot afford to get wrong, Devil's Advocacy can provide further confidence that the current analytic line will hold up to close scrutiny. An individual analyst can often assume the role of the Devil's Advocate if he or she has some doubts about a widely held view, or a manager might designate a courageous analyst to challenge the prevailing wisdom to reaffirm the group's confidence in those judgments. In some cases, the analyst or a team can review a key assumption of a critical judgment during their work, or more likely, a separate analytic product can be generated that arrays all the arguments and data that support a contrary hypothesis. While this can involve some analytic time and effort, when a group of analysts have worked on an issue for a long period of time, it is probably wise to assume that a strong mind-set exists that deserves the closer scrutiny provided by Devil's Advocacy. See Timeline for Using Structured Analytic Techniques graphic above.

Benefits

Analysts have an obligation to policymakers to understand where their own analytic judgments might be weak and open to future challenge. Hence, the Devil's Advocacy process can highlight weaknesses in a current analytic judgment or alternatively help to reaffirm one's confidence in the prevailing judgments by:

- Explicitly challenging key assumptions to see if they will not hold up under some circumstances.
- Identifying any faulty logic or information that would undermine the key analytic judgments.
- Presenting alternative hypotheses that would explain the current body of information available to analysts.

Its primary value is to serve as a check on a dominant mind-set that can develop over time among even the best analysts who have followed an issue and formed strong consensus that there is only one way of looking at their issue. This mind-set phenomenon makes it more likely that contradictory evidence is dismissed or not given proper weight or consideration. An exercise aimed at highlighting such evidence and proposing another way of thinking about an issue can expose hidden assumptions and compel analysts to review their information with greater skepticism about their findings. The analyst could come away from the exercise more certain that:

- The current analytic line was sound;
- The argument is still the strongest, but that there are areas where further analysis is needed; or
- Some serious flaws in logic or supporting evidence suggest that the analytic line needs to be changed or at least caveated more heavily.

Related Techniques

Premortem Analysis, Structured Self-Critique.

Premortem Analysis

Used to reduce the risk of surprise and the subsequent need for a post-mortem examination of what went wrong. It is an easy-to-use technique that allows a group of analysts working on any future-oriented analysis of project to effectively challenge the accuracy of their own conclusions.

---

[904] United States Government, *A Tradecraft Primer: Structured Analytic Techniques for Improving Intelligence Analysis*, (Washington: Center for the Study of Intelligence, March 2009), 17. **Rated A1.**

When to Use

Premortem Analysis[905] should be used by analysts who can devote a few hours to challenging their own conclusions about the future to see where they might be wrong. It is most effective when used by a small group. A premortem as an analytic aid was first used in the context of decision making by Gary Klein in his 1998 book Sources of Power: How People Make Decision. See Timeline for Using Structured Analytic Techniques graphic above.

Benefits

The Premortem Analysis approach helps analysts identify potential causes of error that previously had been overlooked. There are two creative processes at work here. First, the questions are reframed; this exercise typically elicits responses that are different from the original ones. Second the premortem approach legitimizes dissent. For various reasons, many members of small groups suppress dissenting opinions, leading to premature consensus. Research has documented that an important cause of poor group decisions is the desire for consensus.

> It is not bigotry to be certain we are right; but it bigotry to be unable to imagine how we might possibly have gone wrong – G.K. Chesterton, English writer.

The primary value of Premortem Analysis is that it legitimizes dissent. Group members who may have previously suppressed opinions, questions, or doubts because they lack confidence are empowered by the technique to express previously hidden divergent thoughts. If this change in perspective is handled well, each group member will know that they have added value to the exercise for being critical of the previous judgement, not for supporting it.

Related Techniques

Reframing method, Nominal Group Technique, Structured Self-Critique.

Nominal Group Technique

A process for generating and evaluating ideas. It is a form of brainstorming, but Nominal Group Technique[906] has always had its own identity as a separate technique. The goals of Nominal Group Technique and Structured Brainstorming are the same – the generation of good, innovative, and viable ideas. The Nominal Group Technique was developed by A.L. Dulbecco and A.H. Van de Ven.[907]

When to Use

The Nominal Group Technique prevents the domination of a discussion by a single person. Use it whenever there is concern that a senior analyst, executive, or outspoken member of the group will control the direction of the meeting by speaking before anyone else. Conversely, it is also appropriate to use the Nominal Group Technique rather than Structured Brainstorming if there is concern that some members

---

905 Richards J. Heuer, Jr., and Randolph H. Pherson. *Structured analytic techniques for intelligence analysis, Second Edition* (Thousand Oaks CA: CQ Press, 2015), 240. **Rated A1.**

906 Richards J. Heuer, Jr., and Randolph H. Pherson. *Structured analytic techniques for intelligence analysis, Second Edition* (Thousand Oaks CA: CQ Press, 2015), 110. **Rated A1.**

907 A.L. Delbecq and A.H. Van de Ven, "A Group Process Model for Problem Identification and Program Planning," Journal of Applied Behavioural Science VII (July-August, 1971): 46-491, quoted in Richards J. Heuer, Jr., and Randolph H. Pherson. *Structured analytic techniques for intelligence analysis, Second Edition* (Thousand Oaks CA: CQ Press, 2015), 122. **Rated A1.**

of the group may not speak up; the session is likely to be dominated by the presence of one or two well-known experts in the field, or the issue under discussion in controversial, and may provoke heated debate.

Benefits

The Nominal Group Technique can be used to generate ideas, and to provide backup support in a decision-making process where all participants are asked to rank or prioritize the ideas that are generated. If necessary, all ideas and votes can be kept anonymous. Unlike Structured Brainstorming, which usually intends to generate the greatest possible number of ideas, the Nominal Group Technique may be used to focus on a limited number of carefully selected opinions or options.

The technique allows participants to focus on each idea as it is presented by the facilitator, rather than having to think simultaneously about preparing their own ideas and listening to what others are proposing. This situation often occurs with Structured Brainstorming.

Related Techniques

Structured Brainstorming, Virtual Brainstorming.

INDEX

"Lady Al Qaeda" ... 282
"Party of Liberation" ... 285
1979 Iranian revolution ... 77, 98
1991 Explanatory Memorandum on the General Strategic Goal for the Brotherhood in North America ... 42
9/11 ... 7, 87, 118, 256, 274, 275, 283
Aafia Siddiqui ... 282
Aaron Driver ... 275
Abdallah Idris Ali ... 167
Abdi Hersy ... 89, 96
Abdul Rahman Abdul Khaliq ... 48
Abdullah Almalki ... 138, 139
Abdullah Azzam ... 72
Abdullah Hamoud ... 167
Abdul-Rahman al-Sheha ... 86
Abdulrahman El Bahnasawy ... 275, 283
Abdur-Rahman Muhammad ... 78
Abu Ameenah Bilal Philips ... 89, 96
Abu Bakr al-Razi ... 74
Abu Bakr al-Siddiq ... 54, 56
Abu Bakr Musallah ... 89
Abu Bakr Shikawa ... 72
Abul A'la Maududi ... 9, 106, 286
ACH ... 295, 297, 299, 301, 302
Adolph Hitler ... 133
Afghanistan5, 17, 47, 56, 72, 106, 107, 187, 190, 191, 195, 206, 262, 266, 271, 276
Ahmad El Maati ... 138, 139
Ahmaddies ... 29
Ahmadiyya ... 65
Ahmed Hussen ... 65, 118
Ahmed Ressam ... 274, 283
Ahmed Said Khadr ... 16, 17, 186, 187, 189, 190, 249
Air India Inquiry ... 3
Al Aqsa Martyrs Brigades ... 115
Al Balagh Foundation ... 175, 176
Al Jazeera ... 109, 114, 115, 136, 172, 177, 224, 225, 226, 227, 230, 282
Al Jazeera Arabic ... 114, 225
al Qaeda.. 13, 16, 17, 42, 51, 119, 138, 236, 244, 256, 279, 285
Al Qaida ... 84, 125, 160, 169, 195
Al Quds ... 25
Al Sunnah Mosque ... 119, 255
Al-Azhar University ... 71, 72, 147, 256
al-Banna ... 14, 16, 180, 181, 214, 259, 260
Alex Schmid ... 40, 41
Alexander Cloutier ... 66
Algeria ... 16, 77, 278
Al-Hallaj ... 49
Ali bin Abi Talib ... 58
Ali ibn Abi Talib ... 54, 56, 288
Almalki ... 139
al-Qaeda.... 18, 72, 118, 187, 190, 191, 192, 256, 260, 286
Am Shinrikyo ... 302
Amos Tversky ... 294
Analysis of Competing Hypotheses ... 294, 295, 297, 299, 301
analytic methodologist ... 5
Anthony Furey ... 120, 121
Anwar Sadat ... 41
Anwarul Haque ... 167
apostate... 13, 19, 29, 42, 49, 137, 260, 263, 284
apostates 6, 42, 210, 262, 263, 279, 281, 282, 284
Apostates ... 19, 210
Arab ...27, 41, 48, 55, 57, 60, 70, 79, 82, 88, 115, 120, 121, 125, 127, 147, 148, 150, 160, 169, 181, 184, 186, 195, 196, 206, 207, 214, 218, 220, 223, 224, 228, 229, 233, 235, 237, 242, 243, 245, 260, 266
Arab League ... 48
Aramaic Syriac ... 74
Aruna Papp ... 100
asylum centres ... 36
Australia ... 3, 6, 30, 278
Ayatollah Khamenei ... 286
Ayatollah Khomeini ... 47, 77, 98, 174, 286
Ayman al Zawahiri ... 43
Badawi ... 88, 163, 192, 213, 214
Baha'i ... 65
Bangladesh ... 60, 106, 157, 200, 234, 262, 278
Bani Quraiza Judaism ... 74
Bank of Canada ... 3

Barack Obama ... 56
Barbara Perry ... 83
Bashar Assad ... 69
bayat ... 255, 256, 284
BBC ... 21, 33, 34, 35, 115, 163, 198, 264, 265
Belgium ... 6, 15, 17, 18, 178, 264, 268, 269, 276, 279, 280
Benni Antoine Norris ... 274
Bielefeld ... 36
Bill C-24 ... 117
Bill C-6 ... 117
Bill Clinton ... 56
Bill Roggio ... 107
Birmingham ... 125, 159, 269
blasphemy laws ... 103, 105, 281
Boko Haram ... 13, 72
Boston Marathon bombing ... 81
brainstorming ... 296, 297, 298, 299, 304
burka ... 23, 26, 27
burkas ... 23
CAIR CAN . 76, 82, 83, 84, 87, 116, 144, 149, 150, 151, 152, 153, 154, 155, 156, 165, 203, 228, 229, 233, 234, 236, 237
CAIR USA . 76, 79, 82, 83, 84, 149, 150, 151, 153, 155, 218, 229, 233, 236, 237
Calgary.. 27, 69, 89, 153, 179, 189, 190, 191, 249
caliphate.... 42, 44, 48, 52, 57, 58, 61, 63, 68, 73, 74, 76, 91, 171, 176, 237, 241, 259, 285
CAMP ... 110
Canada Revenue Agency. 31, 128, 157, 164, 165, 182, 193, 203, 204, 249
Canadian Alliance Party ... 131
Canadian Armed Forces ... 3, 5
Canadian Association of Journalists ... 282
Canadian Broadcasting Corporation 64, 211, 225
Canadian Charter of Rights and Freedoms 104
Canadian Chiefs of Police Association ... 282
Canadian Council of Imams ... 90, 129, 265
Canadian Council on American---Islamic Relations ... 82
Canadian Islamic Congress ... 70, 71, 82
Canadian Muslim organizations ... 25
Canadian Security Intelligence Service ... 283
Canadian Thinkers' Forum ... 3, 20, 116
Canadian University of Egypt ... 4
Carleton University ... 98, 174
Carnegie Endowment for International Peace 30
Carol Christian ... 81
Catholics ... 63, 65
CATO Institute ... 106
CBC News 99, 104, 118, 123, 127, 141, 182, 191, 195, 197, 211, 226, 249, 256, 271
CCIQ mosque ... 64, 251
Center for Cyber and Homeland Security ... 128
Charles Taylor ... 22
Charlie Hebdo ... 56, 226, 227, 263, 268
Charter of Rights..... 16, 18, 32, 40, 87, 111, 116, 142, 178, 215, 218, 228, 237, 267, 285
Charter of Rights and Freedoms. 20, 32, 40, 169, 178, 215, 218, 237, 267, 281, 285
chauvinism ... 38
Chechnya ... 51
Chiheb Esseghaier ... 179, 191, 275
China ... 20, 51, 107, 114, 274, 278
Chinese ... 23, 27, 274
Christians ... 29, 54, 68, 72, 228, 266
Christoph Luxemburg ... 74
chronologies and timelines ... 300
CIJ News..... 86, 87, 89, 90, 91, 92, 93, 117, 124, 129, 130, 134, 262
CIN News ... 91, 117, 130
Citizenship and Immigration Canada (War Crimes) ... 3
Colin Powell ... 274
Cologne ... 33, 35, 36, 37, 38
Conventional Forces in Europe Treaty ... 3
Côte-des-Neiges ... 119
Council for Muslims Facing Tomorrow ... 7
Council for the Advancement of Muslim Professionals ... 110
Council on American-Islamic Relations 79, 83, 132, 136, 149, 151, 152, 153, 154, 155, 184, 194, 218
Council on American-Islamic Relations USA 79
Criminal Code of Canada 32, 116, 174, 178, 191, 228, 285
CSIS ... 187, 188, 191, 236, 237, 244, 283
Cultural Centre of the Islamic Republic of Iran (Ottawa) ... 174
cultural relativism ... 35, 124, 284
culture of denial ... 33, 34
da'wa ... 142
Dabiq magazine ... 42
Daesh ... 84, 125, 160, 169, 230
Dagens Nyheter ... 37
Dame Louise Casey ... 21

Daniel Kahneman....294
Daniel Pipes....30, 56, 58
Dar Al-Arqam Mosque....48
Dar Al-Arqam schools....48
Dar al-Islam....72
Dar Al-Uloom University....50
David and Mary Thomson Collegiate....175
David Barrett....78
David Cameron....56, 228
Dawa....14, 15, 181, 213
Dawah (invitation to Islam)....170
Deception Detection....301
Delphi Method....301
democratic society....22, 44
Denis McShane....34, 265
Denise Helly....82, 83
Denmark....137
Department of Foreign Affairs and International Trade....99
Department of Justice....3, 131, 158, 200, 275
Devil's Advocacy....302
Devil's Advocate....296, 302
DFAIT....99
Diagnostic Reasoning....302
Divergent/Convergent Thinking....298
Djamila Ben Habib....66
Don Valley East....136
Dortmund....36
Douglas Murray....78
Dr. Soad Saleh....71
Dundas Street Mosque....9, 125, 255, 256, 257
Düsseldorf....36
East End Madrassa....174, 175
Ebtisam Al Ketbi....125, 160
Edmonton....27, 229, 249, 276
Egypt. 4, 6, 41, 43, 48, 49, 51, 57, 60, 69, 71, 72, 73, 125, 127, 132, 148, 160, 163, 170, 180, 186, 189, 194, 226, 228, 234, 237, 259, 263, 266, 267, 278, 280, 287
Ehsan Mohammadi....173
El Maati....139
El-Mahdi Jamali....81
El-Tantawi Attia....9, 147, 256
El-Tantawy Attia....125, 128, 147, 193, 194, 256
Embassy of Iran....173
Emirates Policy Centre....125, 160
Emmanuel Macron....271
Enbala Power....134
Entryism....16, 17, 43, 112, 132, 133, 134, 137, 273, 285
Erdogan....50, 60, 69
Erin Mills....95, 103
Ernst Rohm....133
Essam al-Haddad....162
Etienne Dinet....77
EU head of counter terrorism....279
Europe..3, 6, 7, 9, 14, 17, 30, 32, 35, 39, 62, 133, 142, 148, 160, 181, 230, 262, 266, 267, 271, 279, 285, 287
European Commission....113
extrajudicial killings....105
extremists 40, 41, 46, 53, 56, 59, 60, 61, 68, 134, 137, 179, 187
Fatima Alawadi....79
fatwas....20, 30, 71, 230
FBI....78, 84, 158, 184, 185, 195, 234, 270, 283
Fedayeen....77
female genital mutilation..76, 99, 123, 124, 269
Female Genital Mutilation....6, 39, 99, 269, 281
FGM....99, 269, 270
Fidel Castro....20, 114, 274
Filipinos....23
Financial Post....126, 127, 141, 162, 245
Finland....36
Fiona Jarvis....100
France....6, 15, 17, 18, 27, 49, 51, 56, 141, 178, 226, 230, 241, 264, 268, 276, 278, 279, 281, 282
Francois Hollande....56
Frank Baylis....103
Frankfurt....36
Gaza Strip....126, 161
Gazi Ibrahim Abu Mezer....275
Gehad al-Haddad....162, 163
Gender equality....22
General Electric Canada....134
George Soros....113
George W. Bush....56
George Washington University 16, 104, 128, 280
George Zimmerman....80
Gerard Bouchard....22
German Workers' Party (DAP)....133
Germany 3, 6, 15, 17, 18, 27, 35, 37, 38, 51, 141, 276, 279
Gilles de Kerchove....279
Global News....107, 141, 204, 248

Government of Canada.....31, 94, 102, 124, 128, 129, 198, 209, 230, 250, 251, 254
Government of Pakistan 105
Government of Saudi Arabia.........................115
Government of the United Kingdom 128
Grand Imam of al-Azhar.................................46
Green Light Committee.........................108, 112
Gulf States..69, 70
Hadith.............................52, 54, 73, 74, 92, 288
Hafiz Khalid 107
Halal Certification 280, 281
Hamas 17, 79, 104, 114, 115, 125, 126, 127, 134, 139, 144, 145, 146, 149, 150, 157, 158, 159, 160, 161, 162, 165, 173, 182, 184, 185, 186, 192, 198, 199, 200, 201, 207, 208, 217, 222, 228, 233, 237, 241, 245, 249, 250, 251
Hamburg 36
Hamid Mohammadi 173
Hamilton 27
Haqqani network 106
Harry Potter Syndrome..................................32
Harvard University 128
Hassan al Banna 13
Hassan al-Banna 9, 14, 16, 48, 65, 106, 146, 147, 170, 171, 180, 192, 195, 213, 223, 242, 243, 244, 259, 260, 263, 287
Hassan Jamali..66
hate crimes 15, 39, 62, 64, 122, 123, 131, 281
HCI..165
Hedy Fry 130, 131
Helsingborg 37
Helsinki..36
Henriette Reker..38
Het Laatste Nieuws 269
High Impact / Low Probability Analysis..........299
hijab 73, 77, 122, 170
Hijrah...285
Hillary Clinton..275
Hindus 29, 215
Hizb ut-Tahrir 13, 16, 39, 57, 76, 91, 137, 176, 177, 238, 266, 278, 285, 286
Hizbul Mujahideen.........165, 202, 203, 208, 238
Holy Land Relief 42, 79, 108, 165, 201, 213, 214, 237, 251
Holy Land Relief Foundation...........84, 201, 251
Home Office 133
Home Secretary 34, 133, 265
homophobia..78
honor killings 76
House of Commons 3, 24, 103, 104, 109, 117, 130, 134, 248
Houssein Muhammad Amer...................87, 262
Houston 80, 81
Huffington Post........... 3, 33, 114, 115, 116, 120
Human Concern International165, 187, 190, 203
Humanists 29
Husain Haqqani...30
Hussein Qasti 70
hypotheses.................... 297, 298, 299, 301, 302
Ibn Rushd 49, 74
Ibnoun Baz 119
ICNA .9, 17, 41, 42, 90, 91, 92, 95, 110, 111, 116, 117, 129, 130, 132, 138, 165, 169, 170, 193, 203, 221, 265
ICNA Canada Sisters Wing 170
ICTY 3
IDF..165, 166, 203
IIIT 78, 146, 195, 268
Ikhwan 16, 42, 149, 207, 257, 285
Ikhwani 273, 285
Ilkka Koskimaki 36
Imam Abu Yusuf...38
Imam As'ad Jafri...47
Immigration and Refugee Board of Canada 3
India 6, 50, 70, 71, 106, 202, 266, 278, 286
indicators . 20, 157, 200, 232, 298, 299, 300, 302
Indicators Validator tm..................................300
Indonesia 234, 276, 278
infidel 29, 54, 63
infidels24, 52, 53, 54, 55, 67, 68, 72, 73, 92, 269, 286, 288
information credibility.......... 229, 290, 292, 293
INSET 3, 188
Inside Toronto Magazine....................75, 95, 96
Integrated National Security Enforcement Team 188
integration 21, 22, 28, 63, 78, 116, 142, 145, 264, 271, 273
intelligence analyst 5
International Criminal Tribunal for the former Yugoslavia 3
International Institute for Islamic Thought 78, 146
International Institute of Islamic Thought.... 195, 268
International Islamic Forum 171

International Relief Fund for the Afflicted and Needy 128, 138, 157, 158, 199, 200, 201, 222, 242, 249
International Relief Fund for the Afflicted and Needy – Canada 128
International Union of Muslim Scholars 9, 51, 192, 257
Interpol 122, 181, 227
INTERPOL Red Notice 142, 148, 227, 257
Iqaluit 70
Iqbal Al-Nadvi 90, 129, 265
Iqra Khalid . 15, 24, 25, 75, 95, 96, 103, 106, 107, 108, 109, 110
Iran 29, 31, 47, 51, 55, 56, 58, 60, 65, 69, 97, 98, 99, 114, 117, 172, 173, 174, 175, 176, 262, 273, 274, 276, 283
Iranian Cultural Association of Carleton University 173, 174
Iranian Revolution 76, 172
Iranian Revolutionary Guards Council ... 173, 280
Iraq 47, 56, 79, 80, 91, 98, 187, 189, 191, 192, 212, 262, 266, 276
IRB Canada 105
IRFAN 17, 116, 128, 138, 139, 140, 144, 148, 157, 158, 159, 182, 198, 199, 200, 201, 207, 220, 222, 223, 236, 238, 242, 249, 250, 251, 253, 273, 279, 280
IRGC 172, 280
IRW 125, 161
Ishaan Gardee 83, 84, 150
ISIS. 13, 16, 25, 42, 47, 51, 56, 57, 58, 62, 68, 71, 95, 169, 189, 190, 211, 212, 219, 221, 222, 227, 230, 235, 236, 249, 260, 262, 263, 267, 268, 270, 273, 276, 279, 283, 285, 288
Islam 14, 15, 30, 42, 47, 77, 86, 87, 88, 91, 98, 99, 106, 111, 121, 130, 142, 166, 170, 174, 177, 189, 214, 221, 262, 269
Islam Awareness Week 86, 109, 189
Islamic Caliphate 46, 50, 54, 61, 71, 137
Islamic Center in Quebec 69
Islamic Center in Toronto 69
Islamic Centre of Southwest Ontario 70, 205
Islamic Circle of North America 9, 17, 24, 25, 41, 90, 91, 110, 129, 131, 132, 136, 169, 170, 265
Islamic Congress of Canada 70
Islamic Development Bank 168, 219
Islamic Development Foundation 166
Islamic fundamentalism 119
Islamic Group 72, 135
Islamic Jihad 134, 186, 195
Islamic jurisprudence 50, 59, 60, 61, 68
Islamic Maghreb 279
Islamic Relief ... 83, 124, 125, 126, 128, 144, 159, 160, 161, 162, 163, 193, 194, 219, 220, 242, 245
Islamic Relief Canada 83, 124, 125, 126, 128, 159, 160, 162, 219, 242, 245
Islamic Relief Worldwide 124, 125, 159, 160, 161, 162, 242, 245
Islamic Republic of Iran 174, 286
Islamic Shia Ithna Asheri Jamaat of Toronto . 175
Islamic Society of Greater Houston 80
Islamic Society of North America ... 70, 106, 110, 132, 135, 163, 164, 166, 167, 194, 199, 201, 204, 217, 238
Islamic State..... 95, 187, 188, 189, 220, 230, 233
Islamic University "Dar Al Uloom" 71
Islamic University of Pakistan 50, 71
Islamism 17, 58, 229, 254, 259, 266, 282, 287
Islamist.4, 6, 7, 13, 14, 15, 16, 17, 19, 20, 21, 23, 24, 29, 30, 32, 35, 40, 41, 42, 43, 44, 46, 47, 50, 51, 52, 53, 56, 59, 60, 62, 68, 72, 75, 76, 82, 83, 84, 85, 87, 88, 90, 91, 95, 98, 100, 103, 105, 106, 107, 108, 109, 111, 112, 113, 115, 116, 119, 120, 122,123, 126, 129, 130, 131, 132, 133, 135, 137, 138, 141, 142, 144, 146, 148, 160, 161, 169, 176, 178, 179, 180, 181, 182, 183, 184, 185, 186, 188, 191, 196, 198, 208, 210, 212, 216, 217, 221, 226, 228, 230, 232, 235, 236, 237, 238, 240, 248, 249, 253, 254, 255, 258, 262, 263, 265, 266, 267, 268, 269, 270, 271, 273, 274, 275, 276, 278, 279, 280, 281, 282, 283, 284, 285, 286, 287, 288, 289
Islamist ideology . 6, 7, 16, 17, 19, 21, 32, 46, 51, 60, 68, 75, 76, 84, 95, 103, 105, 106, 115, 131, 137, 146, 148, 178, 180, 182, 186, 188, 210, 212, 232, 253, 258, 263, 267, 268, 273, 278, 280, 281, 282, 283
Islamist terrorism 46, 59, 60, 62, 278
Islamists .6, 13, 14, 15, 17, 18, 19, 20, 24, 26, 27, 29, 30, 31, 32, 39, 40, 43, 46, 47, 50, 51, 52, 55, 56, 59, 60, 61, 62, 63, 64, 65, 66, 67, 68, 69, 70, 72, 73, 74, 76, 78, 84, 85, 89, 92, 94, 95, 99, 102, 103, 104, 105, 106, 112, 113, 116, 119, 120, 123, 130, 133, 137, 138, 142,

146, 208, 210, 211, 215, 227, 229, 230, 234, 262, 263, 265, 266, 267, 268, 270, 272, 273, 276, 277, 278, 279, 280, 284, 285, 286, 287, 288
Islamophobia..... 7, 15, 20, 24, 25, 63, 64, 65, 66, 67, 68, 76, 77, 78, 79, 81, 82, 83, 84, 85, 87, 89, 91, 92, 93, 94, 103, 104, 105, 111, 121, 122, 130, 207, 263, 265, 270, 286
Ismail al-Faruqi....................................146, 268
ISNA... 70, 79, 107, 109, 110, 111, 116, 132, 135, 136, 163, 164, 165, 166, 167, 168, 169, 190, 192, 193, 194, 198, 199, 201, 202, 203, 204, 217, 218, 219, 222, 223, 224, 229, 237, 238, 281
ISNA Canada... 116, 164, 166, 167, 193, 202, 217
ISNA Canada school 169
ISNA development fund...............................107
ISNA Development Fund.......................238, 273
ISNA High School..136
Israel.... 25, 53, 55, 114, 115, 125, 126, 146, 149, 161, 180, 182, 183, 184, 186, 268
Italy 278
IUMS.................. 9, 120, 121, 147, 255, 257, 258
Jaafar Sheikh Idris 48
Jaffari Mosque 39, 97, 173, 174, 175
Jamaat al Fuqra 274
Jamaat-e-Islami..... 9, 14, 21, 24, 29, 31, 41, 106, 107, 111, 116, 132, 135, 165, 202, 203, 238, 241, 260, 286
Jamal Badawi..... 87, 88, 163, 192, 194, 213, 214, 222
Jay Report 33, 34, 35, 85, 233, 264
Jean Charest...22
Jean-Claude Juncker......................................113
Jeremy Corbyn 133
Jews15, 16, 54, 55, 62, 64, 65, 68, 71, 72, 74, 92, 131, 176, 183, 185, 208, 255, 256, 257, 265, 270, 279, 281
jihad 9, 13, 14, 16, 25, 26, 42, 43, 44, 48, 55, 60, 72, 75, 77, 92, 104, 106, 119, 148, 171, 176, 180, 181, 185, 188, 189, 192, 204, 230, 249, 257, 271, 285, 286
jihad against evil (asy-syarr)..........................286
jihad for goodness (al khair) 286
Jihadists..13
Jim Fitzpatrick 133
John Geddes..83
John Maguire 16, 179, 188, 189, 236, 249
John McCain...275
John McCallum 90, 117, 129
Jordan 51, 98, 195, 278
Josh Gerstein 84
Justin Trudeau 9, 23, 56, 64, 112, 113, 114, 117, 118, 120, 124, 129, 136, 138, 182, 197, 270, 276
Kaaba 63
Kalim Siddiqui 77
Kalmar..37
Karlstad 37
Kassim Alhimidi..80
Katherine Bullock.......................... 168, 218, 219
Kathleen Harris 104
Kellie Leitch...21
Kennedy School of Government...................128
Key Assumptions Check........................ 298, 299
Khaleel Mohammad 30
Khalid Durán 30
Khilafah Islamiyah...284
Khomeinism 69
Khomeneism 283
Khomeneists 13, 16, 39, 76, 97, 99, 171, 174, 238, 258, 260, 273
King Faysal bin Abdul Aziz Al Saud..................69
Kingston 100
Kingston Mills 100
kirpans 23
Kitchener Masjid...127
Kitchener Mosque 127
kuffars 131
Kuwait.. 29, 31, 48, 69
Labour Party 34, 133
Latinos..23
Leah Binkovitz...81
Lebanon 262, 278
LGBT... 22, 183
Liberal Party...... 56, 64, 107, 108, 109, 112, 117, 131, 132, 136, 140, 141, 143, 216
Liberal Party of Canada......................... 108, 132
Libya...................... 198, 199, 204, 205, 266, 280
Lorenzo Vidino 16, 104, 128, 144, 146, 213, 229, 232, 241, 280, 287
Los Angeles 79, 181, 183, 186, 189, 220, 274, 275, 283
Los Angeles Airport (LAX) 274, 283
Louise Casey... 21, 34
lovers of death.................................. 9, 60, 171

M-103............15, 20, 24, 93, 103, 104, 105, 111
M-103 Islamophobia motion 105, 111, 281
Maclean's Magazine 83, 174
Macleans Magazine 83, 98, 101, 173
Majlis-As-Shura 166
Malaysia 266, 278
Malmö 37
Mansoo Raza 105
Marie-Claude Bibeau 124
Mark Roth 56
Martin Luther 287
martyrdom 9, 41, 43, 171, 185, 192, 288
martyrs..............26, 41, 138, 180, 192, 230, 249
MAS 88, 163, 169, 193, 224
Masuma Jessa 175, 176
Matthew J. Goodwin......................................43
Maududi..........................14, 106, 241, 243, 263
Maulana Asad Jafri..10
Maxime Bernier 104
Mazin Abdul-Adhim 91, 177
Mecca........................46, 51, 52, 54, 73, 75, 223
Medina46, 50, 51, 52, 53, 75, 223, 234, 235, 255
MEMRI............................43, 109, 180, 237, 257
Michael Petrou...............................98, 173, 174
Middle East 4, 6, 7, 14, 17, 25, 47, 48, 49, 56, 57, 115, 119, 155, 180, 191, 199, 256, 271, 282, 285
military intelligence 5
Minister for the Status of Women................130
Minister of Immigration..........65, 117, 124, 129
Minister of Immigration, Refugees and Citizenship....................90, 117, 118, 124, 129
Minister of International Development and La Francophonie 124
Mirza Ghulam Ahmad 284
misogyny 38, 215
Mississauga . 25, 95, 97, 103, 109, 111, 134, 136, 139, 164, 166, 168, 170, 176, 177, 199, 201, 202, 204, 205, 217, 219, 220, 241, 275, 283
Mississauga-Centre 134
Mobin Foundation 173
Modernist Muslims 29
Mohamed Bekkari.........................167, 193, 202
Mohamed Ibrahim al-Masri 71
Mohamed Ibrahim Al-Masri............................70
Mohamed Mahmoud Taha 75
Mohamed Sifaoui.................................119, 255
Mohammad Anwar Yaqubi 100
Mohammad Shafia 100, 101
Montreal ... 4, 27, 81, 83, 87, 117, 118, 119, 139, 146, 149, 151, 189, 211, 212, 236, 240, 241, 242, 243, 244, 246, 247, 249, 251, 255, 256, 268
Moro Islamic Liberation Front 72, 267
Morocco.......................................51, 193, 278
Mostazafan Foundation of New York 175, 176
MPAC-NY 110
MSA... 75, 96, 108, 109, 168, 179, 180, 181, 182, 183, 184, 185, 186, 187, 188, 189, 190, 191, 193, 194, 195, 196, 197, 221, 222, 236, 282
Muayyed Nureddin 138, 139
Muhammad Aabid 70
Muhammad Badi 47
Muhammad ibn Abd al-Wahhab 289
Muhammad Rizvi.......................98, 99, 174, 175
Muhammad Shahrour 74
Mullah Syndrome 232, 238, 286, 287
Multiculturalism 27, 113, 131
Multiple Hypotheses Generator tm 301
Munir Al Qasim 70
Musleh Khan 90, 234, 235
Muslim American Society 87, 163, 169, 193, 214
Muslim Association of Canada......125, 127, 128, 136, 144, 146, 165, 194, 242, 247
Muslim Brotherhood 4, 9, 13, 14, 16, 17, 19, 21, 24, 25, 31, 39, 41, 42, 43, 44, 47, 48, 51, 57, 58, 60, 64, 65, 69, 76, 78, 79, 84, 88, 90, 91, 104, 106, 109, 110, 111, 115, 116, 120, 121, 124, 125, 127, 128, 129, 132, 134, 135, 136, 137, 140, 141, 142, 144, 145, 146, 147,148, 149, 150, 158, 160, 161, 162, 163, 166, 169, 170, 176, 179, 180, 182, 187, 188, 190, 192, 193, 194, 195, 197, 198, 201, 202, 206, 207, 212, 213, 214, 215, 217, 218, 219, 221, 222, 223, 225, 226, 227, 228, 229, 230, 232, 236, 237, 238, 240, 241, 242, 243, 244, 245, 246, 247, 248, 249, 250, 251, 252, 253, 256, 257, 258, 259, 260, 270, 273, 280, 281, 282, 285, 286, 287, 288
Muslim Centre for Social Support and Integration 70
Muslim Public Affairs Council 110
Muslim Reform Movement 20, 116
Muslim reformers 63
Muslim Student Association . 25, 75, 86, 95, 108, 109, 131, 135, 162, 179, 180, 184, 185, 191,

194, 221, 222, 226, 235, 236, 249, 253, 258, 275, 282
Muslim World League 69, 86, 179, 190, 221, 236
Muslims Facing Tomorrow....................20, 116
Mustafa Kemal Ataturk..............................60
muta marriages..................................98, 281
Mu'tazilah 49, 74
MWL...86
NAIT..........................79, 165, 217, 229, 237
Najamuddin Mohammed..........................110
Nanyang Technological University, Singapore...3
Nasr Hamed Abu Zaid 74
National Council of Canadian Muslims 83, 84, 127, 144, 149, 194, 218, 233, 242
National Energy Board 141
National Public Radio.................................98
NCCM 76, 82, 84, 87, 116, 136, 149, 150, 151, 152, 153, 157, 194, 213, 218, 228, 229, 233, 234, 236, 237, 242
Netherlands..............................3, 15, 17, 27
New Islam Movement 30
New York City............................191, 275, 276
New York Post 30
niqab 26, 221
Niqab...110, 287
Nominal Group Technique............298, 301, 304
non-believers 15, 27, 131, 210, 265, 288, 289
NORAD 274
North Africa...6, 7, 17
North Africans 38
North American Air Defence Command 274
North American Islamic Trust 165
Norway..137
Nunavut..70
Nureddin 139
Oakville...92
ODIHR...84
Office for Democratic Institutions and Human Rights 84
Office for Standards in Education 282
Office of the United States Trade Representative 276
OFSTED 282
Omar Abdul Rahman...................................72
Omar Alghabra..........25, 65, 112, 134, 135, 136
Omar ibn al-Khattab...................................56
Omar Khadr.... 138, 179, 187, 189, 224, 225, 226
Omar Soufyane 119, 255
Ontario......9, 10, 23, 86, 89, 90, 91, 92, 96, 100, 122, 125, 135, 139, 164, 179, 193, 202, 216, 219, 230, 236, 241, 249, 270, 283
Ontario Energy Board 134
Operation Sentinelle....................................15
oppression of women 35, 120, 265
Organization of the Islamic Conference ..51, 206
OSCE...84
Ottawa .. 9, 16, 27, 69, 71, 82, 99, 120, 121, 128, 139, 141, 144, 149, 151, 153, 156, 160, 168, 172, 173, 174, 187, 188, 189, 193, 194, 196, 213, 216, 219, 229, 236, 237, 241, 248, 249, 263
Ottawa Islamic Society.................................69
Ottawa Mosque 119
Oussama El-Saadi......................................137
Pakistan..... 29, 30, 49, 51, 60, 69, 105, 106, 107, 157, 165, 172, 187, 189, 190, 191, 193, 195, 196, 200, 202, 203, 262, 266, 267, 271, 276, 278
Pakistan Today 30
Pakistani.. 29, 33, 34, 85, 93, 105, 107, 108, 135, 187, 190, 204, 264, 274
Pakistani Student Association......................108
Parliamentary Motion 103.....................15, 111
Pashtun 29
Patty Hajdu 130
People's Mojahedin 77
Pervez Nasim 167
Peterborough Mosque 122, 123
Philippines 6, 51, 72, 262, 266, 278
PMO 19, 121, 122, 252
political correctness.. 6, 7, 17, 19, 20, 32, 34, 35, 38, 39, 100, 102, 105, 211, 216, 230, 232, 233, 265, 287
Political correctness......................32, 232, 264
political entryism 39, 131
Political Entryism 284
political Islam .. 46, 48, 50, 54, 55, 56, 59, 61, 63, 69, 74, 206
Political Islam 14, 51, 55, 59
Postmedia News 100, 101
post-national state..............................113, 272
Premortem Analysis...................................303
PressTV 114
Prime Minister Justin Trudeau.....................121
Prime Minister of Canada 120, 141
Prime Minister's Office 19, 121

Prince George 131
probability 298, 300
Project Sapphire 17, 139
Prophet Muhammad... 49, 50, 51, 52, 53, 54, 55, 58, 59, 61, 68, 73, 227
Protestant Reformation 287
Psychology of Intelligence Analysis 294, 295, 297
Public Safety and National Security Committee 91
Punjabi 4, 29
Qatar 29, 31, 39, 69, 89, 106, 114, 115, 136, 142, 192, 209, 225, 226, 227, 278, 280, 282, 283, 289
Qazi Hussain Hamad 165, 203
Qazi Hussein Ahmad 135
Quds Forces 280
Quebec 19, 22, 64, 65, 66, 81, 83, 118, 138, 139, 140, 151, 191, 227, 240, 241, 248, 249, 250, 251, 252, 253, 262, 270
Quebec City 19, 64, 138, 140, 248, 249, 250, 251, 253, 270
Quillian Foundation 287
Quran .. 49, 52, 54, 66, 67, 70, 72, 73, 74, 75, 88, 92, 108, 170, 177, 180, 288
Quraysh 49
racism.. 24, 33, 66, 76, 78, 79, 80, 103, 104, 105, 123, 263, 284
radicalization... 16, 104, 172, 186, 187, 188, 189, 190, 217, 236, 269
Rahim Yar Khan District 107
Rand Corporation 128
Randy Pherson 295
RCMP 17, 139, 140, 148, 188, 189, 191, 195, 196, 236, 244, 249
Reviving the Islamic Spirit conference 138
Richard Martino 66
Richard Stone 77
Richards J. Heuer, Jr. 294, 295, 300, 303, 304
Rideau Canal 100
Riyad us Saliheen 111
Roger Eatwell 43
Rona Amir Mohammed 100
Ronald Wibtrope 43
Rotherham . 33, 34, 38, 39, 84, 85, 233, 264, 265
Royal Canadian Mounted Police 3, 235
Rukanpur 107
Runnymede Trust 77, 78
Russia 51, 125, 127, 160, 276, 278
Russian 4, 267
Ryerson University 134
S. Rajaratnam School of International Studies .. 3
Saadollah Ghaussy 30
Sabrine Djaermane 81
Saddam Hussein 79, 98
Saeed Ramadan 65
Said al-Ashmawi 74
Sajid al-Abdali 48
Sajid Javid 21
Salaf 108
Salafi Jihadist 57
Salafism 108, 109, 234, 282
Salafist Movement 48
Salafists 13, 57, 58, 268
Salim Mansur 30
Salma Zahid 25, 137
Salman Ashrafi 16, 179, 190, 236, 249
Salman Rushdie 77, 230
Samia Shameem 80
San Diego State University 30
Saudi Arabia 29, 31, 41, 50, 51, 54, 56, 60, 62, 63, 65, 69, 70, 71, 98, 105, 106, 107, 115, 125, 127, 134, 160, 168, 179, 196, 206, 207, 209, 221, 223, 228, 234, 236, 246, 262, 267, 276, 278, 283, 289
Saudi Ministry of Culture and Information 168
Sayed Abul A'la Maududi 106
Sayed Qutb 72
Sayyed Tantawi 72
Sayyid Muhhamad Rizvi 97
Sayyid Qutb 170, 171, 241
Sean Craig 107, 204
Secretary of State for Foreign Affairs 65
Secretary of State for Multiculturalism 131
self-censorship 20, 39, 66, 211, 230
sexual assaults 35, 36, 37, 38, 39
Shafqat Ali 109
shaheed 288
Shaima Alawadi 76, 79, 80
Sharia ...13, 15, 21, 24, 26, 44, 46, 47, 48, 56, 58, 72, 75, 76, 108, 109, 112, 135, 147, 174, 176, 180, 186, 189, 196, 217, 218, 219, 262, 278, 279, 280, 281, 282, 283
sharia law 282, 283
Shazim Khan 96, 123
Sheema Khan 151, 153, 154, 155, 228, 229, 236, 237

Sheikh Ahmed al-Tayeb 46
Sheikh Ali Abdul Razek 74
Shiite 47, 49, 58, 63, 65, 80
Shiite Muslim 47
Shiites 47, 49
Shinzo Abe 56
Sikhs 23
Sindhi 29
Singapore 3, 278
Siraj Wahhaj 116
Somalia 16, 56, 70, 124, 266, 276
Soner Chagatai 55
Sophia University 30
source reliability 229, 290, 291, 292
South Asia 6, 7, 17, 30, 106, 238, 286
South Asian 3, 27
South Sudan 124
South Yorkshire Police 85
Soviet Union 17
Spain 49, 278, 279
St Jean sur Richelieu 27, 229
Stephen Harper 118
Stephen Schwartz 30
Steven Stalinsky 109, 257
Stewart Bell 107, 173, 176, 204, 255, 256
Stockholm 37
structured analytic techniques 294
Structured analytic techniques 294, 295, 296, 300, 303, 304
Structured Analytic Techniques for Intelligence Analysis 295, 296
structured brainstorming 298
Structured Self-Critique 303, 304
Stuttgart 36
Submission 15, 20, 51, 262, 272, 288
Sudan 47, 51, 56, 60, 172, 190, 266
Sufi 29, 74, 259, 288
Sufism 288
suicide bomber 16, 137, 179, 190, 229, 236, 249
suicide bombers 16, 41, 179, 183, 184, 191, 221, 222, 230, 236, 270, 271, 288
Sunna 49, 70
Sunnah 108, 118, 119, 177, 255
Sunni Muslim 47, 63, 117
Sunnis 47, 49, 98, 288
Sweden 137, 271, 280
Swedish newspaper Dagens Nyheter 37
Switzerland 279
Syed Abul A'la Maududi 14
Syed Imitiaz Ahmad 166
Syed Mohammed Rizvi 176
Syracuse 274
Syria .. 47, 56, 172, 187, 189, 191, 212, 262, 266, 276, 278
Tahir Aslam Gora 30
Tahir Gora 1, 3, 21, 29, 91, 131
Takfir 74, 288
Takfirist 260, 285, 286, 287
Takfirists 13
Taliban 47, 56, 107, 187, 190, 195, 206
Tarbiyah (education & training) 170
Tarek Abdel Halim 48
Tariq Ramadan 65, 116, 135, 222, 244
Tashbih Sayyid 30
Tazkiyah (personal development) 170
Terrorism Prevention Branch 40
The Blind Sheik 72
The Guardian 34, 38, 77, 269, 271
The Post 30
The Weekly Standard 30
Theresa May 34, 133
Thornhill Mosque 174
Thucydides 18
Times Square 275
Tony Blair 57
Tony Perry 79
Tooba Yahya 101
Toronto 7, 9, 10, 25, 26, 27, 39, 69, 70, 75, 86, 93, 95, 97, 107, 110, 116, 118, 124, 125, 128, 134, 135, 136, 147, 168, 169, 172, 173, 174, 182, 183, 189, 191, 193, 194, 196, 197, 198, 202, 203, 204, 211, 212, 213, 214, 215, 216, 217, 219, 221, 222, 223, 224, 225, 226, 229, 230, 233, 234, 235, 248, 249, 255, 256, 257, 270, 273, 274, 282
Toronto 18 ..... 118, 249, 275
Toronto District School Board 175, 215
Toronto Star.. 134, 136, 169, 172, 193, 194, 202, 203, 211, 212, 213, 214, 215, 216, 217, 221, 223, 224, 225, 226, 230, 233, 270, 273, 282
Trayvon Martin 80
Tunisia 51, 241, 278
Turkey 43, 50, 51, 55, 60, 69, 180, 187, 189, 237, 267, 276, 278, 280
Twelver Jafariya doctrine 47
U.S. Institute of Peace 128

UAE.. 41, 60, 79, 82, 84, 121, 125, 147, 150, 160, 161, 169, 220, 229
UK 3, 6, 18, 21, 22, 32, 33, 35, 41, 42, 51, 78, 99, 125, 126, 133, 159, 161, 162, 163, 172, 176, 206, 220, 228, 233, 238, 245, 249, 264, 265, 266, 269, 270, 276, 280, 281, 282, 290, 291, 292
UK Admiralty rating system 290, 291, 292
UK Prime Minister David Cameron 21
Umar ibn al-Khattab.................................. 54, 73
Umm Al-Qura Universities 71
Umm Al-Qura University in Saudi Arabia......... 50
Ummah.................................. 42, 111, 176, 289
United Arab Emirates 41, 60, 79, 82, 83, 88, 115, 120, 121, 125, 127, 147, 150, 160, 164, 169, 195, 214, 218, 220, 224, 228, 229, 233, 237, 242, 245
United Journalists 4
United Kingdom .. 6, 17, 32, 33, 41, 77, 115, 125, 127, 128, 141, 160, 162, 206, 219, 238, 245, 264, 269, 278, 282
United Nations 40, 206, 266
United Nations Protection Force in Yugoslavia . 3
Université de Montréal............................. 81, 83
University of Calgary 16
University of Ottawa16, 179, 186, 187, 189, 190, 226, 249
University of Toronto 168, 194
University of Vienna 16, 104, 280
University of Western Ontario. 30, 182, 197, 205
Urdu 4
USA.... 3, 6, 17, 30, 39, 42, 51, 68, 79, 80, 81, 82, 83, 84, 96, 108, 116, 135, 146, 149, 150, 151, 152, 153, 155, 156, 158, 161, 163, 164, 166, 169, 170, 200, 201, 202, 206, 207, 208, 213, 217, 218, 221, 222, 229, 233, 234, 236, 237, 245, 263, 268, 270, 274, 275, 276, 277, 278, 280, 281, 282, 283
Usama Al-Shiraida 167
Uthman ibn Affan...................................... 54, 56
Uzbek 4
Valerie Amiraux.. 81
Valerie Jarrett 273
Vancouver... 27, 71, 113
Vatican 50, 63
Via Rail 275
victimhood narrative 103
victimization 76
Victims' Commissioner 34
Vidino............................ 128, 144, 145, 229, 241
Virginia 78
Virtual Brainstorming 298, 304
Vulnerable Children's Consular Policy Consular, Policy and Programs 100
Wahhabism... 69, 289
Walk-in Islamic Info Centre............................. 86
West Bank.................................... 125, 161, 183
What if? Analysis 298
white slavery... 38
Wife Disciplining 87, 109
WIIC 86
Wilayat al-Faqih 47
World Assembly of Muslim Youth .. 86, 199, 205, 206
World Union of Muslim Scholars..................... 48
Yasmin Ratansi.. 136
Yemen 124, 266
York Regional Police 175, 233, 234
York University75, 86, 95, 96, 108, 109, 134, 258
York University Muslim Student Association... 96
Young Muslims Brothers................................ 170
Young Muslims in Canada............................. 170
Young Muslims Sisters 170
Yousef Qaradawi................................... 109, 192
Yusuf al-Qaradawi................................. 121, 181
Yusuf Qaradawi..... 9, 14, 48, 142, 147, 148, 170, 181, 227, 257, 258, 281
Zakaria Amara 118
Zakaria Zubeidi.. 115
Zakaruya Yahya Bin Sharaf An-Nawawi 92
Zazi Hussain Hamad 165, 203
ZDF 38
Zeba Iqbal 110
Zweites Deutsches Fernsehen 38

10081230R00166

Manufactured by
Amazon.ca
Bolton, ON